INVESTMENT TAXATION

Practical Tax Strategies for
Financial Instruments

ARLENE M. HIBSCHWEILER
MARION KOPIN

McGraw-Hill
New York   Chicago   San Francisco   Lisbon   London
Madrid   Mexico City   Milan   New Delhi   San Juan
Seoul   Singapore   Sydney   Toronto

1 2 3 4 5 6 7 8 9 0   DOC/DOC   0 9 8 7 6 5 4 3

ISBN 0-07-139696-9

McGraw-Hill books are available at special quantity discounts to use as premiums and sales promotions, or for use in corporate training programs. For more information, please write to the Director of Special Sales, Professional Publishing, McGraw-Hill, Two Penn Plaza, New York, NY 10121-2298. Or contact your local bookstore.

Library of Congress Cataloging-in-Publication Data

Hibschweiler, Arlene M. (Arlene Mary),
  Investment taxation : practical tax strategies for financial instruments / by Arlene Hibschweiler and Marion Kopin — 1st ed.
    p. cm.
  Contents: Capital gains versus ordinary income — Passive activity losses and passive activity credits — At risk limitations — Investment expenses — Alternative minimun tax — Evaluation investment opportunities — Special issues for corporate investors — Dividend taxation — Taxation of redemptions — Distributions of stock and stock rights.
  ISBN 0-07-139696-9 (hardcover : alk paper)
    1. Investments—Taxation—Law and legislation—United States. 2. Financial instruments—Taxation—Law and legislation—United States. I. Kopin, Marion. II. Title

KF6415.H53 2003
336.2'07—dc21
                                           2003007822

This book is printed on acid-free paper.

To my family, with love and gratitude beyond both words and measure.
Arlene Hibschweiler

To my husband, Chet; my mother, Florence; my children, Therese and her spouse, Rigoberto; Colette; Yevonne and her spouse, Adam; Matthew and his spouse, Beth; and my grandchildren, Nicholas and Serina.
Marion Kopin

CONTENTS

INTRODUCTION

BACKGROUND

Recent years have seen an increasing interest in investments like stocks, bonds, and even more complicated transactions involving options, or futures contracts, for example. There are many reasons for this. To start, the stock market experienced unprecedented growth in the early-to-mid-1990s. At the time, technology stocks were leading the boom, but other sectors and industries were doing very well also. The stock market attracted millions of new investors because no one wanted to be left behind and miss opportunities to make money.

Additionally, retirement plans such as 401(k)s offered employees investments beyond traditional company stock, certificates of deposit, and mutual funds. These plans now are self-directed, meaning that the employee determines where and how much is invested. This type of exposure has prompted employees to begin additional investing of their own funds in the stock market. Further, more types of financial instruments have become available, and taxpayers have been learning about them through their brokers and the Internet. A number of taxpayers have opened their own brokerage accounts through the Internet and do their own on-line trading.

Increased activity means an increasing need to understand the tax effects of the investment decisions taxpayers make. This can be challenging under any circumstances, as when trying to gauge the alternative minimum tax consequences of a potential holding. However, the complexity of some opportunities now being offered in the markets and elsewhere make the task of predicting tax results even more daunting. Moreover, many financial instruments have been developed to circumvent the impact of certain tax rules or to avoid taxes completely. Congress has passed a number of laws to prevent these abuses, thereby limiting the possibilities for manipulation. If investors are not aware of these regulations, they may find themselves losing money even during a seemingly lucrative transaction.

Congress also has passed laws to stimulate growth in small businesses. These laws create opportunities for tax-smart investors to enjoy profits that are treated very favorably by the Tax Code. However, many of these provisions have strict guidelines and contain some inherent downsides. In other words, a taxpayer only vaguely familiar with these rules might be disappointed. This could occur, for example, when an investment expected to qualify for advantageous tax treatment does not.

WHY THIS BOOK WAS WRITTEN

As the number of people becoming active in various investments grows, so does the number of sources for advice. Although professional advisors such as accountants, attorneys, financial planners, and brokers are available, it is astonishing to see so many people take advice from family, friends, bartenders, hairdressers, magazines, TV, and the Internet. Unfortunately, these informal advisers are not familiar with the taxpayer's particular financial situation. Worse yet, they are almost completely unaware of the tax implications of the advice they are so freely giving. This book serves as a guide for taxpayers to navigate through the myriad tax rules and regulations inherent in financial instruments.

In a declining stock market, fortunes are lost. This has caused most investors to become highly nervous about their investment choices. Taxpayers are asking more questions regarding available alternatives for investments, and they are accepting responsibility for these decisions. The focus is now on being an informed investor. Taxpayers want to know about the risks, projected returns, and tax implications of the financial instruments under consideration. This book provides the methods by which financial instruments may be understood along with an analysis of the corresponding tax impacts.

Because of corporate downsizing that has taken place over the past several decades, more people have decided to open their own businesses. Huge investments have been made in privately controlled corporations, partnerships, and limited liability corporations by shareholders, partners, family, and friends. The Internet has made international commerce a reality rather than a possibility, bringing additional opportunities for investments. This book assists investors in these businesses with issues such as taxation of dividends, redemptions, and distributions. We bring out circumstances when the personal holding company tax and accumulated earnings tax would apply, as well as explanations of tainted stock and preferred stock bailouts.

Finally, this book serves as a resource for financial planners, attorneys, accountants, brokers, traders, bankers, entrepreneurs, investors, potential investors, and students. In many cases, these advisors or market participants are looking for an understandable, yet thorough, explanation of various financial investments. The book describes potential investments and also discusses the tax rules applicable to gains or losses that might result. Each chapter contains numerous examples, illustrating the consequences of the tax rules being discussed.

LAYOUT OF THE BOOK

The book initially describes general concepts and then discusses financial instruments in stock/equities, debt, and other financial instruments. The book can be read in sequence from beginning to end. Alternatively, it can be used as a reference. The chapters can be read individually in any succession. However, each chapter cross-references to other chapters that contain additional information on the topic being discussed.

OBJECTIVE

Our objective has been to provide a simple, easy-to-understand guide for the taxation of financial instruments. To this end, we admit that we have only partially been successful. The quagmire of tax laws and regulations that impact each investment is dense and confusing. It was difficult to compress the complexity of the tax laws into a simple narrative or delineate them on a short list. We tried to mitigate this problem through the use of practical examples and illustrations. Our wish is for our readers to be more informed and confident of their investment decisions with full knowledge of the associated tax implications. This guide should provide, at the very least, a starting point for understanding investment taxation. We hope and believe it to be a useful reference.

Tax Considerations and Concepts Generally Acceptable

CAPITAL GAINS VERSUS ORDINARY INCOME

INTRODUCTION

American citizens are generally taxed on their worldwide income. Most earnings are taxed as regular (generally referred to as ordinary) income, and the tax rates increase depending on the amount of taxable income per year. The rates in effect as a result of the Jobs and Growth Tax Relief Reconciliation Act of 2003 (JGTRRA) that was signed into law on May 28, 2003, are: 10 percent, 15 percent, 25 percent, 28 percent, 33 percent, and 35 percent. However, gains from the sale or exchange of a capital asset are taxed at a lower rate than ordinary income. These gains, known as capital gains, receive preferential tax treatment from being used primarily for capital appreciation. Gains derived from the ordinary course of business and from speculation are taxed as ordinary income.

Capital gains rates range from 5 percent to 28 percent. For most transactions, taxpayers in the 25 percent and higher tax bracket are taxed 15 percent on capital gains. Lower income taxpayers have a capital gains rate of 5 percent. These rates are in effect for sales and exchanges on or after May 6, 2003 through December 31, 2007. The 15 percent rate continues in 2008 but the 5 percent rate drops to zero percent for one year only. On January 1, 2009, the old rates of 10 percent and 20 percent are scheduled to return.

Example—Florence is in the 25 percent tax bracket and has just sold her stock in America Utility. She has a gain of $10,000. The saving in tax is:

Tax at ordinary income	$2,500
Capital gains 15% rate	1,500
Tax Savings	$ 1,000

The saving is more significant as one's tax bracket goes up. Let's say that Florence's tax bracket was 35 percent. The saving in tax increases to:

Tax at ordinary income	$3,500
Capital gains 15% rate	1,500
Tax Savings	$ 2,000

With such significant tax savings, there is strong incentive to aggressively search for transactions that allow capital gains treatment.

WHAT IS A CAPITAL ASSET?

When we look for the definition of a capital asset, the code sections and regulations merely indicate what a capital asset is not. IRC (Internal Revenue Code) §1221 states that a capital asset is "property held by the taxpayer," with the exception of the following eight classes of property:

1. Inventory or other property held primarily for sale to customers in the ordinary course of the taxpayer's trade or business
2. Depreciable or real property used in the taxpayer's trade or business
3. Certain literary or artistic property
4. Accounts or notes receivable arising from the taxpayer's trade or business
5. Certain publications of the federal government
6. Commodity financial instruments held by dealers
7. Hedging transactions
8. Supplies of a type regularly consumed in the ordinary course of the taxpayer's trade or business.

Property held longer than one year yields long-term gains or losses, which are taxed at lower rates. Property held less than one year is treated as a short-term gain or loss.[1] Short-term capital gain is taxed at ordinary income rates. In computing the holding period of the property, the day of acquisition is not counted. The holding period begins the day after the property is acquired. However, the date of disposition is counted.[2] Under §1222, net short-term capital gain is the excess of short-term capital gains over short-term capital losses for the taxable year, and net short-term capital loss is the excess of short-term losses over short-term gains. The same is true of long-term capital gains and losses.

Example—In 2002, Chet sells stock that he held less than one year for a gain of $5000. Later in the year he sells investments that he owned for more than one year, which included stock, at a gain of $10,000 and bonds at a loss of $6000. At the end of the year he sells additional stocks, held less than one year, for a loss of $6000.

Short-term capital gain	$5,000	Long-term capital gain	$10,000
Short-term capital loss	(6,000)	Long-term capital loss	(6,000)
Net short-term capital loss	(1,000)	Net long-term capital gain	4,000

Chet has a net capital gain of $3000 for the year. Exhibit 1-1 shows the computation of his Schedule D of his Form 1040 for the 2002 tax year. Additionally, Chet's salary is $65,000, his dividends are $500 and he received a capital gain distribution of $1500.

Chet's taxable income is $62,300, after taking into account his deductions and exemptions. Schedule D separates the capital gain components of income from the ordinary tax component. Chet has total capital gains of $4500. This includes capital gain distributions paid out by mutual funds. They are taxed as long-term capital gains, regardless of how long a taxpayer has held the investment. This is because they represent the net realized long-term capital gains earned by the mutual fund itself.

CAPITAL GAIN TAX RATES—INDIVIDUALS

The significance of the net capital gain in the previous example is that it is taxed at capital gain rates. Long-term capital gains can be from 15-percent, 25-percent, and 28-percent rates. The 15-percent rate is reduced to 5 percent for taxpayers currently in the 15-percent tax bracket but only to the extent that the net capital gains would be subject to the 15-percent tax rate. Therefore, Chet's $3000 gain from the previous example would be taxed at 5 percent or 15 percent depending on Chet's tax bracket.

The 28-percent capital gains bracket applies to the sale or exchange of collectibles held longer than one year. Collectibles include works of art, antiques, gems, stamps, and coins.[3]

Example—Therese purchased a wooden statue for $5000 and sold it for $12,000 thirteen months later. She has a net capital long-term gain of $7000, and the maximum tax rate that she will pay on that gain is 28 percent, depending on her regular tax bracket.

Unrecaptured §1250[4] gain, which results from the sale of depreciable

Exhibit 1-1

SCHEDULE D (Form 1040) Department of the Treasury Internal Revenue Service (99)	**Capital Gains and Losses** ▶ Attach to Form 1040. ▶ See Instructions for Schedule D (Form 1040). ▶ Use Schedule D-1 to list additional transactions for lines 1 and 8.	OMB No. 1545-0074 **2002** Attachment Sequence No. **12**

Name(s) shown on Form 1040	Your social security number
Chester Doe	111-22-3333

Part I   Short-Term Capital Gains and Losses-Assets Held One Year or Less

(a) Description of property (Example: 100 sh. XYZ Co.)	(b) Date acquired (Mo., day, yr.)	(c) Date sold (Mo., day, yr.)	(d) Sales price (see page D-5 of the instructions)	(e) Cost or other basis (see page D-5 of the instructions)	(f) Gain or (loss) Subtract (e) from (d)	
1 ABC Corp.	3/01/02	6/15/02	10,000	5,000	5,000	
Very Nice Corporation	1/05/02	8/04/02	4,000	10,000	−6,000	

2 Enter your short-term totals, if any, from Schedule D-1, line 2	2			
3 Total short-term sales price amounts. Add lines 1 and 2 in column (d)	3	14,000		
4 Short-term gain from Form 6252 and short-term gain or (loss) from Forms 4684, 6781, and 8824	4			
5 Net short-term gain or (loss) from partnerships, S corporations, estates, and trusts from Schedule(s) K-1	5			
6 Short-term capital loss carryover. Enter the amount, if any, from line 8 of your 2001 Capital Loss Carryover Worksheet	6	(		)
7 Net short-term capital gain or (loss). Combine lines 1 through 6 in column (f)	7	−1,000		

Part II   Long-Term Capital Gains and Losses-Assets Held More Than One Year

(a) Description of property (Example: 100 sh. XYZ Co.)	(b) Date acquired (Mo., day, yr.)	(c) Date sold (Mo., day, yr.)	(d) Sales price (see page D-5 of the instructions)	(e) Cost or other basis (see page D-5 of the instructions)	(f) Gain or (loss) Subtract (e) from (d)	(g) 28% rate gain or (loss) (see instr. below)
8 DEF Corp.	9/20/00	10/15/02	25,000	15,000	10,000	
American Bonds	6/02/00	11/09/02	10,000	16,000	−6,000	

9 Enter your long-term totals, if any, from Schedule D-1, line 9	9			
10 Total long-term sales price amounts. Add lines 8 and 9 in column (d)	10	35,000		
11 Gain from Form 4797, Part I; long-term gain from Forms 2439 and 6252; and long-term gain or (loss) from Forms 4684, 6781, and 8824	11			
12 Net long-term gain or (loss) from partnerships, S corporations, estates, and trusts from Schedule(s) K-1	12			
13 Capital gain distributions. See page D-1 of the instructions	13	1,500		
14 Long-term capital loss carryover. Enter in both columns (f) and (g) the amount, if any, from line 13 of your 2001 Capital Loss Carryover Worksheet	14	(		)
15 Combine lines 8 through 14 in column (g)	15			
16 Net long-term capital gain or (loss). Combine lines 8 through 14 in column (f)	16	5,500		

Next: Go to Part III on the back.

* **28% rate gain or loss** includes all "collectibles gains and losses" (as defined on page D-6 of the instructions) and up to 50% of the eligible gain on qualified small business stock (see page D-4 of the instructions).

For Paperwork Reduction Act Notice, see Form 1040 instructions.   Schedule D (Form 1040) 2002

DAA

Exhibit 1-1 (Continued)

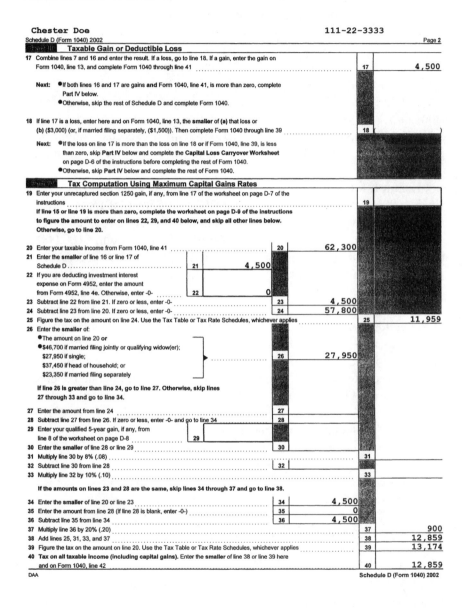

real estate, is taxed at a maximum rate of 25 percent. Examples of depreciable real estate include an apartment complex or an office building. Taxpayers who own depreciable real estate placed in service after 1986 recover its cost using a straight-line method over either $27\frac{1}{2}$ years, for residential rental property, or 39 years, for nonresidential real property holdings. (Straight-line depreciation means the cost of the property is recovered evenly over the recovery period.) Gain to the extent of this depreciation is taxed at 25 percent. Depreciable real estate placed in service in earlier periods may have been eligible for depreciation on a faster, or accelerated, schedule. To the extent that depreciation claimed exceeds straight-line, gain from the sale of depreciable real estate will be taxed as ordinary income.

Example—Colette sells a commercial building that she has owned since 1980 for $1,500,000. She originally paid $500,000 for it and has taken $400,000 of depreciation[5] on the building of which $100,000 was accelerated.[6] Colette's total gain is $1,400,000; of this amount, $100,000 is treated as ordinary income, $300,000 is taxed at 25 percent as unrecaptured §1250 gain, and $1,000,000 is treated as long-term capital gain at 15 percent.

We assume that Colette has a salary of $65,000 plus gain from the sale of the building. Exhibit 1-2 is the Schedule D from Colette's Form 1040 and Form 4797—Sales of Business Property. Page 2 of Form 4797 shows the details of the sale including dates of acquisition and disposition, sales price, cost, depreciation allowed, basis, gain, and any accelerated depreciation that would be recaptured as ordinary income. In our example this is $100,000.

Colette's total taxable income is $1,460,300, computed as follows:

Salary	$ 65,000
Capital Gains	1,300,000
Ordinary Income	100,000
Total Income	1,465,000
Less:	
Standard Deduction	(4,700) (changes each year)
Exemption	0
Taxable income	$1,460,300

Due to income exceeding a threshold of $137,300, Colette is not allowed a deduction for herself or any dependents.[7]

Since $1,300,000 is subject to capital gains tax rates, $160,300 is taxed as ordinary income. $1,000,000 of the gain is taxed at capital gains of 15 percent which is $150,000 and $300,000 is unrecaptured §1250 gain taxed at a rate of 25 percent for $75,000.

LIMITATION ON CAPITAL LOSSES FOR INDIVIDUALS

A noncorporate taxpayer may use short-term or long-term capital losses to offset short-term or long-term capital gains. If losses exceed the gains, $3000 of the excess may be deducted against ordinary income. Under §1212(b), the remaining losses may be carried forward indefinitely and used to offset capital gains or ordinary income (up to the $3000) in future years. The losses that are carried forward retain their character as short-term or long-term in future years and are combined with the future gains and losses to determine the taxpayer's net capital gains and losses.[8]

Example—Yevonne has a net long-term capital gain of $3000, a net short-term capital loss of $10,000, and ordinary income of $40,000. She will use $3000 of her loss to offset the $3000 of capital gain. Also, she may deduct an additional $3000 of the losses against her ordinary income, reducing the $40,000 figure to $37,000. The remaining $4000 of Yevonne's loss must be carried forward and can be used indefinitely to offset capital gains or ordinary income arising in the future.

TRANSACTIONS BETWEEN RELATED PERSONS

Under §267, there is no capital loss deduction allowed from the sale or exchange of property, directly or indirectly, between the following parties:

- Members of a family defined as brothers and sisters (whether by whole or half blood), spouse, ancestors, and lineal ancestors
- A corporation and an individual who, directly or indirectly, owns more than 50 percent of the value of the outstanding stock of the corporation
- A grantor and fiduciary of any trust
- A fiduciary of a trust and a beneficiary of another trust, if the same person is a grantor of both trusts
- A fiduciary of a trust and a corporation if more than 50 percent of the value of outstanding stock is owned, directly or indirectly, by or for the trust or by or for the person who is a grantor of the trust

EXHIBIT 1-2

SCHEDULE D (Form 1040)		Capital Gains and Losses				OMB No. 1545-0074 2002

Department of the Treasury
Internal Revenue Service (99)

▶ Attach to Form 1040.   ▶ See Instructions for Schedule D (Form 1040).
▶ Use Schedule D-1 to list additional transactions for lines 1 and 8.

Attachment Sequence No. **12**

Name(s) shown on Form 1040: **Colette Doe**

Your social security number: **111-22-3333**

Part I — Short-Term Capital Gains and Losses—Assets Held One Year or Less

(a) Description of property (Example: 100 sh. XYZ Co.)	(b) Date acquired (Mo., day, yr.)	(c) Date sold (Mo., day, yr.)	(d) Sales price (see page D-5 of the instructions)	(e) Cost or other basis (see page D-5 of the instructions)	(f) Gain or (loss) Subtract (e) from (d)
1					

2 Enter your short-term totals, if any, from Schedule D-1, line 2 ...... **2**
3 Total short-term sales price amounts. Add lines 1 and 2 in column (d) **3**
4 Short-term gain from Form 6252 and short-term gain or (loss) from Forms 4684, 6781, and 8824 ...... **4**
5 Net short-term gain or (loss) from partnerships, S corporations, estates, and trusts from Schedule(s) K-1 ...... **5**
6 Short-term capital loss carryover. Enter the amount, if any, from line 8 of your 2001 Capital Loss Carryover Worksheet **6**
7 Net short-term capital gain or (loss). Combine lines 1 through 6 in column (f) **7**   **0**

Part II — Long-Term Capital Gains and Losses—Assets Held More Than One Year

(a) Description of property (Example: 100 sh. XYZ Co.)	(b) Date acquired (Mo., day, yr.)	(c) Date sold (Mo., day, yr.)	(d) Sales price (see page D-5 of the instructions)	(e) Cost or other basis (see page D-5 of the instructions)	(f) Gain or (loss) Subtract (e) from (d)	(g) 28% rate gain or (loss) * (see instr. below)
8						

9 Enter your long-term totals, if any, from Schedule D-1, line 9 ...... **9**
10 Total long-term sales price amounts. Add lines 8 and 9 in column (d) **10**
11 Gain from Form 4797, Part I; long-term gain from Forms 2439 and 6252; and long-term gain or (loss) from Forms 4684, 6781, and 8824 ...... **11**   **1,300,000**
12 Net long-term gain or (loss) from partnerships, S corporations, estates, and trusts from Schedule(s) K-1 ...... **12**
13 Capital gain distributions. See page D-1 of the instructions **13**
14 Long-term capital loss carryover. Enter in both columns (f) and (g) the amount, if any, from line 13 of your 2001 Capital Loss Carryover Worksheet **14**
15 Combine lines 8 through 14 in column (g) **15**
16 Net long-term capital gain or (loss). Combine lines 8 through 14 in column (f) **16**   **1,300,000**
   Next: Go to Part III on the back.

* 28% rate gain or loss includes all "collectibles gains and losses" (as defined on page D-6 of the instructions) and up to 50% of the eligible gain on qualified small business stock (see page D-4 of the instructions).

For Paperwork Reduction Act Notice, see Form 1040 instructions.

Schedule D (Form 1040) 2002

DAA

EXHIBIT 1-2 (Continued)

Colette Doe   111-22-3333

Schedule D (Form 1040) 2002   Page 2

■ Taxable Gain or Deductible Loss

17	Combine lines 7 and 16 and enter the result. If a loss, go to line 18. If a gain, enter the gain on Form 1040, line 13, and complete Form 1040 through line 41	**17**	1,300,000

Next: ● If both lines 16 and 17 are gains and Form 1040, line 41, is more than zero, complete Part IV below.
        ● Otherwise, skip the rest of Schedule D and complete Form 1040.

18	If line 17 is a loss, enter here and on Form 1040, line 13, the **smaller** of (a) that loss or (b) ($3,000) (or, if married filing separately, ($1,500)). Then complete Form 1040 through line 39	**18**	( )

Next: ● If the loss on line 17 is more than the loss on line 18 or if Form 1040, line 39, is less than zero, skip **Part IV** below and complete the **Capital Loss Carryover Worksheet** on page D-6 of the instructions before completing the rest of Form 1040.
        ● Otherwise, skip **Part IV** below and complete the rest of Form 1040.

■ Tax Computation Using Maximum Capital Gains Rates

19	Enter your unrecaptured section 1250 gain, if any, from line 17 of the worksheet on page D-7 of the instructions	**19**	300,000

If line 15 or line 19 is more than zero, complete the worksheet on page D-9 of the instructions to figure the amount to enter on lines 22, 29, and 40 below, and skip all other lines below. Otherwise, go to line 20.

20	Enter your taxable income from Form 1040, line 41	**20**		
21	Enter the **smaller** of line 16 or line 17 of Schedule D	**21**		
22	If you are deducting investment interest expense on Form 4952, enter the amount from Form 4952, line 4e. Otherwise, enter -0-	**22**	0	
23	Subtract line 22 from line 21. If zero or less, enter -0-		**23**	
24	Subtract line 23 from line 20. If zero or less, enter -0-		**24**	
25	Figure the tax on the amount on line 24. Use the Tax Table or Tax Rate Schedules, whichever applies		**25**	
26	Enter the **smaller** of:		**26**	

    ● The amount on line 20 or
    ● $46,700 if married filing jointly or qualifying widow(er);
        $27,950 if single;
        $37,450 if head of household; or
        $23,350 if married filing separately

If line 26 is greater than line 24, go to line 27. Otherwise, skip lines 27 through 33 and go to line 34.

27	Enter the amount from line 24	**27**		
28	Subtract line 27 from line 26. If zero or less, enter -0- and go to line 34	**28**		
29	Enter your qualified 5-year gain, if any, from line 8 of the worksheet on page D-8	**29**		
30	Enter the **smaller** of line 28 or line 29		**30**	
31	Multiply line 30 by 8% (.08)		**31**	
32	Subtract line 30 from line 28	**32**		
33	Multiply line 32 by 10% (.10)		**33**	

If the amounts on lines 23 and 28 are the same, skip lines 34 through 37 and go to line 38.

34	Enter the **smaller** of line 20 or line 23	**34**		
35	Enter the amount from line 28 (if line 28 is blank, enter -0-)	**35**		
36	Subtract line 35 from line 34	**36**		
37	Multiply line 36 by 20% (.20)		**37**	
38	Add lines 25, 31, 33, and 37		**38**	
39	Figure the tax on the amount on line 20. Use the Tax Table or Tax Rate Schedules, whichever applies		**39**	
40	**Tax on all taxable income (including capital gains).** Enter the **smaller** of line 38 or line 39 here and on Form 1040, line 42		**40**	318,358

DAA   Schedule D (Form 1040) 2002

Exhibit 1-2

Form **4797**	**Sales of Business Property**	OMB No. 1545-0184
	(Also Involuntary Conversions and Recapture Amounts Under Sections 179 and 280F(b)(2))	**2002**
Department of the Treasury Internal Revenue Service (99)	▶ Attach to your tax return. ▶ See separate instructions.	Attachment Sequence No. **27**

Name(s) shown on return	Identifying number
Colette Doe	111-22-3333

1 Enter the gross proceeds from sales or exchanges reported to you for 2002 on Form(s) 1099-B or 1099-S (or substitute statement) that you are including on line 2, 10, or 20 (see instructions) .... | **1** |

Part I **Sales or Exchanges of Property Used in a Trade or Business and Involuntary Conversions From Other Than Casualty or Theft—Most Property Held More Than 1 Year** (See instructions.)

(a) Description of property	(b) Date acquired (mo., day, yr.)	(c) Date sold (mo., day, yr.)	(d) Gross sales price	(e) Depreciation allowed or allowable since acquisition	(f) Cost or other basis, plus improvements and expense of sale	(g) Gain or (loss) Subtract (f) from the sum of (d) and (e)
2						

3	Gain, if any, from Form 4684, line 39	**3**
4	Section 1231 gain from installment sales from Form 6252, line 26 or 37	**4**
5	Section 1231 gain or (loss) from like-kind exchanges from Form 8824	**5**
6	Gain, if any, from line 32, from other than casualty or theft	**6**	1,300,000
7	Combine lines 2 through 6. Enter the gain or (loss) here and on the appropriate line as follows:	**7**	1,300,000

Partnerships (except electing large partnerships). Report the gain or (loss) following the instructions for Form 1065, Schedule K, line 6, or Form 1120S, Schedule K, line 5. Skip lines 8, 9, 11, and 12 below

All others. If line 7 is zero or a loss, enter the amount from line 7 on line 11 below and skip lines 8 and 9. If line 7 is a gain and you did not have any prior year section 1231 losses, or they were recaptured in an earlier year, enter the gain from line 7 as a long-term capital gain on Schedule D and skip lines 8, 9, 11, and 12 below.

8	Nonrecaptured net section 1231 losses from prior years (see instructions)	**8**
9	Subtract line 8 from line 7. If zero or less, enter -0-. If line 9 is zero, enter the gain from line 7 on line 12 below. If line 9 is more than zero, enter the amount from line 8 on line 12 below and enter the gain from line 9 as a long-term capital gain on Schedule D (see instructions)	**9**

Part II **Ordinary Gains and Losses**

10 Ordinary gains and losses not included on lines 11 through 17 (include property held 1 year or less):

11	Loss, if any, from line 7	**11**	
12	Gain, if any, from line 7 or amount from line 8, if applicable	**12**	
13	Gain, if any, from line 31	**13**	100,000
14	Net gain or (loss) from Form 4684, lines 31 and 38a	**14**	
15	Ordinary gain from installment sales from Form 6252, line 25 or 36	**15**	
16	Ordinary gain or (loss) from like-kind exchanges from Form 8824	**16**	
17	Recapture of section 179 expense deduction for partners and S corporation shareholders from property dispositions by partnerships and S corporations (see instructions)	**17**	
18	Combine lines 10 through 17. Enter the gain or (loss) here and on the appropriate line as follows:	**18**	100,000
a	For all except individual returns. Enter the gain or (loss) from line 18 on the return being filed.		
b	For individual returns:		
	(1) If the loss on line 11 includes a loss from Form 4684, line 35, column (b)(ii), enter that part of the loss here. Enter the part of the loss from income-producing property on Schedule A (Form 1040), line 27, and the part of the loss from property used as an employee on Schedule A (Form 1040), line 22. Identify as from "Form 4797, line 18b(1)." See instructions	**18b(1)**	
	(2) Redetermine the gain or (loss) on line 18 excluding the loss, if any, on line 18b(1). Enter here and on Form 1040, line 14	**18b(2)**	100,000

For Paperwork Reduction Act Notice, see page 7 of the Instructions.   Form **4797** (2002)

DAA

EXHIBIT 1-2 (Continued)

Form 4797   **Page 1 of 1**

(2002)   **Colette Doe**   **111-22-3333**   Page 2

Part III   **Gain From Disposition of Property Under Sections 1245, 1250, 1252, 1254, and 1255**

19	(a) Description of section 1245, 1250, 1252, 1254, or 1255 property:	(b) Date acquired (mo., day, yr.)	(c) Date sold (mo., day, yr.)
A	Commercial Building	3/02/80	6/16/02
B			
C			
D			

	These columns relate to the properties on lines 19A - 19D. ►		Property A	Property B	Property C	Property D
20	Gross sales price (Note: See line 1 before completing.)	20	1,500,000			
21	Cost or other basis plus expense of sale	21	500,000			
22	Depreciation (or depletion) allowed or allowable	22	400,000			
23	Adjusted basis. Subtract line 22 from line 21	23	100,000			
24	Total gain. Subtract line 23 from line 20	24	1,400,000			
25	**If section 1245 property:**					
a	Depreciation allowed or allowable from line 22	25a				
b	Enter the **smaller** of line 24 or 25a	25b				
26	**If section 1250 property:** If straight line depreciation was used, enter -0- on line 26g, except for a corporation subject to section 291.					
a	Additional depreciation after 1975 (see instructions)	26a	100,000			
b	Applicable percentage multiplied by the **smaller** of line 24 or line 26a (see instructions)	26b	100,000			
c	Subtract line 26a from line 24. If residential rental property or line 24 is not more than line 26a, skip lines 26d and 26e	26c	1,300,000			
d	Additional depreciation after 1969 and before 1976	26d				
e	Enter the **smaller** of line 26c or 26d	26e				
f	Section 291 amount (corporations only)	26f				
g	Add lines 26b, 26e, and 26f	26g	100,000			
27	**If section 1252 property:** Skip this section if you did not dispose of farmland or if this form is being completed for a partnership (other than an electing large partnership).					
a	Soil, water, and land clearing expenses	27a				
b	Line 27a multiplied by applicable percentage (see instr.)	27b				
c	Enter the **smaller** of line 24 or 27b	27c				
28	**If section 1254 property:**					
a	Intangible drilling and development costs, expenditures for development of mines and other natural deposits, and mining exploration costs (see instructions)	28a				
b	Enter the **smaller** of line 24 or 28a	28b				
29	**If section 1255 property:**					
a	Applicable percentage of payments excluded from income under section 126 (see instructions)	29a				
b	Enter the **smaller** of line 24 or 29a (see instructions)	29b				

Summary of Part III Gains. Complete property columns A through D through line 29b before going to line 30.

30	Total gains for all properties. Add property columns A - D, line 24	30	1,400,000
31	Add property columns A through D, lines 25b, 26g, 27c, 28b, and 29b. Enter here and on line 13	31	100,000
32	Subtract line 31 from line 30. Enter the portion from casualty or theft on Form 4684, line 33. Enter the portion from other than casualty or theft on Form 4797, line 6	32	1,300,000

Part IV   **Recapture Amounts Under Sections 179 and 280F(b)(2) When Business Use Drops to 50% or Less** (See instructions.)

			(a) Section 179	(b) Section 280F(b)(2)
33	Section 179 expense deduction or depreciation allowable in prior years	33		
34	Recomputed depreciation. See instructions	34		
35	Recapture amount. Subtract line 34 from line 33. See the instr. for where to report	35		

DAA   Form **4797** (2002)

- A person and a §501 tax exempt organization that is controlled directly or indirectly by such person or by the members of the family of that person
- A corporation and a partnership if the same persons own more than 50 percent of the value of the outstanding stock of the corporation and more than 50 percent of the capital or profits interest in the partnership
- An S corporation and another S corporation if the same persons own more than 50 percent in the value of the outstanding stock of each corporation
- An S corporation and a C corporation, if the same persons own more than 50 percent in the value of the outstanding stock of each corporation; and
- An executor and beneficiary of an estate, (except to satisfy a pecuniary bequest).

Example—Nicholas purchases land from his mother, Colette, at its fair market value of $10,000. Colette's basis in the land is $12,000. Since they are mother and son, Colette is unable to deduct the $2000 loss on her tax return.

Example—Landco Development Co. purchases a building for $250,000 from B.A.D. Partnership. B.A.D. purchased the building for $300,000. Since Brad Davis is a partner of B.A.D. with a 60-percent profits interest in the partnership and also owns 75 percent of the outstanding stock in Landco, the $50,000 loss is not deductible by the Partnership, and the loss cannot be passed on to the partners.

As will be explained later in this chapter, it is possible that Nicholas and Landco may be able to use the losses that Colette and B.A.D. Partnership were unable to deduct. However, in general the related party rules are unfavorable to taxpayers, meaning that sales of loss property to a related buyer should be avoided.

CONSTRUCTIVE OWNERSHIP OF STOCK

IRC §267 further states that stock owned by one entity is deemed as being owned by another, through association. This is known as constructive ownership. This rule applies only to stock and not partnership interests, for example. It is used in economic relationships where the tax law deems common interests are present. This rule prevents individuals from disposing of ownership of a corporation among family members while still maintaining control. The constructive ownership rules include:

- Stock owned, directly or indirectly, by or for a corporation, partnership, estate, or trust is considered as being owned proportionately by or for its shareholders, partners, or beneficiaries;

    Example—Quad Partnership owns 1000 shares of Microtech Corporation. Quad has 4 partners, each owning 25 percent of the capital interest in the partnership. Each partner is deemed to own 250 shares of Microtech.

- An individual is treated as owning the stock owned, directly or indirectly, by or for his family;

- An individual owning stock in a corporation is considered to own the stock owned, directly or indirectly, by or for his partner.

    Example—Lois and Clark are equal partners in Duo Partnership. Lois owns 60 percent of the stock of Microtech, and Clark owns the remaining shares. If Clark sells property at a loss to Microtech, he cannot take the loss because he is treated as owning constructively the shares (60 percent) owned by Lois plus the 40 percent of the shares he owns directly for a total of 100 percent.

Amount of Gain Where the Loss Was Previously Disallowed

If a loss is disallowed under the §267 rules, the original seller received no tax deduction. However, the disallowed loss has no effect on the purchaser's basis in the property. His basis is equal to his purchase price. There is partial relief if the related party later sells the property in that he may reduce his gain by the amount of the previously disallowed loss.

Example—Yevonne sells a cottage to her daughter Serina for $100,000. Yevonne paid $125,000 for the cottage but is unable to deduct the loss on her tax return because of constructive ownership rules. Five years later Serina sells the cottage for $150,000. Serina's taxable long-term capital gain is:

Selling price	$150,000
Serina's basis	(100,000)
Yevonne's loss previously disallowed	(25,000)
Serina's recognized gain	$ 25,000

If Yevonne's previously disallowed loss was larger than Serina's gain, then the unused loss is not deductible. Note that the related party rules here have two effects: They delay the loss's use and also shift the deduction from Yevonne to Serina.

LOSSES THAT DO NOT QUALIFY FOR A DEDUCTION

The following losses are not deductible:

1. Personal losses, such as losses incurred on assets that are not used in a trade or business or held in a transaction engaged in for profit, do not qualify for a loss deduction. [9] For example, no loss is allowed to a taxpayer who bought a car for personal use, drove the vehicle for four years, and then sold it at $12,000 less than her purchase price.

    An exception is a casualty loss resulting from an asset destroyed by fire, storm, etc., or theft. A loss is allowed under the Personal Casualty Rules after reduction by an initial nondeductible amount of $100. The net casualty loss will only be allowed to the extent that it exceeds 10 percent of a taxpayer's adjusted gross income.

2. Unregistered Securities. If a taxpayer sustains a loss on securities or other obligations that are required to be in registered form, but are not, then the loss deduction generally will not be allowed. [10] In general, registration is required for obligations issued to the public by an entity, including a government, with a maturity beyond one year. An obligation is considered to be in registered form, for example, if the right to principal and stated interest may be transferred only through a book entry system the issuer maintains. An exception to the rule denying the loss deduction is when broker-dealers hold obligations for sale to customers in the ordinary course of business and sell them to certain financial institutions or exempt organizations.

3. Frustration of Public Policy. A loss is not deductible if it is in contrast to state or federal public policy. This includes fines or penalties paid for violating any law, illegal bribes, kickbacks, lobbying and political expenditures paid for influencing legislation. [11]

4. Inventory losses are not deductible. Losses incurred in inventories will be reported through the taxpayer's accounting records as an adjustment to opening inventory or to purchases.

5. Estates cannot claim the same loss for estate tax purposes and income tax purposes.

6. Demolition losses incurred from a building or other structure are not deductible. Instead the taxpayer is required to capitalize the loss

by adding the cost of the demolition to the basis of the land upon which the building or structure stood. The adjusted basis of the building prior to demolition should also be added to the basis of the land.[12] No loss is allowed when the value of property declines after it is acquired. This loss is unrealized and the gain or loss is not recognized until the property is sold or exchanged.[13]

WHEN IS A LOSS INCURRED?

A loss is allowed as a deduction only for the taxable year in which the loss is sustained. A loss must be evidenced by closed and completed transactions and by identifiable events occurring in that taxable year in order to be deductible.[14]

Example—Matthew owned property containing a fresh water stream in Love Canal, Niagara Falls. He allowed fishermen to fish there during the summer for a flat fee. In the fall of 1995, it was revealed that chemical leakage may have affected the area. In spring of 1997, Matthew could see substantial dead fish in his stream and could determine that the spring could no longer support wildlife. Although the leakage was discovered in 1995, the actual effects to Matthew's stream were not able to be determined until 1997, therefore his loss occurred in 1997. If there is a reasonable prospect for recovery, then a loss is not deductible until the situation is resolved.

If a taxpayer deducts a loss in one year and then is compensated for the loss in a later year, the taxpayer must include the recovery in gross income to the extent the taxpayer received a benefit from the deduction.[15]

§1231 PROPERTY USED IN A TRADE OR BUSINESS AND INVOLUNTARY CONVERSIONS

IRC §1231 is related to property used in a trade or business and involuntary conversions by individuals and corporations. This is property that is subject to the allowance for depreciation and that has been held more than one year. It does not include:

- Property that constitutes inventory
- Property held by the taxpayer primarily for sale to customers in the ordinary course of his trade or business

- A copyright, literary, musical, or artistic composition, a letter or memorandum, or similar intellectual property
- A publication of the U.S. government, or any agency thereof, other than purchased by the taxpayer at the price offered for sale to the public

Trade or business property also includes timber, coal, domestic iron ore, livestock, and unharvested crop.

The excess of §1231 gains over §1231 losses is treated as long-term capital gain. The excess of §1231 losses over §1231 gains, is treated as ordinary loss.

Example—Melissa, a sole proprietor, sells her office desk, which she has owned for over a year for $5000. Her basis is $3500, so she has a net gain of $1500. This is a long-term capital gain. If her basis was $10,000, Melissa would be able to take a $5000 ordinary loss. If it was a capital loss (without any other capital gains), she would only be able to deduct $3000 against ordinary income.

For tax years beginning after 1984, any net §1231 gain is ordinary income up to the amount of any nonrecaptured net §1231 losses from the previous five years. This is known as the Lookback Rule.

Example—Melissa sells her office desk for $10,000. Her basis is $5000. Additionally, she had a §1231 loss in 1999 of $3000 with no subsequent transactions. The resulting gain of $5000 is treated as a capital gain of $2000 and ordinary income of $3000. Melissa must recapture the $3000 §1231 loss from 1999 as ordinary income.

IRC §1400F RENEWAL COMMUNITY CAPITAL GAIN

The Community Renewal Tax Relief Act of 2000 authorizes up to 40 renewal communities. Renewal communities are part of an effort by Congress to encourage development in economically distressed areas. Information about designated communities is available through the IRS Web site (*www.irs.gov*). Businesses located in renewal communities will be eligible for tax incentives.[16] To qualify, a renewal community business must meet all of the following requirements:

- Every trade or business of the corporation or partnership is the active conduct of a qualified business within a renewal community not including a sole proprietorship.

- At least 50 percent of its total gross income is from the active conduct of a qualified business within a renewal community.
- A substantial part of the use of its tangible property is within a renewal community.
- A substantial part of its intangible property is used in the active conduct of the business.
- A substantial part of the employees' services are performed within a renewal community.
- At least 35 percent of the employees are residents of a renewal community.
- Less than 5 percent of the average of the total unadjusted bases of the property owned by the business is from:
  (a) Nonqualified financial property (generally, debt, stock, partnership interests, options, futures contracts, forward contracts, warrants, notional principal contracts, and annuities), or
  (b) Collectibles not held primarily for sale to customers.[17]

Benefits to renewal community investors include a full exclusion of any qualified capital gain derived from the sale of a qualified community asset held for more than five years.[18] This includes stock, a partnership interest, and business property located in the qualified community.

To qualify, the stock, partnership interest, and business property must have the following characteristics:

- Acquired by the taxpayer after December 31, 2001 and before January 1, 2010 at its original issue or purchased for cash
- At the time of issuance or purchase, the corporation, partnership, or property was designated as a renewal community business or for use thereof, and
- The corporation, partnership or property remained a renewal community business interest during the taxpayer's entire holding period[19]

The qualified excluded gain means any gain recognized on the sale or exchange of the qualified stock, partnership interest or §1231(b)[20] business property. However, special attention must be paid to the dates. The gain derived from the appreciation of the property applicable to periods before January 1, 2002 and after December 31, 2014 is not excluded.[21] Additionally, the gain that must be recognized as a result of depreciation recapture, is not excluded. The Secretary of HUD has designated the renewal communities, which can be located on their Web site at *www.hud.gov*.

CORPORATIONS

The netting of short-term gains and losses and long-term gains and losses is the same for individuals and corporations. Also, §1231 rules on gains and losses on sales and exchanges of business property are the same for individuals and corporations. However, under §1201(a), if the maximum regular corporate rate exceeds 35 percent, the tax is the lesser of:

1. The tax computed on taxable income including the gain, or
2. The tax computed on taxable income excluding capital gains, plus tax at 35 percent of the capital gains.

In other words, a corporation's capital gains are not eligible for taxation at the favorable rates available to individuals. A second important difference is in the treatment of capital losses. Under §1212(a), corporations may deduct capital losses up to the amount of their capital gains. If a corporation has a net capital loss for a taxable year, it may carry it back to the three preceding years and forward to the next five years. There is no $3000 offset against ordinary income comparable to what individuals enjoy.

Example—BKC Corporation has a net capital loss of $10,000 in 2000 with no offsetting capital gains. BKC first must carryback this loss to 1997 and offset any capital gains for that year. It is considered a short-term capital loss and offsets capital gain net income. There were no capital gains in 1997 but there were $3000 of capital gains in 1998 and $2000 in 1999, which must be offset by the $10,000. The remaining $5000 is carried forward to 2001. If there is no capital gain net income from 2001 to 2005, the loss carryover will expire. A carryback capital loss may not increase or produce a net operating loss for the taxable year to which it is carried back.[22] Additionally, a corporation may not carry back a net capital loss to a taxable year in which it is a foreign personal holding company, regulated investment company (mutual fund), or a real estate investment trust. Regulated investment companies have eight-year carryforward periods.

S CORPORATIONS AND PARTNERSHIPS

S Corporations and Partnerships are not subject to capital gains taxes at the entity level. They are aggregated and reported on Schedule D of Form

1120S in the case of the S Corporation and Form 1065 for the Partnership. Each shareholder's or partner's proportionate share of the long-term and short-term capital gain or loss is reported on Schedule K-1 of the 1120S or 1065. The amounts indicated on the K-1 are then reported on the Schedule D of the shareholder's or partner's individual Form 1040.

TRUSTS AND ESTATES

Trusts and Estates must report their capital gain income on Schedule D of Form 1041. If there is a net capital loss, a maximum of $3000 may be taken against ordinary income. The remaining amount is a capital loss carryover. Under the tax law, if an estate terminates with unused capital loss carryovers, the deductions can be claimed by the estate beneficiaries.[23]

LIMITED LIABILITY COMPANIES

A Limited Liability Company (LLC) reports its capital gains depending on how it elects to be treated for tax purposes. The LLC can choose to be taxed as a partnership or a corporation. A one-member limited liability company can be taxed as a sole proprietorship or as a corporation.

CONCLUSION

Because of the tax rate differential that exists between capital gain transactions and ordinary income, investors always try to determine how to appropriately plan for capital gains. The timing of transactions is particularly important whereby planning for capital losses to offset capital gains effectively eliminates taxes. However, the use of losses is often hampered by the passive activity rules, which are covered in Chapter 2.

NOTES

[1] §1222 (1), (2)

[2] Rev. Rul. 66-7, 1966-1 C.B. 188, amplifying I.T. 3985, 1949-2 C.B. 51

[3] §1(h)(6)(A)

[4] §1250 outlines the rules for depreciating real property.

[5] Taxpayers are not permitted to deduct the cost of an asset acquired for business or investment use. Instead they must deduct a certain portion of the purchase price each year over the expected life of the asset. This deduction is known as depreciation.

[6] There are several methods of depreciation. Straight-line depreciation is generally used for financial statements prepared under generally accepted accounting principles. Under this method the asset is depreciated over its useful life. However, the modified accelerated cost recovery system (MACRS) is often used for tax purposes for assets placed in service after 1986. Under this method, larger amounts of depreciation are calculated at the beginning period when an asset is first placed into service. Therefore, the depreciable amount is accelerated.

[7] Phaseouts exist for taxpayers in higher income brackets. When income exceeds a certain threshold, the exemption is reduced to zero. In 2002 the thresholds were: $137,300 for a single person, $206,000 for a married couple filing jointly or a qualified widow(er), and $171,650 for head of household.

[8] Reg. §1.1212-1(b)(1)

[9] §165(c)(3)

[10] §165(j)

[11] §162

[12] §280B(a)(2)

[13] §165(b)

[14] §1.165.1(d)(1)

[15] §111

[16] IRS Publication 954, Pg. 1

[17] IRS Publication 954

[18] §1400F(a)

[19] §1400F(b)(2)

[20] §1231(b) property is property used in a trade or business and subject to the allowance for depreciation. It cannot be inventory, a copyright, literary, musical, or artistic composition, or a letter or memorandum. It also cannot be a publication of the US Government not purchased directly from the US Government.

[21] §1400F(c)

[22] §1212(a)(1)(A)(ii)

[23] See Tax Code §642(h) and the accompanying regulations.

2

PASSIVE ACTIVITY LOSSES AND PASSIVE ACTIVITY CREDITS

INTRODUCTION

In 1986, restrictions on the use of passive activity losses ("PALs") and passive activity credits ("PACs") were enacted. These rules were designed to prevent taxpayers from using losses generated by certain investments to offset income from other sources, like salary. The passive activity rules can create unexpected tax consequences for investors. For example, an investor who purchases an interest in an activity that initially is expected to throw off losses may be unable to use those losses to offset other income. Similarly, a taxpayer whose investments in rental property are generating large depreciation deductions may be unable to use those deductions to offset income from a stock purchase that he or she is contemplating. In order to evaluate both existing and potential new investments, a taxpayer has to understand how the passive activity rules affect the use of any deductions or credits that may be involved.

Example—Helen is a successful executive. On the advice of her broker, in Year One Helen decides to purchase a limited partnership interest for $100,000. Helen holds the interest strictly as an investment; she is not involved in actual partnership operations. Helen also owns stock in various corporations that produces dividends of $7500. She has no other investments. Although ultimately expected to be profitable, the limited partnership in which Helen holds an interest generates losses in Year One. Helen's share is $15,000. Assuming Helen's marginal tax rate is 35 percent, the losses would have a value to her of $5250 if she can use them to offset her salary and dividend income ($15,000 × .35). However, because the passive activity rules apply, Helen's share of the limited partnership's deductions can offset only income from other passive activities.[1] This means Helen's $100,000 investment produces no return to her in the current year.

Helen will carry losses and credits not useable under the passive activity rules to later years. Assuming that Helen sells the limited partnership interest in five years, the losses frozen under the passive activity rules must be used first to offset any passive income Helen may have. After that, the deductions will reduce income from nonpassive sources. However, restrictions still remain on the use of any passive activity credits that Helen's limited partnership investment may have created.

Passive activities are activities that involve the conduct of a trade or business in which a taxpayer does not "materially participate." Special rules apply to rental activities, which also may be treated as passive. Passive activities are distinguished from activities that generate active income, like salary or other compensation for services. Portfolio income, like interest, dividends, annuities, royalties, income from mutual funds, or similar items not derived in the ordinary course of a trade or business, and expenses associated with such income, also fall outside the passive activity calculations.[2] Deductions or credits that can't be taken in the current year under passive activity restrictions have a reduced value because of the time value of money. For example, because she has no passive income in Year One, Helen will be unable to claim the $15,000 loss on her Year One Form 1040, meaning she will receive no tax benefit from that loss until some later period. In the case of passive activity losses, however, the deductions ultimately may be useable against nonpassive income, when the taxpayer disposes of the passive activity. This rule does not apply to passive activity credits.

TAXPAYERS TO WHICH THE PAL AND PAC RULES APPLY

In evaluating the potential impact of the passive activity restrictions on investors, the first step is to determine if the rules, which are found in §469 of the Tax Code, even apply. Individuals, estates, and most trusts are subject to these limitations.[3] The rules apply to pass-through entities, like partnerships, S corporations, and grantor trusts, at the taxpayer level. In other words, an investor considering the purchase of a partnership interest must consider the effect of §469 when evaluating the tax impact of his or her projected share of partnership income, gain, deduction, loss, and credit. Since the partnership itself does not pay taxes, however, it is not affected by the rules other than for how it reports income and other items to the partners.

With the exception of closely held and also personal service corporations, the IRC §469 provisions do not apply to C corporations.[4] A corporation is closely held if at any time during the last half of the tax year, five or fewer individuals own more than half of its stock directly or indirectly.[5] Attribution rules apply, under which a taxpayer is treated as owning stock held by his or her spouse, siblings, ancestors, and lineal descendants. In addition, stock owned directly or indirectly by or for a corporation, partnership, estate, or trust is attributed, in proportion, to the shareholders, partners, or beneficiaries. Also, a taxpayer owns any stock on which he or she holds an option. The effect of these rules is that many small corporations owned by members of one family, or by a limited number of people, will have to consider the impact of §469 on any passive activities the corporation holds.

Example—Bill owns 10 percent of the stock of Cook, Inc. Bill's daughters, Donna and Sheila, and his sons, John and Jim, own 9 percent each. Suffolk Company owns 8 percent of Cook. Bill is a 90-percent stockholder in Suffolk. The remaining 46 percent of the Cook shares are owned by 46 unrelated employees, each of whom holds 1 percent.

Looking only at direct stock ownership, Cook, Inc. is not a closely held corporation. The five largest shareholders own only 46 percent of the company. However, under the attribution rules, Cook falls within the closely held rules. This is because Bill is treated as owning all of the shares held by his children, plus 90 percent of Suffolk's holdings. This means Bill owns 53.2 percent of the stock (10 percent directly plus 36 percent owned by Bill's children, plus 90 percent of Suffolk's 8 percent), and therefore Cook, Inc. is subject to the passive activity restrictions.

Personal service corporations also fall within the passive activity rules. A doctor who incorporates his medical practice would be a good example of a personal service corporation. A personal service corporation's principal activity is the performance of personal services. The services must be substantially performed by employee-owners, who must hold more than 10 percent, by value, of the corporation's stock.[6] An employee-owner is any employee who owns any of the outstanding stock on any day of the tax year. As is the case with closely held corporations, attribution rules apply, but these rules are somewhat different than those discussed previously. For example, under the personal service corporation rules, an individual is *not* treated as owning stock held by a sibling.

If a publicly traded partnership is taxed like a corporation, the PAL and PAC rules generally will not apply. (A partnership is publicly traded if interests are traded on an established securities market or on a secondary market or its substantial equivalent.[7]) Where a publicly traded partnership *is* treated as a partnership under the Tax Code, the passive activity restrictions will apply at the partner level, meaning investors must consider their potential impact. However, the rules apply *separately* for each publicly traded partnership interest that an investor holds. In other words, passive losses from one publicly traded partnership cannot offset passive income generated by another. In addition, passive losses cannot be used against any portfolio income that the publicly traded partnership interest might generate. Publicly traded partnerships will be treated as partnerships under the Tax Code if certain income rules are met.

PASSIVE ACTIVITIES

To apply the passive activity rules, an investor first must understand what investments fall within the definition of passive activities.

What Is an Activity?

After determining that a taxpayer is subject to the passive activity restrictions, the next step in applying the §469 provisions is to identify the various activities in which the taxpayer owns an interest. In many cases, this may not be as clear as one might think. For example, an investor who purchases an interest in a partnership actually may hold an interest in several activities, depending on the number of operations and businesses with which the partnership is involved. How a taxpayer's operations are grouped, into one or several activities, can affect whether the passive activity restrictions apply, when activities are treated as sold, etc.

The IRC §469 regulations adopt a facts-and-circumstances approach, providing that the trade or business or rental activities should be considered as a single activity if they constitute an "appropriate economic unit" for measuring gain or loss.[8] Any reasonable method can be used in grouping a taxpayer's activities. Among the factors given the most weight in making this determination are the similarities and differences in the types of activities, the degree of common control, the extent of common ownership, the geographic location, and the level of interdependence among the activities. Not all the factors need to be present to support classifying a taxpayer's actions as a single activity.[9]

Example—Agnes holds a significant ownership interest in a restaurant/bookstore in New York City. She also owns a significant interest in a similar operation located in Buffalo. Analysis of the facts and circumstances may permit Agnes to treat the operations as one activity, as four separate activities, as a restaurant activity and a bookstore activity, or as a New York activity and a Buffalo activity.[10] Assuming Agnes can support any one of these potential groupings, how she chooses to characterize her actions can affect the application of the passive loss rules. For example, if Agnes participates heavily in the bookstore located in Buffalo, she may wish to group all of the operations into one activity. By doing so, she might be able to avoid application of the passive activity restrictions to any of the business operations, on the grounds her work in Buffalo constitutes material participation. On the other hand, if Agnes cannot satisfy the material participation standard under any grouping, she may want to treat the four activities separately if she expects that she will sell one of them soon. This is because the rules permitting use of passive losses upon disposition apply only when a taxpayer disposes of all or substantially all of the activity. If Agnes decides to treat the restaurants as one activity and the bookstore operations as a second, she must continue to use these combinations in the future on a consistent basis. The regulations do not allow a taxpayer to change groupings unless the original categorization was clearly inappropriate or there has been a material change in the facts and circumstances that makes the original grouping clearly inappropriate.[11]

Even if two operations represent an appropriate economic unit, a rental activity generally cannot be grouped with a trade or business unless either the rental or the trade or business is insubstantial in comparison to the other. Unfortunately, Treasury regulations do not define the term "insubstantial." [12] Assuming that both activities are substantial, the rule prohibits a sole proprietor, for example, from combining his business operations with the results of rental real estate activities he conducts, even if the rental property is located on the upper floors of the building housing the business. A taxpayer cannot combine an activity involving the rental of personal property with an activity involving the rental of real property.

Under the regulations, limited partners and limited entrepreneurs are restricted in their ability to group certain activities with unrelated operations. The activities subject to these limitations include the following:

- Holding, producing, or distributing motion pictures or videos.
- Farming.
- Leasing §1245 property. (In general, §1245 property is depreciable personal property.)
- Exploring for or exploiting oil and gas resources as a trade or business or for the production of income.
- Exploring for or exploiting geothermal deposits.[13]

Example—Trini is a member of a limited liability company involved in a cattle-feeding business. She does not materially participate in the operation and therefore for tax purposes is characterized as a limited entrepreneur. Additionally, Trini is a limited partner in an oil and gas partnership. Under the §469 regulations, Trini can combine her cattle-feeding (farming) activities only with other farming operations. The same rule applies to the oil and gas interest. Therefore Trini cannot group the results from her two investments into one activity. However, if Trini owned a second oil and gas limited partnership interest, in addition to the investments above, she could treat the oil and gas holdings as one activity.[14]

A partnership or S corporation groups its activities under the general rules. Then the partner or shareholder, as the case may be, groups those activities with each other, with activities he or she conducts directly, or with activities conducted by other partnerships or S corporations in which he or she has invested.[15] These rules give substantial flexibility to investors who hold partnership or S corporation interests. In other words, an S corporation shareholder who materially participates in the corporation's manufacturing business could combine those activities with a partnership interest that he or she holds in another manufacturing operation, assuming the two activities together represent an appropriate economic unit. This could help the taxpayer satisfy one of the material participation tests and avoid the passive activity restrictions.

When Is an Activity "Passive?"

Under the tax law two types of activities fall within the restrictions of §469: trade or business activities in which a taxpayer does not materially participate and rental activities.[16] Special rules apply to rental activities, including exceptions for real estate professionals. A trade or business can involve both operations conducted for profit or for the production of income, provided that in either case the operations entail activities like making tangible property available for use by customers or other activities constituting a trade or business. Trading personal property, like stocks or bonds, for the taxpayer's own account is not a passive activity, regardless of whether the trading rises to the level of a trade or business.[17] This means, for example, that a taxpayer's investment gains cannot be offset by passive losses, even where the taxpayer's investment activities could properly be called a business.

Material participation is defined as involvement in an activity on a regular, continuous, and substantial basis.[18] The Treasury regulations contain seven tests that can be used to prove material participation on the part of a taxpayer. Any work done in any capacity in connection with any activity in which a taxpayer owns an interest at the time the work is done is treated as participation, although not where the interest is owned indirectly through a C corporation.[19] Work not usually done by an owner of such an activity, where the work was done principally to avoid application of the passive loss rules, does not count.[20] Also, work done by a taxpayer as an investor is not treated as participation unless the taxpayer is directly involved in the daily management of the activity. Therefore, time spent reviewing financial statements is not participation.[21] Participation by a taxpayer's spouse counts as participation by the taxpayer, even where the spouses do not file joint returns for the tax year.[22]

Tests for Material Participation

The taxpayer has the burden of proof in showing the amount of participation for purposes of the passive activity rules.[23] In other words, an investor who acquires an interest in an activity and tries to use losses from it to offset nonpassive income will be subject to the IRC §469 restrictions, unless he or she can prove that a material participation test was met. Detailed records are advisable. This is because six of the seven tests described below are quantitative, focusing on factors like the amount of time the taxpayer devotes to the activity.

1. 500-Hours—A taxpayer materially participates in an activity if he or she devotes more than 500 hours to it during the taxable year.[24] Hours worked by other individuals in connection with the activity are not relevant under this test.
2. 100-Hours—Where an individual is involved in an activity for more than 100 hours during the year, he or she materially participates,

provided the amount of the individual's involvement is no less than anyone else, including persons who do not own an interest in the activity.[25]

Example—Margaret devotes 400 hours to her catering activities in the current year. Margaret has one employee, Lucille Marie, who worked 130 hours in the catering operations. Margaret is treated as materially participating, even though she fails the 500-hour requirement. If Lucille Marie had worked 420 hours for the business, Margaret could not rely on this test to prove material participation. If Margaret has passive losses from investments she has made in other passive activities, she might want to reduce the hours she devotes to her catering in order to fail this and other material participation tests. This might enable Margaret to offset income from the catering operation with the losses from the other passive activities.

3. "Substantially All"—If a taxpayer's participation represents substantially all the participation by anyone during the tax year, the taxpayer is treated as materially participating in the activity.[26] The regulations do not define what is meant by "substantially all." However, it is clear that hours worked by others must be taken into consideration.

   Example—Mary operates a small business out of her garage, arranging floral bouquets for special occasions. She devoted 80 hours to this activity during the current year. Since no one else is involved in the business, Mary materially participated. However, if Mary employs Mike to help her and Mike works 50 hours this year, it is likely Mary would be treated as failing this test. This means the passive activity restrictions would apply to the deductions and credits arising from Mary's operations, unless she meets another material participation standard.

4. Significant Participation Activities—Under this test, a taxpayer whose total involvement in all "significant participation activities" exceeds 500 hours is treated as materially participating. A "significant participation activity" is any trade or business in which the taxpayer is involved for more than 100 hours but for which the taxpayer does not satisfy any other material participation test.[27]

   Example—John participates in four businesses during the current year. He devotes 130 hours to each business but does not meet any of the other material participation tests found in the regulations.

Since John's involvement with each activity exceeds 100 hours, each can be counted as a significant participation activity. Further, because John in total works more than 500 hours in the four businesses, he is treated as materially participating as to each, even if the businesses are unrelated.[28] However, if John only works 120 hours in connection with each activity, he would be unable to qualify under this standard, as his total involvement would not exceed the 500 hours required for this test. John would not be treated as materially participating, and any aggregate gain he has from the significant participation activities would be treated as nonpassive. Therefore, it could not be offset by passive losses that John might have from other sources. However, if John had an aggregate loss, it *would* be treated as passive, meaning it could not offset active or portfolio income.[29]

5. Five out of Ten Years—This test examines a taxpayer's participation in prior years. Specifically, if a taxpayer materially participated without regard to this test for at least five of the preceding ten tax years, he or she is treated as materially participating in the current year.[30] The five years of participation need not be consecutive in order to meet this standard, but an individual is not treated as participating in any year in which he or she did not hold an ownership interest in the activity. The test limits a taxpayer's ability to characterize an activity as passive or nonpassive by varying the number of hours worked in a specific tax year.

   Example—Bea is a successful executive. Eight years ago, she purchased a partnership interest in Puzzle Pieces as an investment. Puzzle Pieces is a general partnership that designs and manufactures puzzles. For each of the eight years, Bea has met the 500-hour material participation test. This year, Bea anticipates that some of her other activities will generate passive losses. Therefore she reduces her involvement in Puzzle Pieces, in order that her share of partnership income will be treated as passive. Unfortunately, because Bea materially participated for at least five of the past ten years, her Puzzle Piece income will continue to fall outside the passive activity rules. In other words, she will be unable to use it to offset the passive losses she will receive from her other activities.

6. Three-Year Test—Like the five-out-of-ten-year rule, this test also examines prior activity but applies only in the context of a "personal service activity." A personal service activity is an activity involving

the performance of services in a trade or business where capital is not a material income-producing factor, like law, health, engineering, or accounting. Under this test, a taxpayer who materially participates for any three prior tax years will be treated as materially participating in the current year.[31] For example, assume the taxpayer is a partner in a medical practice in which she materially participated for at least three years in the past. She will continue to be treated as meeting the material participation standards for so long as she remains a partner, regardless of the number of hours devoted to her practice. This taxpayer should not acquire an interest in a passive activity that she expects will generate losses initially if she anticipates that those losses could be claimed against her partnership income. The investment should be made only if the taxpayer has passive activities generating income, or if the passive investment being contemplated ultimately is expected to be profitable, notwithstanding the initial losses.

7. Facts and Circumstances—This test is subjective, meaning that unlike the other rules, there is no quantity of hours or involvement that must be proven to meet this standard. Instead, the facts and circumstances must show that a taxpayer's involvement in an activity for the year was regular, continuous, and substantial.[32] Management services cannot be taken into account under this test, unless no one else who performed management work received compensation in connection with such service and no other individual provided more management services, measured by hours, than the taxpayer. The regulations do not define what constitutes "management services." A taxpayer who participates 100 hours or less in an activity during the current year cannot meet the facts and circumstances test.[33]

    Example—Rita is a partner in a landscaping business. She is regularly involved in making management decisions, based on information forwarded to her by the general manager, Tom. Tom receives a salary from the partnership for his management work. Rita cannot rely on her management activities as establishing material participation under the facts and circumstances test because Tom is compensated for his management efforts. Further, if Rita devoted less than 100 hours to the landscaping operations, she could not rely on this test, even if Tom did not receive earned income for managing the partnership. This means any deductions or credits generated by the business would be subject to the §469 restrictions, and Rita could not use them to offset dividend income that she expects to receive on a stock investment, for example.

Material Participation by Entities

Passive loss rules apply at the partner, not partnership level. In other words, to determine whether a general partner's income or loss from a partnership's activities will be subject to the restrictions of IRC §469, the partner's own involvement in each activity is tested under the material participation standards found in the regulations. The material participation tests are applied based on the tax year of the partnership, not the partner.[34] A similar rule applies for purposes of assessing an S corporation shareholder's level of participation. A limited partner can show material participation only by meeting the more than 500 hours test, the material participation for five of the prior ten-year test, or, if a personal service activity is involved, the three-taxable year test. The other standards for material participation are not applicable.[35]

Example—Vince decides to invest as a limited partner in County Limited Partnership. In the event the partnership generates a loss, Vince wants to avoid the passive activity restrictions, as he has no passive income from other sources. Therefore he participates for 110 hours in one of County's activities this year, which is not less than any other individual. Although Vince meets the 100-hour test, he is not treated as materially participating, and any losses he receives from County Limited Partnership will be subject to the PAL restrictions. This is because as a limited partner Vince cannot rely on the 100-hour test to show material participation.

Whether a personal service corporation meets the material participation requirement is dependent on the participation of the corporation's shareholders. If individuals who materially participate in an activity own in the aggregate more than 50 percent by value of the corporation's stock, the firm is treated as materially participating. Therefore the passive activity restrictions would not apply to the deductions and credits the corporation claims in connection with the activity.[36] A similar rule applies to closely held corporations. However, closely held companies also can demonstrate material participation based on the work of their employees, provided certain conditions are met.[37]

Rental Activities

Unless an exception applies, rental activities, by definition, will be treated as passive.[38] This means the deductions and credits a rental activity generates will be subject to the restrictions of §469, and an investor who holds both rental and portfolio investments will not be able to use losses from the rental activities to offset the portfolio income. Under the regulations, a rental activity involves holding tangible property for use by customers where the activity's gross income principally represents payments received for the use of such property.[39]

Certain activities will *not* be treated as rental, however, meaning a taxpayer who materially participates in the activity under one of the seven tests discussed previously will avoid application of the passive activity restrictions. These nonrental activities include the following:

1. Seven-day exception—If the average period of customer use is seven days or less, the activity is classified as nonrental. For example, an activity involving the rental of ski equipment to customers for an average period of three days will not be a rental activity under this exception.[40]

2. 30-day exception—Where the average period of rental is 30 days or less and significant personal services are provided, the activity is not rental. Under this exception, a taxpayer who rents out equipment, including the services of an operator, for an average period of 20 days would qualify, assuming the operator's work is significant in comparison to the equipment.[41]

3. Extraordinary personal services—Regardless of the period of customer use, if "extraordinary personal services" are provided, the activity is not rental. Extraordinary personal services must be provided by individuals. Services are extraordinary if the customers' use of the property is incidental to the receipt of the service. This means, for example, that a closely held corporation that operates a hospital would not be treated as participating in rental activities, even though part of its revenue actually arises from the rental of its rooms.[42]

4. Incidental rental activities—In certain cases, rental activities that are incidental to nonrental operations will not invoke the passive activity restrictions. For example, a taxpayer who holds land primarily to realize a gain from its expected appreciation can rent the

property without triggering a characterization as rental. Certain conditions must be met to take advantage of this rule, which also applies to the rental of business property.[43]

5. Nonexclusive use—If the property is made available for nonexclusive use by customers during defined business hours, the activity is not rental. This means a golf course available to golfers who pay for the right to play on an annual, monthly, weekly, or per-use basis would not be a rental activity.[44]

6. Property rented to a pass-through entity—Income derived from renting property to a partnership or S corporation in which the taxpayer owns an interest is not rental. This rule applies where the entity is using the property in a nonrental activity and the taxpayer is making the property available in his capacity as an owner of an interest in the partnership or S corporation.[45]

7. Rental real estate activities of real estate professionals—If more than half of the personal services performed by a taxpayer in trades or businesses during the taxable year are performed in real property trades or businesses in which the taxpayer materially participates and the taxpayer works more than 750 hours in such trades or businesses, the taxpayer's rental real estate activities will fall outside the passive activity restrictions.[46] This exception recognizes that persons in real estate trades or businesses should not be treated as passive investors subject to the restrictions of Tax Code §469.[47]

In addition to the rules described previously, a further provision pertains to rental activities. Specifically, if a taxpayer "actively participates" in rental real estate activities, he or she may offset nonpassive income with up to $25,000 of losses from rental real estate.[48] This rule applies only if the taxpayer owns at least 10 percent, by value, of the rental real estate activity. "Active participation" is also required; this can be met by showing that the taxpayer participates in making management decisions in a significant and bona fide manner.[49]

Where a taxpayer has credits from a rental real estate activity, he or she must convert them into equivalent deductions in order to take advantage of this rule.[50] This is done by dividing the amount of credit by the taxpayer's marginal tax rate. Where the total of the deductions and credits exceeds $25,000, the losses are used first.

Example—Mary has $20,000 of losses and $4000 of credits from a rental real estate activity in which she actively participates. If Mary's marginal tax rate is 35 percent, her credits are equivalent to $11,429 in deductions ($4000/.35). Since the total of Mary's deductions and credits exceeds the $25,000 limit, she uses the losses ($20,000) first. This means Mary will use $1750 of credits ($5000 * .35) and will carry forward $2250 in credits to next year.

In order to apply the $25,000 exception, a taxpayer must first offset income and loss from all rental real estate activities in which he or she actively participates for the tax year. If a net loss results, it must be used to offset any passive income from other sources. Any loss remaining is then eligible for the $25,000 offset. Note that the $25,000 figure is reduced by 50 percent of the amount by which the taxpayer's adjusted gross income exceeds $100,000.[51]

Example—Wally has an interest in three passive activities. Activities A and B are rental real estate, and Wally satisfies the requirements for the active participation rule as to both. Activity A generates $5000 income, while B gives rise to $23,000 of loss. Activity C, which does not involve rental real estate, produces income of $2000 for Wally in the current year. Wally's adjusted gross income (AGI) is $140,000.

In applying the $25,000 exception, Wally first offsets the income and loss from activities A and B. This leads to a loss of $18,000 ($23,000-$5000). He then uses $2000 of this loss to zero out the passive income he received from Activity C. This leaves $16,000 of loss eligible for the $25,000 rule. In Wally's case, however, the $25,000 ceiling must be reduced because his AGI exceeds $100,000. This means Wally will be allowed to deduct only $5000 of his losses against nonpassive income [$25,000 - .5*($140,000–$100,000)]. The remaining $11,000 of loss will be carried over to next year.

CALCULATING PASSIVE ACTIVITY LOSSES

For taxpayers other than closely held corporations, passive activity losses represent the amount by which passive activity deductions exceed passive activity gross income for the tax year.[52] (A closely held corporation can use its passive activity losses to offset both passive income and active income.[53]) All passive activity income and losses are combined in determining whether there is an overall passive activity loss for the year. Passive activity credits are credits related to passive activities that exceed the amount of regular tax liability attributable to passive income.[54] They include general business credits, like the research credit of §41, and the Low Income Housing Credit, found at §42.[55] Where losses and credits cannot be used under the passive activity restrictions, they are carried forward and treated as arising from the same passive activities in later years. When the taxpayer disposes of his or her interest in a passive activity, special rules apply that generally permit deduction of PALs, although use of PACs will still be restricted.

Example—Doug has the following income and losses from the three passive activities in which he has an interest in the current year:

Activity A	$40,000
Activity B	(60,000)
Activity C	2,000

Doug also has an investment in stocks and bonds, which produced $24,000 of income this year. Under the passive loss rules, Doug offsets the $60,000 of loss arising from Activity B with the $42,000 of income generated by A and C. This leaves Doug with passive activity losses of $18,000. Unless a special rule applies, like the $25,000 active participation provision for rental real estate, Doug must carry the unused loss to the following year. He cannot use it to offset the $24,000 of portfolio income from the stocks and bonds he holds.

Passive activity gross income includes gain from the disposition of an interest in property used in a passive activity.[56] Whether the activity is passive depends on its character in the year of disposition. For example, if a taxpayer materially participates in the activity in the year of sale, the gain is not passive, even if the taxpayer did not meet any of the material participation tests for any of the prior tax years in which he owned an interest in the activity. If property was used only partially in a passive activity, the gain or loss resulting upon sale must be allocated in a reasonable manner.[57] Likewise, allocation is required if the use of the property changes within the 12 months preceding the date of sale.[58]

The sale of a partnership interest or S corporation stock is treated as gain from the disposition of interests in all of the activities in which the partnership or S corporation is involved. In other words, gain arising from the sale is allocated to each activity in which the partnership or S corporation has an interest and which would have produced gain had the activity been sold at fair market value. The gain is then characterized as passive or nonpassive, depending on the partner or shareholder's level of involvement.[59]

Passive activity losses arise when passive activity deductions exceed passive activity gross income. Passive activity deductions encompass both deductions arising currently from passive activities and those carried over from a prior taxable year.[60] Passive deductions include interest expense, where the interest is allocable to a passive activity under the tracing rules discussed in Chapter 4. Certain other deductions, like taxes or charitable contributions, are excluded.[61] These items are deductible under the usual rules. In other words, if an S corporation donates $12,000 to charity, shareholders who do not materially participate in the corporation's activities will not add the contribution to their share of passive activity losses but instead will deduct the gift under the regular rules for charitable donations.

Passive deductions include losses arising from the sale of an interest in property used in a passive activity and an interest in an activity held through a partnership or S corporation. The rules discussed previously, for selling property at a gain, also apply here. In other words, whether the activity is passive depends on the taxpayer's involvement in the year of sale.[62] Also, the taxpayer will have to make allocations, where the asset is used in more than one activity during the 12 months preceding the sale,[63] and where a partnership interest or S corporation stock is sold at a loss.[64]

To the extent that a taxpayer has flexibility in his or her level of involvement, the sale of passive activity property or a passive activity interest may present real planning opportunities. This is because the taxpayer in certain cases may be able to characterize expected losses or gains arising from the sale as passive or nonpassive, depending upon what is most advantageous, just by meeting or failing the material participation requirement for the year of sale.[65]

Passive activity deductions do not include losses disallowed under at-risk rules.[66] This also would apply to a partner or S corporation shareholder who is unable to deduct his or her share of passive losses because of insufficient basis.[67] Instead, the losses are carried over to the next tax year. Their characterization as passive or nonpassive will depend on the taxpayer's level of participation in the year to which the losses are carried.

Example—Marge is a partner in the Medina Limited Partnership. This year, Marge's share of partnership losses amounts to $5000. Marge is unable to deduct these losses because her basis in her partnership interest is $0. (A taxpayer's basis in her partnership interest serves as a limit on the amount of partnership deductions and losses she can claim. This means a partner with a zero basis is unable to take any deductions passed through from the partnership until her basis increases.) If next year Marge's basis rises to $3000, Marge will be able to deduct $3000 of suspended losses.

However, if Marge does not materially participate in the Medina Limited Partnership next year, the $3000 of losses she deducts will be subject to passive activity restrictions.[68]

Individual taxpayers are allowed to deduct up to $3000 of capital losses against ordinary income. This limitation is applied after the passive activity rules.[69] For example, assume a taxpayer has $10,000 of capital losses that are suspended under the Tax Code §469 restrictions until a later year, when the passive activity is sold for a $1000 capital gain. The $9000 loss ($10,000 loss less $1000 gain) is fully deductible in the year of disposition under the passive activity provisions, but the capital loss rules limit the deduction to $3000. The remaining $6000 of loss is carried forward to later years.

DISPOSITION OF PASSIVE ACTIVITY INTERESTS

When a taxpayer disposes of his or her entire interest in a passive activity, the restrictions of IRC §469 no longer prohibit using losses from that activity to offset income from active or portfolio sources.[70] This rule applies not only to loss from the activity arising in the year of disposition but also to suspended losses generated by the activity in prior years. The losses must be used first to offset any passive income the taxpayer has from other activities. A passive activity is treated as disposed of in the year that gain or loss is recognized.

Example—Ann maintains an interest in four passive activities: A, B, C, and D. In the current year, A and B generate a total of $30,000 of passive income. C produces a loss of $4000 for Ann. She sells Activity D. Taking into account both D's current year performance and the loss Ann incurs in connection with the sale, D gives rise to a total loss for the year of $14,000. Additionally, Ann has $50,000 of losses suspended under the §469 rules that are attributable to D.

Under passive activity provisions, Ann uses D's losses to offset the $26,000 of net passive income she has from Activities A, B, and C. This leaves her with $38,000 of losses that can offset nonpassive income.

In order for the rule concerning dispositions to apply, the taxpayer must dispose of his or her complete interest in the activity, in a taxable transaction to an unrelated taxpayer.[71] This means the taxpayer must dispose of all assets that are used in the activity. If the taxpayer owns an interest in a passive activity through a pass-through entity like a partnership or S corporation, he or she must dispose of the entire interest in the entity, or the entity must liquidate all assets used in the activity.[72] A tax-free disposition, as where property is transferred to a corporation in exchange for stock under Tax Code §351, would not trigger application of the rule permitting use of the losses.[73] Likewise, if the passive activity is sold to the taxpayer's spouse or to some other buyer considered to be related to the taxpayer under the tax law rules, passive losses allocable to the activity cannot be used until the activity is acquired by someone unrelated to the taxpayer.[74] Making a gift of a passive activity does not permit the donor to use the suspended losses. Instead, the losses are added to the basis taken in the property by the donee.[75]

When a passive activity is sold, any unused credits still are limited, in their use, to tax attributable to passive income. Unused credits continue to be carried forward. A taxpayer can elect to increase the basis of the passive activity interest by the amount of unused credit, if the credit reduced the interest's basis in the year the credit arose. This will affect the amount of gain or loss reported from the disposition. If the election is made, the passive activity credits are lost permanently.[76]

Example—Tom has $6000 of tax credits attributable to a passive activity in which he holds an interest. Tom's basis in the passive activity is $20,000. He sells the activity this year for $25,000. Tom has no other passive investments. Assuming a 35-percent marginal tax rate, the sale will generate an additional $1750 of tax liability for Tom. This means he would continue to carry $4250 of unused credit to later years. Alternatively, Tom could elect to increase the basis of his passive activity interest to $26,000, creating a loss of $1000 on the sale. This loss could offset nonpassive income in the year of sale, under the §469 disposition rules. Effectively, this election requires Tom to trade a dollar of credit for a dollar of deduction. Since a dollar of credit is worth a dollar, while a dollar of deduction generally is worth a fraction equal to the taxpayer's marginal tax rate, Tom must decide whether the immediate tax benefit offered by the election outweighs the reduced value of the credit. In Tom's case, the credit will be worth only $2100 ($6000 $\times$ .35=$2100) if this election is made.

FORMER PASSIVE ACTIVITIES

Special rules apply to former passive activities. For example, assume a taxpayer did not meet any of the material participation tests for the first three years he owned an interest in an activity but thereafter satisfies the 500-

hour test. In this case the suspended losses and credits can be used against the activity's current income and its resulting tax liability, even though it now is nonpassive. However, the losses cannot be used against nonpassive income from other sources.[77]

IMPACT OF THE PASSIVE ACTIVITY RULES

Taxpayers hope to make money from investments, not lose it. However, where an individual or corporation decides to enter into a risky investment, based in part on the ability to use the resulting losses should the holding prove unprofitable, passive activity rules must be consulted. This is because these rules can delay, or in some cases deny, the use of losses or credits generated by passive investments. This means taxpayers need to understand both when these rules apply and if an investment that is being considered is subject to these restrictions. Where the PAL and PAC provisions do apply, an investment needs to make economic sense, since it's likely that the use of any resulting losses will be limited.

NOTES

[1] The passive activity rules almost always apply to taxpayers who invest in a trade or business as a limited partner. This is because limited partners are presumed not to "materially participate" unless they meet one of three tests. These tests (the 500-hour rule, the 5-of-10 year test or the 3-year standard) are discussed in detail in this chapter. (See text accompanying notes 24, 30, and 31.) Since Helen is not involved in partnership operations, she won't satisfy any of the three tests and therefore is subject to the passive activity restrictions. See Treasury Regulation §1.469-5T(e) and the discussion accompanying note 35.

[2] Tax Code §469(e)(1). Portfolio income does not include income earned in the ordinary course of a trade or business. This would include, for example, interest on accounts receivable arising from the performance of services in a taxpayer's regular business, where credit is customarily offered to customers. Treasury Regulation §1.469-2T(c)(3).

[3] Tax Code §469(a)(2)

[4] Tax Code §469(a)(2). A C corporation is taxed under the regular Tax Code rules, unlike an S corporation, which is taxed like a partnership.

[5] Tax Code §469(j)(1)

[6] Tax Code §469(j)(2)

[7] Tax Code §469(k)

[8] Treasury Regulation §1.469-4(c)(1)

[9] Treasury Regulation §1.469-4(c)(2)

[10] Treasury Regulation §1.469-4(c)(3)

[11] Treasury Regulation §1.469-4(e)

[12] Treasury Regulation §1.469-4(d)

[13] Treasury Regulation §1.469-4(d)(3). The term "geothermal deposits" is defined in Tax Code §613(e)(2).

[14] Treasury Regulation §1.469-4(d)(3)(ii), Ex. A taxpayer may group one of the listed activities with another activity in the same business, assuming he or she is a limited partner or limited entrepreneur as to both operations. Treasury Regulation §1.469-4(d)(3)(i). In addition, grouping may occur with an activity in the same business although the taxpayer is not a limited partner or limited entrepreneur, if appropriate under the general facts and circumstances test.

[15] Treasury Regulation §1.469-4(d). Where personal property is provided as part of the real estate rental, or vice versa, the activities may be combined. *Id.* The regulations do contain restrictions on certain groupings by limited partners or limited entrepreneurs. See Treasury Regulation §1.469-4(d).

[16] Tax Code §469(c)

[17] Treasury Regulation §1.469-1T(e)(6). Activities involving deductible research expenses may also qualify as a trade or business. Code §469(c)(5).

[18] Tax Code §469(h)

[19] Treasury Regulation §1.469-5

[20] Treasury Regulation §1.469-5T

[21] Treasury Regulation §1.469-5T

[22] Treasury Regulation §1.469-5T

[23] Form 8582, Instructions (Year 2001) at p. 4

[24] Treasury Regulation §1.469-5T(a)(1)

[25] Treasury Regulation §1.469-5T(a)(3)

[26] Treasury Regulation §1.469-5T(a)(2)

[27] Treasury Regulation §1.469-5T(a)(4). See §1.469-5T(c) for the definition of a significant participation activity.

[28] See Treasury Regulation §1.469-5T(k), Ex. 4. In that example, the taxpayer works 400 hours in a restaurant activity and 150 hours in a shoe store. Since the taxpayer's aggregate participation exceeds 500 hours, the material participation test is met for both activities.

[29] Under Treasury Regulation §1.469-2T(f)(2), a taxpayer's aggregate net passive income from significant participation activities that fail the material participation requirement is treated as active. For example, assume a taxpayer works 150 hours in an activity but does not satisfy any material participation standard. The income from the activity would be treated as active, and could not be offset by any passive losses the taxpayer has. If a taxpayer has more than one significant participation activity but again does not meet a material participation test, a pro rata portion of each activity's net passive income is recharacterized.

[30] Treasury Regulation §1.469-5T

[31] Treasury Regulation §1.469-5T

[32] Treasury Regulation §1.469-5T(a)(7)

[33] Treasury Regulation §1.469-5T(b)

[34] Treasury Regulation §1.469-2T(e).When the partnership and partner both use the same tax year, that 12-month period is the time over which the partner's activity is mea-

sured. However, if a partnership year ends on November 30, for example, and the partner is a calendar year taxpayer, material participation will be tested by looking at the 12 months ending on November 30th.

[35] Treasury Regulation §1.469-5T(e). An estate or trust materially participates in an activity if the executor or trustee does.

[36] Treasury Regulation §1.469-1T(g). Note that in applying the significant participation test under this rule, the shareholder's participation in activities other than the personal service corporation's is disregarded. This means, for example, that a taxpayer's involvement outside the context of the corporation could not be combined with his or her corporate work in order to meet the 100-hour requirement for significant participation.

[37] Tax Code §469(h)(4)(B). In order to rely on this provision, the closely held corporation must have at least one full-time employee substantially all of whose time is spent actively managing the business and at least three full-time nonshareholder employees who spend substantially all their time working in the business. In addition, the corporation's deductions for ordinary business expenses relating to the business must exceed 15 percent of the business' gross income.

[38] Tax Code §469(c)(2)

[39] Treasury Regulation §1.469-1T(e)(3)

[40] Treasury Regulation §1.469-1T(e)(3)

[41] Treasury Regulation §1.469-1T(e)(3). Under the regulations, only services performed by individuals count. Significance is determined by examining the facts and circumstances, including the value of the service and the frequency with which it is provided. Some services are excluded, like those required in order to use the property legally.

[42] Treasury Regulation §1.469-1T(e)(3)

[43] Treasury Regulation §1.469-1T(e)(3). In order to use this exception, the principal purpose for owning the property must be for investment and the gross rent must be less than 2 percent of the lesser of the property's unadjusted basis or its fair market value. Business property can also qualify for this exception, provided that the 2-percent test is met, the taxpayer owns an interest in the trade or business, and the property was used predominantly in a business activity during the current taxable year or during at least two of the immediately preceding five tax years. Property rented to an employee for the employer's convenience also is treated as incidental to a nonrental activity.

[44] Treasury Regulation §1.469-1T(e)(3)

[45] Treasury Regulation §1.469-1T(e)(3)

[46] Tax Code §469(c)(7)

[47] In order to take advantage of this exception, the taxpayer must own an interest in rental real estate. Personal services performed by the taxpayer as an employee do not count, unless the taxpayer owns more than 5 percent of the employer. For purposes of determining whether the 750-hour and more than half of personal services tests are met, a taxpayer's participation cannot be aggregated with his or her spouse's. However, the involvement of both spouses can be counted toward the material participation requirement. The determination of what activities constitute real property trades or businesses is done on a facts and circumstances basis. A taxpayer can elect to treat all rental real estate interests as a single activity. See generally, Code Section 469(c)(7); Treasury Regulation Section 1.469-9.

[48] Tax Code §469(i)

[49] Publication 925, *Passive Activity and At-Risk Rules* (2001), p. 3

[50] The active participation requirement is not applicable to certain kinds of credits, like the low-income housing credit. Tax Code §469(i)(6).

[51] Tax Code §469(i)(3). For taxpayers who are married but file separately, the phase-out begins when adjusted gross income exceeds $50,000 and the limit is $12,500, assuming the taxpayers lived apart throughout the tax year. Code Section 469(i)(5). There are special phase-out rules for some credits.

[52] Tax Code §469(d)(1). For special rules applicable where a taxpayer engages in a lending transaction with a partnership or S corporation in which the taxpayer owns an interest and the loan proceeds are used in a passive activity, see Treasury Regulation §1.469-7.

[53] Tax Code §469(e)(2). Similarly, PACs can be used to offset tax liability on net active income.

[54] Tax Code §469(d)(2)

[55] Treasury Regulation §1.469-3T(b). General business credits are nonrefundable and also include the Investment Credit (§46), the Alcohol Fuels Credit (§40), and the Work Opportunity Credit (§51).

[56] Treasury Regulation §1.469-2T(c)

[57] Treasury Regulation §1.469-2T(c)

[58] No allocation is required for small sales, in which case the entire amount realized may be allocated to the activity in which the property was used predominantly during the 12 months preceding sale. A small sale is where the fair market value of the interest in property is no more than $10,000 or 10 percent of the fair market value of all property used in the activity, whichever is lesser. Treasury Regulation §1.469-2T(c)(2).

[59] Treasury Regulation §1.469-2T(e)

[60] Treasury Regulation §1.469-2T

[61] Treasury Regulation §1.469-2T(d)(2). Passive activity deductions also do not include the dividends received deduction (on dividends not included in passive income), miscellaneous itemized deductions subject to the 2-percent disallowance rule, certain casualty and theft losses, etc.

[62] Treasury Regulation §1.469-2T(d)(5)

[63] Treasury Regulation §1.469-2T(d)(5)

[64] Treasury Regulation §1.469-2T(e). The regulations contain a default rule, if gain or loss cannot be allocated under the procedure described in the text.

[65] Note, however, that if a taxpayer materially participated in an activity for at least five of the preceding ten years, the activity will fall outside of the §469 restrictions, regardless of the level of participation in the year of sale. See endnote no. 30 and accompanying text.

[66] Treasury Regulation §1.469-2T(d)(6). The at-risk rules are discussed in Chapter 3.

[67] Recall that both partners and S corporation shareholders are limited in their ability to use losses that flow down from the entity by their basis in the partnership interest or S corporation stock. See Tax Code §704(d) and §1366(d), respectively.

[68] See the example at Treasury Regulation §1.469-2T(d)(1).

[69] Treasury Regulation §1.469-1(d)(2)

[70] Tax Code §469(g)

[71] Under the regulations, a taxpayer who disposes of "substantially all of an activity" can treat the transaction as a complete disposition, triggering use of the suspended loss. This rule applies only if the taxpayer can establish the income and deductions, etc., allocable to

the part of the activity disposed of, with reasonable certainty. See Treasury Regulation §1.469-4(g).

[72] Publication 925, *Passive Activity and At-Risk Rules*, (2001), p. 9

[73] Publication 925, *Passive Activity and At-Risk Rules* (2001), p. 8

[74] Tax Code §469(g)(1)(B)

[75] Tax Code §469(j)(6)

[76] Tax Code §469(j)(9)

[77] Tax Code §469(f)(1)

AT-RISK LIMITATIONS

INTRODUCTION

Deductions are often allowed that do not represent what the taxpayer actually has invested in the activity. For instance, equipment costing $12,500 may be purchased by $1500 in cash and a loan for the balance. If the loan is a nonrecourse loan, meaning that the loan is secured by the equipment and not guaranteed by the taxpayer personally, then the taxpayer only has $1500 of his own funds invested in the equipment. However, the taxpayer is enjoying tax deductions in the form of depreciation on the full purchase price of $12,500. Additionally, part or all of the purchase price, for certain property used in a trade or business, may be expensed in the year of purchase using a §179 deduction up to $24,000 in 2001 or 2002 and up to $100,000 in 2003, 2004, and 2005. The amounts will be adjusted for inflation for 2004 and 2005.[1] Additionally, bonus depreciation is available under §168(k) that allows an additional 50 percent for new property acquired after May 5, 2003 and before January 1, 2005.

Example—Beth purchased a computer and printer for her consulting business for $5000 and a desk, chair, and credenza for $7500. She had $1500 in cash and borrowed $11,000 from a financial institution. The furniture and computer equipment secures the loan. After a very successful and profitable year, Beth decided to take a §179 deduction of $12,500 to offset her income. She was able to take this deduction in spite of the fact that she only had $1500 of her own cash, which represents her true economic outlay, invested in the furniture and equipment.

The underlying principle of the at-risk rules is that a taxpayer should not be allowed to claim tax losses for transactions in which he/she is not at risk economically.

Example—Assume the same facts as the previous example except that Beth became seriously ill and could not work. The lender repossessed the furniture and computer, having a balance due on the loan of $10,000. The tax gain/(loss) on her tax return would be:

Sales/ Exchange Price		$10,000
Less Purchase Price of		
computer and printer	$5,000	
Purchase Price of furniture	7,500	
Less §179 depreciation	(12,500)	
Beth's basis		0
Beth's gain		$10,000

However, assuming that she took a regular instead of §179 depreciation deduction, her loss would be:

Sales/Exchange Price		$10,000
Purchase price		
of computer and printer	5,000	
Purchase price of furniture	7,500	
Less depreciation	(890)	
Beth's basis		11,610
Beth's loss		1,610
Beth's tax loss		$ 1,500

Her loss is limited by the at-risk rules to the cash, which represents her economic outlay. She was not personally responsible for the remaining $10,000 loan, which was secured by the furniture and equipment.[2]

ACTIVITIES WHERE THE AT-RISK RULES APPLY

The At-Risk Rules apply to each activity engaged in by the taxpayer in carrying on a trade or business or for the production of income.[3] Activities of a personal nature, such as qualified residence interest, casualty losses, theft losses, and charitable contributions are governed by their own rules and are not affected by the at-risk rules.

Amounts Considered At Risk

The following are the amounts that are considered at risk:

- Cash contributed by the taxpayer to the activity
- Adjusted basis of other property contributed by the taxpayer to the activity[4]

- Borrowed amounts—Funds borrowed for use in an activity to the extent that the taxpayer is personally liable for the repayment of such amounts or has pledged property, other than the property used in the activity, as security for the loan[5]

The following are not considered at risk:

- Interested persons—A taxpayer is not at risk for money borrowed from a lender who has an interest in the activity other than merely being a creditor. This is because the creditor may not insist on his rights as a creditor since he has a personal stake in the activity. This limitation applies even though the creditor maintains that he will enforce his rights as a creditor.[6]

  Example—Sarah purchases commercial property from Land Development Co. for $500,000. Sarah pays $100,000 in cash and Land Development takes a mortgage for the remaining $400,000 with full recourse against Sarah. The terms of the note provide that Land Development will receive an additional interest of 15 percent of the operating cash flow that Sarah's property generates and 30 percent of the sales proceeds when the property is sold. Since there is an additional right to participate in additional profits, the note may be disqualified for the at-risk rules.

- Related persons—If a lender is "related" to a person with an interest in the activity, the borrowed money is not considered to be "at risk." For example, assume Adam and Jenna are partners in a business. Funds loaned by Erika, Adam's daughter, are not at risk. In determining whether a lender is a related person, the following rules apply:

  1. The at-risk rules incorporate the definition of related parties found at Code §267(b) and §707(b), with some modifications. Consequently, related persons under the at-risk provisions include members of a family and also a trustee and beneficiary of a trust. A corporation and an individual who owns, directly or indirectly, more than 10 percent by value of the firm's outstanding stock also are related. Similarly, a partnership and a more than 10-percent partner are related parties, as are two partnerships where the same persons directly or indirectly own more than 10 percent of the capital or profits interest.[7]

2. A lender and taxpayer will be considered related if they are engaged in a trade or business under common control with a 10-percent ownership test.[8]

C CORPORATIONS

IRC §465(a)(1)(B) states that a C Corporation is subject to at-risk rules if it is closely held. The test to determine whether a C corporation is closely held is whether there are five or fewer individuals who among them own more than 50 percent of the value of the corporation's stock at any time during the last half of the corporation's tax year. Attribution rules apply. This means stock owned, directly or indirectly, by or for a corporation, partnership, estate, or trust shall be considered as being owned proportionately by its shareholders, partners, or beneficiaries.[9] However, for purposes of the at-risk rules, stock owned by one partner is not deemed to be owned by another partner solely because of this relationship.

Example—Christopher owns 20 percent of the stock of Clean Socks Manufacturing Co., Linus owns 15 percent, Joanne owns 10 percent, and Tim owns 10 percent. Clean Socks Manufacturing is subject to the at-risk rules because five or fewer individuals own more than 50 percent of the stock.

Example—Pat owns 55 percent of the stock of Great Soccer Inc., a calendar year corporation. In June of 2001 she sold 5 percent of her stock to Jenna, 10 percent to Chandra, 10 percent to Natalie, 10 percent to Michael, and 10 percent to Ford. The general public holds the remainder of the stock. Great Soccer is not subject to the at-risk rules because more than five people own more than 50 percent of the stock during some period in the last half of the corporation's taxable year.

Exemption

There is an exemption from the at-risk rules for qualifying C corporations. A C corporation can offset losses incurred in an active business against income from investments and other business activities.[10] The term qualifying business means any active business if:

(i) During the entire 12-month period ending on the last day of the taxable year, the corporation had at least one full-time employee who was active in the management of the business.[11]

(ii) During that same period, the corporation had at least three full-time, nonowner employees who actively performed services for the business.[12]

(iii) Ordinary and necessary business expenses must exceed 15 percent of the corporation's gross income for the year.[13] However, compensation paid to an employee who owns more than 5 percent of the corporation's stock or to any member of the employee's family, meaning his/her spouse, children, grandchildren, and parents, may not be counted as part of the 15 percent.[14] This includes contributions to the pension plan of an employee who owns more than 5 percent of the corporation's stock. Additionally, interest, most taxes, and depreciation cannot be counted toward the 15 percent.[15]

(iv) The business cannot involve the use, sale, lease, or disposition of master sound recordings, motion picture films, video tapes, or tangible or intangible assets associated with literary, artistic, musical, or similar properties.[16]

Example—RW Painting Inc. employs 10 people including Bob Winbig the owner. Its ordinary and necessary business expenses, including shareholder compensation, interest, taxes, and depreciation are 65 percent of total revenues. Bob's daughter and son are employed by the business. Their compensation is 10 percent of gross revenues. Since business expenses exceed 15 percent of gross revenues, the company qualifies for an active business exemption from the at-risk rules.

Example—Assume the same facts as above except that the name of the company is RW Studios, Inc. and is involved in the sale of films and musical CDs and tapes. Since this is not an exempt activity, the company will be subject to the at-risk rules.

Equipment Leasing by C Corporation

At-risk rules do not apply to a closely held C corporation's losses from equipment leasing if at least 50 percent of the corporation's gross receipts are derived from equipment leasing and it has at least three full-time employees devoted to the business.[17] Equipment leasing means leasing, servicing, and selling equipment that is tangible, personal property, like machinery, trucks, or office furniture.[18] All corporations under common control must be treated as a single corporation for meeting the 50-percent gross receipts test. In other words, an investor who owns 100 percent of Tool Co. and 80 percent of Equipment Co. must show that at least half of the combined gross receipts of both companies are derived from equipment leasing in order to meet the 50-percent gross receipts requirement.

Example—Rebecca owns 80 percent of Kresse Corporation and 90 percent of Buffalo Company. Kresse has gross receipts in the current year of $5 million, of which $4 million are attributable to the firm's office furniture leasing operations. Buffalo grossed $1 million in the current tax year, 10 percent of which arose from the company's truck leasing business.

Kresse Corporation and Buffalo Company are members of a controlled group, since Rebecca owns at least 80 percent of the stock in each firm.[19] Therefore the companies' gross receipts must be combined for purposes of the 50-percent test. The total receipts from both corporations amount to $6 million. Of this figure, $4,100,000 arises from equipment leasing activities. As a result, the at-risk rules do not apply to either Buffalo's or Kresse's equipment-leasing operations. However, if Buffalo's gross receipts amounted to $6 million, with only $100,000 attributable to equipment leasing, *both* companies would be subject to the at-risk limitations with respect to their leasing activities. This is because gross receipts now would total $11 million ($5 million + $6 million), but only $4,100,000, or less than 50 percent, arises from equipment leasing.

Leasing Subsidiaries The at-risk rules will not apply to the equipment leasing losses of a member of a controlled group if each of the following conditions are met:

1. At least 80 percent of the member's gross receipts must come from equipment leasing[20]
2. During the entire year and each of the two immediately preceding taxable years the group had at least three full-time employees devoted to equipment-leasing activities[21]
3. During the entire year and each of the two immediately preceding taxable years, the group in the aggregate had at least $1,000,000 in gross receipts from equipment leasing[22]

Example—Small Business Leasing, Inc., a division of Big Business Leasing, Inc., leases computer systems. They employ three part-time installers, one administrative person, and two electricians. They earn

$1,100,000 in rentals, $100,000 in repairs, and $100,000 in other activities. Since they had at least 80 percent of their gross income in revenues from leasing, and they have at least three full-time employees, they are not subject to the at-risk rules.

Separate Activity

Taxpayers cannot combine results from different activities in order to avoid the at-risk restrictions. Losses from one activity may not be used to offset income from other activities. Losses incurred from activities within the same activity from which income is derived may be used to offset that income.[23]

Example—Assume the same facts as in the previous example, except that the Small Business Leasing had a loss in their Repair Dept. of ($190,000). Since the loss is derived from the activity of servicing computers, it can be used to offset the $1,100,000 income from computer rental.

S CORPORATION

A taxpayer is often advised to elect S Corporation status when initially incorporating a new business. The logic is that a business probably will incur losses in the first several years, and these losses may be taken by the shareholders on their personal tax returns to offset their other income.

However, the at-risk rules apply, and these losses are deductible only to the extent of the aggregate amount that the shareholder is at risk for at the close of the corporation's taxable year. This aggregation does not include different activities of an S Corporation. Losses from one of the corporation's operations cannot offset income from another.

Example—Assume the same facts as in the previous example except that the Small Business Leasing, Inc. is an S Corporation. Besides its services to small businesses, it also is engaged in Christmas tree farming to generate additional revenue. The Christmas trees are sold to retail lots in the United States and are sold also through a lot owned by the Small Business Leasing. The losses from computer system repairs can only offset revenue from computer leasing. They may not be used to offset revenue from the Christmas tree farm because the tree farming and computer operations represent separate activities.

Shareholder Basis in the S Corporation

Under the subchapter S rules, losses can generally be deducted on the tax returns of shareholders of an S Corporation to the extent that the shareholder has basis in the corporation. Additionally, shareholders are subject to at-risk rules, passive activity loss rules, discussed in Chapter 2, and hobby loss limitations.[24] The hobby loss limits mean that taxpayers may take deductions only up to income from hobby-related activities.

However, we first begin with the calculation of basis in applying the at-risk rules. S corporation shareholders have two types of basis: stock and debt. Debt basis means funds lent directly to the corporation by the shareholder. A personal guarantee of a loan from a financial institution is not counted. A shareholder who guarantees a $10,000 loan made by a bank to an S corporation cannot increase her basis in her S investment by the $10,000. However, if the shareholder winds up paying the bank loan because the corporation defaults on its obligation, then the basis increase is appropriate.

The calculation of stock basis is as follows:[25]

1. Initial investment in the corporation
2. Plus: Additional capital contributions made during the year
   Allocable share of ordinary income
   Allocable share of separately stated income items
3. Less: Distributions not included in shareholder's gross income
   Allocable share of expenses not used in calculating income
   Allocable share of ordinary loss
   Allocable share of separately stated loss and deduction items

Example—Tim of E & M Distributors, Inc. is the only shareholder of that S Corporation. His initial investment in the corporation is $25,000. During its first year Tim added another $5000 to the corporation, and the corporation had a loss of $15,000. The corporation made charitable contributions of $500. Tim's basis the first taxable year is:

Initial contribution	$25,000
Additional contribution	5,000
Less operating loss	(15,000)
Less charitable contributions	(500)
Basis	$14,500

The calculation of debt basis is:

1. Initial loan by shareholder to the corporation
2. Less: Allocable remainder share of loss and deduction items after stock basis is reduced to zero. If a shareholder has given several loans to the corporation, the reduction in basis is applied to each loan in the same proportion that the basis of each indebtedness bears to the aggregate basis of the loans.[26]

Example—Aladdin's Cleaning Corp. is an S Corporation. Jerry, the sole shareholder, has stock basis of $40,000. He personally loaned the corporation $100,000 over the years. In 2002, Aladdin's had a bad year and lost $150,000. Jerry will be able to deduct $140,000 of the loss on his personal tax return. This is the total amount for which he is at risk. The calculation of Form 6198, Schedule E, Page 2, and Form 1040, Page 1 of Jerry's personal tax return for 2002 is attached. (See Exhibit 3-1).

Real Property

In general, the proceeds of a nonrecourse loan are not considered to be at risk. This is because an investor is not personally responsible for paying off a nonrecourse obligation. When a lender makes a nonrecourse loan in connection with an office building, for example, it expects the money for repayment to come from the real estate, rather than the building owner's personal resources. This means the owner is not at risk as to the borrowed funds. However, there is an exception for "qualified nonrecourse financing," secured by real property (real estate).[27] This exception means a nonrecourse loan backed by a mortgage on the underlying real estate may be at risk, if it meets the qualified nonrecourse financing requirements. Those requirements are:

- The loan is borrowed by the taxpayer with respect to the activity of holding real property;[28]
- The lender is a person/entity actively engaged in lending money or the loan is from any federal, state, or local government or instrumentality, or is guaranteed by any federal, state, or local government;[29]
- No person is personally liable for repayment except to the extent provided for in regulations;[30] and
- The obligation is not convertible debt.[31]

Example—Assume the same facts as the previous example, except that Jerry bought a building for the corporation for $250,000, for which he paid $50,000 in cash and had a $200,000 nonrecourse mortgage on the property from a bank. Jerry would be able to take the entire $150,000 loss on his personal tax return because he would now have a basis of $140,000 plus $250,000 for a total of $390,000.

PARTNERSHIPS

IRC §704(d) states that a partner's distributive share of partnership losses shall be allowed only to the extent of the adjusted basis of such partner's interest in the partnership at the end of the year. However, partners are faced with the limitations of the at-risk rules in determining the amount of allowable losses they can deduct on their personal tax returns.

A partner's beginning basis in a partnership interest depends on how the interest was obtained. If it was purchased, then the partner's basis is merely the purchase price paid. If the interest was a gift, then the basis is the donor's carryover basis.[32] If the interest was inherited, then, under current law, the basis would be the fair market value as of the decedent's date of death or the alternate valuation date, if elected by the executor.[33]

Under §752(a), basis is increased by a partner's share of the liabilities of a partnership, or by any increase in debt that a partner incurs on behalf of the partnership, or by a partner assuming partnership liabilities. This assumption of liabilities is synonymous to the contribution of money by the partner to the partnership. Liabilities of a firm increase the basis of each partner generally to the extent of each partner's interest. For example, if a partnership's liabilities increase by $100,000, a 10-percent partner's basis in his partnership interest goes up by $10,000. A partner that loans money to a partnership does not increase his or her basis by the entire amount of the loan. Instead, the loan becomes a partnership obligation and all the partners are responsible for its repayment. The partner who loans the money would have basis to the extent that he or she is personally responsible to repay the loan. Using the previous facts, this means that a 10-percent partner who loans $100,000 to the partnership again would increase his basis by $10,000. However, if the loan is a nonrecourse loan, then the loan is allocable entirely to the lending partner.[34]

Example—Rita and Louis are general partners in Partnership R & L. At the inception of the partnership, each partner contributed $10,000. The

EXHIBIT 3-1

Form **1040**	Department of the Treasury- Internal Revenue Service **U.S. Individual Income Tax Return**	**2002**	(99)	IRS Use Only- Do not write or staple in this space.

For the year Jan. 1-Dec. 31, 2002, or other tax year beginning ____ , 2002, ending ____ , 20 ____ OMB No. 1545-0074

Label (See instructions on page 21.)

L A B E L

Your first name and initial — Jerry
Last name — Aladdin
Your social security number — 111-22-3333

If a jt. rtn., sp. first name & initial
Last name
Spouse's social security number

Use the IRS label. Otherwise, please print or type.

H E R E

Home address (number and street). If you have a P.O. box, see page 21. — 12 Back St.   Apt. no.

City, town or post office, state, and ZIP code. If you have a foreign address, see page 21. — Buffalo   NY 14226

▲ **Important!** ▲ You **must** enter your SSN(s) above.

Presidential Election Campaign (See page 21.)

Note. Checking "Yes" will not change your tax or reduce your refund.
Do you, or your spouse if filing a joint return, want $3 to go to this fund? ▶ You ☐ Yes ☐ No Spouse ☐ Yes ☐ No

Filing Status

Check only one box.

1 ☒ Single
2 ☐ Married filing jointly (even if only one had income)
3 ☐ Married filing separately. Enter spouse's SSN above and full name here. ▶
4 ☐ Head of household (with qualifying person). (See pg. 21.) If the qualifying person is a child but not your dependent, enter this child's name here. ▶
5 ☐ Qualifying widow(er) with dependent child (year spouse died ▶ ____). (See page 21.)

Exemptions

6a ☒ **Yourself.** If your parent (or someone else) can claim you as a dependent on his or her tax return, do not check box 6a
b ☐ **Spouse**
c **Dependents:**

(1) First name Last name	(2) Dependent's social security number	(3) Dependent's relationship to you	(4) Ck. if qual. child for child tax credit (see pg. 22)

If more than five dependents, see page 22.

No. of boxes checked on 6a and 6b — 1
No. of children on 6c who:
● lived with you
● did not live with you due to divorce or separation (see page 22)
Dependents on 6c not entered above
Add numbers on lines above ▶ — 1

d Total number of exemptions claimed

Income

Attach Forms W-2 and W-2G here. Also attach Form(s) 1099-R if tax was withheld. If you did not get a W-2, see page 23.

Enclose, but do not attach, any payment. Also, please use Form 1040-V.

7	Wages, salaries, tips, etc. Attach Form(s) W-2	7	
8a	Taxable interest. Attach Schedule B if required	8a	
b	Tax-exempt interest. Do not include on line 8a	8b	
9	Ordinary dividends. Attach Schedule B if required	9	
10	Taxable refunds, credits, or offsets of state and local income taxes (see page 24)	10	
11	Alimony received	11	
12	Business income or (loss). Attach Schedule C or C-EZ	12	
13	Capital gain or (loss). Attach Schedule D if required. If not required, check here ▶ ☐	13	
14	Other gains or (losses). Attach Form 4797	14	
15a	IRA distributions 15a ____ b Taxable amount (see page 25)	15b	
16a	Pensions and annuities 16a ____ b Taxable amount (see page 25)	16b	
17	Rental real estate, royalties, partnerships, S corporations, trusts, etc. Attach Schedule E	17	-140,000
18	Farm income or (loss). Attach Schedule F	18	
19	Unemployment compensation	19	
20a	Social security benefits 20a ____ b Taxable amount (see page 27)	20b	
21	Other income. List type & amt. (see page 29)	21	
22	Add the amounts in the far right column for lines 7 through 21. This is your **total income** ▶	22	-140,000

Adjusted Gross Income

23	Educator expenses (see page 29)	23	
24	IRA deduction (see page 29)	24	
25	Student loan interest deduction (see page 31)	25	
26	Tuition and fees deduction (see page 32)	26	
27	Archer MSA deduction. Attach Form 8853	27	
28	Moving expenses. Attach Form 3903	28	
29	One-half of self-employment tax. Attach Schedule SE	29	
30	Self-employed health insurance deduction (see page 33)	30	
31	Self-employed SEP, SIMPLE, and qualified plans	31	
32	Penalty on early withdrawal of savings	32	
33a	Alimony paid b Recipient's SSN ▶	33a	
34	Add lines 23 through 33a	34	
35	Subtract line 34 from line 22. This is your **adjusted gross income** ▶	35	-140,000

For Disclosure, Privacy Act, and Paperwork Reduction Act Notice, see page 76.
DAA
Form **1040** (2002)

EXHIBIT 3-1 (Continued)

Form **6198**	**At-Risk Limitations**	OMB No. 1545-0712
	▶ Attach to your tax return.	**2002**
Department of the Treasury Internal Revenue Service	▶ See separate instructions.	Attachment Sequence No. **31**

Name(s) shown on return	Identifying number
Jerry Aladdin	111-22-3333

Description of activity (see page 2 of the instructions)
Aladdin's Cleaning Corp.

Part I   **Current Year Profit (Loss) From the Activity, Including Prior Year Nondeductible Amounts** (see instructions).

1	Ordinary income (loss) from the activity (see page 2 of the instructions)	**1**	−150,000
2	Gain (loss) from the sale or other disposition of assets used in the activity (or of your interest in the activity) that you are reporting on:		
a	Schedule D	**2a**	
b	Form 4797	**2b**	
c	Other form or schedule	**2c**	
3	Other income and gains from the activity, from Schedule K-1 of Form 1065, Form 1065-B, or Form 1120S, that were not included on lines 1 through 2c	**3**	
4	Other deductions and losses from the activity, including investment interest expense allowed from Form 4952, that were not included on lines 1 through 2c	**4**	( )
5	Current year profit (loss) from the activity. Combine lines 1 through 4. See page 3 of the instructions before completing the rest of this form	**5**	−150,000

Part II   **Simplified Computation of Amount At Risk.** See instructions before completing this part.

6	Adjusted basis (as defined in section 1011) in the activity (or in your interest in the activity) on the first day of the tax year. Do not enter less than zero	**6**	140,000
7	Increases for the tax year (see page 4 of the instructions)	**7**	
8	Add lines 6 and 7	**8**	140,000
9	Decreases for the tax year (see page 4 of the instructions)	**9**	
10a	Subtract line 9 from line 8 ▶	**10a**	140,000
b	If line 10a is **more** than zero, enter that amount here and go to line 20 (or complete Part III). Otherwise, enter -0- and see **Pub. 925** for information on the recapture rules	**10b**	140,000

Part III   **Detailed Computation of Amount At Risk.** If you completed Part III of Form 6198 for 2001, see page 4 of the instructions.

11	Investment in the activity (or in your interest in the activity) at the effective date. Do not enter less than zero	**11**	
12	Increases at effective date	**12**	
13	Add lines 11 and 12	**13**	
14	Decreases at effective date	**14**	
15	Amount at risk (check box that applies):		
a	☐ At effective date. Subtract line 14 from line 13. Do not enter less than zero.	**15**	
b	☐ From 2001 Form 6198, line 19b. Do not enter the amount from line 10b of the 2001 form.		
16	Increases since (check box that applies):		
a	☐ Effective date b ☐ The end of your 2001 tax year	**16**	
17	Add lines 15 and 16	**17**	
18	Decreases since (check box that applies):		
a	☐ Effective date b ☐ The end of your 2001 tax year	**18**	
19a	Subtract line 18 from line 17 ▶	**19a**	
b	If line 19a is **more** than zero, enter that amount here and go to line 20. Otherwise, enter -0- and see **Pub. 925** for information on the recapture rules	**19b**	0

Part IV   **Deductible Loss**

20	Amount at risk. Enter the **larger** of line 10b or line 19b	**20**	140,000
21	**Deductible loss.** Enter the **smaller** of the line 5 loss (treated as a positive number) or line 20. See page 8 of the instructions to find out how to report any deductible loss and any carryover.	**21**	140,000)

Note: If the loss is from a passive activity, see **Form 8582,** Passive Activity Loss Limitations, or **Form 8810,** Corporate Passive Activity Loss and Credit Limitations, to find out if the loss is allowed under the passive activity rules. If only part of the loss is subject to the passive activity loss rules, report only that part on Form 8582 or Form 8810, whichever applies.

For Paperwork Reduction Act Notice, see page 8 of the instructions.   Form **6198** (2002)

EXHIBIT 3-1 (Continued)

| Schedule E (Form 1040) 2002 | | | | | Attachment Sequence No. **13** | | Page 2 |

Name(s) shown on return. Do not enter name and social security number if shown on other side.

Your social security number

Jerry Aladdin

111–22–3333

Note. If you report amounts from farming or fishing on Schedule E, you must enter your gross income from those activities on line 41 below. Real estate professionals must complete line 42 below.

Part II   Income or Loss From Partnerships and S Corporations Note. If you report a loss from an at-risk act., you **must** check either col. **(e)** or **(f)** on ln. 27 to describe your investment in the activity. See page E-1. If you check col. **(f)**, you must att. Form 6198.

27	(a) Name	(b) Enter P for partnership; S for S corp.	(c) Check if foreign partnership	(d) Employer identification number	(e) All is at risk	(f) Some is not at risk
A	Aladdin's Cleaning Corp.	S				X
B						
C						
D						
E						

	Passive Income and Loss		Nonpassive Income and Loss		
	(g) Passive loss allowed (attach Form 8582 if required)	(h) Passive income from Schedule K-1	(I) Nonpassive loss from Schedule K-1	(j) Section 179 expense deduction from Form 4562	(k) Nonpassive income from Schedule K-1
A	* 0		140,000		
B					
C					
D					
E					
28a	Totals				
b	Totals		140,000		

29	Add columns (h) and (k) of line 28a	29	0
30	Add columns (g), (i), and (j) of line 28b	30	(140,000)
31	Total partnership and S corporation income or (loss). Combine lines 29 and 30. Enter the result here and include in the total on line 40 below	31	−140,000

Part III   Income or Loss From Estates and Trusts

32	(a) Name	(b) Employer identification number
A		
B		

	Passive Income and Loss		Nonpassive Income and Loss	
	(c) Passive deduction or loss allowed (attach Form 8582 if required)	(d) Passive income from Schedule K-1	(e) Deduction or loss from Schedule K-1	(f) Other income from Schedule K-1
A				
B				
33a	Totals			
b	Totals			

34	Add columns (d) and (f) of line 33a	34	
35	Add columns (c) and (e) of line 33b	35	( )
36	Total estate and trust income or (loss). Combine lines 34 and 35. Enter the result here and include in the total on line 40 below	36	

Part IV   Income or Loss From Real Estate Mortgage Investment Conduits (REMICs)-Residual Holder

37	(a) Name	(b) Employer identification number	(c) Excess inclusion from Schedules Q, line 2c (see page E-6)	(d) Taxable income (net loss) from Schedules Q, line 1b	(e) Income from Schedules Q, line 3b

38	Combine columns (d) and (e) only. Enter the result here and include in the total on line 40 below	38	

Part V   Summary

39	Net farm rental income or (loss) from Form 4835. Also, complete line 41 below	39	
40	Total income or (loss). Combine lines 26, 31, 36, 38, and 39. Enter the result here and on Form 1040, line 17 ▶	40	−140,000
41	Reconciliation of Farming and Fishing Income. Enter your gross farming and fishing income reported on Form 4835, line 7; Schedule K-1 (Form 1065), line 15b; Schedule K-1 (Form 1120S), line 23; and Schedule K-1 (Form 1041), line 14 (see page E-6)	41	
42	Reconciliation for Real Estate Professionals. If you were a real estate professional (see page E-1), enter the net income or (loss) you reported anywhere on Form 1040 from all rental real estate activities in which you materially participated under the passive activity loss rules	42	

DAA   *Loss limited by amount at risk   Schedule E (Form 1040) 2002 partnership subsequently borrowed $50,000 from a bank. The basis in the partnership is $35,000 each, $10,000 capital contribution plus $25,000 of each partner's responsibility of the loan.

Example—Assume the same facts as above, except that the loan was provided by Louis instead of the bank. The partners' bases would continue to be $35,000 each since each partner would be liable for one half of the loan.

Example—Assume the same facts as above, except that Rita is not responsible to repay any part of the debt, because it is a nonrecourse loan. The entire loan of $50,000 would be allocated to Louis and his basis would be $60,000; Rita's would be her initial $10,000 contribution.

The effects of liabilities on a partner's basis can be summed up as follows:

Starting with the partner's initial basis:

Add:	Increases in partner's share of partnership liabilities
	Increases in partnership liabilities assumed by this partner
	Nonrecourse loans made by the partner to the partnership
Subtract:	Decreases in partner's share of partnership liabilities
	Liabilities of the partner assumed by the partnership

The final result is the partner's basis in the partnership. This number represents the maximum amount of losses a partner can deduct on the personal tax return due to his/her interest in the partnership. At-risk rules allow partners to take losses on their personal tax returns only to the extent of their basis for which the partner is personally at risk. Basis is dissected into that derived from recourse and nonrecourse financing to determine the partner's risk limitation. Basis attributable to a nonrecourse loan is not at risk unless it represents qualified nonrecourse financing with respect to real estate, as described previously. This means that an investor in a partnership may be able to deduct far fewer losses in a tax year than he/she otherwise would expect because of the at-risk constraints.

Example—Charlene is an investor in the DOC Partnership. Her share of losses for the current year is $15,000. Since her basis in the partnership interest is $20,000, she plans on making full use of the losses that flow through to her on a K-1.[35] However, if $13,000 of Charlene's basis is attributable to nonrecourse financing, she is at risk for only $7000. This means that Charlene will be unable to deduct more than $7000 of her current-year losses until her at-risk basis increases.

Contribution of a Note to a Partnership

Partners are often required to contribute capital at various intervals over a period of time. Amounts at risk consist of capital actually contributed, and do not include personal promissory notes to the partnership.[36]

Limited Partnerships

A limited partnership has two classes of partners, general and limited. The general partners are responsible for all the liabilities of the partnership and for the management of the partnership. A limited partner cannot lose more than he/she has invested into the partnership plus any additional commitment of capital or assumption or liability that he/she has made. Therefore, the at-risk rules apply only to the actual contribution and assumption of liabilities of the limited partner.

   Example—Helen and Ron have a limited partnership, HR. Helen is a limited and Ron a general partner. Each contributed $20,000. The partnership subsequently incurs a $100,000 recourse loan. Helen is at risk for her initial investment of $20,000 and Ron is at risk for $120,000. As a general partner, Ron assumes the entire risk of loss since he would have to repay the obligation if the partnership lacked sufficient capital to satisfy the debt.

LIMITED LIABILITY COMPANIES

A limited liability company (LLC) is a relatively new form of business designed to offer investors both protection from personal liability and favorable tax treatment. LLCs do not include entities classified as a trust or subject to other special treatment under the Code. Most limited liability companies can elect to be taxed as either corporations or partnerships regardless of whether they possess or lack traditional corporate characteristics.[37] Under the regulations, a separate business entity with two or more members can generally elect to be classified as a corporation or a partnership.[38] Certain entities may not be treated as partnerships. These include: (a) entities whose classification is determined under the Code; (b) trusts; (c) entities that are taxed as corporations under the law.

   An LLC with only one member does not qualify as a partnership but may choose to be classified as a corporation or as a sole proprietorship.

   The at-risk rules of the elected entity would prevail. If a new entity fails to elect a type of tax treatment, then a default classification is used. The default rules are that entities created or organized in the United States[39] with two or more members are classified as partnerships, and domestic single-member entities are treated as sole proprietorships. Foreign entities with two or more members are classified as corporations unless any member has unlimited liability.[40]

The election is made under the "check-the-box" regulations by filing Form 8832, Entity Classification Election with the service center designated on the form. An election will not be accepted unless all of the information required by the form and instructions, including the taxpayer identifying number of the entity, is provided.[41] If the default classification is used, then an election is not necessary.

An election is effective on the date specified by the entity, and a classification cannot be changed during the 60 months following the effective date of the election unless more than 50 percent of the ownership interest in the entity has changed.[42]

DISALLOWED LOSSES

Under the at-risk rules, any losses that are disallowed in a taxable year are suspended and treated as a deduction allocable to the activity the next year.[43] This means that at the very least, use of the loss is deferred for one year. However, depending on the circumstances, the disallowed losses may or may not be deductible the following year. As a result, application of the at-risk rules can result in long-term suspension of loss use.

Example—Rigo purchases computers for business use during 2001 for $25,000. He pays $5000 of his own cash and borrows $20,000 on a non-recourse note. During 2001 he receives computer lease income from his business of $40,000 and deductions of $46,000. He can claim a loss of $5000. The remaining loss of $1000 is suspended until 2002. In 2002 he receives lease payments of $50,000 and has expenses of $48,500. He can claim total deductions of $49,500 (including the $1000 carryover from 2001) and has net taxable income of $500.

Losses suspended under the at-risk rules can be carried over indefinitely. Gain from the disposition of an investment constitutes income from the activity, and the taxpayer can offset that gain with any losses that have been suspended under the at-risk rules.

An activity may continue to generate losses from year to year. Consequently, the amount by which a taxpayer is at risk must be calculated each year. The following adjustments may have to be made:

- The amount permitted as a deduction by the at-loss rules reduces the amount at risk.
- If an activity generates taxable income that is not distributed, the at-risk amount is increased.[44]
- The taxpayer may contribute additional money or property, which increases the amount at risk.
- The taxpayer may withdraw money from the activity, which decreases the amount at risk.
- The taxpayer's liabilities related to an activity may decrease or the taxpayer may withdraw property from the activity.

The task of keeping track of amounts at risk is cumbersome and similar to keeping track of partner or shareholder basis.

CONCLUSION

When considering an investment or business activity that appears attractive because losses may be generated that can offset income, the investor must be wary of the at-risk rules. S corporation shareholders are particularly vulnerable to this rule because it is common to incur operating losses within the first several years of a new corporation. Alternatively, an investment in a limited partnership may appear attractive because of inherent losses that the investor would like to utilize against income. However, the at-risk rules severely curtail the losses that may ultimately be claimed.

NOTES

[1] Tax Code §179 allows a taxpayer to expense, rather than depreciate, the cost of tangible "§1245 property" used in the active conduct of a trade or business. Subject to certain limits, this means the cost of an asset the taxpayer bought for $20,000, for example, can be recovered in the year the property is placed in service, rather than over several years, as would be the case if the taxpayer depreciated the item. Depreciable personal property items like computers, automobiles, or equipment are common examples of §1245 property, although §179 does contain some limitations on what assets qualify. Property is "placed in service" when it is ready for its intended use. See Tax Code §179 for further details.

[2] This example represents the theory. In reality, a financial institution would undoubtedly insist on Beth's personal guarantee.

[3] §465(c)(3)(A)(i)

[4] §465(b)(A)

[5] §465(b)(1)(B)(2)

[6] §465(b)(3)(A)

[7] §267(b) defines related persons as (1) members of a family; (2) an individual who owns more than 50 percent of the value of the standing stock of a corporation; (3) two corporations which are members of the same controlled group; (4) a grantor and a fiduciary of any trust; (5) a fiduciary of a trust and a fiduciary of another trust, if the same person is a grantor of both trusts; (6) a fiduciary of a trust and a beneficiary of such trust; (7) a fiduciary of a trust and a beneficiary of another trust, if the same person is a grantor of both trusts; (8) a fiduciary of a trust and a corporation more than 50 percent in value of the outstanding stock of which is owned, directly or indirectly, by or for the trust or by or for a person who is a grantor of the trust; (9) a person and an organization to which §501 applies and which is controlled directly or indirectly by such person or by members of the family of such individual; (10) a corporation and partnership if the same person owns more than 50 percent in value of the outstanding stock of the corporation, and more than 50 percent of the capital interest, or the profits interest, in the partnership. IRC §707, described in the text, deals with controlled partnerships.

[8] §465(b)(3)(C)(i) and (ii)

[9] §544(a)(1)

[10] §465(c)(7)(a) A C corporation will qualify if it is not a personal holding company, foreign personal holding company, and personal service corporation tested with a 5-percent employee-owner threshold.

[11] §465(c)(7)(c)(i)

[12] §465(c)(7)(c)(ii)

[13] §465(c)(7)(iii)

[14] §318(a)(1)

[15] §465(c)(7)(c)(iii)

[16] §465(c)(7)(c)(iv)

[17] §465(c)(4)(B)

[18] For purposes of this exception to the at-risk rules, "equipment leasing" does not include the leasing of master sound recordings or similar contractual arrangements involving tangible or intangible assets associated with literary, artistic, or musical properties. §465(c)(6)(B).

[19] Kresse and Buffalo are referred to as brother/sister corporations. A 50-percent test also applies, which looks only at the individual shareholders' identical stock ownership in each company. Since Rebecca owns more than 50 percent of the stock in each firm, this test also is met. See Tax Code §1563(a)(2).

[20] §465(c)(5)(A)(i)

[21] §465(c)(5)(B)(i)

[22] §465(c)(5)(B)(iii)

[23] §465(a)(1)(B)

[24] The hobby loss limitations are found in Tax Code §183. A hobby is an activity not en-

gaged in for profit. For example, assume a college professor raises and trains pedigreed poodles for pleasure. If she earns $5,000 from her canine activities in the current year, she can deduct only $5,000 of the related expenses. In other words, a net loss cannot be reported in connection with a hobby.

[25] §1.1367-1

[26] §1.1367-2(b)(1)

[27] §465((b)(6)(A)

[28] §465(b)(6)(B)(i)

[29] §465(b)(6)(B)(ii)

[30] §465(b)(6)(B)(iii)

[31] §465(b)(6)(B)(iv)

[32] If the carryover basis is less than fair market value, then the carryover basis becomes the fair market value.

[33] The estate tax is scheduled to be repealed December 31, 2009. At that time a carryover basis would be used.

[34] Reg.§1.465-27

[35] A partnership does not pay taxes. It files a Form 1065 listing all of its income, deductions, and net income, as well as other items. Each partner receives a Form K-1 that lists each individual partner's share of these items.

[36] §465(b)

[37] The attractiveness of a limited liability company is the flexibility that can be exercised in the operating agreement and the limited liability it delivers to each member.

[38] Reg. §301.7701-3(a)

[39] These are considered to be "domestic" entities. Domestic entities also include entities created or organized under the laws of the United States or any state. Treasury Regulation §301.7701-1(d).

[40] Reg. §301.7701-3(b)

[41] Reg. §301.7701-3(c)(i)

[42] Reg. §301.7701-3(c)(1)(iii)

[43] §465(a)(2)

[44] Reg. §1.465-22(c)(1)

4

INVESTMENT EXPENSES

INTRODUCTION

In order to prevent what was perceived as abuses, certain limits have been adopted in connection with the deduction of expenses related to investments. Depending on the taxpayer and the nature of the investment held, the rules might limit the amount of an expense that can be deducted or prohibit the deduction completely. These restrictions are designed to ensure that investments make economic sense, independent of their tax consequences.

Example—Marie buys a tax-exempt bond that pays 6.6 percent. She is a single taxpayer with a marginal tax rate of 35 percent. The bond is financed by a loan, on which Marie pays 7 percent interest. Although on first glance Marie appears to be losing money as a result of her investment, because she is paying 7 percent interest in order to receive a 6.6-percent return, the arrangement is profitable, after taking into account the tax implications. This is because the after-tax cost of the interest is only 4.55 percent. The after-tax cost is calculated by multiplying the stated interest rate (7 percent in this example) by one less the marginal tax rate (1 -.35). When this figure is compared to the bond's return of 6.6 percent, the transaction actually makes money for Marie. In comparison, if the bond's interest income were subject to tax, the after-tax return on the bond would be only 4.29 percent. (6.6 percent times (1 -.35)) and Marie would not make the investment.

Congress has adopted various restrictions on deducting expenses associated with investments. These include rules under §265 of the Tax Code, relating to tax-exempt income; the investment interest limitations, found at §163; and certain other provisions. These limitations must be considered when making decisions about potential investments, particularly if the investment will be debt financed. Otherwise, it is possible that a taxpayer will either lose money or receive an after-tax return that is less than desired because expenses expected to be deductible are not.

COSTS ASSOCIATED WITH TAX-EXEMPT INTEREST INCOME

Under the Tax Code, costs otherwise deductible for investment advice or safe deposit box rentals, for example, are disallowed when allocable to tax-exempt interest income. Specifically, the law bars deduction of expenses that otherwise would be authorized under §212 of the Tax Code.[1] That section permits taxpayers to deduct the costs of producing or collecting income and also the costs of managing, keeping, or maintaining property held for income production. This provision typically is used by taxpayers to deduct expenses like investment advice, custodial fees, clerical help, or similar expenses incurred in connection with investment activities.[2] However, where these expenditures are properly allocable to tax-exempt income, no deduction is allowed.[3]

Under a second disallowance provision, a taxpayer cannot deduct interest on debt connected to investments that generate tax-exempt interest.[4] (The Tax Code also specifically disallows a deduction for interest where loan proceeds are used to purchase shares in a mutual fund that pays tax-exempt interest dividends.[5]) In determining whether a loan was incurred, or continued, to purchase or carry tax-free bonds, the focus is on the taxpayer's purpose in either taking out a loan or not repaying a debt. According to the IRS, this is a determination based on the facts and circumstances, and can be established either directly or by circumstantial evidence.[6]

Using tax-exempt bonds to secure the debt is considered direct evidence of a tainted purpose, meaning that the interest on the loan will be nondeductible. Likewise, where the proceeds of the obligation are used to purchase a tax-exempt security, no deduction will be permitted. Where there is no direct evidence of a taxpayer's purpose, "insubstantial" investments in tax-free obligations will not trigger a disallowance. This means the average amount of the tax-exempt bonds, valued at adjusted basis, is no more than 2 percent of the average adjusted bases of both portfolio investments and trade or business assets.[7]

For purposes of this 2-percent exception, portfolio investments include stocks, bonds, and interests in for-profit ventures not tied to the active conduct of a trade or business. The term also includes investments in real estate. A substantial ownership interest in the voting stock of a corporation conducting an active trade or business is not a portfolio investment. For corporate taxpayers, the 2-percent test is applied by reference only to the average adjusted bases of trade or business assets.[8]

Example—Jean holds tax-exempt securities with a fair market value of $5000 and an adjusted basis of $4700. She owes money on certain loans; there is no direct evidence linking these debts to her tax-exempt bonds. Jean has portfolio investments, consisting of stocks and bonds, with an average adjusted basis of $200,000. She also actively operates a business; the associated assets, on average, have a basis of $200,000. Because the adjusted basis of Jean's tax-exempt bonds ($4700) is less than 2 percent of the bases of her portfolio and business assets (2 percent * $400,000= $8000), none of her interest will be disallowed. However, if Jean were a corporation, the company could not take advantage of the 2-percent rule. This is because the $4700 basis of the exempt bonds exceeds 2 percent of the bases of the corporation's trade or business assets ($4000).

Where there is no direct evidence concerning the purpose of a debt and the taxpayer cannot rely on the 2-percent rule, indirect, or circumstantial, proof will be used. The deduction will be lost if the evidence shows a "sufficiently direct relationship" between the loan and the tax-free bonds. Interest on obligations incurred for personal reasons, like a mortgage on a residence, should be deductible even if the taxpayer holds tax-exempt securities at the same time. Likewise, debt incurred in connection with the active conduct of a trade or business should generate deductible interest. However, if a taxpayer borrows more than business needs would dictate, the IRS will presume the loan is connected to his or her tax-exempt securities. Similarly, if tax-exempt bonds were purchased at a time when the taxpayer could have foreseen that debt would be needed in the future to meet regular, recurring business obligations, the subsequent loan will be considered tainted unless the taxpayer can show a business purpose.[9]

Where a taxpayer's debt is not directly connected to personal reasons or a trade or business, it is presumed that the purpose of the loan is to carry the tax-exempt obligations owned.[10] This means that in order to deduct the interest, the taxpayer would have to show the loan was for another reason.[11] For example, a taxpayer who borrows money to finance a stock investment, while owning tax-exempt bonds, will lose the interest deduction. This is because the taxpayer could have sold the tax-exempt investment in order to purchase the bonds. To avoid this presumption, the taxpayer would have to show that the bonds could not have been sold. It is not sufficient to show that they could have been liquidated only at a loss or that the taxpayer had other, taxable, investments that could have been sold.[12]

A taxpayer can make a temporary investment of borrowed moneys in tax-exempt securities without losing the interest deduction. Also, where only part of a debt is incurred or continued to buy or hold a tax-exempt security, the interest deduction will be only partially disallowed. The calculation of the disallowed portion differs, depending on whether direct or circumstantial evidence is available concerning the purpose of the loan.[13]

Example—Jim borrows $150,000 and uses $100,000 of the proceeds to buy tax-free bonds. He has no other debt. Jim pays $10,000 of interest this year. Since direct evidence exists linking two-thirds of the debt to tax-exempt securities, Jim will lose a corresponding amount of the interest deduction. In other words, because two-thirds of the debt proceeds were used to purchase tax-exempt obligations, only one-third of the interest on the debt is potentially deductible. However, if only indirect proof were available regarding the loan's purpose, the disallowed portion of the debt would be calculated using the following formula:

Total Interest *   Average amount of tax-exempt bonds for the year, valued at adjusted basis

Average amount of total assets for the year, valued at adjusted basis, less debt not subject to disallowance

If, apart from the bonds, Jim's other assets have a total basis of $1,000,000, the disallowed interest would be $909. This is $10,000 * $100,000/ $1,100,000.[14]

The rules limiting the deduction of interest on debts incurred or continued in order to buy or hold tax-free bonds also apply to partners and corporations. A partner's share of partnership debt and partnership tax-exempt obligations flows down to him or her from the partnership. The partnership's purpose in incurring the debt is attributed to the general partners. Where there is no direct evidence of a corporate taxpayer's purpose in borrowing funds, moneys needed for an active trade or business not involving the holding of tax-exempt securities will not be tainted unless the loan exceeded business needs. If a corporation continued debt that could be repaid partially or completely by liquidating tax-exempt holdings, the interest will be nondeductible unless the liquidation would affect capital required for regular business activities. Likewise, the deduction will be lost if a corporation invests a disproportionately large amount of its liquid assets in tax-free bonds, unless the bonds are related to the reasonable needs of the corporation's business or are required by its financial condition.[15]

INVESTMENT INTEREST LIMITATIONS APPLICABLE TO NONCORPORATE TAXPAYERS

Taxpayers that are not corporations are subject to certain restrictions on the deduction of interest arising from loans relating to investments. These rules are found at Tax Code §163(d).

Allocation Rules

Noncorporate taxpayers can deduct only certain types of interest expense, including home mortgage interest,[16] interest arising in a trade or business, and passive activity interest. Investment interest also can be deducted, but within limits.[17] Because different rules apply depending on the type of loan generating the interest obligation, the first issue in determining how much, if any, interest that can be claimed as an expense is to assign the interest among the various categories. The IRS has developed allocation rules used to characterize debt as investment, passive, trade or business, or personal. These rules use a tracing principle under which interest on a debt typically is allocated according to how the proceeds of the underlying obligation were spent.[18]

Under regulations issued by the IRS, debt proceeds are used for investment purposes where they are spent on expenditures properly chargeable to capital in connection with assets held for investment or on costs tied to holding investment property. Investment expenditures also include amounts spent for assets that produce portfolio income that is excluded from the passive activity rules of §469. (These rules are discussed in Chapter 2.) For this purpose, portfolio income includes interest, dividends, royalties, etc., that are not derived in the ordinary course of a trade or business.[19]

If money is borrowed initially for one purpose but later is put to another use, the interest on the loan will be reallocated at the time the use changes. For example, interest on a trade or business loan, the proceeds of which are later used for investment expenditures, will be recharacterized as an investment interest loan. This can lead to somewhat complicated calculations because of the effect of the accrued interest.[20] The example below, found in the regulations, is illustrative:

Example—On January 1, a calendar year taxpayer borrows $1000 at 11-percent interest, compounded semiannually. The money is used immediately for an investment. On July 1, the investment is sold for $1000 and the proceeds used to acquire a passive activity. Accrued interest is paid on December 31.

Total interest for the first six months is $55 ($1,000 $\times$ $\frac{1}{2}$ $\times$ .11). Interest for the second half of the year is $58 ($1,055 $\times$ $\frac{1}{2}$ $\times$ .11). However, the taxpayer has $58 of investment interest, not $55. This is because $3 of the interest obligation arising in the second half of the year is attributable to interest that accrued during the first six months of the loan, when the debt was used for an investment expenditure.

Instead of this procedure, the regulations allow a taxpayer to assign interest accruing in the year for the purpose of a debt change, on a straight-line basis. This would mean an equal amount of interest is assigned to each day. The amount of investment interest then would be the number of days in the year the loan was used for investment purposes, multiplied by the amount of interest treated as accruing each day. In the example above, half of the interest would be allocated to investment expenditures and half to passive activities.[21]

Reallocation rules apply if the debt proceeds are used to create, improve, or purchase a capital asset and that asset is either disposed of or its use or character changes. For example, if an investment property that is a capital asset is sold, the loan used to finance it will be reallocated according to how the sale proceeds are used. If the asset is sold for less than the outstanding loan obligation, the reallocation will apply only to the extent of the proceeds. If the use of property changes, as where an investment is converted into a trade or business asset, the amount of debt recharacterized will be equal to the fair market value of the property at the time of conversion. If more than one debt is associated with an asset, a pro rata portion of each obligation will be recharacterized at the time of reallocation. When a taxpayer sells a capital asset and receives an installment obligation, the deferred payments are treated as an investment expenditure.[22]

Example—Charley holds a capital asset for investment purposes that was debt financed. He sells the asset for $30,000, at a time when the outstanding debt also amounts to $30,000. The proceeds are used to buy a car to be used by Charley and his wife. The $30,000 loan is now treated as personal, and the interest Charley pays on it will no longer be deductible. Assume instead that Charley had sold the asset for $10,000 cash, which he used in his business, and an installment note of $20,000. As to the outstanding debt, $10,000 is now treated as a loan incurred in Charley's business. The remaining $20,000 continues to be viewed as tied to an investment, now the installment obligation. As the $20,000 of payments are received, the loan will be recharacterized, depending on how Charley uses the money the payments represent.[23]

Often the proceeds of a loan are received as cash, paid directly to the debtor. In order to figure out whether any of the interest on the loan is deductible, a 15-day rule applies. Any money used within 15 days of receiving the borrowed cash may be treated as having been funded by the loan proceeds. If the borrowed money is not spent within 15 days, debt proceeds held as cash are allocable to a personal expenditure.[24] This means the interest on the debt is not deductible.

Example—Intisar borrows $15,000 and receives the proceeds on March 1. On March 10, she uses $13,500 to purchase an investment. Intisar can treat interest on $13,500 of the $15,000 loan as investment interest. Since the remaining loan proceeds are held as cash, however, interest on $1500 of the debt is not deductible. Intisar is treated as having acquired her investment on March 1, meaning interest on the $13,500 portion of the loan is deductible as investment interest right from the outset.

Loan proceeds held in a bank account are treated as an investment expenditure. When the proceeds are withdrawn, the loan is recharacterized according to the way the debtor uses the funds. If the bank account contains both borrowed and unborrowed moneys, the borrowed money is treated as having been spent first. If the bank account holds the proceeds of more than one debt, the borrowed money is withdrawn on a first-in-first-out basis. If funds from loans incurred on two different days are deposited in the account on the same day, the debtor is treated as having deposited the funds from the older loan first. Money taken out of an account by check is treated as withdrawn at the time the draft was written, provided the instrument was delivered or mailed to the payee within a reasonable period. A taxpayer may treat checks drafted on the same day as written in any order.[25]

Example—Rita received $25,000 of loan proceeds on May 1. She deposited the funds into an account containing $5000 from an earlier loan, received on April 15, and $40,000 of her own money. On May 25, Rita wrote a check for $20,000 to purchase a used car for personal use. On May 28, Rita wrote a second check for $40,000 to purchase an investment asset.

Both of Rita's loans are characterized initially as tied to investment expenditures. When Rita writes the check on May 25th, she is treated as having spent the April 15th loan proceeds, meaning the interest on that debt will no longer be deductible. She also is treated as now having spent $15,000 of the $25,000 loan on personal purposes. The remaining $10,000 of the May 1 $25,000 debt will be treated as an investment obligation. This is because the money stays in the account until the May 28th check is written. However, since the May 28th expenditure is for an investment asset, the $10,000 will continue to be treated as an investment obligation even after the funds are withdrawn.

The result above is unfavorable to Rita. She would prefer to be treated as having spent the unborrowed money on the car, since that was a personal expenditure, meaning a loan to finance it would generate nondeductible interest. To avoid the ordering rules applicable to accounts holding both borrowed and unborrowed funds, Rita should deposit the loan proceeds in a separate account. This would permit her to show that unborrowed money was used to buy the car and borrowed funds financed part or all of the investment asset. If a segregated account has only the proceeds of the borrowing and the interest the borrowed funds generated, the depositor can treat any withdrawal as coming first from interest. In the previous example, this means that if Rita deposited the $30,000 of loan proceeds in a separate account, she could use the interest income the bank pays her on the deposited moneys for personal purposes without jeopardizing the deductions for the interest expense she pays on the two obligations.[26]

When a debt allocated exclusively to one purpose is repaid, as where a debtor pays off a loan taken out to acquire an investment asset, no special issues arise. However, if the obligation were used for several different kinds of expenditures, the debtor needs to know which part of the loan is treated as being repaid first. Under ordering rules contained in the §163 regulations, the debt is treated as paid back in the following order:

1. Personal expenditures
2. Moneys spent on investments and most passive activities
3. Amounts spent on rental real estate passive activities where the debtor actively participates
4. Expenditures associated with former passive activities and
5. Trade or business expenditures.[27]

Rules relating to passive activities are discussed in Chapter 2 of this book. If money is allocated to more than one activity falling within the same category, the repayment is treated as having been made in the same order as the initial allocation.[28]

Example—On August 31, Josh borrows $250,000, which he deposits immediately in a checking account. On September 30, Josh withdraws $50,000 to make an investment in a passive activity that does not involve rental real estate. On October 10, he uses $100,000 of the funds in his business. An additional withdrawal of $60,000 is made on October 20 to acquire an investment. The final $40,000 is used on November 1, when Josh purchases a yacht for personal use. On March 31, Josh repays $100,000, followed by a second $100,000 payment on April 30. The balance of the loan is repaid on May 31.

Under these facts, the $100,000 repayment made on March 31st is allocated first to the $40,000 yacht. This rule is favorable to Josh, since it means he retires the portion of the debt on which the interest is not deductible first. The remaining $60,000 of the repayment is assigned to the second category, investment and passive activity expenditures. Josh has two items in this class, the $50,000 passive activity and the $60,000 investment. The repayment is allocated first to the passive activity, since that expenditure was made on September 30, before Josh purchased the October 20th investment. This leaves $10,000 of the March 31st payment to be allocated to the investment portion of the loan. The April 30th payment retires that portion of the debt allocable to the investment ($50,000) and half of the business debt ($50,000). The final payment Josh makes on May 31st extinguishes the remaining balance of the loan, all of which is now treated as a trade or business debt.

Funds borrowed through a line of credit are treated as one loan so long as interest accrues on the borrowed money at the same fixed or variable rate. According to the IRS regulations, this means that if the actual interest payable on a loan changes because of a change in an underlying index on which the interest is based, more than one loan exists. These "separate" debts are treated as repaid in the same order as provided in the loan agreement.[29] If debt is refinanced, the new obligation is allocated in the same way as the loan it replaces. If the refinanced debt is more than the original loan, the excess is allocated based on how it is used.[30]

Under temporary rules, where a taxpayer holds an interest in a pass-through entity, like a partnership or S corporation, tracing occurs at both the owner and the entity levels. For example, if a taxpayer borrows money in order to acquire a partnership interest, the debt proceeds must be allocated. The allocation will be to assets of the partnership or to expenditures made by the entity, as though the taxpayer/partner's debt actually was an obligation of the partnership. The options available depend on whether the partnership receives the debt proceeds from the taxpayer as a contribution to capital.[31]

If the pass-through entity uses debt to make a distribution to its owners, the obligation must be allocated using either a general or an optional rule. Under the general rule, debt used for distributions, plus the associated interest, is assigned according to how the owner uses the proceeds. In other words, if a debt-financed partnership distribution is used by a partner for personal purposes, the partner's share of the partnership's interest expense on the loan is not deductible. Under the optional rule, a pass-through entity may assign distributed debt proceeds, plus the corresponding interest, to expenditures, other than distributions, made during the same year, to the extent loans have not already been allocated to the expenditure. For example, if a partnership borrows $175,000 to make a distribution in the same year it acquired a business asset for $200,000, it could treat the entire loan as trade or business related. This option would not be available if other debt proceeds had already been assigned to the $200,000 asset.[32]

Investment Interest Limitations

Under §163, the deduction for interest on investment debt is limited to net investment income. This limitation applies to individuals, estates, and trusts.[33] Interest on investment debt held by a pass-through entity, like a partnership or S corporation, flows down to the owners. In other words, if a partnership borrows money to buy an investment asset, the partners treat the interest paid on the debt as investment interest.[34] The investment interest rules do not apply to C corporations, which are corporations taxed under the regular income tax rules.[35]

Interest not deductible because of the investment interest limitations is carried forward and treated as paid or accrued in the next tax year.[36] The length of the carryforward period is unlimited. The investment interest rules are designed to prevent taxpayers from taking deductions for interest on debt used in connection with investment property that is producing little or no current income.

Example—Theresa buys stock in Peanut Company as an investment. Peanut does not pay dividends, but shares in the corporation are expected to appreciate substantially in the future. Theresa pays $5000 of interest in the current year on the loan she incurred to buy the Peanut stock.

Without the investment interest rules, Theresa would deduct $5000, generating a tax loss in connection with the shares. If Theresa were in a 35-percent tax bracket, the loss would create tax savings of $1750. Eventually, when Theresa sells the appreciated stock, she will have to report a gain for income tax purposes. However, assuming Theresa holds the Peanut shares for more than one year, this gain would be taxed at the lower rates applicable to net capital gains. If capital gains are taxed at 15 percent, for example, this means Theresa has generated deductions against income otherwise taxed at a 35 percent rate, at a cost of later reporting gain taxed at 15 percent.

Investment interest is interest paid or accrued on debt allocable to property held for investment, under the rules discussed previously. It includes amounts deductible in connection with personal property used in a short sale.[37] Assets that generate interest, dividends, annuities, or royalties that are not derived in the ordinary course of a trade or business are considered investment property.[38] Similarly, assets that would yield capital gain or loss on disposition, like options or futures contracts, also would be considered to be property held for investment, unless they are part of a taxpayer's trade or business. If an asset is used for a trade or business[39] or as part of a passive activity,[40] it is not investment property. However, if the taxpayer does not materially participate in the trade or business, the associated interest expense falls within the investment interest limitations, unless the passive activity rules apply.[41]

Interest on a loan will be subject to the investment interest limitations so long as the taxpayer had a "substantial investment motive;" it does not matter that the dominant reason for incurring the debt was business related. Under these rules, a taxpayer who borrows money in order to buy stock in her employer may be subject to the investment interest restrictions, even though her primary reason in acquiring the stock was to protect her job.[42] Interest on debt incurred to buy tax-exempt securities is excluded from the investment interest calculations. The deduction for this interest is disallowed under the §265 rules discussed previously. Likewise excluded is qualified residence interest, even if it is tied to an investment. This means a taxpayer who uses the proceeds of a home equity loan to buy stock can deduct the interest, assuming all of the qualified residence interest requirements are met.[43]

"Net investment income" is defined by the tax law as investment income less investment expenses. Investment income generally includes all gross income from property held for investment; however, dividends taxed at the reduced rates (15% for most individual taxpayers) contained in the

2003 tax legislation are excluded from this definition. Individual investors can elect to characterize dividends as income from investments but only at a cost of giving up the lower 2003 Act dividend tax rates. Gain arising from the disposition of investment assets is included as investment income to the extent that it is not net capital gain. A taxpayer can elect to treat net capital gain arising from the disposition of a capital asset as ordinary income, in order to maximize the amount of the investment interest deduction.[44] However, like the dividend option, a taxpayer who makes this election loses the favorable tax rate that otherwise might apply to the sale proceeds.

Investment expenses are deductible expenditures, other than interest, that are directly connected with producing investment income. Deductible investment expenditures are those that exceed the 2-percent adjusted gross income floor that applies to miscellaneous itemized deductions. This floor is first applied to noninvestment expenditures.[45] This rule minimizes the amount of investment interest a taxpayer can deduct.

Example—Cecelia has the following income and expense information for the current year:

Salary	$118,000
Investment income	12,000
Investment interest expense	11,400
Miscellaneous itemized deductions relating to Cecelia's investment	1,000
Other miscellaneous itemized deductions	2,500

Cecelia's miscellaneous itemized deductions that are unrelated to her investment activities are reduced to $0 ($2500 less 2 percent of Cecelia's adjusted gross income of $130,000 {$118,000 + $12,000}). This means her net investment income is $11,100 ($12,000 - $900 of deductible investment expenditures) and she can only deduct that amount of investment interest expense. The remaining $300 will be carried over to the following year as investment interest. If Cecelia had been able to offset the $1000 of noninterest investment expenses by 2 percent of her AGI, she could have deducted all of the investment interest expense.

DEDUCTION OF INTEREST BY CORPORATE TAXPAYERS

The §163(d) rules limiting the deduction of investment interest do not apply to corporations. However, corporate investors may face restrictions on the deduction of interest expense under other provisions of the Tax Code. For example, like individuals, closely held and personal service corporations are both subject to the passive activity rules.[46] This means interest incurred by a closely held corporation, for example, in connection with a passive activity will be subject to the restrictions found in §469. (The passive activity rules are discussed in Chapter 2.)

Under IRC §279, deductions for interest paid or incurred by a corporation on "corporate acquisition indebtedness" are limited to $5 million, less interest arising during the same year on certain other acquisition debt. The other acquisition debt refers to obligations used to finance a stock or asset purchase that does not meet the corporate acquisition indebtedness requirements. These rules target situations where a corporation makes an acquisition by issuing obligations that have both debt and equity features. Various requirements must be met before an instrument will be treated as a Code §279 obligation. In general, the debt must be evidenced by documentation like a bond, debenture, or note. The instrument must be subordinated to certain other obligations, and convertible into stock of the debtor corporation or part of an investment arrangement that includes options to acquire stock directly or indirectly. Also, certain requirements must be met concerning either the debt-equity ratio of the debtor corporation or its projected earnings-annual interest ratio.[47]

OTHER RESTRICTIONS

In addition to the rules discussed previously, other provisions may limit the deduction of interest expense. For example, a taxpayer who borrows money to buy a market discount bond is subject to the limitations of §1277. That section restricts the interest deduction to the amount by which the net direct interest expense exceeds the market discount allocable to the taxpayer for the year under consideration. The "net direct interest expense" is the interest paid or accrued on a debt to buy or carry the bond, over the interest, including OID, includible in income.[48] (Market discount bonds are discussed in Chapter 13.) A similar rule applies where short-term obligations are debt financed, under §1282. The at-risk rules (see Chapter 3) also may limit the deduction of interest on certain loans incurred to finance investments.

CAUTIONS TO CONSIDER

A taxpayer who plans on using debt to acquire or continue an investment or plans on deducting any costs associated with his or her investment holdings should research all possible disallowance provisions before assuming that the item(s) can be claimed against income. Limits under the tax law on deducting expenses associated with assets that generate tax-exempt income, and also restricting the amount of deductions associated with other investments, can impact the after-tax return an asset generates. This means it's important to estimate the expenses involved with a potential holding, and to determine whether those expenses are deductible, before committing to the investment.

NOTES

[1] Tax Code §265(a)(1)

[2] Treasury Regulation §1.212-1

[3] Tax Code §265(a)(1)

[4] Tax Code §265(a)(2). The language of the Tax Code prohibits a deduction for "[i] interest on indebtedness incurred or continued to purchase or carry obligations the interest on which is wholly exempt from the taxes imposed by this subtitle.

[5] Tax Code §265(a)(4)

[6] Rev. Proc. 72-18, 1972-1 C.B. 740, clarified by Rev. Proc. 74-8, 1974-1 C.B. 419, modified by Rev. Proc. 87-53, 1987-2 C.B. 669

[7] Rev. Proc. 72-18, 1972-1 C.B. 740

[8] Rev. Proc. 72-18, 1972-1 C.B. 740

[9] Rev. Proc. 72-18, 1972-1 C.B. 740

[10] Rev. Proc. 72-18, 1972-1 C.B. 740

[11] *Indian Trail Trading Post, Inc. v. Commissioner.*, 60 T.C. 497 (1973), aff'd. per curiam, 503 F.2d 102 (6th Cir. 1974).

[12] Rev. Proc. 72-18, 1972-1 C.B. 740

[13] Rev. Proc. 72-18, 1972-1 C.B. 740

[14] Rev. Proc. 72-18, 1972-1 C.B. 740

[15] Rev. Proc. 72-18, 1972-1 C.B. 740

[16] "Qualified residence interest," including interest on debt to acquire a residence or on a home equity loan, is deductible provided certain requirements are met. See Tax Code §163(h).

[17] Tax Code §163

[18] Treasury Regulation §1.163-8T

[19] Treasury Regulation §1.163-8T

[20] Treasury Regulation §1.163-8T

[21] Treasury Regulation §1.163-8T(c)(2)(ii)

[22] Treasury Regulation §1.163-8T(j)

[23] Treasury Regulation §1.163-8T(j)(4)

[24] Treasury Regulation §1.163-8T(c)(5)

[25] Treasury Regulation §1.163-8T(c)(4). A 15-day rule also applies to expenditures made from an account within 15 days after debt proceeds were deposited in that account. See Treasury Regulation §1.163-8T(c)(4)(iii)(B).

[26] Treasury Regulation §1.163-8T(c)(4)(iii)

[27] Treasury Regulation §1.163-8T(d)(1)

[28] Treasury Regulation §1.163-8T(d)(2)

[29] Treasury Regulation §1.163-8T(d)(3)

[30] Treasury Regulation §1.163-8T(e)

[31] Notice 88-20, 1988-1 C.B. 487; Notice 88-37, 1988-1 C.B. 522; Notice 89-35, 1989-1 C.B. 675.

[32] *Id*

[33] Tax Code §163(d)(1)

[34] See Form 4952, *Investment Interest Expense Deductions,* (2002) Instructions.

[35] Tax Code §163(d)(1)

[36] Tax Code §163(d)(2)

[37] Tax Code §163(d)(3)

[38] Tax Code §163(d)(5)

[39] See Tax Code §162 for a discussion of interest deductible as a trade or business expense.

[40] Tax Code §163(d)(4)

[41] Tax Code §163(d)(5)(A)

[42] *Miller v. Commissioner,* 70 T.C. 448(1978). Where an employer is in financial distress, a taxpayer/employee may believe that a loan will offer sufficient liquidity to see the company through its cash crisis. Therefore the taxpayer might agree to loan money to his employer in order to keep the firm open and preserve his job.

[43] Tax Code §163(d)(3)(B)

[44] Tax Code §163(d)(4)

[45] See Form 4952, *Investment Interest Expense Deductions*, (2002) Instructions.

[46] Tax Code §469(a)(2)

[47] Tax Code §279

[48] Tax Code §1277(a)(1)

5 | ALTERNATIVE MINIMUM TAX

INTRODUCTION

Years ago, Congress passed legislation that provided favorable tax treatment to certain taxpayers. This preferential treatment included accelerated depreciation, artificial deductions such as percentage of depletion, incentive stock options, certain itemized deductions, installment sales of some property, and others. Congress soon became concerned that many taxpayers were using these tax preference items as tax planning tools to avoid paying taxes. They felt that the tax burden was being shifted onto other taxpayers. To counteract that, Congress installed the AMT.

The alternative minimum tax (AMT) was enacted as a separate tax system that runs parallel to our regular tax system. It is used to equalize our tax structure so that everyone pays his or her fair tax on true economic income.

The effect of AMT must be considered by investors evaluating potential holdings. This is because certain financial instruments that appear to be good investments are particularly vulnerable to impact of the alternative minimum tax. These include: tax-exempt interest from private activity bonds, incentive stock options, capital gains, installment sales, tax shelters, and certain credits.

After calculating the regular tax liability, the alternative minimum tax must be determined. After all required adjustments and tax preference modifications are made for AMT purposes, a minimum tax is calculated. If the regular tax is higher than the minimum tax, then there is no AMT liability. However, if the minimum tax is higher, then AMT is the difference between the minimum tax and regular tax. This chapter discusses all of the required calculations that are necessary to compute the alternative minimum tax.

OVERVIEW OF THE ALTERNATIVE MINIMUM TAX CALCULATION

The following steps are required in the calculation of AMT:

1. Start with taxable income, then add the tax preferences.
2. Next, add personal and dependency exemptions and the standard deduction (if the taxpayer doesn't itemize).
3. Then add/subtract the adjustments for AMT. The results are alternative minimum taxable income (AMTI).
4. Take alternative minimum taxable income (AMTI) and subtract the exemption amount. (The exemption amount varies depending on filing status. Additionally, it is phased out as a taxpayer's income exceeds certain levels.) Then multiply the first $175,000 ($87,500 for married individuals filing separately) by 26 percent and the excess of $175,000 by 28 percent.
5. Then subtract any AMT foreign tax credit. This results in the tentative minimum tax.
6. Take the tentative minimum tax and subtract the regular tax (calculated under the regular tax system). The results are the alternative minimum tax.

Example—Matthew, a single taxpayer, has taxable income of $150,000. His regular tax liability is $41,065 and he has tax preferences of $20,000 and disallowed itemized deductions for AMT of $10,000. His alternative minimum tax is:

Taxable Income	$150,000
Plus Tax Preferences	20,000
Plus Disallowed Itemized Deductions	10,000
Plus Personal Exemption	2,900
Alternative Minimum Taxable Income	182,900
Less: Exemption	
($ 40,250[1] − (25% × ($182,900 − $112,500))	(22,650)
Alternative Minimum Taxable Income after exemption	$160,250
Tentative Minimum Tax @ 26%	41,665
Less Regular Tax	(41,065)
Alternative Minimum Tax	$ 600

Matthew's total tax will be $42,265 of which $41,065 is regular tax and $600 is alternative minimum tax.

RECOMPUTATION OF TAXABLE INCOME

Some forms of income and deductions will receive different tax treatment for AMTI purposes than for regular taxable income calculations. As a result, taxable income for regular tax purposes differs from alternative minimum taxable income. Unfortunately, this means taxpayers are expected to recompute certain items for AMT purposes. These items, all of which are limited or in some way affected by it, include:

- IRC §179[2] expenses, where a taxpayer's deduction is limited by the net profit of the business.
- Expenses for business or rental use of a home.
- Conservation expenses, where a taxpayer's deduction is limited to a percentage of gross income from farming.
- Taxable IRA distributions, if prior-year IRA deductions were different for AMT and regular tax.
- Self-employed health insurance deduction.
- Keogh retirement plan or self-employed SEP deduction; and
- IRA deductions affected by the earned income limitation of §219(b)(1)(B).[3]

Example—Ann purchases equipment for her business for $130,000 and decides to expense its cost in the current year, under §179. Ann's deduction, by statute, is capped at $100,000. However, the deduction is further limited to Ann's taxable income from the conduct of any trade or business during the year. (This would include wages earned by her husband and other businesses that Ann may own.) If Ann's total business income for regular tax purposes is $128,000, she will expense $100,000 and depreciate the remaining amount according to her regular depreciation schedule. However, if Ann's alternative minimum taxable income from her business is only $90,000, her §179 deduction for AMT purposes is limited to $90,000. The remaining cost will be recovered for AMT in future years.

ADJUSTMENTS APPLICABLE TO ALL TAXPAYERS

Adjustments that must be made to regular taxable income are primarily related to timing differences, whereby income is deferred or deductions are accelerated. These include: depreciation, mining exploration and development costs, treatment of certain long-term contracts, the alternative tax net operating loss deduction, pollution control facilities, and the adjusted basis in property.

Depreciation

Depreciation refers to the method by which the cost of property is recovered for tax purposes. The method used to calculate regular tax depreciation depends on when the asset was placed in service, meaning when it was ready for its intended function. Property placed in service after 1986 is depreciated using "MACRS," the Modified Accelerated Cost Recovery System. MACRS divides assets up into classes, which determine the period over which the cost will be recovered. Property in the 3, 5, and 7 year classes is depreciated using an accelerated method,[4] with a switch to straight-line when the straight-line deduction becomes larger.[5] The cost of depreciable real estate is recovered over $27\frac{1}{2}$ years (for residential rental property) or 39 years (for nonresidential property) on a straight-line basis.

For AMT, depreciation of property placed in service after 1986 must be calculated using ADS, or the Alternative Depreciation System.[6] ADS recovers the cost of personal property over its class life and real property over 40 years. (The class life usually is longer than the MACRS recovery period.) In most cases, straight-line depreciation applies.[7] However, for tangible personal property placed in service before 1999, ADS is applied for AMT purposes using 150-percent declining balance, a somewhat accelerated method of cost recovery.[8] Post 1998 personal property is also depreciated for AMT purposes using 150-percent declining balance, but over the MACRS recovery period rather than the asset's class life.

This means adjustments for AMT purposes will be necessary because of depreciation for

(a) Property placed in service after 1998 that is depreciated under MACRS for regular tax purposes;

(b) Property, like office buildings or apartment complexes,[9] that was placed in service after 1998 and depreciated using a method other than straight-line; and

(c) Tangible property placed in service after 1986 and before 1999.

A few general rules can be helpful for understanding the depreciation adjustment.[10]

1. Property placed in service before 1999
   a. Real property is depreciated using straight-line over 40 years.[11]
      Example—Tom purchased residential rental property in 1996. For regular tax purposes, the property is depreciated over $27\frac{1}{2}$ years. Since the AMT depreciation must be over a period of 40 years, an adjustment is necessary.
   b. Tangible property like desks, computer equipment, etc., that was depreciated using straight-line for regular tax purposes. AMT cost recovery for these assets also is calculated using straight-line, but over the property's AMT class life, not its MACRS recovery period.[12]
   c. Other tangible personal property—Use the 150-percent declining balance method, switching to straight-line the first tax year that it gives a larger deduction. The depreciation is calculated using the property's class life, not the MACRS period.
      Example—Laura placed an asset in service in 1998 that has a class life of 10 years. For AMT purposes, Laura must depreciate the asset using the 150-percent declining balance method. This means her AMT depreciation deduction in 2003 is $8740, assuming that the asset initially cost $100,000.
2. For property placed in service after 1998, depreciation is refigured using the same conventions and recovery period as for regular tax purposes. However, the depreciation method may be different for regular tax and AMT. For property other than §1250 property, use the 150-percent declining balance, switching to straight-line in the first year that it yields a larger deduction. For §1250 property, like an apartment building, use straight-line.

Mining Exploration and Development Costs

Mining exploration costs are those paid or incurred during the taxable year for the purpose of ascertaining the existence, location, extent, or quality of any deposit of ore or other minerals, and paid or incurred before the beginning of the development stage of the mine.[13] Under §616(a), development costs of a mine or other natural deposits (other than an oil or gas well) are those paid after the existence of ores or minerals, in commercially marketable quantities, has been disclosed.

These expenses would normally be deducted in the year in which they were paid or incurred. However, a taxpayer may elect under §616 to deduct these costs on a ratable basis as the units of produced ores or minerals are sold. Expenditures paid or incurred with respect to the development of a mine or other natural deposit (other than an oil, gas, or geothermal well) located outside of the United States may be deducted ratably over 10 years.[14]

However, a taxpayer may have to recapture some or all of the expensed costs as ordinary income, or through disallowance of depletion of the property, under the following circumstances:

1. When a mine reaches the producing stage, a taxpayer may elect to include in income an amount equal to the adjusted exploration expenditures of that mine. When these expenditures are included in income, the taxpayer may add these costs to the basis of the mine. If this income inclusion is not made, then the taxpayer must forego its depletion deduction with respect to the mine until the foregone depletion equals the amount of the exploration expenditure.[15]
2. If a taxpayer receives a bonus or royalty with respect to mining property, the deduction for depletion is disallowed, on that mine, until the amount of depletion equals the amount of the adjusted exploration expenditures.[16]
3. Upon disposition of the mine, the taxpayer must report as ordinary income the lesser of the basis of the adjusted exploration costs or the gain realized on the disposition[17]

In addition to expensing the costs in the current year or deferring them as units are sold, a taxpayer may also elect to expense mining development and exploration costs over a 10-year period. A taxpayer can choose to make this election for only some costs.

Example—Gary incurs mining development costs of $10,000 and exploration costs of $10,000. He can elect to expense $13,000 over a 10-year period.

Alternative Minimum Tax treatment for mining exploration and development costs incurred after December 31, 1986 is that these costs are capitalized and amortized ratably over the 10-year period beginning with the taxable year in which the expenditures were made.[18] This requirement applies to all exploration and development costs incurred relative to each mine.

Treatment of Certain Long-Term Contracts

In the case of any long-term contracts entered into by the taxpayer after March 1, 1986, the taxable income is computed using the percentage of completion method of accounting as described in §460(b).[19] This code section covers construction, installation, federal contracts, and manufacturing contracts that are not completed in the same year in which the contract originated. Contracts for services are not included since something must actually be constructed or built.

Percentage of Completion Method   Under the percentage of completion method, the taxpayer must include in income the amount of the contract price that the taxpayer completed during the taxable year in proportion to the total contract price.[20] The calculations include:[21]

1. Compute the completion factor for the contract by calculating a ratio. The numerator is the total costs incurred in the taxable year and the denominator is the estimated total contract costs that the taxpayer expects to incur under the contract.
2. Compute the cumulative gross receipts from the contract by multiplying the completion factor by the total price.
3. Compute the current-year gross receipts, which is the difference between the amount of cumulative gross receipts for the current taxable year and the amount of cumulative gross receipts for the immediately preceding taxable year.
4. Subtract the allocable contract costs incurred during the current year from the current-year gross receipts to determine current-year taxable income.

Example—Chet, whose taxable year ends December 31, determines the income from long-term contracts using the percentage of completion method. During 2001, Chet agrees to manufacture for his customer a unique item for a total contract price of $1,000,000. Under Chet's contract, his customer is entitled to retain 10 percent of the total contract price until it accepts the item. By the end of 2001, Chet has incurred $200,000 of allocable contract costs and estimates that the total allocable contract costs will be $800,000. By the end of 2002, Chet has incurred $600,000 of allocable contract costs and estimates that the total allocable contract costs will be $900,000. In 2003, after completing the contract, Chet determines that the actual cost to manufacture the item was $750,000. Chet's income from the contract is computed as follows:

	2001	*2002*	*2003*
(A) Cumulative incurred costs	$200,000	$600,000	$750,000
(B) Estimated total costs	800,000	900,000	750,000
(C) Completion factor: (A)/(B)	25%	66.67%	100.00%
(D) Total contract price	1,000,000	1,000,000	1,000,000
(E) Cumulative gross receipts: (C) × (D)	250,000	666,667	1,000,000
(F) Cumulative gross receipts (prior year)	(0)	(250,000)	(666,667)
(G) Current year gross receipts	250,000	416,667	333,333
(H) Cumulative incurred costs	200,000	600,000	750,000
(I) Cumulative incurred costs (prior year)	(0)	(200,000)	(600,000)
(J) Current year costs	200,000	400,000	150,000
(K) Gross Income: (G)–(J)	$50,000	$16,667	$183,333[22]

Exempt Contracts A contract is not required to use the percentage-of-completion method if it is a home construction contract or a construction contract with a contractor whose average gross receipts for the three preceding taxable years do not exceed $10,000,000.[23] Exempt contracts may be calculated under the exempt-contract percentage of completion method or the completed contract method.

Under the exempt-contract percentage-of-completion method, the percentage of completion may be determined using any method of cost comparison or by comparing the work performed on the contract with the estimated total work to be performed.[24]

Under the completed contract method, the total price of the contract is taken into income in the year the contract is completed.

Determining Alternative Minimum Tax in Long-Term Contracts A taxpayer must use the percentage-of-completion method for long-term contracts when calculating AMTI. However, AMT costs must be used when calculating the amount of completion. Depreciation is the primary contributory factor for this difference.

Example—A taxpayer expects to incur total costs of $1,000,000 on a long-term contract. At the end of the first year, total costs incurred were $300,000. The percentage of completion is determined as follows:

Regular Tax
Costs incurred $300,000/Total costs expected $1,000,000 = 30 percent.

Alternative Minimum Tax
Costs incurred $200,000(AMT depreciation)/Total costs expected due to difference in depreciation $600,000 = 33.3 percent.

These percentages would then be used to determine the amount of income for regular tax and AMT purposes.

Election to Use Regular Methods and Regular Costs
Instead of calculating different percentages for regular tax and AMT as discussed previously, a taxpayer may elect to use the same percentage for the calculation of AMT and regular tax. This election must be made on the taxpayer's federal income tax return for the first taxable year in which the taxpayer is subject to AMT. This election is then treated as electing a method of accounting and shall not be revoked without obtaining the consent of the Commissioner.[25] The primary disadvantage is that a taxpayer recognizes a greater amount of income in the early years after an asset has been acquired. He foregoes the benefits of accelerated depreciation and pays more tax in the beginning of an asset's life.

Look-Back Rules
Unless the regular methods and regular costs election is made, a taxpayer must also apply the look-back rules for regular and AMT taxes. In calculating the percentage of completion for regular and AMT purposes, differences between estimated and actual costs for the two calculations may exist. The taxpayer must determine the income that would have been earned in previous years of a contract if the actual total contract price and costs have been used instead of estimates. If income was understated, the taxpayer owes the government interest on the underpayment. If income was overstated, the taxpayer is due interest from the government.[26]

Example—Williams Construction Corp. uses the percentage-of-completion method for accounting for income on a long-term contract. Williams incurred 25 percent, or $100,000, of the estimated $400,000 of total costs at the end of the first year. The price of the contract is $1,000,000. Williams calculates revenues in year one as 25 percent × 1,000,000 = $250,000 and reports a profit for regular tax purposes of $150,000. The contract is completed the following year and actual costs are $600,000. Therefore, 17 percent ($100,000/$600,000) of the total contract price should have been included instead of 25 percent. Consequently the government owes Williams one year of interest on the difference in taxes paid and actually due. The difference may offset AMT in the total tax calculation.

The look-back rules do not apply to contracts that must be completed within two years of the beginning of the agreement and have a gross contract price that does not exceed the lesser of $1,000,000 or 1 percent of the taxpayer's average gross receipts for the three taxable years preceding the year the contract is completed.[27]

Pollution Control Facilities

Congress enacted legislation in the 1960s giving certified pollution control facilities favorable tax treatment to encourage environmental protection. However, these facilities face AMT treatment and are subject to an adjustment in computing AMTI.

A certified pollution facility is a new treatment facility that has been certified by the state and federal governments to abate or control water or atmospheric pollution and other contamination by removing, altering, disposing, storing, or preventing the creation or emission of pollutants, contaminants, wastes, or heat.[28]

The regular tax treatment gives a taxpayer the opportunity to elect to amortize his/her basis in the facility over a 60-month period. However, if the useful life of the facility exceeds 15 years, the amortizable basis is reduced by a ratio that 15 years has to its useful life.[29] The amount in excess of the amortizable basis would be depreciated under MACRS.[30]

The Alternative Minimum Tax Treatment for a facility placed in service after December 31, 1998 is that the straight-line method of depreciation under the MACRS rules is used.[31]

Adjusted Basis in Property

Due to various depreciation methods used in calculating regular tax and AMT, the adjusted basis of an asset will differ. Therefore, calculations of gains and losses are likely to be different under each method.

Example—Ron purchases an asset for his business for $40,000. The asset is five-year property and he claims $35,200 of depreciation for regular tax purposes. AMT depreciation amounts to $22,000 of depreciation. Ron sells the asset after holding it for three years, for $30,000. He reports a regular tax gain of $25,200 ($30,000−($40,000−$35,200)).[32] However, his gain for AMT purposes is $12,000 ($30,000−($40,000−$22,000)).

ADJUSTMENTS IN COMPUTING AMT APPLICABLE TO ALL INDIVIDUAL TAXPAYERS

Individual taxpayers make certain adjustments in computing AMT on Form 6251 of their tax return. Note that these adjustments reflect both an individual's personal and business activities. The following rules apply:

- No deduction is allowed for miscellaneous itemized deductions, taxes, and medical expenses less than 10 percent of adjusted gross income. The standard deduction and personal exemptions also are not allowed for AMT. Interest expenses are deductible for the following purposes:
  1. Qualified housing interest. This is interest paid on indebtedness used to acquire, construct, or improve a taxpayer's principal residence and one other residence. The total amount of debt that qualifies as acquisition indebtedness is $1,000,000 ($500,000 for married individuals filing separately).[33]

     Example—Emily purchases a home for $100,000 with a down payment of $20,000 and a mortgage for $80,000. The interest paid on the mortgage is acquisition interest and is fully deductible. Home equity indebtedness is any indebtedness secured by a qualified residence to the extent that the home equity loan does not exceed the fair market value of the residence reduced by the amount of the acquisition indebtedness. The amount of home equity debt that is deductible is $100,000 ($50,000 in the case of a married couple filing separately).[34]

     Example—Assume the same facts as in the previous example except that it is five years later and Emily decides to take a home equity loan for a trip to Europe and a new car. Her home has appreciated in value to $250,000, so she borrows $125,000 on a home equity loan. Only interest paid on $100,000 qualifies as residence interest and is deductible. Interest on the other $25,000 is considered personal interest and is nondeductible. Alternative Tax Treatment of qualified housing interest requires that only interest paid for acquiring, constructing, or substantially improving a principal residence is deductible. Home equity interest generally does not qualify and is not deductible since it is not used to acquire a principal residence.

2. Investment interest, up to investment income earned, is generally deductible. This is interest paid on indebtedness to acquire property held for investment such as dividends, interest, and royalties. Additionally, this would include income derived from a trade or business in which a taxpayer does not materially participate.[35] Net investment income is the excess of investment income over investment expenses. If expenses exceed income, the excess may be carried forward into succeeding years.[36]

Because of the preferential tax rates associated with capital gains, a taxpayer must make a special election to include capital gains as investment income. By making this election, the taxpayer is electing to have the capital gains taxed at ordinary rates. The purpose of the election is to decrease the amount of total taxable income. The election is made on Form 4952, which must be filed on or before the due date, including extensions, of the income tax return for the taxable year involved.[37]

Example— Bob Doe has taxable interest income of $2425 and dividends of $1400. Additionally, he has $8000 of long-term capital gains for regular tax purposes and $15,000 for AMT purposes from the sale of a depreciable asset. During the year, he incurred $12,000 of investment interest. He decided to have all of his $8000 of capital gains considered as investment income. He would make this election on Form 4952, line 4e (see Exhibit 5-1). The investment interest of $12,000 paid offsets $11,825 of their income and $175 is carried over to the next year. In this case there would be no impact on AMT. Investment interest expense is a preference item to the extent of the difference between regular tax and AMT interest. This would occur in cases where the taxpayer does not materially participate in a business and his or her share of gains from the sale of depreciable assets would be different for regular tax and AMT purposes.

This election does not work well for high-income taxpayers with large home interest and state income and property tax deductions. These individuals are subject to a phase-out of their itemized deductions and therefore may be unable to benefit from the full amount. Additionally, if there are capital loss carryovers from previous years, then capital gains are offset by these losses.

EXHIBIT 5-1

Form **4952**	**Investment Interest Expense Deduction**	OMB No. 1545-0191
Department of the Treasury Internal Revenue Service (99)	▶ Attach to your tax return.	**2002** Attachment Sequence No. **72**

Name(s) shown on return	Identifying number
Bob Doe	111-22-3333

Part I   Total Investment Interest Expense

1	Investment interest expense paid or accrued in 2002. See instructions	1	12,000
2	Disallowed investment interest expense from 2001 Form 4952, line 7	2	
3	**Total investment interest expense.** Add lines 1 and 2	3	12,000

Part II   Net Investment Income

4a	Gross income from property held for investment (excluding any net gain from the disposition of property held for investment)			4a	3,825
b	Net gain from the disposition of property held for investment	4b	8,000		
c	Net capital gain from the disposition of property held for investment	4c	8,000		
d	Subtract line 4c from line 4b. If zero or less, enter -0-			4d	0
e	Enter the amount from line 4c that you elect to include in investment income. Do not enter more than the amount on line 4b. See instructions		▶	4e	8,000
f	Investment income. Add lines 4a, 4d, and 4e			4f	11,825
5	Investment expenses. See instructions			5	
6	**Net investment income.** Subtract line 5 from line 4f. If zero or less, enter -0-			6	11,825

Part III   Investment Interest Expense Deduction

7	Disallowed investment interest expense to be carried forward to 2003. Subtract line 6 from line 3. If zero or less, enter -0-	7	175
8	**Investment interest expense deduction.** Enter the smaller of line 3 or 6. See instructions	8	11,825

For Paperwork Reduction Act Notice, see back of form.

DAA

Form **4952** (2002)

EXHIBIT 5-1 (Continued)

SCHEDULES A&B	Schedule A-Itemized Deductions	OMB No. 1545-0074

(Form 1040)

Department of the Treasury
Internal Revenue Service (99)

2002

(Schedule B is on back)

►Attach to Form 1040. ►See Instructions for Schedules A and B (Form 1040).

Attachment Sequence No. **07**

Name(s) shown on Form 1040
Bob Doe

Your social security number
111-22-3333

Medical and Dental Expenses	Caution. Do not include expenses reimbursed or paid by others.			
	1 Medical and dental expenses (see page A-2)	1		
	2 Enter amt. from Form 1040, ln. 36 **2**			
	3 Multiply line 2 by 7.5% (.075)	3		
	4 Subtract line 3 from line 1. If line 3 is more than line 1, enter -0-		4	0
Taxes You Paid (See page A-2.)	5 State and local income taxes	5	2,500	
	6 Real estate taxes (see page A-2)	6	2,600	
	7 Personal property taxes	7		
	8 Other taxes. List type and amount ►	8		
	9 Add lines 5 through 8		9	5,100
Interest You Paid (See page A-3.)	10 Home mortgage interest & points reported to you on Form 1098	10	3,500	
	11 Home mortgage interest not reported to you on Form 1098. If paid to the person from whom you bought the home, see page A-3 and show that person's name, identifying no., and address ►	11		
Note. Personal interest is not deductible.	12 Points not reported to you on Form 1098. See page A-3 for special rules	12		
	13 Investment interest. Attach Form 4952 if required. (See page A-3.)	13	11,825	
	14 Add lines 10 through 13		14	15,325
Gifts to Charity If you made a gift and got a benefit for it, see page A-4.	15 Gifts by cash or check. If you made any gift of $250 or more, see page A-4	15		
	16 Other than by cash or check. If any gift of $250 or more, see page A-4. You **must** attach Form 8283 if over $500	16		
	17 Carryover from prior year	17		
	18 Add lines 15 through 17		18	
Casualty and Theft Losses	19 Casualty or theft loss(es). Attach Form 4684. (See page A-5.)		19	
Job Expenses and Most Other Miscellaneous Deductions (See page A-5 for expenses to deduct here.)	20 Unreimbursed employee expenses-job travel, union dues, job education, etc. You **must** attach Form 2106 or 2106-EZ if required. (See page A-5.) ►	20		
	21 Tax preparation fees	21		
	22 Other expenses-investment, safe deposit box, etc. List type and amount ►	22		
	23 Add lines 20 through 22	23		
	24 Enter amt. from Form 1040, ln. 36 **24**			
	25 Multiply line 24 by 2% (.02)	25		
	26 Subtract line 25 from line 23. If line 25 is more than line 23, enter -0-		26	0
Other Miscellaneous Deductions	27 Other-from list on page A-6. List type and amount ►		27	
Total Itemized Deductions	28 Is Form 1040, line 36, over $137,300 (over $68,650 if married filing separately)?			
	☒ **No.** Your deduction is not limited. Add the amounts in the far right column for lines 4 through 27. Also, enter this amount on Form 1040, line 38.		28	20,425
	☐ **Yes.** Your deduction may be limited. See page A-6 for the amount to enter.			

For Paperwork Reduction Act Notice, see Form 1040 instructions.

Schedule A (Form 1040) 2002

DAA

3. Under §265, no deduction is allowed for interest expenses associated with tax-exempt income. There is an exception for certain tax exempt obligations from qualified small issuers who have issued obligations less than $10,000,000 in a calendar year. For AMT purposes no deduction is allowed for interest expense associated with private activity bonds. A private activity bond is any bond issued for private business use or for private security or loan financing.[38]

- Circulation Expenses are expenditures paid or incurred to begin, maintain, or increase the circulation of a magazine, newspaper, or periodical.[39] This does not include any expense that must be capitalized, such as the purchase of land, buildings, or acquisition of another publishing business.

  The deduction for these expenses must be taken in the year when the expense is paid or incurred.[40] A taxpayer may elect to capitalize expenses incurred by a publisher to establish or increase circulation. These would not include normal, daily expenses to maintain current circulation.

  Example—Mr. Olson wants to have a special promotion to increase circulation of the *Daily Planet*. He has hired a Web page designer, on a temporary basis, to design a special promotion on the Internet, which would change daily for six weeks. He may elect to capitalize these costs.

  The election is made by attaching a statement to the tax return for the first taxable year in which the election is applicable. Once made, the taxpayer must continue to amortize these expenditures.[41]

  For AMT purposes, circulation expenditures must be amortized over a three-year period beginning with the year the costs were incurred. Consequently, a taxpayer may also elect to amortize these expenses for regular tax purposes also.[42] In doing so, no AMT adjustment would be required.

- Research and Development Costs are those costs incurred in connection with the taxpayer's trade or business, which are experimental. This includes all costs incident to the development or improvement of a product, such as costs of obtaining a patent, producing a pilot model, process, formula, invention, technique, or similar property. This extends to products to be used by the taxpayer in its trade or business as well as products to be held for sale, lease, or license.[43] These costs do not include quality control costs, efficiency surveys, studies, advertising, promotions, or the acquisition or improvement of depreciable or depletable property.

For regular tax purposes, §174 indicates that a taxpayer has several choices:

1. An election may be made to expense research and development expenses in the year in which they incurred. Alternatively, a 10-year write-off may be chosen for all or part of the costs incurred during the year.[44]
2. These expenditures may be treated as deferred expenses and amortized over a 60-month period. This particularly applies to property that has no determinable useful life.
3. These expenses may be capitalized over the property's useful life.

The election must be made no later than the due date for filing the tax return for the year in which the expenditures were incurred. Once an election is made, it may not be changed without IRS approval.

The Alternative Minimum Tax treatment of research and experimental expenditures is that they must be written off over a 10-year period beginning with the year in which the expenses were incurred.

Example—Chet incurs research costs of $50,000 in developing a new plasma coating process for use in soap and detergent manufacturing. He elects to expense these costs in the year in which they were made. His AMT adjustment would be:

Year	Regular Tax Deduction	AMT Deduction	Adjustment
1	$50,000	$5,000	$45,000
2	0	5,000	($5,000)
3	0	5,000	($5,000)
4	0	5,000	($5,000)
5	0	5,000	($5,000)
6	0	5,000	($5,000)
7	0	5,000	($5,000)
8	0	5,000	($5,000)
9	0	5,000	($5,000)
10	0	5,000	($5,000)
	$50,000	$50,000	$ 0

This adjustment is mandated only if the current expensing election is made. It is not required if the 10-year election is made or if the taxpayer elects to treat these expenses as deferred expenses.[45]

- Incentive Stock Options (ISO) are given by an employer to employees and are opportunities to buy stock in the employer's corporation. To quality as an ISO, the following requirements must be met:

  1. The option is granted pursuant to a plan, approved by the shareholders, which indicates the number of shares that may be issued, and the employees, or class of employees, eligible to receive them.
  2. The option is granted within 10 years from the date of the plan's adoption.
  3. The option by its terms is not exercisable after the expiration of 10 years from the date that it is granted.
  4. The option price is not less than the fair market value of the stock at the time the option is granted. (In the case of a closely held corporation, a good approximation of fair market value would be an average of two or more valuations by independent expert appraisers.[46])
  5. The option is not transferable by the individual, except by will or the laws of descent and distribution, and is exercisable during lifetime only by the employee.
  6. The employees, at the time the option is granted, do not own stock possessing more than 10 percent of the total combined voting power of all classes of stock of the employer corporation or its parent or subsidiary.[47]

The stock acquired through the option must not be disposed of within two years from the date the option was granted nor within one year after the transfer of the stock to the employee.[48] Additionally, the individual must be an employee at all times during the period from the date the option was granted through the date ending three months prior to the date of exercise.[49] By satisfying certain holding and employment requirements, an employee receives preferential tax treatment with an ISO. Additionally, an employer may choose to provide ISOs only to key employees, whereas an employee stock purchase plan must be offered to all employees.

Under regular tax treatment of an individual receiving an ISO, no income is recognized upon the grant of the option. Likewise, the employee reports no income when the option is exercised. Instead, income is recognized when the shares, acquired through the ISO, are sold. However, this is a capital gain resulting in the difference between the sale proceeds and the employee's basis in the stock.

Example—Mort receives an incentive stock option to purchase 100 shares of stock at $20/share, which is the stock's fair market value at the time of grant. Mort decides to exercise the option when the fair market value is $35. Mort recognized no income when he was granted the option nor when he exercised it. Three years later Mort sells the stock for $45 per share. He recognizes capital gain of $25 per share ($45−$20).

Regular tax treatment of the employer granting the ISO is that no deduction is allowed for the stock transferred to the employee upon exercise of the option.[50]

If the holding periods or employment periods are not followed, the transaction becomes a disqualifying disposition. An individual has not severed employment if he/she is on military leave, sick leave, or other bona fide leave of absence of up to 90 days, or if the job is guaranteed by statute or contract.[51]

The regular tax treatment of an individual in a disqualifying disposition is that the employee pays ordinary income tax on the difference between the option price and the fair market value at the date of exercise. Additionally, tax is paid on the difference between the exercise price and sales price at the time of disposition.

Example—Using the same facts from the previous example, let's say that Mort sold his shares three months after he exercised his option. Because he sold his shares before the statutory holding period of two years after date of grant and one year after date of exercise, he recognizes a gain of $25, of which $15 is ordinary ($35−$20) and $10 is short term capital gain ($45−$35).

The amount of income that must be recognized when the market value of the stock has declined is the excess of the actual sale proceeds, not the fair market value of the shares on the date of exercise, over the employee's basis in the shares.

Example—Using the same facts as the above examples, let's say that Mort sold the stock for $35 instead of $45. Mort recognizes a gain of $15 per share, which is all ordinary income.

In a disqualifying disposition, the corporation will have a deduction for compensation in the year in which the transaction occurs.[52] This amount is to be reported on the employee's W2 for the year of disposition.

In alternative minimum tax, incentive stock options are adjustments, subject to a set of rules that apply to nonstatutory stock options.[53] Under these rules, the timing of income recognition depends on whether the ISO has a readily ascertainable fair market value at the date of grant.

The readily ascertainable fair market value at date of grant determines the AMT tax impact on income resulting from the excess of the option's fair market value over the amount, if any, that was paid for the option.[54] This income would be ordinary income. An option traded on an established market such as the Chicago Board of Options Exchange has a readily ascertainable fair market value, which is its current trading price.

Non readily ascertainable fair market value at the date of grant will result in no AMT tax consequences until the option is exercised or disposed of. At that time, the employee must report the difference between the fair market value of the stock received and the amount paid for the stock and option as compensation income.[55]

Example—In 2000, Generous, Inc. grants Vance, an employee, an option to purchase 1000 shares of its stock. The stock has a fair market value of $40 per share. The exercise price is $15 per share and may be exercised at any time during a three-year period. On October, 2001, the stock's fair market value was $55 per share, and Vance decided to exercise his option. He acquired 1000 shares for $15 per share. At this point Vance has compensation income of $40,000 (($55−$15)×1000).

Generally, no adjustment will be necessary for AMT purposes if an employee sells the stock the same year as the option is exercised.

ADJUSTMENTS APPLICABLE TO CORPORATIONS

Under the Taxpayer Relief Act of 1997, AMT was effectively repealed for small corporations beginning after December 31, 1997. A small corporation is one that has average annual gross receipts of $5 million or less for the first three taxable years beginning after December 31, 1993. A corporation that ceases to be a small corporation will be subject to AMT.[56]

Adjustments required for corporations are made on Form 4626 and include the following:

- Adjusted Current Earnings (ACE) must be calculated for each corporation except for an S corporation, regulated investment company, real estate investment trust, and real estate mortgage investment conduit.[57] To arrive at this computation, a corporation starts with its alternative minimum taxable income and makes all of the adjustments applicable to all taxpayers listed previously.

Then a set of additional adjustments are made without calculating the alternative tax net operating loss deduction.[58]

These adjustments are:

1. Exclusion income items, which are any items of income that are includible in the corporation's earnings and profits but not in regular taxable income or AMTI. These items must be accounted for in the computation of ACE and include:
   - Proceeds of life insurance contracts, including income on the contract. Income on the contract is the sum of the increase in the contract's net surrender value during the taxable year, plus the cost of life insurance protection during the year reduced by the premiums paid[59]
   - Tax-exempt interest on state and local bonds
   - Compensation for injuries or sickness
   - Income taxes of a lessor of property that are paid by a lessee
   - Income attributable to the recovery of an item deducted in computing earnings and profits in a prior year
   - Amounts received as proceeds from sports programs
   - Certain cost-sharing payments
   - Interest on loans used to acquire employer securities
   - Federal financial assistance[60]
2. Exclusion expense items, which constitute any items normally deductible for regular tax and AMTI purposes but not for computing earnings and profits. In computing ACE, a deduction is not allowed for:
   - Unrecovered losses attributable to certain damages, to the extent that those damages were previously deducted in computing earnings and profits.
   - Deduction for small life insurance companies under §806 (This section states that there is a deduction of 60 percent of so much of the tentative life insurance company taxable income (LICTI) that does not exceed $3,000,000, provided the assets of the company are not greater than $500,000,000.)
   - Certain dividends received by corporations are excluded from the ACE adjustment. (The dividends-received deduction is allowed in computing ACE if it is a 100-percent or 80-percent dividend.[61] This exception only applies if the corporation paying the dividend is subject to U.S. taxation on its income. As discussed in Chapter 8, the dividend-received

deduction is a deduction given to corporations that receive dividends on stock they own. The size of the deduction, 70 percent, 80 percent, or 100 percent, depends on how much stock the corporation owns in the dividend-paying company. If the corporate stockholder owns less than 20 percent of the distributing company, the deduction is 70 percent; if the ownership is between 20 percent and 80 percent, the deduction is 80 percent. Members of an affiliated group of corporations can claim a 100-percent dividend-received deduction.)

- Dividends received on certain preferred stock.
- Dividends received from certain foreign corporations deductible under §245. (This is any foreign corporation if at least 10 percent of the stock is owned by the taxpayer.)
- Dividends paid on certain preferred stock of public utilities.
- Deductible dividends paid to an employee stock ownership plan; and
- Deductible nonpatronage dividends of a cooperative.[62]

3. Other Earnings and Profits Adjustments
- Intangible drilling costs must be capitalized over 60 months, and mineral exploration or development must be capitalized over 120 months, beginning with the month in which production from the deposit begins or the month in which such amounts were paid or incurred.[63]
- Circulation expenditures must be capitalized.
- Organizational expenditures are not deductible.
- LIFO recapture applies to the ACE adjustment.[64]
- Installment method of accounting may not be used for ACE.[65]

4. Losses on the exchange of any pool of debt for another pool of debt of comparable interest rates and maturities are not allowed.[66]

5. Depletion is computed under the cost depletion method of §611.[67] (Depletion is the method of cost recovery used for natural resources, like oil and gas. Cost depletion is calculated by dividing the tax cost of the asset by the amount of the resource the asset is expected to produce. Percentage depletion, by comparison, is calculated, in general, by multiplying the gross income from the property by a statutory percentage.[68])

6. The adjusted basis of each asset, to its proportionate share of the fair market value of the corporation prior to an ownership change, must be calculated for a change of more than 50 percent of the stock of a corporation that has net unrealized built-in losses. This causes a reduction in the basis of the assets of the corporation.[69]

Under §56(g), the ACE adjustment can be either positive or negative. A corporation must increase its AMTI by 75 percent of the excess of its adjusted current earnings over its AMTI. Conversely, a corporation's AMTI must be reduced by 75 percent of the excess of its AMTI over its adjusted current earnings.

- Merchant Marine Capital Construction Funds—Under the Marine Act of 1936, Congress established a capital construction fund program as an incentive for investment in the U.S. shipping industry. Under this program deposits to a capital construction fund for vessels constructed or reconstructed in the United States, under U.S. law, and operated in the foreign or domestic commerce of the United States or in the fisheries of the United States, may be deductible. Additionally, earnings on the deposits can accumulate tax free for regular tax purposes. However, these benefits are not available to corporations for AMT purposes.[70]

AMT NET OPERATING LOSS DEDUCTION

For AMT purposes, the alternative tax net operating loss deduction is different than the regular tax net operating loss. In this calculation, additional modifications must be made to reflect the difference between the regular tax and AMT rules. The same adjustments and tax preferences that are made to calculate a person's AMTI must be made to determine the AMT NOL.

As in the NOL calculation, AMT NOL is carried back and then forward. The AMT NOL deduction cannot exceed 90 percent of the individual's AMTI. However, the 2002 Job Creation and Worker Assistance Act temporarily suspended the 90 percent limit on certain NOLs. This provision allows 100 percent of the taxpayer's AMT NOL to be deducted from NOLs arising in taxable years ending in 2001 and 2002. This includes NOL carryforwards to these taxable years.

PREFERENCE ITEMS

Preference items are the same for individuals and corporations and must be added back to taxable income in calculating AMTI. The most common tax preference items are:

(a) Percentage of depletion in excess of basis—When computing regular tax depletion, taxpayers may choose cost depletion. This is a pro rata recovery, based on the number of mineral units sold in the year, of the taxpayer's depletable basis in the mineral property.[71] Cost depletion is determined by the following formula:

Adjusted basis at end of year of mineral property
Unrecovered units of mineral property × units sold during the year

A taxpayer may decide to use the percentage depletion method, which is a specified percentage of the gross income from the property, excluding rents or royalties paid by the taxpayer.[72]

An AMT preference arises when depletion in excess of basis is taken. This excess is determined on a property-by-property basis.[73]

(b) Excess intangible drilling costs—When a taxpayer elects to currently expense intangible drilling costs (IDCs) for regular tax purposes, an AMT preference results from excess intangible drilling costs that exceed 65 percent of the taxpayer's net income from oil, gas, and geothermal properties.[74] This preference must be computed separately for all geothermal properties and all other oil and gas properties. The excess IDC is the current intangible drilling cost deducted minus the allowed AMT amortization.

(c) Tax exempt interest—When a taxpayer has tax-exempt interest from a private activity bond, this is an AMT preference. Private activity bonds include exempt facility bonds, qualified mortgage bond, qualified veterans' mortgage bond, qualified small issue bond, qualified student loan bond, qualified redevelopment bond, and qualified §501(c)(3) bond. Interest on a private activity bond must be added back to AMTI as a preference item for AMT purposes.

(d) Certain small business stock—When certain qualified small business stock (§1202) is held more than five years, noncorporate taxpayers are generally allowed to exclude 50 percent of the gain on the sale or exchange of the stock. If the stock is acquired after December 21, 2000 and is a qualified business entity, 60 percent of the gain is excluded.[75] (This is repealed after December 31, 2014.) The amount of the gain eligible for this exclusion is limited to $10 million, or 10 times the taxpayer's basis in the stock, whichever is greater. Qualified small business stock means any stock in a C Corporation that was originally issued after August 10, 1993 and is:

- A qualified small business;
- Acquired at the original issue in exchange for money or property or as compensation for services;
- A corporation that meets the active business requirement.[76]
  The AMT treatment requires an inclusion of 42 percent of the amount excluded as a tax preference item. This percentage is reduced to 28 percent for stock acquired after December 31, 2000.[77]

Additional preferences, which will not be discussed, include accelerated depreciation on pre-1981 property, accelerated depreciation on pre-1981 property subject to a lease, accelerated depreciation on ACRS property placed in service after 1980 and before 1987, and amortization of pollution-control facilities placed into service before 1987. These items are not likely to affect many investors.

FOREIGN TAX CREDIT

As noted earlier, the tentative minimum tax is reduced by the regular tax. If a positive balance results from this calculation, the taxpayer owes an AMT equal to the difference.[78] For tentative minimum tax purposes, an AMT foreign tax credit may be claimed. This credit is computed in the same manner as the regular foreign tax credit, only the limit is modified. The foreign source taxable income and worldwide taxable income are computed by factoring in the AMT adjustments and preferences.[79] The maximum AMT credit is equal to the following formula:

Tentative Minimum Tax × Foreign Source AMTI/Worldwide AMTI

The allocation of adjustments and preferences to foreign-source income may produce a different limit for AMT purposes than for regular tax purposes. Additionally, the AMT foreign tax credit cannot offset more than 90 percent of the tentative minimum tax calculated without regard to this credit and the AMT NOL deduction. The excess credit may be carried back two and forward five years.[80]

For taxable years after December 31, 1997, taxpayers may elect to use a simplified §904 limitation in determining the AMT foreign tax credit. Under this method, the foreign tax credit limitation is based on the proportion that the taxpayer's regular taxable income from sources outside the United States (but not in excess of the taxpayer's entire alternative minimum taxable income) bears to the taxpayer's entire alternative minimum taxable income for the tax year.[81] This election may be made only for the taxpayer's first taxable year that begins after 1997 and for which the taxpayer claims this credit.

CREDITS

There are ordering rules in the application of nonrefundable credits and the foreign tax credit to the regular and AMT tax liability. Under §26(a) the individual first reduces his regular tax by his nonrefundable personal credits such as dependent care credit, credit for the elderly and permanently disabled, adoption expense credit, child tax credit, HOPE Scholarship and Lifetime Learning credits, and others. The individual then reduces his regular tax by his regular foreign tax credit and then applies any general business credits he/she may have. The general business credit may not reduce the regular tax liability below the greater of the tentative minimum tax or 25 percent of the amount of the net regular tax liability over $25,000.[82] Additional rules apply to the empowerment zone employment credit where the regular tax liability can be offset but not below 75 percent of the tentative minimum tax.[83] General business credits include rehabilitation credit, energy credit, reforestation credit, work opportunity credit, low-income housing credit, research credit, alcohol fuels credit, enhanced oil recovery credit, disabled access credit, renewable electricity production credit, Indian employment credit, employer social security credit, clinical drug testing credit, new markets tax credit, small employer pension plan startup cost credit, employer-provided child care credit, and RC employment credit.

MINIMUM TAX CREDIT

There could be an inequity in the AMT system when there is minimum tax for one year, and yet those same preference items provide no regular tax benefit to an individual when regular tax exceeds the minimum tax in later years. The minimum tax credit was developed to correct this inequity. To the extent that AMT was attributable to adjustments and preferences associated with timing differences in one year, the minimum tax credit offsets the regular tax liability (but not below the tentative minimum tax) in subsequent years.[84] This credit may be carried forward indefinitely but not carried back.

COMPREHENSIVE EXAMPLE OF INDIVIDUAL AMT

Example—Nicholas has seven dependents, and he and his wife earn $125,000 in wages. His work takes him to three states, where he earns income in each state and pays state withholding taxes of $7700. He received a refund of $750 of state income taxes. Besides owning a home, he owns a summer cottage and some land where his wife raises thoroughbred dogs. His property taxes are $22,000, and charitable contributions are $3500. His wife earns another $30,000 through the sale of her dogs. He has interest income of $5000 of which $2500 is from private activity bonds and $1000 is from a savings account in Canada. He paid $250 in foreign taxes. Nicholas earned dividends of $6500. He has recently sold stock in a small tool company, which he purchased over five years ago when the company was first formed, at a gain of $20,000. Additionally, he received a K-1 from a partnership, which owns a mine, of which he is a general partner. His share of the partnership loss was $5000 and depletion was $500. He also has a sole proprietorship in which he is a consultant in lung research. He incurred $10,000 in research and experimental costs during the year, and his net income in this activity is $47,400. Nicholas incurred child care expenses of $5800 and paid $30,000 in federal estimated taxes.

Exhibit 5-2 shows the computations of Form 1040, Schedule A, Schedule D, Form 6251, and Form 1116 for this example. Itemized deduction, Schedule D, foreign tax credit, and exemption worksheets (Example is for 2002 tax year. The exemption increases to $58,000 for married couples filing jointly for 2003 and 2004 only) are also included for a better understanding of of the computations. Other schedules that would be required for these taxpayers, such as Schedule B (Interest and Dividend Income), Schedule C (Profit or Loss from Business), and Schedule SE (Social Security Self-Employment Tax) are not included since they are not particularly relevant to the AMT calculation. Also, discussion regarding phase-outs and self-employment taxes is beyond the scope of this book.

EXHIBIT 5-2

Form **1040**	Department of the Treasury- Internal Revenue Service **U.S. Individual Income Tax Return**	**2002**	(99)	IRS Use Only- Do not write or staple in this space.

		For the year Jan. 1-Dec. 31, 2002, or other tax year beginning , 2002, ending , 20	OMB No. 1545-0074

Label (See instructions on page 21.)

L A B E L	Your first name and initial	Last name	Your social security number
	Nicholas	Schepperly	111-22-3333
	If a jt. rtn., sp. first name & initial	Last name	Spouse's-social security number
	Betsy	Schepperly	111-22-3333

Use the IRS label. Otherwise, please print or type.

H E R E	Home address (number and street). If you have a P.O. box, see page 21.	Apt. no.	▲ **Important!** ▲
	12 Back St.		You must enter
	City, town or post office, state, and ZIP code. If you have a foreign address, see page 21.		your SSN(s) above.
	Buffalo NY 14226		

Presidential Election Campaign (See page 21.)

Note. Checking "Yes" will not change your tax or reduce your refund.

Do you, or your spouse if filing a joint return, want $3 to go to this fund?   You [ ] Yes [ ] No   Spouse [ ] Yes [ ] No

Filing Status

Check only one box.

1 [ ] Single
2 [X] Married filing jointly (even if only one had income)
3 [ ] Married filing separately. Enter spouse's SSN above and full name here. ▶
4 [ ] Head of household (with qualifying person). (See pg. 21.) If the qualifying person is a child but not your dependent, enter this child's name here. ▶
5 [ ] Qualifying widow(er) with dependent child (year spouse died ▶ _____). (See page 21.)

Exemptions

6a [X] Yourself. If your parent (or someone else) can claim you as a dependent on his or her tax return, do not check box 6a
b [X] Spouse

No. of boxes checked on 6a and 6b	2

c Dependents:

(1) First name	Last name	(2) Dependent's social security number	(3) Dependent's relationship to you	(4) Ck. if qual. child for child tax credit (see pg. 22)
Frank	Schepperly	456-66-0022	Son	[X]
Colette	Schepperly	100-33-4444	Daughter	[X]
Serina	Schepperly	222-33-4444	Daughter	[X]
Yevonne	Schepperly	333-55-6666	Daughter	[X]
Adam	Schepperly	444-66-7777	Son	[X]

If more than five dependents, see page 22.

No. of children on 6c who:	
● lived with you	5
● did not live with you due to divorce or separation (see page 22)	
Dependents on 6c not entered above	
Add numbers on lines above ▶	7

d Total number of exemptions claimed

Income

Attach Forms W-2 and W-2G here. Also attach Form(s) 1099-R if tax was withheld.

If you did not get a W-2, see page 23.

Enclose, but do not attach, any payment. Also, please use Form 1040-V.

7	Wages, salaries, tips, etc. Attach Form(s) W-2	7	125,000
8a	Taxable interest. Attach Schedule B if required	8a	2,500
b	Tax-exempt interest. Do not include on line 8a	8b	2,500	
9	Ordinary dividends. Attach Schedule B if required	9	6,500
10	Taxable refunds, credits, or offsets of state and local income taxes (see page 24)	10	750
11	Alimony received	11	
12	Business income or (loss). Attach Schedule C or C-EZ	12	77,400
13	Capital gain or (loss). Attach Schedule D if required. If not required, check here ▶ [ ]	13	10,000
14	Other gains or (losses). Attach Form 4797	14	
15a	IRA distributions [15a] b Taxable amount (see page 25)	15b	
16a	Pensions and annuities [16a] b Taxable amount (see page 25)	16b	
17	Rental real estate, royalties, partnerships, S corporations, trusts, etc. Attach Schedule E	17	-5,000
18	Farm income or (loss). Attach Schedule F	18	
19	Unemployment compensation	19	
20a	Social security benefits [20a] b Taxable amount (see page 27)	20b	
21	Other income. List type & amt. (see page 29)	21	
22	Add the amounts in the far right column for lines 7 through 21. This is your **total income** ▶	22	217,150

Adjusted Gross Income

23	Educator expenses (see page 29)	23	
24	IRA deduction (see page 29)	24	
25	Student loan interest deduction (see page 31)	25	
26	Tuition and fees deduction (see page 32)	26	
27	Archer MSA deduction. Attach Form 8853	27	
28	Moving expenses. Attach Form 3903	28	
29	One-half of self-employment tax. Attach Schedule SE	29	2,755
30	Self-employed health insurance deduction (see page 33)	30	
31	Self-employed SEP, SIMPLE, and qualified plans	31	
32	Penalty on early withdrawal of savings	32	
33a	Alimony paid b Recipient's SSN ▶	33a	
34	Add lines 23 through 33a	34	2,755
35	Subtract line 34 from line 22. This is your **adjusted gross income** ▶	35	214,395

For Disclosure, Privacy Act, and Paperwork Reduction Act Notice, see page 76.

DAA

Form **1040** (2002)

EXHIBIT 5-2 (Continued)

Form 1040 (2002)		Nicholas & Betsy Schepperly		111-22-3333 Page 2
Tax and Credits	36	Amount from line 35 (adjusted gross income)	36	214,395
	37a	Check if: ☐ You were 65 or older, ☐ Blind; ☐ **Spouse** was 65 or older, ☐ Blind.		
		Add the number of boxes checked above and enter the total here ▶ 37a ☐		
	b	If you are married filing separately and your spouse itemizes deductions, or you were a dual-status alien, see page 34 and check here ▶ 37b ☐		
Standard Deduction for-	38	**Itemized deductions** (from Schedule A) or your **standard deduction** (see left margin)	38	38,887
	39	Subtract line 38 from line 36	39	175,508
● People who checked any box on line 37a or 37b or who can be claimed as a dependent, see page 34.	40	If line 36 is $103,000 or less, multiply $3,000 by the total number of exemptions claimed on line 6d. If line 36 is over $103,000, see the worksheet on page 35	40	19,320
	41	**Taxable income.** Subtract line 40 from line 39. If line 40 is more than line 39, enter -0-	41	156,188
	42	**Tax** (see page 36). Check if any tax is from: a ☐ Form(s) 8814		
		b ☐ Form 4972	42	37,067
● All others:	43	**Alternative minimum tax** (see page 37). Att. Form 6251 ▶	43	8,177
Single, $4,700	44	Add lines 42 and 43 ▶	44	45,244
Head of household, $6,900	45	Foreign tax credit. Attach Form 1116 if required	45	185
	46	Credit for child and dependent care expenses. Attach Form 2441	46	960
Married filing jointly or Qualifying widow(er), $7,850	47	Credit for the elderly or the disabled. Attach Schedule R	47	
	48	Education credits. Attach Form 8863	48	
	49	Retirement savings contributions credit. Attach Form 8880	49	
	50	Child tax credit (see page 39)	50	
Married filing separately, $3,925	51	Adoption credit. Attach Form 8839	51	
	52	Credits from: a ☐ Form 8396 b ☐ Form 8859	52	
	53	Other credits. Check applicable box(es): a ☐ Form 3800		
		b ☐ Form 8801 c ☐ Specify _____	53	
	54	Add lines 45 through 53. These are your **total credits**	54	1,145
	55	Subtract line 54 from line 44. If line 54 is more than line 44, enter -0- ▶	55	44,099
Other Taxes	56	Self-employment tax. Attach Schedule SE	56	5,508
	57	Social security and Medicare tax on tip income not reported to employer. Attach Form 4137	57	
	58	Tax on qualified plans, including IRAs, and other tax-favored accounts. Attach Form 5329 if required	58	
	59	Advance earned income credit payments from Form(s) W-2	59	
	60	Household employment taxes. Attach Schedule H	60	
	61	Add lines 55 - 60. This is your **total tax** ▶	61	49,607
Payments	62	Federal income tax withheld from Forms W-2 and 1099	62	19,500
If you have a qualifying child, attach Schedule EIC.	63	2002 estimated tax payments & amount applied from 2001 return	63	30,000
	64	**Earned income credit (EIC)**	64	
	65	Excess social security and tier 1 RRTA tax withheld (see page 56)	65	
	66	Additional child tax credit. Attach Form 8812	66	
	67 68	Amount paid with request for extension to file (see page 56) Otr. pymt. from: a ☐ Form 2439 b ☐ Form 4136 c ☐ Form 8885 68	67	
	69	Add lines 62 through 68. These are your **total payments** ▶	69	49,500
Refund	70	If line 69 is more than line 61, subtract line 61 from line 69. This is the amount you **overpaid**	70	
Direct deposit? See page 56 and fill in 71b, 71c, and 71d.	71a	Amount of line 70 you **want refunded to you** ▶	71a	
	▶ b	Routing number ▶ c Type: ☐ Checking ☐ Savings		
	▶ d	Account number		
	72	Amount of ln. 70 you want **applied to your 2003 estimated tax** ▶ 72		
Amount You Owe	73	**Amount you owe.** Subtract line 69 from line 61. For details on how to pay, see page 57 ▶	73	107
	74	Estimated tax penalty (see page 57) 74		

Third Party Designee — Do you want to allow another person to discuss this return with the IRS (see page 58)? ☒ **Yes. Complete the following.** ☐ No

Designee's name ▶ Preparer   Personal identification number (PIN) ▶   Phone no. ▶

Sign Here
Under penalties of perjury, I declare that I have examined this return and accompanying schedules and statements, and to the best of my knowledge and belief, they are true, correct, and complete. Declaration of preparer (other than taxpayer) is based on all information of which preparer has any knowledge.

Your signature	Date	Your occupation	Daytime phone number
Joint return? See page 21.		Research Consultant	
Spouse's signature. If a joint return, **both** must sign.	Date	Spouse's occupation	
Keep a copy for your records.		Dog Breeder	

EXHIBIT 5-2 (Continued)

SCHEDULES A&B	Schedule A-Itemized Deductions	OMB No. 1545-0074
(Form 1040)	(Schedule B is on back)	2002
Department of the Treasury Internal Revenue Service (99)	▶Attach to Form 1040. ▶See Instructions for Schedules A and B (Form 1040).	Attachment Sequence No. 07

Name(s) shown on Form 1040
Nicholas & Betsy Schepperly

Your social security number
111-22-3333

Medical and Dental Expenses
Caution. Do not include expenses reimbursed or paid by others.
1 Medical and dental expenses (see page A-2) ... **1**
2 Enter amt. from Form 1040, ln. 36 **2**
3 Multiply line 2 by 7.5% (.075) ... **3**
4 Subtract line 3 from line 1. If line 3 is more than line 1, enter -0- ... **4** | 0

Taxes You Paid
(See page A-2.)
5 State and local income taxes ... **5** | 7,700
6 Real estate taxes (see page A-2) ... **6** | 22,000
7 Personal property taxes ... **7**
8 Other taxes. List type and amount ▶ ... **8**
9 Add lines 5 through 8 ... **9** | 29,700

Interest You Paid
(See page A-3.)
Note. Personal interest is not deductible.
10 Home mortgage interest & points reported to you on Form 1098 **10** | 8,000
11 Home mortgage interest not reported to you on Form 1098. If paid to the person from whom you bought the home, see page A-3 and show that person's name, identifying no., and address ▶ ... **11**
12 Points not reported to you on Form 1098. See page A-3 for special rules ... **12**
13 Investment interest. Attach Form 4952 if required. (See page A-3.) ... **13**
14 Add lines 10 through 13 ... **14** | 8,000

Gifts to Charity
If you made a gift and got a benefit for it, see page A-4.
15 Gifts by cash or check. If you made any gift of $250 or more, see page A-4 ... **15** | 3,500
16 Other than by cash or check. If any gift of $250 or more, see page A-4. You must attach Form 8283 if over $500 ... **16**
17 Carryover from prior year ... **17**
18 Add lines 15 through 17 ... **18** | 3,500

Casualty and Theft Losses
19 Casualty or theft loss(es). Attach Form 4684. (See page A-5.) ... **19**

Job Expenses and Most Other Miscellaneous Deductions
(See page A-5 for expenses to deduct here.)
20 Unreimbursed employee expenses-job travel, union dues, job education, etc. You must attach Form 2106 or 2106-EZ if required. (See page A-5.) ▶ ... **20**
21 Tax preparation fees ... **21**
22 Other expenses-investment, safe deposit box, etc. List type and amount ▶ ... **22**
23 Add lines 20 through 22 ... **23**
24 Enter amt. from Form 1040, ln. 36 **24**
25 Multiply line 24 by 2% (.02) ... **25**
26 Subtract line 25 from line 23. If line 25 is more than line 23, enter -0- ... **26** | 0

Other Miscellaneous Deductions
27 Other-from list on page A-6. List type and amount ▶ ... **27**

Total Itemized Deductions
28 Is Form 1040, line 36, over $137,300 (over $68,650 if married filing separately)? *
☐ No. Your deduction is not limited. Add the amounts in the far right column for lines 4 through 27. Also, enter this amount on Form 1040, line 38.
☒ Yes. Your deduction may be limited. See page A-6 for the amount to enter. } ▶ **28** | 38,887

For Paperwork Reduction Act Notice, see Form 1040 instructions.   * Limited by AGI   Schedule A (Form 1040) 2002

DAA

EXHIBIT 5-2 (Continued)

SCHEDULE D						OMB No. 1545-0074	
(Form 1040)		**Capital Gains and Losses**				**2002**	
Department of the Treasury Internal Revenue Service (99)		▶ Attach to Form 1040. ▶ See Instructions for Schedule D (Form 1040). ▶ Use Schedule D-1 to list additional transactions for lines 1 and 8.				Attachment Sequence No. **12**	

Name(s) shown on Form 1040: Nicholas & Betsy Schepperly

Your social security number: 111-22-3333

Part I — Short-Term Capital Gains and Losses-Assets Held One Year or Less

(a) Description of property (Example: 100 sh. XYZ Co.)	(b) Date acquired (Mo., day, yr.)	(c) Date sold (Mo., day, yr.)	(d) Sales price (see page D-5 of the instructions)	(e) Cost or other basis (see page D-5 of the instructions)	(f) Gain or (loss) Subtract (e) from (d)	
1						

2 Enter your short-term totals, if any, from Schedule D-1, line 2 .... **2**

3 Total short-term sales price amounts. Add lines 1 and 2 in column (d) **3**

4 Short-term gain from Form 6252 and short-term gain or (loss) from Forms 4684, 6781, and 8824 .... **4**

5 Net short-term gain or (loss) from partnerships, S corporations, estates, and trusts from Schedule(s) K-1 .... **5**

6 Short-term capital loss carryover. Enter the amount, if any, from line 8 of your 2001 Capital Loss Carryover Worksheet .... **6** (   )

7 Net short-term capital gain or (loss). Combine lines 1 through 6 in column (f) **7**   0

Part II — Long-Term Capital Gains and Losses-Assets Held More Than One Year

(a) Description of property (Example: 100 sh. XYZ Co.)	(b) Date acquired (Mo., day, yr.)	(c) Date sold (Mo., day, yr.)	(d) Sales price (see page D-5 of the instructions)	(e) Cost or other basis (see page D-5 of the instructions)	(f) Gain or (loss) Subtract (e) from (d)	(g) 28% rate gain or (loss) * (see instr. below)
8 Great Company	5/04/97	6/15/02	50,000	30,000	20,000	10,000
Section 1202 exclusion					-10,000	

9 Enter your long-term totals, if any, from Schedule D-1, line 9 .... **9**

10 Total long-term sales price amounts. Add lines 8 and 9 in column (d) **10**   50,000

11 Gain from Form 4797, Part I; long-term gain from Forms 2439 and 6252; and long-term gain or (loss) from Forms 4684, 6781, and 8824 .... **11**

12 Net long-term gain or (loss) from partnerships, S corporations, estates, and trusts from Schedule(s) K-1 .... **12**

13 Capital gain distributions. See page D-1 of the instructions **13**

14 Long-term capital loss carryover. Enter in both columns (f) and (g) the amount, if any, from line 13 of your 2001 Capital Loss Carryover Worksheet .... **14** (   ) (   )

15 Combine lines 8 through 14 in column (g) **15**   10,000

16 Net long-term capital gain or (loss). Combine lines 8 through 14 in column (f) **16**   10,000
    Next: Go to Part III on the back.

* 28% rate gain or loss includes all "collectibles gains and losses" (as defined on page D-6 of the instructions) and up to 50% of the eligible gain on qualified small business stock (see page D-4 of the instructions).

For Paperwork Reduction Act Notice, see Form 1040 instructions.   Schedule D (Form 1040) 2002

DAA

EXHIBIT 5-2 (Continued)

Nicholas & Betsy Schepperly   111-22-3333

Schedule D (Form 1040) 2002   Page 2

Part III   Taxable Gain or Deductible Loss

17 Combine lines 7 and 16 and enter the result. If a loss, go to line 18. If a gain, enter the gain on
Form 1040, line 13, and complete Form 1040 through line 41 .... | 17 | 10,000

Next: • If both lines 16 and 17 are gains and Form 1040, line 41, is more than zero, complete
Part IV below.
• Otherwise, skip the rest of Schedule D and complete Form 1040.

18 If line 17 is a loss, enter here and on Form 1040, line 13, the **smaller** of (a) that loss or
(b) ($3,000) (or, if married filing separately, ($1,500)). Then complete Form 1040 through line 39 .... | 18 | ( )

Next: • If the loss on line 17 is more than the loss on line 18 or if Form 1040, line 39, is less
than zero, skip Part IV below and complete the **Capital Loss Carryover Worksheet**
on page D-6 of the instructions before completing the rest of Form 1040.
• Otherwise, skip Part IV below and complete the rest of Form 1040.

Part IV   Tax Computation Using Maximum Capital Gains Rates

19 Enter your unrecaptured section 1250 gain, if any, from line 17 of the worksheet on page D-7 of the
instructions .... | 19 |
If line 15 or line 19 is more than zero, complete the worksheet on page D-9 of the instructions
to figure the amount to enter on lines 22, 29, and 40 below, and skip all other lines below.
Otherwise, go to line 20.

20 Enter your taxable income from Form 1040, line 41 .... | 20 |
21 Enter the smaller of line 16 or line 17 of
Schedule D............................. | 21 |
22 If you are deducting investment interest
expense on Form 4952, enter the amount
from Form 4952, line 4e. Otherwise, enter -0- ..... | 22 | 0
23 Subtract line 22 from line 21. If zero or less, enter -0- .... | 23 |
24 Subtract line 23 from line 20. If zero or less, enter -0- .... | 24 |
25 Figure the tax on the amount on line 24. Use the Tax Table or Tax Rate Schedules, whichever applies .... | 25 |
26 Enter the smaller of:
• The amount on line 20 or
• $46,700 if married filing jointly or qualifying widow(er);
$27,950 if single;
$37,450 if head of household; or
$23,350 if married filing separately | 26 |

If line 26 is greater than line 24, go to line 27. Otherwise, skip lines
27 through 33 and go to line 34.

27 Enter the amount from line 24 .... | 27 |
28 Subtract line 27 from line 26. If zero or less, enter -0- and go to line 34 ..... | 28 |
29 Enter your qualified 5-year gain, if any, from
line 8 of the worksheet on page D-8 .... | 29 |
30 Enter the smaller of line 28 or line 29 .... | 30 |
31 Multiply line 30 by 8% (.08) .... | 31 |
32 Subtract line 30 from line 28 .... | 32 |
33 Multiply line 32 by 10% (.10) .... | 33 |

If the amounts on lines 23 and 28 are the same, skip lines 34 through 37 and go to line 38.

34 Enter the smaller of line 20 or line 23 .... | 34 |
35 Enter the amount from line 28 (if line 28 is blank, enter -0-) .... | 35 |
36 Subtract line 35 from line 34 .... | 36 |
37 Multiply line 36 by 20% (.20) .... | 37 |
38 Add lines 25, 31, 33, and 37 .... | 38 |
39 Figure the tax on the amount on line 20. Use the Tax Table or Tax Rate Schedules, whichever applies .. | 39 |
40 Tax on all taxable income (including capital gains). Enter the **smaller** of line 38 or line 39 here
and on Form 1040, line 42 .... | 40 | 37,067

DAA   Schedule D (Form 1040) 2002

EXHIBIT 5-2 (Continued)

Form 6251	Alternative Minimum Tax-Individuals	OMB No. 1545-0227
Department of the Treasury	▶ See separate instructions.	**2002**
Internal Revenue Service (99)	▶ Attach to Form 1040 or Form 1040NR.	Attachment Sequence No. 32

Name(s) shown on Form 1040: **Nicholas & Betsy Schepperly**
Your social security number: **111-22-3333**

Part I Alternative Minimum Taxable Income (See instructions for how to complete each line.)

1	If filing Schedule A (Form 1040), enter the amount from Form 1040, line 39, and go to line 2. Otherwise, enter the amount from Form 1040, line 36, and go to line 7. (If zero or less, enter as a negative amount.)	1	175,508
2	Medical and dental. Enter the **smaller** of Schedule A (Form 1040), line 4, **or** 2 1/2% of Form 1040, line 36	2	
3	Taxes from Schedule A (Form 1040), line 9	3	29,700
4	Certain interest on a home mortgage **not** used to buy, build, or improve your home	4	
5	Miscellaneous deductions from Schedule A (Form 1040), line 26	5	
6	If Form 1040, line 36, is over $137,300 (over $68,650 if married filing separately), enter the amount from line 9 of the worksheet for Schedule A (Form 1040), line 28	6	(2,313)
7	Tax refund from Form 1040, line 10 or line 21	7	(750)
8	Investment interest expense (difference between regular tax and AMT)	8	
9	Depletion (difference between regular tax and AMT)	9	500
10	Net operating loss deduction from Form 1040, line 21. Enter as a positive amount	10	
11	Interest from specified private activity bonds exempt from the regular tax	11	2,500
12	Qualified small business stock (42% of gain excluded under section 1202)	12	4,200
13	Exercise of incentive stock options (excess of AMT income over regular tax income)	13	
14	Estates and trusts (amount from Schedule K-1 (Form 1041), line 9)	14	
15	Electing large partnerships (amount from Schedule K-1 (Form 1065-B), box 6)	15	
16	Disposition of property (difference between AMT and regular tax gain or loss)	16	
17	Depreciation on assets placed in service after 1986 (difference between regular tax and AMT)	17	
18	Passive activities (difference between AMT and regular tax income or loss)	18	
19	Loss limitations (difference between AMT and regular tax income or loss)	19	
20	Circulation costs (difference between regular tax and AMT)	20	
21	Long-term contracts (difference between AMT and regular tax income)	21	
22	Mining costs (difference between regular tax and AMT)	22	
23	Research and experimental costs (difference between regular tax and AMT)	23	1,000
24	Income from certain installment sales before January 1, 1987	24	( )
25	Intangible drilling costs preference	25	
26	Other adjustments, including income-based related adjustments	26	
27	Alternative tax net operating loss deduction	27	( )
28	**Alternative minimum taxable income.** Combine lines 1 through 27. (If married filing separately and line 28 is more than $173,000, see page 7 of the instructions.)	28	210,345

Part II Alternative Minimum Tax

29 Exemption. (If this form is for a child under age 14, see page 7 of the instructions.)

IF your filing status is . . .	AND line 28 is not over . . .	THEN enter on line 29 . . .		
Single or head of household	$112,500	$35,750		
Married filing jointly or qualifying widow(er)	150,000	49,000	29	33,914
Married filing separately	75,000	24,500		

If line 28 is **over** the amount shown above for your filing status, see page 7 of the instructions.

30	Subtract line 29 from line 28. If zero or less, enter -0- here and on lines 33 and 35 and stop here	30	176,431
31	• If you reported capital gain distributions directly on Form 1040, line 13, **or** you had a gain on both lines 16 and 17 of Schedule D (Form 1040) (as refigured for the AMT, if necessary), complete Part III on the back and enter the amount from line 57 here. • **All others:** If line 30 is $175,000 or less ($87,500 or less if married filing separately), multiply line 30 by 26% (.26). Otherwise, multiply line 30 by 28% (.28) and subtract $3,500 ($1,750 if married filing separately) from the result.	31	45,272
32	Alternative minimum tax foreign tax credit (see page 7 of the instructions)	32	213
33	Tentative minimum tax. Subtract line 32 from line 31	33	45,059
34	Tax from Form 1040, line 42 (minus any tax from Form 4972 and any foreign tax credit from Form 1040, line 45)	34	36,882
35	**Alternative minimum tax.** Subtract line 34 from line 33. If zero or less, enter -0-. Enter here and on Form 1040, line 43	35	8,177

For Paperwork Reduction Act Notice, see page 8 of the instructions. Form **6251** (2002)
DAA

EXHIBIT 5-2 (Continued)

Form 6251 (2002) Nicholas & Betsy Schepperly   111-22-3333 Page **2**

Part III   **Tax Computation Using Maximum Capital Gains Rates**

Caution: If you **did not** complete Part IV.of Schedule D (Form 1040), see page 8 of the instructions before you complete this part.

36 Enter the amount from Form 6251, line 30	**36**	176,431
37 Enter the amount from Schedule D (Form 1040), line 23, or line 9 of the Schedule D Tax Worksheet on page D-9 of the instructions for Schedule D (Form 1040), whichever applies (as refigured for the AMT, if necessary) (see page 8 of the instructions)	**37** 10,000	
38 Enter the amount from Schedule D (Form 1040), line 19 (as refigured for the AMT, if necessary) (see page 8 of the instructions)	**38**	
39 If you did not complete a Schedule D Tax Worksheet for the regular tax or the AMT, enter the amount from line 37. Otherwise, add lines 37 and 38, and enter the **smaller** of that result or the amount from line 4 of the Schedule D Tax Worksheet (as refigured for the AMT, if necessary).	**39** 10,000	
40 Enter the **smaller** of line 36 or line 39	**40**	10,000
41 Subtract line 40 from line 36	**41**	166,431
42 If line 41 is $175,000 or less ($87,500 or less if married filing separately), multiply line 41 by 26% (.26). Otherwise, multiply line 41 by 28% (.28) and subtract $3,500 ($1,750 if married filing separately) from the result	**42**	43,272
43 Enter the amount from Schedule D (Form 1040), line 28, or line 16 of the Schedule D Tax Worksheet on page D-9 of the instructions for Schedule D (Form 1040), whichever applies (as figured for the regular tax) (see page 8 of the instructions)	**43**	
44 Enter the **smaller** of line 36 or line 37	**44**	
45 Enter the **smaller** of line 43 or line 44. If zero, go to line 51	**45**	
46 Enter your qualified 5-year gain, if any, from Schedule D (Form 1040), line 29 (as refigured for the AMT, if necessary) (see page 8 of the instructions)	**46**	
47 Enter the **smaller** of line 45 or line 46	**47**	
48 Multiply line 47 by 8% (.08)	**48**	
49 Subtract line 47 from line 45	**49**	
50 Multiply line 49 by 10% (.10)	**50**	
51 Subtract line 45 from line 44	**51** 10,000	
52 Multiply line 51 by 20% (.20)	**52**	2,000
If line 38 is zero or blank, skip lines 53 and 54 and go to line 55. Otherwise, go to line 53.		
53 Subtract line 44 from line 40	**53**	
54 Multiply line 53 by 25% (.25)	**54**	
55 Add lines 42, 48, 50, 52, and 54	**55**	45,272
56 If line 36 is $175,000 or less ($87,500 or less if married filing separately), multiply line 36 by 26% (.26). Otherwise, multiply line 36 by 28% (.28) and subtract $3,500 ($1,750 if married filing separately) from the result	**56**	45,901
57 Enter the **smaller** of line 55 or line 56 here and on line 31	**57**	45,272

Form **6251** (2002)

DAA

Exhibit 5-2 (Continued)

Form 1116	Foreign Tax Credit	OMB No. 1545-0121
	(Individual, Estate, or Trust)	
Department of the Treasury Internal Revenue Service (99)	▶ Attach to Form 1040, 1040NR, 1041, or 990-T. ▶ See separate instructions.	**2002** Attachment Sequence No. 19

Name	Identifying number as shown on page 1 of your tax return
Nicholas Schepperly	111-22-3333

Use a separate Form 1116 for each category of income listed below. See **Categories of Income** on page 3 of the instructions. Check only one box on each Form 1116. Report all amounts in U.S. dollars except where specified in Part I below.

- a ☒ Passive income
- b ☐ High withholding tax interest
- c ☐ Financial services income
- d ☐ Shipping income
- e ☐ Dividends from a DISC or former DISC
- f ☐ Certain distributions from a foreign sales corporation (FSC) or former FSC
- g ☐ Lump-sum distributions
- h ☐ Section 901(j) income
- i ☐ Certain income re-sourced by treaty
- j ☐ General limitation income

k Resident of (name of country) ▶

Note: If you paid taxes to only one foreign country or U.S. possession, use column A in Part I and line A in Part II. If you paid taxes to more than one foreign country or U.S. possession, use a separate column and line for each country or possession.

Part I   Taxable Income or Loss From Sources Outside the United States (for Category Checked Above)

		Foreign Country or U.S. Possession			Total
		A	B	C	(Add cols. A, B, and C.)
l	Enter the name of the foreign country or U.S. possession ▶	Canada			
1	Gross income from sources within country shown above and of the type checked above (see page 7 of the instr.):	1,000			1 1,000
	Deductions and losses (Caution: See pages 9, 12, and 13 of the instructions):				
2	Expenses definitely related to the income on line 1 (attach statement)				
3	Pro rata share of other deductions not definitely related:				
a	Certain itemized deductions or standard deduction (see instructions)	24,069			
b	Other ded. (att. stmt.)				
c	Add lines 3a and 3b	24,069			
d	Gross foreign source inc. (see instr.)	1,000			
e	Gross inc. from all sources (see instr.)	236,650			
f	Divide line 3d by line 3e (see instr.)	0.0042			
g	Multiply line 3c by line 3f	101			
4	Pro rata share of interest expense (see instructions):				
a	Home mortgage interest (use worksheet on page 12 of the instructions)	32			
b	Other interest expense				
5	Losses from foreign sources				
6	Add lines 2, 3g, 4a, 4b, and 5	133			6 133
7	Subtract line 6 from line 1. Enter the result here and on line 14, page 2 ▶				7 867

Part II   Foreign Taxes Paid or Accrued (see page 13 of the instructions)

Credit is claimed for taxes (you must check one)			Foreign taxes paid or accrued								
(m) ☒ Paid		In foreign currency					In U.S. dollars				
(n) ☐ Accrued		Taxes withheld at source on:			(s) Other foreign taxes paid or accrued	Taxes withheld at source on:			(w) Other foreign taxes paid or accrued	(x) Total foreign taxes paid or accrued (add cols. (t) through (w))
	(o) Date paid or accrued	(p) Dividends	(q) Rents and royalties	(r) Interest		(t) Dividends	(u) Rents and royalties	(v) Interest		
A	Various							250		250
B										
C										

8	Add lines A through C, column (x). Enter the total here and on line 9, page 2 ▶	8	250

DAA   For Paperwork Reduction Act Notice, see page 16 of the instructions.   Form **1116** (2002)

EXHIBIT 5-2 (Continued)

Nicholas Schepperly 111-22-3333

Form 1116 (2002) Page 2

	Part III **Figuring the Credit**			
9	Enter the amount from line 8. These are your total foreign taxes paid or accrued for the category of income checked above Part I	9	250	
10	Carryback or carryover (att. detailed computation)	10		
11	Add lines 9 and 10	11	250	
12	Reduction in foreign taxes (see page 13 of the instructions)	12		
13	Subtract line 12 from line 11. This is the total amount of foreign taxes available for credit		13	250
14	Enter the amount from line 7. This is your taxable income or (loss) from sources outside the United States (before adjustments) for the category of income checked above Part I (see page 14 of the instructions)	14	867	
15	Adjustments to line 14 (see page 14 of the instructions)	15		
16	Combine the amounts on lines 14 and 15. This is your net foreign source taxable income. (If the result is zero or less, you have no foreign tax credit for the category of income you checked above Part I. Skip lines 17 through 21. However, if you are filing more than one Form 1116, you must complete line 19.)	16	867	
17	**Individuals:** Enter the amount from Form 1040, line 39. If you are a nonresident alien, enter the amount from Form 1040NR, line 37. **Estates and trusts:** Enter your taxable income without the deduction for your exemption	17	172,762	
	Caution: If you figured your tax using the special rates on capital gains, see page 15 of the instructions.			
18	Divide line 16 by line 17. If line 16 is more than line 17, enter "1"		18	0.0050
19	**Individuals:** Enter the amount from Form 1040, line 42. If you are a nonresident alien, enter the amount from Form 1040NR, line 40. **Estates and trusts:** Enter the amount from Form 1041, Schedule G, line 1a, or the total of Form 990-T, lines 36 and 37		19	37,067
	Caution: If you are completing line 19 for separate category **g** (lump-sum distributions), see page 15 of the instr.			
20	Multiply line 19 by line 18 (maximum amount of credit)		20	185
21	Enter the **smaller** of line 13 or line 20. If this is the only Form 1116 you are filing, skip lines 22 through 30 and enter this amount on line 31. Otherwise, complete the appropriate line in Part IV (see page 16 of the instructions) ▶		21	185
	Part IV **Summary of Credits From Separate Parts III** (see page 16 of the instructions)			
22	Credit for taxes on passive income	22		
23	Credit for taxes on high withholding tax interest	23		
24	Credit for taxes on financial services income	24		
25	Credit for taxes on shipping income	25		
26	Credit for taxes on dividends from a DISC or former DISC and certain distributions from a FSC or former FSC	26		
27	Credit for taxes on lump-sum distributions	27		
28	Credit for taxes on certain income re-sourced by treaty	28		
29	Credit for taxes on general limitation income	29		
30	Add lines 22 through 29		30	
31	Enter the **smaller** of line 19 or line 30		31	185
32	Reduction of credit for international boycott operations. See instructions for line 12 on page 13		32	
33	Subtract line 32 from line 31. This is your **foreign tax credit.** Enter here and on Form 1040, line 45; Form 1040NR, line 43; Form 1041, Schedule G, line 2a; or Form 990-T, line 40a ▶		33	185

Form **1116** (2002)

DAA

EXHIBIT 5-2 (Continued)

Form **1116**	Alt. Min. Tax **Foreign Tax Credit** (Individual, Estate, or Trust)	OMB No. 1545-0121
Department of the Treasury Internal Revenue Service (99)	▶ Attach to Form 1040, 1040NR, 1041, or 990-T. ▶ See separate instructions.	**2002** Attachment Sequence No. **19**

Name	Identifying number as shown on page 1 of your tax return
Nicholas Schepperly	111-22-3333

Use a separate Form 1116 for each category of income listed below. See **Categories of Income** on page 3 of the instructions. Check only one box on each Form 1116. Report all amounts in U.S. dollars except where specified in Part II below.

a [X] Passive income
b [ ] High withholding tax interest
c [ ] Financial services income

d [ ] Shipping income
e [ ] Dividends from a DISC or former DISC
f [ ] Certain distributions from a foreign sales corporation (FSC) or former FSC

g [ ] Lump-sum distributions
h [ ] Section 901(j) income
i [ ] Certain income re-sourced by treaty
j [ ] General limitation income

k   Resident of (name of country) ▶

Note: If you paid taxes to only one foreign country or U.S. possession, use column A in Part I and line A in Part II. If you paid taxes to more than one foreign country or U.S. possession, use a separate column and line for each country or possession.

Part I   Taxable Income or Loss From Sources Outside the United States (for Category Checked Above)

		Foreign Country or U.S. Possession			Total
		A	B	C	(Add cols. A, B, and C.)
l	Enter the name of the foreign country or U.S. possession ▶	Canada			
1	Gross income from sources within country shown above and of the type checked above (see page 7 of the instr.):	1,000			1 1,000
	Deductions and losses (Caution: See pages 9, 12, and 13 of the instructions):				
2	Expenses **definitely related** to the income on line 1 (attach statement)				
3	Pro rata share of other deductions **not definitely related:**				
a	Certain itemized deductions or standard deduction (see instructions)	3,500			
b	Other ded. (att. stmt.)				
c	Add lines 3a and 3b	3,500			
d	Gross foreign source inc. (see instr.)	1,000			
e	Gross inc. from all sources (see instr.)	236,650			
f	Divide line 3d by line 3e (see instr.)	0.0042			
g	Multiply line 3c by line 3f	15			
4	Pro rata share of interest expense (see instructions):				
a	Home mortgage interest (use worksheet on page 12 of the instructions)	34			
b	Other interest expense				
5	Losses from foreign sources				
6	Add lines 2, 3g, 4a, 4b, and 5	49			6 49
7	Subtract line 6 from line 1. Enter the result here and on line 14, page 2 ▶				7 951

Part II   Foreign Taxes Paid or Accrued (see page 13 of the instructions)

Country	Credit is claimed for taxes (you must check one)		Foreign taxes paid or accrued								
			In foreign currency				In U.S. dollars				
	(m) [X] Paid (n) [ ] Accrued	(o) Date paid or accrued	Taxes withheld at source on:			(s) Other foreign taxes paid or accrued	Taxes withheld at source on:			(w) Other foreign taxes paid or accrued	(x) Total foreign taxes paid or accrued (add cols. (t) through (w))
			(p) Dividends	(q) Rents and royalties	(r) Interest		(t) Dividends	(u) Rents and royalties	(v) Interest		
A	Various								250		250
B											
C											
8	Add lines A through C, column (x). Enter the total here and on line 9, page 2 .... ▶								**8**		250

DAA   **For Paperwork Reduction Act Notice, see page 16 of the instructions.**   Form **1116** (2002)

116 *Chapter 5*

Exhibit 5-2 (Continued)

Alt. Min. Tax
Nicholas Schepperly   111-22-3333
Form 1116 (2002)   Page 2
Part III   Figuring the Credit

9	Enter the amount from line 8. These are your total foreign taxes paid or accrued for the category of income checked above Part I	**9** 250	
10	Carryback or carryover (att. detailed computation)	**10**	
11	Add lines 9 and 10	**11** 250	
12	Reduction in foreign taxes (see page 13 of the instructions)	**12**	
13	Subtract line 12 from line 11. This is the total amount of foreign taxes available for credit	**13**	250
14	Enter the amount from line 7. This is your taxable income or (loss) from sources outside the United States (before adjustments) for the category of income checked above Part I (see page 14 of the instructions)	**14** 951	
15	Adjustments to line 14 (see page 14 of the instructions)	**15**	
16	Combine the amounts on lines 14 and 15. This is your net foreign source taxable income. (If the result is zero or less, you have no foreign tax credit for the category of income you checked above Part I. Skip lines 17 through 21. However, if you are filing more than one Form 1116, you must complete line 19.)	**16** 951	
17	**Individuals:** Enter the amount from Form 1040, line 39. If you are a nonresident alien, enter the amount from Form 1040NR, line 37. **Estates and trusts:** Enter your taxable income without the deduction for your exemption	**17** 202,780	
	Caution: If you figured your tax using the special rates on capital gains, see page 15 of the instructions.		
18	Divide line 16 by line 17. If line 16 is more than line 17, enter "1"	**18**	0.0047
19	**Individuals:** Enter the amount from Form 1040, line 42. If you are a nonresident alien, enter the amount from Form 1040NR, line 40. **Estates and trusts:** Enter the amount from Form 1041, Schedule G, line 1a, or the total of Form 990-T, lines 36 and 37	**19**	45,272
	Caution: If you are completing line 19 for separate category g (lump-sum distributions), see page 15 of the instr.		
20	Multiply line 19 by line 18 (maximum amount of credit)	**20**	213
21	Enter the **smaller** of line 13 or line 20. If this is the only Form 1116 you are filing, skip lines 22 through 30 and enter this amount on line 31. Otherwise, complete the appropriate line in Part IV (see page 16 of the instructions) ▶	**21**	213

Part IV   Summary of Credits From Separate Parts III (see page 16 of the instructions)

22	Credit for taxes on passive income	**22**	
23	Credit for taxes on high withholding tax interest	**23**	
24	Credit for taxes on financial services income	**24**	
25	Credit for taxes on shipping income	**25**	
26	Credit for taxes on dividends from a DISC or former DISC and certain distributions from a FSC or former FSC	**26**	
27	Credit for taxes on lump-sum distributions	**27**	
28	Credit for taxes on certain income re-sourced by treaty	**28**	
29	Credit for taxes on general limitation income	**29**	
30	Add lines 22 through 29	**30**	
31	Enter the **smaller** of line 19 or line 30	**31**	213
32	Reduction of credit for international boycott operations. See instructions for line 12 on page 13	**32**	
33	Subtract line 32 from line 31. This is your **foreign tax credit.** Enter here and on Form 1040, line 45; Form 1040NR, line 43; Form 1041, Schedule G, line 2a; or Form 990-T, line 40a ▶	**33**	213

Form **1116** (2002)
DAA

EXHIBIT 5-2 (Continued)

Form **1040**	**Exemption and Deduction Worksheets**	**2002**

Name	Taxpayer Identification Number
Nicholas & Betsy Schepperly	111-22-3333

Exemptions Worksheet

1.	Multiply $3,000 by the total number of exemptions claimed on Form 1040, line 6d	1.	21,000
2.	Enter the amount from Form 1040, line 36	2.	214,395
3.	Enter on line 3 the amount shown below for your filing status:		
	• Single - $137,300		
	• Married filing jointly or Qualifying widow(er) - $206,000	3.	206,000
	• Married filing separately - $103,000		
	• Head of household - $171,650		
4.	Subtract line 3 from line 2. If zero or less, **stop here**; enter the amount from line 1 above on Form 1040, line 40	4.	8,395
	Note: If line 4 is more than $122,500 (more than $61,250 if married filing separately), **stop here;** you cannot take a deduction for exemptions. Enter -0- on Form 1040, line 40.		
5.	Divide line 4 by $2,500 ($1,250 if married filing separately). If the result is not a whole number, round it up to the next higher whole number (for example, increase 0.0004 to 1)	5.	4
6.	Multiply line 5 by 2% (.02) and enter the result as a decimal amount	6.	0.08
7.	Multiply line 1 by line 6	7.	1,680
8.	**Deduction for exemptions.** Subtract line 7 from line 1. Enter the result here and on Form 1040, line 40	8.	19,320

Itemized Deductions Worksheet

1.	Add the amounts on Schedule A, lines 4, 9, 14, 18, 19, 26, and 27	1.	41,200
2.	Add the amounts on Schedule A, lines 4, 13, and 19, plus any gambling and casualty or theft losses included on ln 27.	2.	
	Caution: Be sure your total gambling and casualty or theft losses are clearly identified on the dotted line next to line 27.		
3.	Subtract line 2 from line 1. If the result is zero, **stop here**; enter the amount from line 1 above on Schedule A, line 28	3.	41,200
4.	Multiply line 3 above by 80% (.80)	4.	32,960
5.	Enter the amount from Form 1040, line 36	5.	214,395
6.	Enter $137,300 ($68,650 if married filing separately)	6.	137,300
7.	Subtract line 6 from line 5. If the result is zero or less, **stop here;** enter the amount from line 1 above on Schedule A, line 28	7.	77,095
8.	Multiply line 7 above by 3% (.03)	8.	2,313
9.	Enter the **smaller** of line 4 or line 8	9.	2,313
10.	**Total itemized deductions.** Subtract line 9 from line 1. Enter the result here and on Schedule A, line 28	10.	38,887

Standard Deduction Worksheet for Dependents

1.	Add $250 to your **earned income.** Enter the total	1.	
2.	Minimum standard deduction	2.	
3.	Enter the **larger** of line 1 or line 2	3.	
4.	Enter the amount shown below for your filing status.		
	• Single - $4,700		
	• Married filing separately - $3,925	4.	
	• Married filing jointly or qualifying widow(er) - $7,850		
	• Head of household - $6,900		
5.	**Standard deduction.**		
	a. Enter the **smaller** of line 3 or line 4. If under 65 and not blind, **stop here** and enter this amount on Form 1040, line 38 (Form 1040A, line 24). **Otherwise, go to line 5b**	5a.	
	b. Check if: ☐ You were 65 or older, ☐ Blind; ☐ Spouse was 65 or older, ☐ Blind. **Total boxes checked** ☐ If 65 or older or blind, multiply $1,150 ($900 if married or qualifying widow(er) with dependent child) by the number in the box above	5b.	
	c. Add lines 5a and 5b. Enter the total here and on Form 1040, line 38 (Form 1040A, line 24)	5c.	

EXHIBIT 5-2 (Continued)

Form **1040**	**Schedule D Tax Worksheet - Line 40**	**2002**

Name	Taxpayer Identification Number
Nicholas & Betsy Schepperly	111-22-3333

1. Enter your taxable income from Form 1040, line 41 .... **1.** _156,188_
2. Enter the **smaller** of line 16 or line 17 of Schedule D .... **2.** _10,000_
3. If you are filing Form 4952, enter the amount from Form 4952, line 4e. Otherwise, enter -0-. **Also enter this amount on Schedule D, line 22** .... **3.** _0_
4. Subtract line 3 from line 2. If zero or less, enter -0- .... **4.** _10,000_
5. Combine lines 7 and 15 of Schedule D. If zero or less, enter -0- **5.** _10,000_
6. Enter the **smaller** of line 5 above or Schedule D, line 15, but not less than zero .... **6.** _10,000_
7. Enter the amount from Schedule D, line 19 .... **7.**
8. Add lines 6 and 7 .... **8.** _10,000_
9. Subtract line 8 from line 4. If zero or less, enter -0- .... **9.** _0_
10. Subtract line 9 from line 1. If zero or less, enter -0- .... **10.** _156,188_
11. Enter the **smaller** of:

    • The amount on line 1 **or**
    • $46,700 if married filing jointly or qualifying widow(er);
      $27,950 if single;
      $37,450 if head of household; or
      $23,350 if married filing separately .... **11.** _46,700_

12. Enter the **smaller** of line 10 or line 11 .... **12.** _46,700_
13. Subtract line 4 from line 1. If zero or less, enter -0- .... **13.** _146,188_
14. Enter the **larger** of line 12 or line 13 ▶ **14.** _146,188_
15. Figure the tax on the amount on line 14. Use the Tax Table or Tax Schedules, whichever applies ▶ **15.** _34,267_

    If lines 11 and 12 are the same, skip lines 16 through 21 and go to line 22. Otherwise, go to line 16.
16. Subtract line 12 from line 11 ▶ **16.**
17. Enter your qualified 5-year gain, if any, from the worksheet on page D-8. **Also enter this amount on Schedule D, line 29** **17.**
18. Enter the **smaller** of line 16 above or line 17 above .... **18.**
19. Multiply line 18 by 8% (.08) .... **19.**
20. Subtract line 18 from line 16 **20.**
21. Multiply line 20 by 10% (.10) .... **21.**

    If lines 1 and 11 are the same, skip lines 22 through 34 and go to line 35. Otherwise, go to line 22.
22. Enter the **smaller** of line 1 or line 9 .... **22.**
23. Enter the amount from line 16 (if line 16 is blank, enter -0-) .... **23.** _0_
24. Subtract line 23 from line 22 ▶ **24.**
25. Multiply line 24 by 20% (.20) **25.**

    If line 7 is zero, skip lines 26 through 31 and go to line 32. Otherwise, go to line 26.
26. Enter the **smaller** of line 4 or line 7 .... **26.**
27. Add lines 4 and 14 .... **27.**
28. Enter the amount from line 1 above ...... **28.**
29. Subtract line 28 from line 27. If zero or less, enter -0- **29.**
30. Subtract line 29 from line 26. If zero or less, enter -0- .... ▶ **30.**
31. Multiply line 30 by 25% (.25) **31.**

    If line 6 is zero, skip lines 32 through 34 and go to line 35. Otherwise, go to line 32.
32. Add lines 14, 16, 24, and 30 .... **32.** _146,188_
33. Subtract line 32 from line 1 .... **33.** _10,000_
34. Multiply line 33 by 28% (.28) **34.** _2,800_
35. Add lines 15, 19, 21, 25, 31, and 34 **35.** _37,067_
36. Figure the tax on the amount on line 1. Use the Tax Table or Tax Rate Schedules, whichever applies .... **36.** _37,267_
37. **Tax on all taxable income (including capital gains).** Enter the **smaller** of line 35 or line 36. Also enter this amount on Schedule D, line 40, and Form 1040, line 42 .... **37.** _37,067_

DAA

EXHIBIT 5-2 (Continued)

Form **1116**	Foreign Tax Credit Worksheet	**2002**

Name	Taxpayer Identification Number
Nicholas & Betsy Schepperly	111-22-3333

If you are filing a Schedule D (Form 1040) with your tax return or you reported capital gain distributions on Form 1040, line 13, you must use the worksheet on this page to figure the amount to enter on line 17 of Form 1116. If you figured your tax using the **Capital Gain Tax Worksheet** complete the worksheet as follows: Skip lines 2 through 5. On line 6, enter the amount from line 2 of the **Capital Gain Tax Worksheet.** Complete the rest of the Worksheet for Line 17 as instructed.

Worksheet for Form 1116, Page 2, Line 17

1.	Enter the amount from Form 1040, line 39 or Form 1040NR, line 37		1.	175,508
2.	Enter your worldwide 28% gains (see instr on pg 15)	2. 10,000		
3.	Multiply line 2 by .2746	3. 2,746		
4.	Enter your worldwide 25% gains (see instr on pg 15)	4.		
5.	Multiply line 4 by .3523	5.		
6.	Enter your worldwide 20% gains (see instr on pg 15)	6.		
7.	Multiply line 6 by .4819	7.		
8.	Add lines 3, 5 and 7		8.	2,746
9.	Subtract line 8 from line 1. Enter the result here and on Form 1116, line 17		9.	172,762

Please refer to the Schedule D AMT Worksheets for the alternative minimum tax amounts reported on this worksheet

Worksheet for AMT Form 1116, Page 2, Line 17

1.	Enter the amount from Form 6251, line 28		1.	210,345
2.	Enter your worldwide 28% gains (see instr on pg 15)	2. 10,000		
3.	Multiply line 2 by .2746	3. 2,746		
4.	Enter your worldwide 25% gains (see instr on pg 15)	4.		
5.	Multiply line 4 by .3523	5.		
6.	Enter your worldwide 20% gains (see instr on pg 15)	6. 10,000		
7.	Multiply line 6 by .4819	7. 4,819		
8.	Add lines 3, 5 and 7		8.	7,565
9.	Subtract line 8 from line 1. Enter the result here and on AMT Form 1116, line 17		9.	202,780

EXHIBIT 5-2 (Continued)

Form **1040**	AMT Exemption and Sch D Line 25 Worksheets	**2002**

Name	Taxpayer Identification Number
Nicholas & Betsy Schepperly	111-22-3333

Exemption Worksheet - Form 6251, Line 29

1. Enter $35,750 if single or head of household; $49,000 if married filing jointly or qualifying widow(er); $24,500 if married filing separately **1.** 49,000
2. Enter your alternative minimum taxable income (AMTI) from Form 6251, line 28 .... **2.** 210,345
3. Enter $112,500 if single or head of household; $150,000 if married filing jointly or qualifying widow(er); $75,000 if married filing separately **3.** 150,000
4. Subtract line 3 from line 2. If zero or less, enter -0- **4.** 60,345
5. Multiply line 4 by 25% (.25) **5.** 15,086
6. Subtract line 5 from line 1. If zero or less, enter -0-. If this form is for a child under age 14, go to line 7 below. Otherwise, **stop here** and enter this amount on Form 6251, line 29 and go Form 6251, line 30 ▶ **6.** 33,914
7. Child's minimum exemption amount .... **7.**
8. Enter the **child's earned income**, if any. See instructions .... **8.**
9. Add lines 7 and 8 .... **9.**
10. Enter the **smaller** of line 6 or line 9 here and on Form 6251, line 29, and go to Form 6251, line 30 ▶ **10.**

Schedule D Line 19 Refigured for AMT Worksheet - Form 6251, Line 38

All forms referenced are the AMT version of the form. **If you are not reporting a gain on Form 4797, ln 7, skip lines 1-9 and go to ln 10**

1. If you have a section 1250 property in Part III of Form 4797 for which you made an entry in Part I of the Form 4797 (but not Form 6252), enter the **smaller** of line 22 or line 24 of Form 4797 for that property. .... **1.** *
2. Enter the amount from Form 4797, ln 26g, for the property for which you made an entry in line 1 .... **2.** *
3. Subtract line 2 from line 1. *(Total amount is reported. See the Unrecaptured Section 1250 Gains stmt for detail) .... **3.**
4. Enter the total unrecaptured section 1250 gain included on line 26 or line 37 of Form(s) 6252 from installment sales of trade or business property held more than 1 year .... **4.**
5. Enter the total of any amounts reported to you on Sch K-1 from partnership/S corp as unrecap sect 1250 gain .... **5.**
6. Add lines 3 through 5 .... **6.**
7. Enter the **smaller** of line 6 or gain from Form 4797, line 7 .... **7.**
8. Enter the amount, if any, from Form 4797, line 8 .... **8.**
9. Subtract line 8 from line 7. If zero or less, enter -0- **9.** 0
10. Enter the amount of any gain from the sale/exchange of a partnership interest attributable to unrecaptured section 1250 gain .... **10.**
11. Enter the total AMT amount reported to you on a Schedule K-1, Form 1099-DIV or Form 2439 as "unrecaptured section gain" from an estate, trust, real estate investment trust, or mutual fund (or other regulated invest co) .... **11.**
12. Enter the total of any unrecaptured sect 1250 gain from sales (including installment sales) or other dispositions of section 1250 property held more than 1 year for which you did not make an entry in Form 4797 for the yr of sale .... **12.**
13. Add lines 9 through 12 .... **13.**
14. Enter the gain or (loss), if any, from the AMT Schedule D, line 15 .... **14.**
15. Enter the (loss), if any, from the AMT Schedule D, line 7. If zero or gain enter -0- **15.** 0
16. Combine lines 14 and 15. If result is zero or a gain, enter -0-. If result is a (loss), enter it as a positive amount **16.** 0
17. Subtract line 16 from line 13. If zero or less, enter -0-. Enter the result on Form 6251, page 2, line 38 .... **17.** 0

AMT Qualified 5-Year Gain Worksheet - Form 6251, Line 46

1. Enter the total of all gains that you reported on line 8, column (f), of Schedules D and D-1 from dispositions of property held more than 5 years. **Do not reduce these gains by any losses** **1.** 10,000
2. Enter the total of all gains from dispositions of property held more than 5 years from Form 4797, Part I, but **only** if Form 4797, line 7, is more than zero. **Do not reduce these gains by any losses** .... **2.**
3. Enter the total of all capital gains from dispositions of property held more than 5 years From Form 4684, line 4, but if Form 4684, line 15 is more than zero. **Do not reduce these gains by any losses** .... **3.**
4. Enter the total of all capital gains from dispositions of property held more than 5 years from Form 6252; Form 6781, Part II; and Form 8824. **Do not reduce these gains by any losses** .... **4.**
5. Enter the total of any qualified 5-year gain reported to you on:
   - Form 1099-DIV, box 2c;
   - Form 2439, box 1c; and
   - Schedule K-1 from a partnership, S corporation, estate, or trust (do not include gains from section 1231 property; take them into account on line 2 above, but **only** if Form 4797, line 7, is more than zero) .... **5.**
6. Add lines 1 through 5 .... **6.** 10,000
7. Enter the part, if any, on line 6 that is:
   - Attributable to 28% rate gain or
   - Included on line 6, 10, 11, or 12 of the Unrecaptured Sect 1250 Gain Wrk **7.** 10,000
8. **Qualified 5-Year Gain.** Subtract line 7 from line 6. Enter the result here and on Form 6251, line 46 .... **8.**

DAA

Regular tax on Page 2 Line 40 of Form 1040 for 2002 is $37,067. However, due to all of the preference items required in the AMT calculation on Form 6251, there is an AMT tax of $8177. This tax brings Nicholas's liability in line with that of other taxpayers who do not have these preference items.

CONCLUSION

Alternative minimum tax is a pervasive tax system developed to equalize tax liability among taxpayers, prevent abuse, and discourage overuse of preferential items. However, it has added to the proliferation of financial instruments developed to assist investors with economic and tax benefits not currently realized under this system.

NOTES

[1] The Jobs and Growth Tax Relief Reconciliation Act of 2003 changed the AMT exemption amount to 440,250 for single taxpayers from $35,750 previously. However, this is effective only for tax years beginning in 2003 and 2004.

[2] §179 allows a taxpayer to expense, instead of capitalize, up to $100,000 in 2002 and 2004 and 2005. The amounts will be indexed for inflation in 2004 and 2005. This expensing is for tangible personal property used in a trade or business.

[3] A deduction for a regular IRA is generally limited to $3000 or earned income, whichever is less. However, if a taxpayer has a qualified pension plan with his/her employer, then there may be a phase-out of this amount depending on the amount of income. Additionally, there is a catch-up rule for individuals age 50 and older where they may contribute an additional $500.

[4] Three-, five-, and seven-year property is depreciated using 200-percent declining balance, with a switch to straight line when straight line becomes larger. The 200 percent means twice the rate of recovery if a straight line system were being applied. The depreciation rate remains constant, and is applied to the cost of the asset, reduced by previous depreciation deductions. For example, the recovery percentage for the first year of 5-year property is 20 percent. MACRS uses a half-year convention, so that regardless of when the property was placed in service during the year, the taxpayer can get half a year of depreciation. (Note that in some cases, a midquarter convention may apply.) Therefore the depreciation calculation is $\frac{1}{2}$ of 40 percent in the first year. (Assuming a five-year recovery, straight line depreciation would amount to 20 percent per year.) 40 percent is double what a taxpayer would deduct if he were depreciating the property over five years using straight-line.

[5] Straight-line depreciation means the asset's cost is recovered evenly over the relevant time period. For five-year property, 10 percent of the cost is recovered in year one (assuming that a half-year convention applies) 20 percent in years two, three, four, and five, and finally 10 percent again in year six.

[6] Taxpayers can avoid making depreciation adjustments for AMT by using slower depreciation for regular tax purposes. For example, no adjustment would be necessary if a taxpayer uses the 150-percent declining balance method to depreciate personal property placed in service in 1998.

[7] See note 4, above. Appropriate conventions (half year or midquarter) apply.

[8] Declining balance depreciation reflects a multiple of the figure that would apply under a straight line calculation. (See the discussion of 200-percent declining balance, in note 1, above.) The depreciation rate stays constant, and is applied to the reduced book value each year. For example, for ten-year property, straight-line depreciation would amount to 10 percent per year, ignoring the midyear convention. 150-percent declining balance therefore uses a rate equal to 15 percent of the asset's cost, which figure drops to 7.5 percent if a half-year convention applies. Assuming an asset costs $100,000 with a 10-year class life, depreciation in the first year would be $7,500 [$100,000*.15*$\frac{1}{2}$; because of the half year convention]. In year two, $13,875 of depreciation would be claimed [(100,000 − 7,500)*.15]. Under the 150-percent declining balance method, the taxpayer switches to straight-line when that yields a higher allowance.

[9] This rule applies to "§1250 property." See the discussion in the note below.

[10] Depreciation that is not refigured for AMT includes

    i. Residential rental property placed in service after 1998.

    ii. Nonresidential real property with a class life of 27.5 years or more placed in service after 1998. This rule applies if the property is depreciated for regular tax purposes using the straight-line method.

    iii. Other §1250 property placed in service after 1998 that is depreciated for regular tax purposes using straight line.

    iv. Property (other than §1250 property) placed in service after 1998 that is depreciated for regular tax purposes using 150-percent declining balance or straight line.

    v. Property for which an election to use the ADS system was made, any part of the cost of any property for which a §179 election was made.

    vi. Motion picture films, videotapes, or sound recordings.

    vii. Property depreciated under the unit-of-production method or any other method not expressed in a term of years.

    viii. Qualified Indian reservation property.

Tax Code §56(a). §1250 property is depreciable real property that doesn't fall under §1245. It includes office buildings, warehouses, apartment complexes, and low-income housing. Nonresidential real estate, like an office building, put in service after 1980 and before 1987 is considered §1245 property, assuming accelerated depreciation was claimed.

[11] This rule applies to §1250 property. IRC §1250 property generally includes office buildings, warehouses, apartment complexes, and low-income housing. See note 9, above, for a fuller discussion.

[12] This rule does not apply to §1250 property.

[13] §617(a)(1)

[14] §616(d)

[15] §617(b)(1)(B)

[16] §617(c)

[17] §617(d)(1)

[18] 56(a)(2)(A)

[19] §56(a)(3)

[20] §1.460-4(b)(1)

[21] §1.460-4(b)(2)

[22] Facts were based on Example in Reg. §1.460-4(h).

[23] The latter exception applies only to construction contracts expected to be completed within two years. See §460(e)(1).

[24] §1.460-4(c)(2)

[25] Notice 87-61, 1987-2 C.B. 370

[26] §460(b)(2)

[27] §460(b) An election may be made not to apply the look-back method if the cumulative taxable income (or loss) is within 10 percent of the cumulative look-back taxable income (or loss).

[28] §169(d)

[29] §169(f)

[30] §169(g)

[31] §56(a)(5)

[32] This gain is subject to depreciation recapture, which is beyond the scope of this book.

[33] §163(h)(3)(B)

[34] §163(h)(3)(C)

[35] §163(d)(5) Interest limits are discussed in Chapter 4.

[36] §163(d)(4)

[37] §1.163(d)-1

[38] §141(a)(1) These bonds are discussed in greater detail later.

[39] §173(a)

[40] §1.173-1(a)(3)

[41] §1.173-1(c)(2)

[42] §59(e)(1)

[43] §1.174-2(a)

[44] §59(e)

[45] Under §56(b)(2)(D) there is an exception for the taxpayer who materially participates in an activity. In this case, the taxpayer may expense research and experimental expenses for AMT and regular tax purposes and does not have to make any adjustments.

[46] §Prop. Regs. §1.422§A-2(e)(2)(ii)

[47] §422 (b)

[48] §422(a)(1)

[49] §422(a)(2)

[50] §1.421-8(a)(I)(ii)

[51] §1.421-7(h)(2)

[52] §1.421-8(b)(1)

[53] §56(b)(3)

[54] §83(a)

[55] §1.83-7(a)

[56] §55(e)(4)

[57] Reg.1.56(g)-1(4)

[58] §56(g)(3)(B)

[59] §7702(g)(1)(B)

[60] Reg. §1.56(g)-1(c)(6)

[61] §56(g)(4)(c)(ii)(I) The dividend received deduction is discussed in Chapter 8.

[62] Reg. 1.56(g)-1(d)(3)

[63] §312(n)(2)(B)

[64] LIFO recapture is the excess of the amount of inventory calculated under the first-in, first-out (FIFO) method over the inventory calculated under the last-in, last-out method (LIFO).

[65] §56(g)(4)(D)

[66] §56(g)(4)(E)

[67] Reg. §1.56(g)-1(j)

[68] See Tax Code §611-613A.

[69] Reg. §1.56(g)-1(k)

[70] 46 USC §1101

[71] Reg. §1.611-1(a)(1)

[72] §613()

[73] §57(a)

[74] §57(a)(2)(A)

[75] §1202(a)(2)

[76] For full discussion of §1202 stock, see Chapter 7.

[77] §57(a)(7)

[78] See the discussion earlier, under "Overview of the Alternative Minimum Tax Calculation."

[79] §59(a)(1)(A)

[80] §59(a)(2)(b)

[81] §59(a)(4)(A)

[82] §38(c)(1)

[83] §38(c)(2) Special rules under this section also apply to the New York Liberty Zone Business Employee Credit.

[84] §53(c)

EVALUATING 6 INVESTMENT OPPORTUNITIES[1]

INTRODUCTION

There are many considerations that can factor into a decision about where or how to invest money. For example, risk is an obvious concern, and investors study statistics or other information relating to variability in gauging the safety of a potential investment. Liquidity also must be considered; an investor who anticipates a need for cash in the near future cannot afford to lock funds into a long-term investment that carries substantial penalties for premature liquidation. Persons with particular religious beliefs may be uncomfortable investing in defense industries, and environmentalists will be unwilling to buy stock or bonds of companies seen as heavy polluters. Obviously, though, the primary goal for every investor is to maximize after-tax profit.

Example—Theresa has $10,000 that she plans to invest for ten years. She can buy tax-free City of Trobert municipal bonds that will pay annual interest at a rate of 5 percent. Alternatively, Theresa, who is in a 30-percent tax bracket, can earn 7.2 percent annually by purchasing corporate bonds issued by Thuman Company. Both of these acquisitions would be funded with after-tax dollars, meaning Theresa is using salary or other moneys on which she has already paid tax. Interest on the Thuman bonds would be taxed currently, so that compounding would be limited to after-tax proceeds, assuming Theresa can reinvest the interest left after paying her tax each year. However, since the Trobert bonds are tax-free, an investment in them could grow at the full 5-percent rate annually, without reduction for taxes.

A third choice for Theresa would be a tax-deferred investment, like an annuity. This also would be funded with after-tax moneys, but Theresa's return, or profit, would not be taxed until the annuity is cashed out. This means the proceeds will be taxed at whatever Theresa's marginal rate is in the year(s) they are received.[2] Finally, Theresa might be able to make an investment on a before-tax basis, such as by making an elective contribution to a pension plan.

Assuming all of these options are comparable to Theresa in terms of risk, her expected liquidity needs over the next 10 years, and any other concerns that influence her investment decisions, she will pick the choice that represents the highest yield, after taking taxes into consideration. This means Theresa needs to be able to calculate the after-tax profit and rate of return for each possible investment option. The formulae presented in this chapter can be used for that purpose. However, these formulae do not take into account transaction costs, which also must be considered. In addition, the models assume after-tax earnings from the holdings are reinvested at the same rate of return as the underlying investment being evaluated. This means an investor who extracts the earnings from his or her holding each year and uses those funds for other purposes will have a lower profit and growth rate than the formulae predict.

One other point should be made in connection with this chapter. In using these models to choose among investment options, Theresa will have to make assumptions, the accuracy of which will affect her conclusions. For example, if Theresa chooses a tax-deferred investment, her ultimate after-tax proceeds will be dependent on her marginal rate in the year(s) the moneys are received. In other words, Theresa will need to estimate what her income level is likely to be, in order to determine what bracket she would be in, and she also will need to anticipate future changes to the Internal Revenue Code, including tax rate revisions, that could impact the tax consequences of her investment.

The need to make assumptions and estimates introduces a degree of uncertainty into the formulae and models discussed here. Calculations used to compare potential investment options can lead to inaccurate conclusions, where numbers are based on assumptions that later prove to be wrong. Nearly all, if not all, decisions investors make, however, are premised on beliefs as to how potential investment choices will perform in the future. The results of the calculations found in this chapter are no different, in that they also are dependent on an investor's ability to predict future events. What all of this means is that using models or formulae to make investment decisions should not lead to overconfidence. The results of these calculations can provide useful information. However, they should not necessarily be viewed as a guarantee that an investor's choice represents the most profitable decision that could have been made.

USING BEFORE-TAX OR AFTER-TAX DOLLARS

In most cases, after-tax dollars are used to make investments. A pretax elective contribution to a Keogh plan (for self-employed taxpayers), 401(k) plan (also known as a cash or deferred arrangement), 403(b) plan (for employees of educational institutions and certain tax-exempt organizations), or a deductible IRA would be examples of investments using before-tax moneys. A simple equation can be used to describe the relationship between before-tax and after-tax funds:

$I_A = I_B * (1 - T_0)$ where

I_A represents the after-tax dollars invested;
I_B stands for before-tax dollars; and
T_0 is the tax rate in year 0, the year the investment is made.

Example—Pauline's marginal tax rate is 40 percent. In 2003, she can elect to contribute up to $12,000 of before-tax funds to a §401(k) plan maintained by her employer. Alternatively, Pauline could decide to take the money as taxable salary and invest the after-tax proceeds in bonds issued by Lorenz Company. If Pauline chooses this second option, she will have $7200 to invest ($12,000, before-tax dollars, * {1 −.4} = $7200). If the minimum amount Pauline can invest in Lorenz Company bonds is $12,000, she will need $20,000 in pretax funds in order to have the required $12,000 remaining after her taxes are paid ($12,000/(1 −.4) = $20,000).

INVESTMENT TAXED CURRENTLY

An investment taxed currently is one where the income must be reported to the IRS each year. This could include stocks that are expected to pay dividends at least annually, bonds issued by corporations, and interest on certificates of deposit or commercial paper. Interest on most obligations of the U.S. government is subject to federal income tax, but in many cases state or municipal bonds are tax-free. This means a potential investment in bonds issued by the state of Maryland, for example, would be analyzed for federal tax purposes using the exempt model rather than the formula presented here.[3]

Assuming after-tax dollars are being used initially to fund the investment, profit where earnings are taxed currently can be calculated using the following formula:

Profit, after tax = $I_A [(1+R) - (R*T)]^n - I_A$ where

I_A stands for after-tax dollars invested;
R is the before-tax rate of return on the investment;
T represents the tax rate assumed to be applicable throughout the investment horizon; and
n is the number of periods for which the investment will be outstanding.

Ignoring the effect of taxes for the moment, the accumulation that will result when moneys are invested at a specific rate, compounded over a number of periods, is equal to the initial amount of funds put in the investment multiplied by the quantity (1 + the rate of return) raised to a power equal to the number of periods the investment is outstanding $\{(1+R)^n\}$. In other words, if a $10,000 investment pays 5 percent, compounded annually, over six years, an investor can expect to receive a total of $13,401 at the end of the sixth year $\{(1.05)^6 = 1.340096 * \$10,000 = \$13,401\}$. When the earnings on an investment are subject to current taxation, the rate of return must be reduced by the taxes expected to be paid each year. This is captured in the formula above by reducing the return by the product of the return rate times the tax rate (R*T). The overall result then is reduced by the amount of the initial investment (I_A) in order to calculate the actual profit net of tax.

Example—Lillian plans on investing $50,000 in Marfurt Company preferred stock for four years. Lillian's dividend tax rate is estimated to be 15 percent throughout this period. The stock is expected to pay annual dividends of 9 percent, which Lillian plans to reinvest in additional Marfurt Company shares. Using the formula above to calculate Lillian's earnings at the end of the four years, she anticipates total profits of $17,147:

$50,000 $[(1+.09) - (.09*.15)]^4$ - $50,000 =
$50,000 $[1.0765]^4$ - $50,000 =
($50,000 * 1.34294) - $50,000 =
$17,147.

Determining a rate of return would be helpful for Lillian to use in comparing potential investment opportunities. In the case of an investment where earnings are taxed currently, the rate of return, here called growth, can be expressed as g in the following formula:

$$I_A [(1+R) - (R*T)]^n = I_A (1+g)^n$$
Simplifying, $(1+R) - (R*T) = 1+g$
$1 + R(1-T) = 1+g$
$R(1-T) = g$ where

R again is the before-tax rate of return;
T is the tax rate applicable throughout the investment horizon; and
g is the growth rate Lillian will use for comparison purposes. In the example above, Lillian's growth rate computes to 7.65 percent $\{.09*(1-.15)\}$.

Note that this model assumes a constant rate of tax and the same before-tax rate of return throughout the investment horizon. If either of these numbers is expected to change, the calculations become more complicated. First, the investor determines his or her total after-tax accumulation, and using that number, then derives the rate of growth.

Example—Continuing with the facts above, Lillian again plans on buying Marfurt Company preferred shares. However, she anticipates that her tax rate in the last year of the investment will increase to 35 percent. This means the total amount Lillian can expect to have accumulated after four years is determined as follows:

Accumulation after three years = $50,000 $[(1+.09) - (.09*.15)]^3 =$ $62,375
Accumulation after the final year = $62,375$[(1+.09) - (.09*.35)]^1 =$ $66,024

This means Lillian's total accumulation will be $66,024, which leaves a profit of $16,024.

Solving for a growth rate yields the following calculation:

$$\$66,024 = \$50,000(1+g)^4$$
$1.32048 = (1+g)^4$
$1.071970803 = 1+g$ and therefore
$g = 7.20\%$

This means Lillian can expect an overall after-tax earnings rate of 7.20 percent on her Marfurt holdings, assuming her dividend tax rate rises from 15 percent to 35 percent in the last year of her investment.[4]

TAX-EXEMPT INVESTMENT

Analysis of tax-exempt investments is easier because the complicating factors introduced in order to take into account the effect of taxes are no longer present. Again assuming investment of after-tax dollars, and based on the previous discussion, the profit from tax-free holdings can be calculated as follows:

$$\text{Profit} = I_A (1+R)^n - I_A \text{ where}$$

I_A stands for after-tax dollars invested;
R is the before-tax rate of return on the investment; and
n is the number of periods for which the investment will be outstanding.

For comparison purposes, "profit," as used in this equation, corresponds to the "profit after tax" result of the formula used when analyzing investment earnings that are subject to current taxation. The before-tax rate of return, symbolized by "R" in both calculations, is not reduced by the tax rate in the exempt model.

Example—Delores plans on investing $50,000 until her retirement in three years, when she intends to use the proceeds to buy a small vacation cottage. Delores can buy taxable bonds issued by Witnauer Company, which will pay 9 percent annually. Alternatively, by buying tax-free City of Clarence bonds, Delores can earn 6.4 percent. If Delores' marginal tax rate is 40 percent, she will have additional earnings by buying the tax-free bonds. This is because her profit on the Clarence investment is $10,228 [$50,000*(1.064)^3 - $50,000]$. By comparison, she will earn only $8545 with the Witnauer instruments $\{50,000*[(1+.09) - (.09*.4)]^3 - \$50,000\}$. However, if Delores' tax rate is only 26 percent, she is better off with the taxable bonds. This is because her after-tax profit on the Witnauer obligations would amount to $10,670 $\{\$50,000[(1+.09)-(.09*.26)]^3 - \$50,000\}$, which is $442 more than she would earn by holding the Clarence bonds.

For an investment where earnings are taxed currently, the formula "$R(1-T) = g$" was used to compute a growth rate for comparison purposes.[5] In the context of a tax-free investment, "T," the tax rate applicable throughout the investment horizon is set equal to 0. This means the growth rate ("g") is equal to the before-tax rate of return ("R").

Example—Continuing with the facts above, the growth rate of Delores' taxable Witnauer investment is 5.4 percent, assuming a 40-percent marginal tax rate $\{g = .09*(1-.4)\}$. If Delores is in a 26-percent tax bracket, her growth rate on the taxable bonds is 6.67 percent. The growth rate of the tax-free Clarence investment is simply the before-tax rate of return, or 6.4 percent in this example. These numbers show that the tax-free investment is more attractive to Delores when she is in a 40-percent tax bracket, while the Witnauer bonds are better if Delores' marginal tax rate is 26 percent. To find the rate of return at which the two investments are equal, Delores uses the following calculation:

$$R^t(1-T) = R^{tf} \text{ where}$$

R^t is the rate of return on the taxable investment;
R^{tf} represents the return on the tax-free obligations; and
T is the investor's marginal tax rate.

If Delores' marginal tax rate is 30 percent, the taxable Witnauer investment paying 9 percent will be equivalent to tax-free bonds paying 6.3 percent annually $[.09*(1- 0.3) = 6.3$ percent]. As expected, the lower Delores' marginal tax rate, the more interest tax-free bonds have to pay in order to be equivalent to her after-tax rate of return on a taxable investment.

As noted above, the calculations become more complicated if changes are expected over the life of the holding.

Example—Gert, whose dividend tax rate is 15 percent, is considering two possible investments for a four-year period. She could buy taxable Baker Company preferred shares, which are expected to pay 8 percent annually for the first two years and 9 percent thereafter. The other option is tax-free bonds issued by the City of Swormville. The Swormville bonds, which mature in four years, pay 5.5 percent annual interest. In both cases, Gert expects to reinvest her profit, after she pays any associated tax, at the same (taxable or tax-free) rate of return. She plans to fund the investment with $10,000 initially.

If Gert buys the Swormville obligations, she will earn a profit of $2388 $[\$10,000(1+.055)^4 - \$10,000]$ and her growth rate, "g" is equal to 5.5 percent. For the Baker investment, Gert makes the following calculations:

Accumulation after the first two years—$\$10,000[(1+.08) - (.08*.15)]^2 = \$11,406$

Accumulation after final two years—$11,406[(1+.09) − (.09*.15)]^2 = $13,218

This means Gert expects an after-tax profit from holding the Baker Company preferred stock of $3218 ($13,218, total amount received after four years, less $10,000 initial investment). Her growth rate for Baker is 7.22 percent [$13,218 = $10,000(1+g)^4]. Assuming the two choices are otherwise comparable for Gert, an investment in the Baker preferred stock is more attractive because it will generate a higher yield.

INVESTMENTS WITH TAX-DEFERRED EARNINGS

A tax-deferred investment is one where the profits are subject to tax but not until the end, when the investor liquidates the investment. Examples of tax-deferred investments include annuities, as mentioned previously, and also capital assets, the appreciation on which is not taxed until a sale or exchange. Tax-deferred investments are acquired with after-tax dollars, like the tax-free and currently taxed investment options discussed previously. However, these opportunities offer a middle ground between the tax-exempt return of a municipal bond, for example, and the currently taxed return generated by a corporate debt instrument or dividend-paying stock.

The following formula can be used to calculate the after-tax profit expected from a deferred investment:

Profit after-tax = $I_A[(1+R)^n − 1](1-T_f)$ where

I_A is the initial investment of after-tax dollars;
R represents the before-tax rate of return;
n is the number of periods the investment is outstanding; and
T_f is the tax rate in the year the deferred investment is liquidated and subject to tax.

The phrase "$I_A(1+R)^n$" describes the total amount of moneys expected to be received when an initial investment of after-tax dollars (I_A) is allowed to grow at a specified before-tax rate of return ("R") for some number of compounding periods ("n"). This amount must be reduced by the initial investment, I_A, in order to reflect the actual profit. The number that results is then multiplied by one less the investor's marginal tax rate in the year of liquidation (1-T_f) in order to determine the funds actually available to the investor after taxes are paid.

Example—Jane buys stock in Fastco. The Fastco shares are not expected to generate dividends, but Jane estimates the stock will appreciate by 7 percent each year. Jane plans on holding the Fastco stock for five years. Her after-tax profit, assuming the shares cost $60,000 initially and Jane pays a tax on long-term capital gain of 18 percent in the year of liquidation, is $19,805 {$60,000*[(1+.07)^5 - 1](1-.18)}. If instead of the stock Jane held an asset not eligible for capital gain treatment, and assuming Jane's marginal tax rate for ordinary income is 35 percent, her after-tax profit would amount to $15,700 {$60,000*[(1+.07)^5 - 1]*(1-.35)}. This means Jane saves $4105 in deferred tax due to the capital gain treatment.

Where an investor cannot use capital gain reporting in connection with a deferred investment, it is possible a higher-than-expected marginal tax rate will apply. This can occur if the appreciation arising over the entire period when the investment was held is reported in only one tax year. This may push the taxpayer into a higher tax bracket.

To calculate the growth rate, so that Jane can compare her Fastco shares to other potential investments, she needs the total accumulation, meaning the entire amount of money she will have when the investment is liquidated and her taxes are paid. This is captured in the left side of the following equation:

$$I_A[(1+R)^n - 1](1-T_f) + I_A = I_A(1+g)^n$$

Simplifying leads to the following:

$$I_A\{1[(1+R)^n - 1](1-T_f) + 1\} = I_A(1+g)^n$$
$$[(1+R)^n - 1](1-T_f) + 1 = (1+g)^n$$
$$(1+R)^n - 1 - T_f(1+R)^n + T_f + 1 = (1+g)^n$$
$$(1+R)^n - T_f(1+R)^n + T_f = (1+g)^n$$

leading to

$$(1+R)^n(1-T_f) + T_f = [1+g]^n$$

R stands for the before-tax return on the investment;
T_f is the tax rate in the final year, when the investment is liquidated;
n is the number of periods the investment is held; and
g represents the rate of growth.

In the first situation involving Jane, where she invests in the Fastco stock that is expected to grow in value at a rate of 7 percent annually, using the calculation above yields a growth rate of 5.87% [(1+.07)^5

$(1-.18)+.18 = (1+g)^5$]. This presumes Jane will be taxed at an 18-percent capital gain rate when she sells the Fastco shares. If instead the gain is not eligible for long-term capital gain treatment and is therefore taxed at an assumed ordinary income rate of 35 percent, Jane's growth rate will be 4.76 percent $[(1+.07)^5(1-.35)+.35] = (1+g)^5$].

As seen earlier, it is possible the investment return is expected to vary over the period during which the asset is held. Again, this introduces an additional complication into the calculations.

Example—Kenny holds stock in Information, Inc., which he bought for $25,000. He expects the shares will grow in value by 10 percent for the first three years of his investment and 12 percent thereafter. Information, Inc. stock historically has not paid dividends. To determine his after-tax profit, if he sells the shares as planned in 10 years, Kenny will use the following calculations:

Accumulation after three years = $I_A(1+R)^n$ where

I_A is the initial after-tax investment;
R represents the before-tax rate of return; and
n is the number of periods the investment is outstanding. A before-tax ("R") rate of return is used because Kenny's investment is not taxed until he sells the shares, in 10 years.

Using this formula, Kenny can expect to have accumulated $33,275 after three years [$25,000(1+.1)^3$]. In seven more years, now at a 12-percent return, Kenny's Information, Inc. shares will have grown in value to $73,560 [$33,275(1+.12)^7$]. Subtracting off his initial after-tax investment of $25,000, Kenny will report a profit of $48,560 when he sells his Information shares. Assuming a 20-percent long-term capital gain tax rate, this means Kenny will pay $9712 in taxes, keeping $63,848 ($73,560 − $9712) from the proceeds. His after-tax profits are $38,848 ($48,560 − $9712) and Kenny's growth rate works out to be 9.83 percent [$63,848 = $25,000(1+g)^{10}$].

INVESTING WITH BEFORE-TAX DOLLARS

The treatment of a before-tax dollars investment is similar to a tax-deferred program. This is because in both cases, the investor is not taxed until the end, when the investment is liquidated. However, unlike the tax-deferred situation, a taxpayer who invests before-tax dollars must report the entire accumulation when the investment ends, and not just his profit. For example, assume an employee elects to make a $10,000 before-tax contribution to the retirement plan in which she participates at work. The contribution grows at a rate of 7.5 percent annually until the employee retires 10 years later. The employee will be taxed on the entire $20,610 [$10,000(1+.075)^{10}], even though this figure represents not only the growth on the contribution but also the initial $10,000 the employee put into the program. This is because the employee is using moneys not previously taxed to fund the investment.

The following formula permits an investor to calculate the profit, net of tax, on a before-tax investment:

$I_B(1+R)^n(1-T_f)$ where

I_B represents the before-tax dollars invested (As discussed above, $I_B = I_A/(1-T_0)$ where T_0 is the tax rate in the year the investment is made.);
R is the before-tax rate of return;
n stands for the number of periods the investment is outstanding; and
T_f is the tax rate in the year the investment is liquidated.

Looking at this formula more closely, $I_B(1+R)^n$ represents the amount of money that will have accumulated at the end of n investment periods, assuming a rate of return equal to R. The quantity is multiplied by $(1-T_f)$, to reflect the tax that must be paid on the entire accumulation, not just the profit, at liquidation. This is because before-tax dollars (I_B) are being used to fund the investment.

Example—John's employer contributes $10,000 in the current year to a pension plan on John's behalf. The plan is qualified under the Tax Code, meaning John does not recognize the $10,000 in current-year income. John expects to retire in 15 years, at which time he believes he is likely to be taxed at a 25-percent rate. The retirement plan in which John participates is a defined contribution program, and he anticipates the funds will earn 8 percent, annually. This means John can expect a profit of $23,791. The funds will grow to a total value of $31,722 [$10,000(1+.08)^{15}]. John will report all of this money as income, meaning he will have $23,791 remaining [(1-.25)*$31,722] after he pays his taxes.

Assuming that John's employer contributes the $10,000 to a §401(k) plan, John has the option of taking the cash up-front instead of receiving a retirement plan contribution. If John's current tax bracket is 30 percent, this would leave him $7000 to invest. In order for John to match his after-tax profits under the §401(k) program, he would have to earn 14.83 percent ("R"), annually if he put the $7000 in an investment, the earnings of which are subject to current taxation at a 30-percent marginal rate:

Profit, after tax $= I_A[(1+R) - (R*T)]^n - I_A$
$23,791 = $7,000[(1+R)-(R*.3)]^{15} - $7,000$
$30,791/$7,000 = [(1+R)-(R*.3)]^{15}$
$1.103794901 = 1+R-.3R$
$R = 14.83$ percent

If instead John invested the $7000 of after-tax moneys in a deferred investment, he would have to earn at least 12.08 percent, as shown:

Profit after-tax $= I_A[(1+R)^n - 1](1-T_f)$
$23,791 = $7000[(1+R)^{15} -1](1-.25)$
$5.531619048 = (1+R)15$
$R = 12.08$ percent

This calculation assumes John is taxed at a 25-percent rate in 15 years, when the investment is liquidated.

To calculate the growth rate, "g," for a before-tax investment, the following formula is used:

$[(1+R)^n + 1/(1-T_f)]^{1/n} = 1+g$ where

R is the rate of return on a before-tax basis;
n is the number of periods the investment remains outstanding; and
T_f represents the tax rate in the final year, when the investment is liquidated.[6]

Example—Linda is eligible to make a deductible contribution of $3000 to an individual retirement account. The IRA is expected to earn 5 percent per year, and Linda is planning on retiring in 20 years. She estimates her marginal tax rate at that time will be about 20 percent. If Linda does make the IRA contribution, she can expect a growth rate of 7.05 percent $[(1+.05)^{20} + 1/(1-.20)]^{1/20} = 1+g]$. However, if Linda withdraws the money from the IRA early and incurs a 10-percent penalty as a result, her growth rate will be smaller. This is because the penalty will have the effect of increasing the tax rate Linda pays on the IRA funds.

Assume that Linda is considering other possible investment vehicles for her funds. She believes that before retiring she will be taxed at a consistent 25-percent rate. Instead of the IRA, Linda could make an investment using the money remaining after she pays tax on the $3,000. If she chooses that option, Linda plans on buying bonds issued by D'Youville Corporation, paying interest at 8.5 percent. A third possibility would be for Linda to buy stock in International, Inc. International typically does not pay dividends, but the shares have been appreciating in value consistently at about 7 percent.

If Linda puts the money in the IRA, she will have an after-tax profit, at the end of 20 years, of $6368 [$3000(1+.05)^{20} (1−.20)]. If she buys the D'Youville bonds, Linda will accumulate a total of $5494 {$2250[(1+.085)−(.085*−.25)]^{20} −$2250}. This calculation presumes that Linda invests $2250, which is what remains of the $3000 after Linda is taxed at a 25-percent rate. If $2250 were invested in the International shares, Linda would calculate her results using the deferred formula {$2,250[(1+.07)^{20} − 1](1−.2)}, yielding an after-tax profit of $5165, assuming a 20% capital gain rate. These numbers suggest that Linda should put her funds in the deductible IRA. However, if she needs to access the money prematurely and penalties become a consideration, the D'Youville bonds make better sense under Linda's specific facts. That is because her after-tax profit with the IRA, when the 10-percent penalty[7] applies {$4928 = [$3000(1+.05)^{19}(1−.35)]}, is less than her expected earnings from the D'Youville holdings ($5030), assuming in both cases that Linda liquidates the investment after 19 years.

TAX PLANNING CAUTIONS

A word of caution must be raised in connection with the formulae discussed in this chapter. Many of the calculations rely on tax rates as the method of predicting the tax impact of potential investments. However, this analysis may be too simple in that it may fail to reflect an investor's unique tax situation.

For example, assume an investor buys corporate bonds. Her AGI will increase by the amount of taxable interest she reports each year (assuming she has no deductible expenses associated with the obligations). This means any itemized deductions the investor claims that are subject to an AGI floor, like medical expenses or miscellaneous itemized deductions, will be reduced. In other words, if the investor reports additional interest income of $4500 each year, for example, because of an investment in taxable bonds, her deductible medical expenses will drop by $337.50 annually. This is because medical expenses are reduced by 7.5 percent of AGI, and the investor's AGI in each year of the investment has increased by the $4500 of interest income she receives.

Additional income also can trigger other, unexpected consequences. For example, if the same investor holds Series EE bonds that she cashes out to pay for the qualifying educational expenses of a dependent grandchild, the additional interest income may trigger a reduction in the EE bond interest exclusion she otherwise would enjoy.[8] To fully capture the different tax consequences of various investment choices, an investor should prepare his tax return both with and without the potential investment income and then compare the results.

NOTES

[1] The authors gratefully acknowledge the contributions of Rita A. Hibschweiler, Ph.D., Department of Mathematics, University of New Hampshire, Durham, New Hampshire, to the material contained in this chapter.

[2] Annuities that are paid out over a period of years or over the annuitant's life expectancy are reported under the rules found at Tax Code §72. Under these rules, a portion of each payment received is treated as a recovery of cost, and therefore is tax-free. The remainder of the payment must be reported as income. Once cost is completely recovered, all payments received are taxable. See IRS Publication 575, *Pension and Annuity Income* (2002) for a further discussion of these rules.

[3] Some tax-exempt bonds may trigger an alternative minimum tax liability. See the discussion of A.M.T. in Chapter 5 of this book.

[4] Calculators and software programs may permit users to take a specified root of a number. Where these tools are not available, the calculation can be done using the y^x key on a calculator. For example, when taking the 5th root of 1.3224, raise the quantity 1.3224 to the "[⅕]" (or ".20") power. This will yield the result given above.

[5] Recall the calculation became more complicated if the rate of return or rate of tax changed while the investment was outstanding.

[6] The formula is derived by setting the total accumulation at the end of the investment equal to the growth rate, taking into account taxes:

$I_B(1+R)^n(1-T_f) + I_B = I_B(1+g)^n(1-T_f)$. The factor "$(1-T_f)$" appears on the right side of the equation because the accumulation is taxed at the end of the investment horizon. Simplifying:

$(1+R)^n(1-T_f) + 1 = (1+g)^n(1-T_f)$
$(1+R)^n + 1/(1-T_f) = (1+g)^n$ and finally
$[(1+R)^n + 1/(1-T_f)]^{1/n} = 1+g$

[7] Tax Code §72(t)
[8] See Tax Code §135

7 SPECIAL ISSUES FOR CORPORATE INVESTORS

INTRODUCTION

In certain circumstances, a closely held C corporation may owe a tax called the personal holding company tax. This is a tax imposed only on C corporations because their shareholders do not pay personal income taxes on undistributed corporate income. This tax arises in three distinctly different situations.

The first situation is when a corporation has large amounts of investment income. Often, corporations are formed for the sole purpose of holding investments. The idea is to hold the earnings within the corporation and have it taxed at corporate versus individual rates. The second situation that generates this tax is when income is attributable to personal services provided by the shareholders who own at least 25 percent of the stock of the company under contracts with third parties. Finally, the personal holding company tax applies to corporations who hold property for their shareholders' use.

Often, there is not a deliberate formation of a personal holding corporation. A company may inadvertently become one through an evolutionary process. After a corporation has been in existence for many years, the owner begins planning for retirement. The assets of the business, including customer lists, intangibles, etc., may be sold over a period of time. While this process is taking place, a corporation may unknowingly find itself subject to the personal holding company tax. Normal operating income may be declining while investment income, earned by the proceeds from the sale of assets, is increasing.

Conversely, when a corporation is formed to hold investments of the shareholders, it may unknowingly fail to distribute adequate amounts of income to those investors and become liable for the personal holding company tax.

Another pitfall facing C corporations is the accumulated earnings tax. This is a tax, in addition to the income tax, that must be paid when a corporation retains its earnings beyond the normal operating requirements of the business. This chapter will explore the circumstances under which a company finds itself subject to the personal holding company tax and the accumulated earnings tax.

PERSONAL HOLDING COMPANY

A personal holding company is any corporation that meets both the stock ownership test and the income test. Since both of these taxes can be precipitated by excessive investment holdings, corporate taxpayers need to ensure that their investment strategies will not trigger either of these potentially punitive liabilities.

Stock Ownership Test

Stock ownership is met when, at any time during the last half of the taxable year, more than 50 percent of the outstanding stock is owned, directly or indirectly, by no more than five individuals.[1] Indirectly means that constructive ownership rules apply in addition to actual ownership. These provisions, also referred to as attribution rules, apply to the stock ownership test only; constructive ownership rules apply to the personal holding company income test.[2] The constructive ownership rules for the stockholding test are:

1. Stock owned, directly or indirectly, by or for a corporation, partnership, estate, or trust is considered as being owned proportionately by its shareholders, partners, or beneficiaries.[3]

    Example: The Cracon Partnership owns 40 percent of the stock of Great Snow Co. Chris, who holds a 50 percent interest in Cracon, is treated as owning 20 percent (40 percent X 50 percent) of the Great Snow stock.

    In the case of a trust, a present or future beneficiary's proportionate share of stock owned by the trust is determined actuarially. Both present and future interests are attributed.[4] In the case of an estate, only present interests owned by the beneficiaries are attributed.[5]

2. Stock owned, directly or indirectly, by or for a family member or partner is attributed to a taxpayer. Family includes siblings (whole or half blood and adopted), spouse, ancestors, and lineal descendants.[6]

   Example—Hook's Co. has 20 shareholders. Two shareholders, Fred and Bob, are brothers, each owning 20 percent of the stock. The other 12 shareholders each own 5 percent. Hook's meets the stock ownership test because Fred is treated as owning Bob's stock.

Fred—Direct ownership	20%
Fred—Indirect ownership (through Bob)	20%
3 other shareholders (5% * 3)	15%
Total	55%

   Since more than 50 percent of the stock is owned by five individuals, the stock ownership test is met.

3. If a person has an option to acquire stock, such stock is treated as being owned by the person for purposes of determining stock ownership.[7] This rule will apply only if the effect is to make the corporation a personal holding company.[8] Additionally, the option rule overrides the family and partner attribution rules.[9]

4. Reattribution is allowed for shares attributed from an entity to an owner or beneficiary. However, reattribution is not allowed for shares owned due to attribution from a relative or partner.[10]

   Example—Gary owns 25 percent of the stock of Baseball Bats Inc. His sister, Annette, is treated as owning this stock under the attribution rules. That stock cannot be reattributed to Annette's daughter because Annette owns it only by family attribution.

5. Convertible securities are treated as stock only if the effect is to make the corporation a personal holding company.[11]

Income Ownership Test

The income ownership requirement is met when 60 percent or more of the corporation's adjusted ordinary gross income is personal holding company income. Personal holding company income includes the following eight categories:

1. Dividends, interest, royalties, and annuities. This does not include interest that constitutes rents (see explanation below), interest on reserve accounts under provisions of the Merchant Marine Act, and certain amounts received by a broker or dealer in connection with inventory of securities held as property, margin accounts, or secured financing for a customer.[12] Active business computer software royalties received by a corporation during the taxable year in connection with the licensing of computer software within the active conduct of the business of developing, manufacturing, or producing the software is excluded from personal holding income.[13]

2. Rents. However, rents will not be considered personal holding company income if it meets a two-part test. First, the adjusted income from rents must equal 50 percent or more of the adjusted ordinary gross income. Second, the dividend distributions for the taxable year must be, at a minimum, equal to the corporation's personal holding company income reduced by 10 percent of its ordinary gross income.

   Example—Adam and Yevonne own all of the stock of Live Well, Inc. The company, which paid no dividends during the year, has the following results:

Rental Income		$100,000
Operating profit from sales		45,000
Dividends		10,000
Interest		8,000
Gross income		$163,000
Less:		
Depreciation	$10,000	
Mortgage interest	20,000	
Real estate taxes	6,000	
Total allowable expenses		(36,000)
Adjusted ordinary gross income (see explanation below)		$127,000

Since it has only two shareholders, Live Well meets the stock ownership test described earlier. This means it will be treated as a personal holding company if 60 percent or more of its adjusted ordinary gross income is personal holding company income. Consequently, it is in the corporation's best interests to try to minimize the amount of its income characterized as personal holding company funds. Live Well will be able to exclude rent from its personal holding company income total if it meets both parts of the test described above. The calculations are as follows:

Test 1— 50% of adjusted ordinary gross income

Rental income	$100,000
Less allowable expenses	(36,000)
Adjusted income from rents	$ 64,000
50% of adjusted ordinary gross income ($127,000 X .50)	$ 63,500
Test 1 satisfied	

Test 2— 10% of ordinary gross income

Dividends	$10,000
Interest	8,000
Total portfolio income	18,000
Less 10% of ordinary gross income (.10 X $163,000)	16,300
Minimum required distributions	$ 1,700
Dividends paid	-0-
Test 2 not satisfied.	

Although Live Well passed the first test, it failed the second. This means the company must include its adjusted income from rent in its personal holding company income. Live Well's total personal holding company income is $82,000 (Dividends of $10,000 + interest ($8000) + adjusted income from rent amounting to $64,000). Since this number exceeds 60 percent of the corporation's adjusted ordinary gross income (60 percent X $127,000 = $76,200), Live Well is a personal holding company. The corporation must file a Schedule PH with its Form 1120 tax return to calculate the amount of personal holding company tax, if any, that it owes.

3. Mineral, oil, and gas royalties are usually personal holding company income. They may be excluded if all of the following is met:
   • They constitute 50 percent or more of the adjusted ordinary gross income;
   • Personal holding company income for the taxable year is not more than 10 percent of the ordinary gross income;
   • Business deductions (excluding shareholder compensation) for these royalties must equal or exceed 15 percent of the adjusted ordinary gross income.[14]

   Example—Bio-mine, Inc. received mineral royalties of $350,000 and $50,000 in dividends. Expenses allocable to the royalties total

$60,000, of which $20,000 was operating expenses. Bio-mine's ordinary gross income is $400,000. However, royalty income is greater than 50 percent of the adjusted ordinary gross income, satisfying the first test. Dividend income is greater than 10 percent of $400,000 = $40,000. Because dividends are greater than 10 percent of the ordinary gross income, the second test failed. Consequently, all of the royalties must be included as personal holding income. Additionally, the third test also failed. Operating expenses of $20,000 are less than 15 percent of the adjusted ordinary gross income of $360,000 ($54,000).

4. Copyright royalties are normally personal holding company income except when a corporation meets each of the following:
   • Royalties that constitute 50 percent or more of the ordinary gross income (not including works created by any shareholder);
   • Corporation's other personal holding income does not exceed 10 percent of its ordinary gross income. Copyright royalties are excluded in this computation, but royalties received for works created by any shareholder owning actually or constructively more than 10 percent of the total outstanding capital stock of the corporation are included.[15] Additionally, adjusted income from rents and from mineral, oil, and gas royalties are included in this purpose even if they would be excluded under the rules applicable to their own categories of income.[16] Finally, the corporation, in certain cases, excludes dividends received from certain corporations in which it owns at least 50 percent of the total value of all classes of the stock.[17]
   • Trade or business deductions allocable to these royalties other than deductions for compensation for personal services rendered by the shareholders, deductions for royalties paid or accrued, and for amortization, must be at least 25 percent of the corporation's ordinary gross income.[18]

5. Produced film rents must be 50 percent or more of the corporation's ordinary gross income to be excluded from personal holding company income.[19]

6. Shareholder rentals that constitute income from use of corporate property by a shareholder owning 25 percent or more of the value of the outstanding stock of the corporation is personal holding company income.[20]

7. Personal service contract income occurs when the corporation enters into a contract that designates who specifically will perform the service. The person providing the service must own at least 25 percent of the value of the corporation's stock at some time during the year.[21]

8. Income from estates and trusts. Funds received by a corporation that represent its share of estate or trust income, as a beneficiary, is personal holding company income.[22]

EXEMPT CORPORATIONS

Certain corporations are exempt from personal holding company status. They are:

- Tax-exempt corporations;
- Banks;
- Life insurance companies;
- Surety companies;
- Foreign personal holding companies;
- Lending or finance companies where 60 percent or more of its ordinary gross income is derived from the active business of lending;
- Foreign corporations owned by nonresident aliens;
- Small business investments companies licensed by the Small Business Administration; and
- Passive foreign investment companies.[23]

Additionally, S corporations. by their nature of having income taxed to the individual shareholders, are also exempt.

PERSONAL HOLDING COMPANY TAX

Personal holding company tax applies to C corporations that have undistributed personal holding company income. This tax is in addition to regular income taxes. The personal holding company tax was equal to the product of the highest rate of tax for unmarried individuals times the undistributed personal holding company income. The maximum rate is now 35 percent. The Jobs and Growth Tax Relief Reconciliation Act of 2003 has now changed the rate for personal holding company tax to 15 percent.

Computation of the personal holding company tax involves making the following adjustments to taxable income:

1. Subtract:
   - Foreign and U.S. taxes not including the accumulated earnings tax (discussed below) and the personal holding company tax.[24]
   - Charitable contributions of up to 50 percent instead of 10 percent of the corporation's contribution base.[25]
   - Net operating loss incurred during the preceding year computed without regard to the dividend-received deduction;[26]
   - Net capital gains less the tax attributed to those gains.[27]
2. Plus:
   - Dividend-received deduction claimed;
   - NOL deduction for the current year;
   - Rental expenses in excess of rental income;
   - Income, less allocable expenses, derived from personal service contracts of a foreign corporation whose stock is owned by non-resident aliens;
   - Excess charitable contributions carried over from a previous year and deducted in the current year to determine regular taxable income.[28]
3. Equals adjusted taxable income
4. Less: dividends paid deduction
5. Equals undistributed personal holding company income (UPHCI)
6. UPHCI X 15 percent = Personal holding company tax

Example—Bio-mine, Inc. is a personal holding company with the following results:

Operating profit		$290,000
Long-term capital gain		40,000
Dividends		50,000
Interest		25,000
Gross income		405,000
Less:		
Salaries	$100,000	
General and administrative		
Expenses	40,000	
Charitable contributions	26,500	

($405,000 − $100,000 − $40,000) X 10% statutory limitation. The total contribution was greater than $26,500, but corporations have a limit of 10% of income that is allowed to be deducted for charitable contributions.

Dividend-received deduction		
($50,000 × 70%)	35,000	
Total deductions		(201,500)
Taxable income		$203,500

PHC Tax Liability:		
Taxable income		$203,500
Plus dividend received deduction		35,000
Minus:		
Excess charitable contributions over 10%		(10,000)
Federal income taxes		(62,615)
Long-term capital gain	$40,000	
Less federal income taxes	(15,600)	(24,400)
Dividends-paid deduction (See discussion below.)		(10,000)
Undistributed personal holding company income		$ 131,485
Times tax rate		X .15 Personal holding company tax
		$ 19,723

As seen in the previous example, the personal holding company tax is a formidable penalty for failing to distribute sufficient income. Total tax for Bio-mine is $ 82,338 ($62,615 + $ 19,723).

ELIMINATING THE PERSONAL HOLDING COMPANY TAX

According to §561(a), a personal holding company may claim a deduction for dividends paid out of accumulated and current earnings and profits. This is known as the dividends-paid deduction. This is the total of dividends paid during the taxable year, consent dividends for the taxable year, and the dividend carryover.

Dividends paid during the taxable year qualify as personal holding dividends if they are treated as dividends for income tax purposes.[29] Dividends paid after the taxable year but on or before the 15th day of the third month following the close of the taxable year are considered paid during the taxable year if the taxpayer makes an election. Additionally, these dividends cannot exceed either (a) the undistributed personal holding company income for the year, or (b) 20 percent of the total dividends actually paid during the taxable year.[30]

Example—Your Design, Inc., a calendar-year taxpayer, pays dividends in January, April, July, and Oct. In 2002 it paid dividends of $12,500 each quarter for a total of $50,000. It has undistributed personal holding income of $150,000 for 2002. It wants to eliminate its personal holding company tax, and makes an election to pay a dividend of $100,000 in January of 2003 to apply to 2002. Unfortunately, Your Design will be able to treat only $10,000 of the January 2003 distribution as having been paid in 2002. This is because the amount of a dividend a corporation can carry back to the prior year is limited to the lesser of its undistributed personal holding company income ($150,000) or 20 percent of the actual dividends paid in 2002 (20 percent × $50,000 = $10,000). The remaining $90,000 of the January 2003 distribution can be used by Your Design in its 2003 personal holding company tax calculations.

Liquidating Dividends

Liquidating dividends[31] are treated differently for a personal holding company. The normal treatment is that these distributions are treated as sales transactions. However, in the case of a personal holding company:

(a) If a plan of complete liquidation is adopted to occur within 24 months, any distribution to corporate shareholders within that period is treated as a dividend for purposes of computing the dividends paid deduction. This distribution must represent the allocable share of the corporate shareholders' undistributed personal holding company income for the taxable year.[32]

(b) The amount allocated to a noncorporate shareholder may not exceed the amount actually distributed. These distributions must be designated as dividends by the corporation, and the shareholder must be notified accordingly.[33] The shareholder must receive a Form 1099 or substitute for the tax year. If these requirements are made, the corporation may then take a dividend-paid deduction.

Preferential Dividends

Preferential dividends do not qualify for the dividend-paid deduction. There can be no preference to any share of stock as compared with other shares of the same class, and no preference to one class of stock over another, except to the extent that the stock is entitled to such preference.[34]

Property Dividends

Property dividends, for the purposes of the dividend-paid deduction, are valued as the corporation's adjusted basis under Reg. §1.562-1.[35]

Consent Dividends

Consent dividends are hypothetical dividends paid by the corporation to a consenting shareholder on the last day of the taxable year and then contributed back to the corporation on the same day.[36] This is done when the corporation is low on cash and it wishes to eliminate the personal holding company tax. The effect on the shareholder is that he/she is taxed as receiving a dividend, and his/her basis in the company's stock is increased. Accordingly, the shareholder may face a cash-flow problem. This election may be made through the due date of the corporation's tax return.

Dividend Carryovers

Dividend carryovers represent amounts paid as dividends in excess of the corporation's taxable income during the previous two years. These excesses may be used to compute the current year dividend-paid deduction whether or not the company was a personal holding company during those years. [37]

Deficiency Dividends

Deficiency dividends are paid after it is established that the taxpayer has liability for the personal holding company tax. Deficiency dividends may not be used to calculate the dividend-paid deduction.[38] In order to use this dividend, there must be a formal determination by the Tax Court or an order by any court of jurisdiction, a closing agreement made under §7121, or a determination under a signed agreement with the government.[39] Deficiency dividends must be paid within 90 days of the determination.

Other Strategies

Other strategies to avoid the personal holding company tax include increasing the number of shareholders, changing the income mix to increase the percentage of operating income, or changing the taxable portfolio interest income to nontaxable interest income. Corporations with significant rental holdings may be able to avoid the personal holding company tax by structuring their income so as to exclude rental moneys from the definition of personal holding company income. Corporate investors with large holdings in nonoperating assets need to monitor their situations carefully to avoid application of this tax.

ACCUMULATED EARNINGS TAX

The Accumulated Earnings Tax is a tax imposed on C corporations to ensure that the company does not maintain profits unnecessarily within the business to avoid paying tax on dividends at the shareholder level. This tax is imposed on C corporations, regardless of the type of income they have. Because dividends are not deductible in determining taxable income, income from C corporations is subject to two levels of tax, one at the corporate level and the other again at the individual shareholder level. The accumulated earnings tax is levied on the current-year accumulated earnings (not total accumulated earnings) that are not needed for the reasonable needs of the business. The amount of the tax was the highest individual income tax rate (currently 35 percent) times the corporation's accumulated taxable income. However, the Jobs and Growth Tax Relief Reconciliation Act of 2003 also changed this tax to a maximum rate of 15 percent.

Exceptions from the Accumulated Earnings Tax

Exceptions for companies from the accumulated earnings tax include:

- Personal holding companies
- Foreign personal holding companies
- Tax-exempt companies
- Passive foreign investment companies[40]
- S corporations, because all of the income is passed through directly to the shareholders.

Reasonable Needs of the Business

Reasonable needs of the business, if supported by sufficient facts, would include:

1. Provide for bona fide expansion of the business or replacement of a plant. This includes expansion into a new location and the purchase of depreciable assets.
2. Acquire a business enterprise through purchasing stock or assets. However, if stock is purchased, a company must be careful that it does not fall into the passive income rules (see Chapter 2). By acquiring a controlling interest, that possibility would be eliminated.
3. Provide for the retirement of indebtedness created in connection with the trade or business. A desire to reduce interest payments, increase cash flow, and possess sound credit ratings would be considered appropriate business reasons for debt reduction.
4. Provide necessary working capital for the business, such as for the procurement of inventories. Working capital is the difference between current assets and current liabilities. Current assets include cash, marketable securities, accounts receivable, inventories, and prepayments. Current liabilities are those debts that generally must be paid within the year. These include accounts payable, payroll and withholding taxes, sales taxes, lines of credit, floor planning[41] of inventory, and notes payable. Cash and marketable securities are normally used to pay dividends, but they are also required to pay both current and long-term liabilities.

   The courts have maintained that cash is always being replenished within the operating cycle of the corporation through purchasing, manufacturing, sales, and receivables. Therefore the immediate needs of the corporation are met through this operating cycle.
5. Provide for investments or loans to suppliers or customers if necessary in order to maintain the business of the corporation; or
6. Provide for the payment of reasonable anticipated product liability losses.[42]

The above list is not exhaustive and there may be other legitimate business requirements to maintain profits within the company. Additionally, the business requirement may not be immediate, but there should be a specific plan for business use of the earnings and profits, which should be updated regularly.

Unreasonable Accumulations of Earnings and Profits

Evidence of unreasonable accumulations of earnings and profits beyond the reasonable needs of the business would include:

1. Loans to shareholders, or the use of funds of the corporation for the personal benefit of the shareholders;
2. Loans having no reasonable relation to the conduct of the business made to relatives or friends of shareholders, or to other persons;
3. Loans to another corporation that has no business relationship to the corporation other than mutual controlling shareholders;
4. Investments in properties or securities that are unrelated to the activities of the business of the corporation; or
5. Retention of earnings and profits to provide against unrealistic hazards.[43]

HOLDING OR INVESTMENT COMPANIES

A corporation having practically no activities except holding property and collecting the income derived from it or investing the income shall be considered a holding company.[44] If the activities of the corporation include buying and selling stocks, securities, real estate, or other investment property so that the income is derived not only from the investment yield but also from profits due to market fluctuations, the corporation shall be considered an investment company.[45] IRC §533(b) states that the fact the taxpayer is a holding or investment company is prima facie evidence of the purpose to avoid income tax with respect to shareholders and, therefore, the corporation is subject to the accumulated earnings tax.

ACCUMULATED EARNINGS TAX

Prior to calculating the accumulated earnings tax, the accumulated taxable income must be determined.

Accumulated Taxable Income

Accumulated taxable income is the corporation's taxable income with the following adjustments:

Add:

- Dividend-Received Deduction—This deduction is added back because it was designed as an incentive to invest in other corporations and to subsequently distribute the dividends to shareholders. This deduction is for 70 percent of dividends received from a corporation if less than 20 percent of its stock is owned by the taxpayer; 80 percent if the taxpayer owns at least 20 percent of the stock; and 100 percent if the taxpayer is a small business investment company or if both the taxpayer and payer of the dividends are members of an affiliated company.[46]
- Net operating loss carrybacks and carryforwards are not allowed because they occurred in a different taxable year.[47]
- Charitable deductions carried over from a preceding year; and
- Capital loss carryovers.[48]

Subtract:

- Federal income taxes and foreign taxes. However, a foreign tax credit may be taken instead of a deduction for foreign taxes.[49]
- Charitable contributions in excess of the 10-percent limit of income allowed to corporations;[50]
- Capital losses in excess of capital gains;[51]
- Capital gains in excess of capital losses minus federal income taxes attributable to those gains.

  Example—Julie's Shoes has taxable income of $200,000 and long-term capital gain of $10,000. There are no current or carryover capital losses. The corporation is in the 34-percent income tax bracket.

Julie's accumulated taxable income	$200,000
Less taxes	(68,000)
Less capital gain less taxes	(6,600)
Accumulated taxable income	$125,400

- Dividends-paid deduction is generally the same as those allowed for the personal holding corporation tax.
- Accumulated Earnings Credit. A C corporation is allowed a minimum credit of $250,000 or $150,000 for service corporations reduced by accumulated earnings and profits as of the close of the

preceding taxable year, or the amount of current earnings and profits required to meet the reasonable needs of the business.[52]

After making these adjustments to taxable income, the result is the accumulated taxable income.

Accumulated Earnings Tax

The accumulated taxable income is multiplied by 15 percent to arrive at the accumulated earnings tax.

Example—Julie's Shoes has the following results for its taxable year:

Taxable income	$200,000
Plus: Dividends received deduction	26,000
NOL carryforward	75,000
Less: Federal income taxes	(42,500)
($200,000 − $75,000) X 34%	
Net long-term capital gain less taxes	(6,600)
Dividends paid deduction	(8,000)
Current year earnings and profits to meet needs of business net of long-term capital gain reduced by taxes	(150,000)
Accumulated taxable income	$93,900
Tax rate	X .15 Accumulated earnings tax
	$14,085

ELIMINATING THE ACCUMULATED EARNINGS TAX

One of the best methods for avoiding the accumulated earnings tax is to document the needs of the corporation. If a capital project will be undertaken in the future, retained earnings should be appropriated for that purpose. A business plan should be done, indicating what the company's cash requirements will be to support the plan. This plan should be specific as to the timetable and resource requirements. Existence of strong documentation will allow corporations to take advantage of attractive investments without triggering accumulated earnings tax concerns.

If there appears to be a growing amount of accumulated earnings, the company should consider a new project, or making an election to become an S corporation. If these options aren't workable, it may be necessary to liquidate an investment in order to make a distribution to shareholders. This is because few assets generate a favorable after-tax return when subject to a combined tax rate of as much as 54 percent (15 percent, plus 39 percent, maximum corporate rate).

CONCLUSION

The personal holding company tax and the accumulated earnings tax are both layers of additional tax levied as a preventive measure against tax avoidance. However, each of these taxes may unknowingly surface when a taxpayer experiences changes in operations or circumstances. From an investment point of view, corporations potentially subject to these layers need to be careful. Holding an asset unrelated to the corporation's business may trigger application of the accumulated earnings tax, turning what was thought to be a sound investment into a tax nightmare. Similarly, income from an investment may mean a corporation meets the personal holding company requirements, and, therefore, is potentially subject to the punitive personal holding corporation tax. Awareness of these rules will assist in preventing payment of these taxes.

The next chapter will examine the rules related to the distribution and receipt of dividends.

NOTES

1 §542(a)(2)
2 §543(a)
3 §544(a)(1)
4 Rev. Rul 62-155, 1962C.B. 132
5 Reg. 1.318-3(a)
6 §544(a)(2)
7 §544(a)(3)
8 §544(4)(A)
9 §544(a)(6)
10 §544(a)(5)
11 §544(b)(1)
12 §543(a)(1)
13 §543(a)(1)(C)
14 §543(a)(3)
15 §543(a)(4)(B)(i)
16 §543(a)(4)(B)(iii)
17 §543(a)(4)(B)(ii) The corporation paying the dividends must receive copyright royal-

ties that are at least equal to 50 percent of its ordinary gross income and have operating expenses from the copyright royalties equal to at least 25 percent of the corporation's ordinary gross income reduced by royalties it pays and by its amortization deductions attributable to the copyright royalties.

[18] §543(a)(C)

[19] §543(a)(5)

[20] §543(a)(6)

[21] §543(a)(7)

[22] §543(a)

[23] §542(c)

[24] §545(b)(1)

[25] §545(b)(2)

[26] §545(b)(4)

[27] §545(b)(5)

[28] Id.

[29] §562(a)

[30] 563(b)

[31] Liquidating dividends are paid to shareholders when a corporation is in the process of dissolving. Part of the dividends is treated as sale proceeds of assets and part is treated as a return of the shareholder's initial investment.

[32] Reg§1.562.1(b)(2)(I)

[33] Reg. §1.316-1(b)(2)

[34] §562(c)

[35] However, the IRS has issued PLR 9335030 for the distribution of appreciated property where the property's fair market value will be used.

[36] §565(c)

[37] §564(b)

[38] §547(d)(1)

[39] §547(c)

[40] §532(b)

[41] Floor planning is a method of financing large inventory items such as cars and boats.

[42] Reg. §1.537.2(b)

[43] Reg. §1.537-2(c)

[44] Reg. §1.533-1(c)

[45] Id.

[46] §243(a) and §243(b)

[47] §535(b)(4)

[48] §535(b)(7)

[49] §275(a)(4) Most often a credit is preferable since it is a dollar for dollar reduction against taxes.

[50] §535(b)(2)

[51] §535(b)(7)

[52] §535(c)(2) This minimum credit is available only once over the life of the corporation. It is not a yearly credit.

Making an Investment in Stock

8

DIVIDEND TAXATION

INTRODUCTION

Buying stock in a corporation is a good investment if it generates a strong return—either the shares grow in value or they throw off dividends or both. In order to realize the return represented by a stock's appreciation in value, however, a taxpayer must liquidate the investment and face the corresponding tax consequences. The profit from the sale of stock usually is eligible for favorable capital gain tax treatment unless the taxpayer is a dealer. This means the gain will be taxed at lower rates, assuming the taxpayer has held the investment for a long enough period. (The capital gains rules are discussed in Chapter 1.) Until the stock is sold, however, the investor pays no tax.

By comparison, a taxpayer who purchases stock that generates regular dividends enjoys income on a recurring and predictable basis. Further, the income is received without the necessity of liquidating the investment. However, the income taxation of dividends varies from how stock sale proceeds are taxed. Assuming that the corporation declaring the dividends has sufficient earnings and profits, the payouts to the shareholders will be taxed at the time of distribution, meaning dividends do not offer the same opportunity for tax deferral that stocks that are held for appreciation do. Under the 2003 tax legislation, most individual taxpayers will pay tax at a 15-percent rate on dividend income. However, if a dividend payout does not qualify under the 2003 rules, or if the investor is a corporation,[1] ordinary income rates will apply. These rates may be higher than capital gain rates.

Example—Pat owns stock in Morgan Company and Ransom, Inc. She paid $10,000 for her shares in each corporation. Morgan is an established company in a mature industry; the shares are considered an income stock.[2] The investment generates an annual dividend of 11 percent. Morgan share prices have moved relatively little in recent years. Pat is in a 15-percent dividend tax bracket and after paying the tax, she spends what's left of the dividend each year on personal expenses. After four years, if there are no changes to either Pat's tax rate or the amount of dividends Morgan pays, Pat's after-tax income will total $3740; she will have paid $660 in taxes. If Pat sells the Morgan shares at the end of the four-year investment period for $10,000, she will report no capital gain because she sold the shares for the price at which they were purchased. Assuming an annual discount rate of 4 percent, reflecting the time value of money, the present value of the $3740 that Pat will receive in income from the investment in Morgan Company is $3393. The present value of the taxes Pat will pay is $600. If instead Pat is in a 35% bracket and her dividends are taxed as ordinary income, she will pay $385 in tax each year, leaving a total of $2860 (present value $2596) in after tax proceeds.

By comparison, Ransom, Inc., the other company in which Pat has invested, is a growth company[3] and does not generally pay dividends. (Ransom is not a personal holding company, and the corporation's accumulated earnings are not beyond the reasonable needs of its business.) Although more volatile than Morgan, in recent years the value of Ransom stock has appreciated at an average annual rate of 11 percent. At the end of four years, Pat's Ransom shares will be worth $15,181, meaning Pat will report capital gain of $5181 when she sells the Ransom stock. If the capital gain rate is 15 percent, Pat will pay $777 in taxes. Again, with an annual discount rate of 4 percent, the present value of Pat's profit on her Ransom shares is $4429. The present value of the $777 of taxes Pat will pay in year four is $664.

The difference between Pat's returns in the above example reflects the differing tax treatment of the two investments. Looking at Pat's situation strictly from the point of view of after-tax profit, and assuming no changes in the tax rate structure, it is clear she should have invested all of her money in Ransom and should not have acquired any Morgan stock. However, an investor also must consider the relative risk of the proposed investments, expected cash flow needs throughout the investment horizon, and various other factors. All of this means that tax considerations should not be the sole factor driving investment decisions. However, a taxpayer who invests in stock without considering the tax consequences is likely to be disappointed.

HOW DIVIDENDS ARE TAXED

Previously, dividends were treated as ordinary income for all investors and taxed at regular rates. However, dividend taxation rules were changed substantially by the 2003 tax legislation. "Qualified dividend income" received by noncorporate taxpayers after 2002 but before 2009 is eligible for a 15 percent tax rate, although low-income taxpayers may pay less.[4] The new reduced rates apply to dividend payments received from domestic and qualified foreign corporations.[5] Mutual fund payouts may be eligible too, assuming certain requirements are met.[6] However, some distributions are not covered under the new rules, meaning they will be taxed at ordinary income rates. These include dividends paid by credit unions and mutual insurance companies.

In order to take advantage of the reduced tax rates, an individual must hold the stock generating the dividend payout for more than 60 days during the 120-day period surrounding the ex-dividend date.[7] (A longer holding period may apply to preferred stock.) Payouts on borrowed funds do not qualify for the reduced rates if the investor chooses to treat the payments as investment income under the rules discussed in Chapter 4. Individuals who do not genuinely own the dividends they receive also cannot take advantage of the reduced rates. This could occur, for example, where an investor sells her shares short and remains in that position when the stock goes ex-dividend.[8]

Individuals who receive one or more dividends qualifying for the 2003 tax rate reductions may wind up reporting long-term capital loss in connection with a later sale of the shares that generated the payout. This rule applies if the dividends are "extraordinary." Generally this means the dividends taxed at the reduced rates equal or exceed 10 percent of the shareholder's adjusted basis in the stock. Long-term capital loss is the least favorable type of tax loss, since it usually offsets long-term capital gain that otherwise would be taxed at reduced capital gain rates. The characterization as long-term applies to the extent of the reduced tax rate dividends received.[9]

The reduced rates of the 2003 Act only apply to "dividends," a term the legislation does not define. Although corporations are not eligible for these reduced dividend rates, special provisions do apply to corporate investors who report dividend income. (These rules are discussed later in this chapter.) This means both corporate and noncorporate investors first must identify which income or payments they receive actually are considered to be dividends under the Tax Code rules. Once that determination is made, the amount of the payment must be calculated. Issues also may arise as to when the dividend should be recognized and which taxpayer should report it.

What Is a Dividend?

A dividend is any distribution made by a corporation in the ordinary course of business from its current or accumulated earnings and profits.[10] Taxpayers who have invested in mutual funds will receive a Form 1099 at the end of the year describing how any income and distributions from the fund are to be reported. This statement will reflect both dividends and capital gains.[11] A "dividend" paid to a policyholder of a life insurance company is not treated as a distribution if it really represents a partial refund of the premium the policyholder paid.[12] However, if the amount distributed exceeds what the policyholder paid for the insurance, the excess is taxable.[13]

How Dividends Are Reported

A shareholder who receives a dividend must include it in his or her gross income; it is taxed at dividend or ordinary income rates. Any part of a distribution that exceeds the earnings and profits is treated as a tax-free return of capital. This causes a corresponding reduction in the shareholder's basis. Once the basis is exhausted, any further amount of distribution is handled for tax purposes as capital gain.[14]

Example—Doug is a shareholder in Electric, Inc. He purchased the stock many years ago, and his current basis in the shares he holds is $2000. Doug receives a distribution of $6000 in the current year. Assuming Doug's share of earnings and profits amounts to $2500, Doug must report dividend income of this amount. If Doug's dividend tax rate is 15 percent, he pays tax of $375 on this part of the distribution. The next $2000 of the payment is a tax-free return of capital, but Doug's basis in the shares is now reduced to $0. This leaves $1500 of the distribution that has yet to be handled. This amount will be treated as a capital gain. If a 15-percent rate applies, Doug will pay an additional $225 of tax, meaning his total tax bill on the amount distributed will be $600.

Property Distributions

A corporation can use either cash or property to make a dividend distribution. Where the dividend is paid out in property, the shareholder reports the fair market value of the assets received, less any liabilities.[15] The term "property" is defined by the Tax Code to include securities, but in general it does not refer to stock in the distributing corporation.[16] (The rules governing distributions of stock in the company declaring the dividend are discussed further in Chapter 10.) A company may issue scrip dividends when profits exist but no cash or property is available for distribution. In that case, the shareholder is taxed on the fair market value of the scrip when it is issued, even though the actual cash or property is not received until later.[17] The basis of property received in a dividend distribution is its fair market value.[18] This amount is *not* reduced by any liability the shareholder assumed as a part of the transaction.

Example—Jim is a shareholder in Lawco, Inc. He receives a distribution of land from the corporation. The land cost Lawco $12,000, and its fair market value at the time of the distribution is $15,000. Jim's basis in his stock is $4000. Of the total distribution, assume that $5000 is paid out of Lawco's earnings and profits and therefore is taxable as dividend income. The land is subject to a $1000 nonrecourse mortgage.

Under these facts, Jim is treated as receiving a $14,000 distribution. He has $5000 of dividend income, and his basis in Lawco drops to $0. Jim also reports $5000 of capital gain. His basis in the land he received from the company is its fair market value of $15,000. This figure is not reduced by the amount of the mortgage to which the land is subject.

Earnings and Profits

In order for a distribution to be treated as a dividend, it must be made out of the declaring corporation's "earnings and profits."[19] This term is not defined in the Tax Code, but generally it represents a measure of the corporation's ability to make payments to shareholders without using its capital. A shareholder to whom a dividend is paid will receive a Form 1099, which will indicate the amount of the distribution that will be subject to dividend treatment. If a shareholder owns more than one type of stock, earnings and profits are assigned first to the dividends paid on the shares with the higher distribution priority. Distributions paid on the lower-priority shares are then treated as dividends, to the extent that earnings and profits remain.[20]

Who Is Taxed on the Dividend?

Dividends are normally taxed to the person who receives the benefit of the distribution. Usually this is the person listed as owning the shares, but in some cases it is not. For example, if an agent holds stock on behalf of a principal, any tax due on a distribution is owed by the principal and not the agent. Likewise, a stockholder whose shares are held in street name by a broker must include in income the total distributions reported to her by the broker.[21]

If stock is sold before a dividend is declared and paid, the distribution is income to the buyer, even if the sale price reflected the expectation of a dividend payment.[22] In other words, the buyer cannot argue that the distribution represents a tax-free return of capital. If the seller reserved the right to receive the payment, then he or she is taxed on it, even if the distribution occurs after the sale is closed.[23]

Assuming the normal case, where the ex-dividend date precedes the record date, a dividend paid on stock sold after the declaration but before the record or ex-dividend date is taxed to the buyer.[24] Dividends paid to the seller as the holder of record, where the shares were sold after the record date but before the distribution is made, must be reported as income by the seller.[25] In order to transfer the obligation to pay tax on a dividend from the seller to the buyer, the sale of the underlying stock must be complete. A distribution made during a period when a put or call option is outstanding is reported by whoever owned the shares when the holder became legally entitled to the payment.[26] If after the option is exercised the seller must pay the distribution to the buyer, the buyer reports the income from the payment, if any.

If a taxpayer lends his stock for use in a short sale, "substitute payments" received before the transaction is closed are treated as "other income" and not dividends. Therefore, these payments are not eligible for reduced taxation under the 2003 dividend rules for noncorporate investors. A substitute payment is made in place of certain dividends, assuming the ex-dividend date is after the stock is transferred for use in the short sale but before the closing of the short sale itself. Substitute payments will be taxed as ordinary income. This is true even if the substitute payment is made in lieu of sums that otherwise would have been reported as dividends or a tax-free return of capital or capital gain. A taxpayer considering a loan of his or her stock for use in a short sale transaction should weigh any possible increased tax burden when deciding upon the amount of compensation he or she wants in order to participate in the transaction.[27]

If a taxpayer disposes of stock by gift, the donee, or recipient, reports any corporate distributions after the gifting transaction is complete.[28] A shareholder cannot escape taxation on dividends by giving away the right to the distribution while retaining the underlying stock. In that case the donor must report the dividend income, and the donee pays no tax.[29]

When Are Dividends Taxed?

Dividends are taxed when received or when available to the shareholder without restriction.[30] This rule applies for both cash and accrual-method taxpayers[31] and even where the distribution is paid by the corporation using notes. If dividends payable on December 31 are mailed per the corporation's usual practice so that shareholders will not receive them until January, the dividends become taxable in the shareholders' tax years that include January.[32] A dividend payment that is restricted because of capital or liquidity concerns is taxed when actually distributed.[33] If stockholders of cumulative preferred shares become entitled to receive common stock once a specified number of accounting periods pass without dividend payments, the shareholders constructively receive income equal to the value of the common stock to which they are entitled. This occurs on the date when the required number of periods passed without a dividend distribution.[34]

When dividends previously in arrears are finally paid, they become taxable, whether the recipient is the stockholder who owned the shares while the arrears accrued or is a buyer who purchased the stock during the time when the dividends weren't being paid.[35] If the arrears are not declared but instead included in the redemption price of the underlying shares, they generally will be treated as part of the sale proceeds, and not a dividend distribution.[36] Where the arrears are paid as part of a recapitalization exchange, the shareholder generally is taxed as a dividend on whichever is less, the gain she realized on the transaction or her share of the corporation's earnings and profits.[37]

DIVIDEND-RECEIVED DEDUCTION

Shareholders that are themselves corporations are entitled to a dividend-received deduction, under rules found in §243 through §246A of the Tax Code. The purpose of this deduction is to ensure that income is taxed no more than twice: at the corporate level and again when received by the shareholder.

Example—Laura owns stock in Parent Corporation, which in turn owns shares of Subsidiary Company. Subsidiary declares a dividend and pays Parent, using after-tax proceeds from its operations. Parent has sufficient capital on hand, and therefore declares a dividend payable to its shareholders, using the Subsidiary distribution. Without a dividend-received deduction, the distribution paid by Subsidiary and ultimately received by Laura would be taxed three times: as part of Subsidiary's taxable income, on receipt by Parent, and again on receipt by Laura. The dividend-received deduction is designed to mute this possibility by providing a deduction to Parent in connection with its receipt of a dividend distribution from Subsidiary.

In order to claim a dividend-received deduction, the distribution must be a dividend, and it generally must be received from a domestic corporation that is subject to federal income tax.[38] Whether a distribution constitutes a dividend is determined in most cases by the rules found in §301 and §316 of the Code, discussed previously. Ordinary distributions from a mutual fund may qualify for the 70-percent dividend-received deduction, provided certain requirements are met.[39]

The amount of the deduction is dependent upon the number of shares of stock in the distributing corporation that are held by the corporate shareholder. If the corporation owns less than 20 percent, then the dividend-received deduction is 70 percent. The deduction rises to 80 percent where the recipient owns 20 percent or more, by reference to both voting power and value of the distributing corporation's shares. Where the distributing and recipient corporations are members of the same affiliated group, a 100-percent dividend-received deduction may be available.[40]

Taxable Income Limitation

There are income limits that may apply to the dividend-received deduction. Specifically, under §246, the deduction for a dividend received from a less than 20-percent owned corporation cannot exceed 70 percent of the recipient corporation's taxable income. Similarly, the deduction for a payment from a 20-percent or more owned corporation is limited to 80 percent of the recipient's taxable income. There is no comparable limitation where the recipient is eligible to take a 100-percent dividend-received deduction. If more than one limitation applies, as where a corporate shareholder owns 10 percent of the stock of one corporation and 25 percent of the stock of another, the limit is applied first to the distribution eligible for the 80-percent deduction. Thereafter, the recipient corporation's taxable income is reduced by the 80 percent dividends before calculating the 70-percent limitation.[41]

Example—Mike Company owns 15 percent of the stock of Rochester, Inc. and 30 percent of the outstanding shares of Batavia Corp. Rochester and Batavia are both domestic corporations, the distributions from which are eligible for the dividend-received deduction. In the current year, Mike Company receives a dividend of $200,000 from Batavia and $15,000 from Rochester. Mike's income for the current year is $205,000, because of a $10,000 loss the company has from its operations.

Mike Company has a potential 80-percent dividend-received deduction for the payment received from Batavia because it owns 30 percent of the outstanding Batavia shares. This would amount to a $160,000 deduction. The dividend-received deduction is limited to 80 percent of Mike Company's income, which is $164,000 (80 percent of $205,000). Therefore, Mike Company can claim the full deduction with respect to the Batavia Corp. distribution. Mike's income then would be reduced by the $200,000 deduction on the distribution from Batavia. This means the deduction on the Rochester payment would be limited to 70 percent of $5000, or $3500. Because 70 percent of $15,000 is $10,500, Mike Company is not able to claim the full dividend-received deduction for the Rochester distribution. The company's taxable income for the current year will be $41,500 ($205,000 income, less dividend-received deductions of $160,000 and $3500).

The taxable income limitations are not applicable in any year in which the recipient corporation reports a net operating loss. In determining if a NOL exists, the full dividend-received deduction is used without regard to the taxable income limit.[42]

Example—Joyce Co. receives a dividend distribution from Blue Jay Inc. of $80,000. Joyce owns 10 percent of Blue Jay. Joyce has a loss from its business operations for the current year of $28,000, meaning the corporation's taxable income is $52,000. Since a full dividend-received deduction of $56,000 (70 percent of $80,000) would create a net operating loss, Joyce Co. escapes the taxable income limit on the deduction and can claim a $56,000 deduction despite §246.

Limits Applicable Where Related Payments Are Required

The dividend-received deduction is not available where the recipient corporation is obligated to make "related payments" in connection with "substantially similar or related property."[43] This rule is designed to prevent corporations from using short sales or other arrangements to generate dividends while also making deductible payments to others.

Example—Marie Company makes a short sale of stock in Les Co. As a result, Marie is obligated to make dividend equivalent payments to the lender of the Les Co stock used in the short sale. Marie also holds shares of its own in Les Co. Les Co. declares a dividend, and Marie makes a $10,000 dividend equivalent payment to the lender of the shares sold short. This payment is deducted in full. At the same time, Marie receives a $10,000 dividend on its own Les holdings and claims a 70-percent dividend-received deduction. This means Marie Company has generated a $10,000 deduction at the cost of recognizing only $3000 in income.

Under these facts, the related payment rules prevent Marie Company from claiming the dividend-received deduction. The limit applies to all or some of the dividends received, depending on the number of shares on which Marie Company is obligated to make related payments because of positions held on substantially similar or related property. The term "substantially similar or related property" is not defined in the Tax Code for purposes of this rule. However, the same language is used elsewhere, in the same section of the Code. Regulations issued under that provision state that whether property is substantially similar or related is dependent on the facts and circumstances.[44] A two-part test is provided. The first part is satisfied when the fair market values of stock and property primarily reflect the performance of a single firm or enterprise, the same industry or industries, or the same economic factor or factors, like interest rates.[45] The second part of the test requires that changes in the value of the stock must be expected to track, directly or inversely, changes in the property's value.[46] The two-part test would be met by the short sale of Les Co. stock in the example above. This is because changes in the values of the shares and the positions are reasonably expected to vary inversely.[47]

Holding Period Requirement

In order to claim the dividend-received deduction, a corporation must meet a holding period requirement. This rule prevents dividend stripping.

Example—Sharon Corporation buys $100,000 worth of stock in Pine Company. The price Sharon pays reflects a dividend expected soon from Pine. The dividend amounts to $10,000, and Sharon Corporation claims a dividend-received deduction of 70 percent. Thereafter Sharon sells the Pine stock for $92,000, the lower price a result of the $10,000 distribution. Sharon takes a loss of $8000 on the sale. Even if the use of this loss is limited, which would be the case for capital losses,[48] Sharon nonetheless has managed to create an $8000 deduction at a cost of reporting only $3000 in income.

To guard against this result, the Tax Code denies the dividend-received deduction where the stock is held 45 days or less during the 90-day period that surrounds the ex-dividend date.[49] In other words, in order to take the deduction, the corporation must own the shares for at least 46 days during the 90-day period that begins 45 days before the stock becomes ex-dividend. In the case of preferred stock, a longer holding period may apply.[50]

When calculating the holding period, the day of disposition counts, but not the day of acquisition.[51] The holding period does not include days where the taxpayer has reduced its risk of loss as to the stock. [52] Under this rule, for example, periods during which the stockholder-corporation has an option to sell substantially identical stock or securities [53] are excluded from the holding period calculation.[54] A similar result applies where the corporation has granted an option to buy substantially identical stock or securities[55] or has otherwise reduced its risk by holding one or more other positions with respect to "substantially similar or related property."[56]

Debt-Financed Stock

The Tax Code contains rules limiting the use of the dividend-received deduction where the underlying stock is debt financed. Without these rules, a shareholder-corporation could purchase or carry stock using the proceeds of a loan and deduct in full the interest it is required to pay on the obligation. At the same time, the corporation would recognize at most only 30 percent of the corresponding dividends generated by the stock investment. To prevent this result, the Tax Code requires a corporation to reduce the dividend-received deduction by a proportion reflecting the amount of debt financing.[57]

The restrictions apply where a corporation holds "debt-financed portfolio stock." Portfolio stock includes any shares of stock owned by a corporation unless as of the beginning of the ex-dividend date, the shareholder-corporation is a 50-percent or more owner of the declaring corporation.[58] Under certain circumstances, stock where the shareholder-corporation meets a 20-percent ownership test may also be excluded.[59] Stock is debt-financed if "portfolio indebtedness" exists during the "base period." "Portfolio indebtedness" is debt directly attributable to a portfolio stock investment.[60] It would include a loan, the proceeds of which were used to buy the portfolio shares.[61] The "base period" means the one-year period ending on the day before the ex-dividend date for the dividend at issue. Alternatively, it refers to the period running from the ex-dividend date for the most recent previous dividend and ending on the day before the ex-dividend date for the dividend at issue, if this is shorter.[62]

Example—Bob, Inc. owns 10 percent of the outstanding shares of stock in Fifth Company. The stock cost $200,000, and Bob borrowed $80,000 in order to partially fund the acquisition. Fifth Company pays a dividend of $10,000 on March 1. The ex-dividend date for the declaration was February 15. The $80,000 debt was outstanding since July. The ex-dividend date for the most recent previous dividend was August 15.

Since Bob, Inc.'s Fifth Company holdings are debt-financed, the company must reduce the dividend-received deduction, which would otherwise amount to 70 percent. This number is multiplied by 100 percent less the average indebtedness percentage. The average indebtedness percentage is the average amount of portfolio indebtedness on the stock during the base period divided by the average adjusted basis during the same time. In Bob, Inc.'s case, this number amounts to 60 percent (100 percent − 40 percent {80,000/200,000}). This means Bob, Inc.'s dividend-received deduction is 42 percent (70 percent * 60 percent). In other words, Bob, Inc. will recognize $5800 in connection with the $10,000 dividend received on March 1. At the same time, Bob, Inc. will be allowed to deduct whatever interest it pays on the $80,000 loan it took out to acquire the Fifth Company shares.[63]

The limitation on the dividend-received deduction for debt-financed stock does not apply to stock eligible for the 100-percent dividend-received deduction.[64] Also, the decrease in the dividend-received deduction is not to exceed the interest deduction allocable to the dividend.[65] In the example above, assume that the interest allocable to the dividend amounts to $2400. Bob, Inc.'s dividend-received deduction is reduced under the debt-financed rules by $2800, from $7000 to $4200. Since this is in excess of the limit, the reduction would be capped at the $2400 interest figure.

Extraordinary Dividends

Under Tax Code § 1059, receipt of an "extraordinary dividend" will trigger a reduction in basis of the underlying stock. A dividend is extraordinary if it is received on stock held for two years or less and it equals or exceeds certain percentages of the shareholder-corporation's adjusted basis in the shares of the declaring corporation.[66] In the case of preferred stock, the percentage is 5 percent, and for other shares the figure is 10 percent.[67] The adjusted basis to which the 5-percent or 10-percent calculation is applied is reduced by the nontaxed portion of prior extraordinary dividends.[68] A taxpayer can elect to use the fair market value of the stock instead of its adjusted basis, if value can be proven to the satisfaction of the IRS.[69] This election would be helpful if the stock has appreciated since the shareholder-corporation acquired it.

Aggregation rules apply, under which dividends paid within certain time periods are combined for purposes of determining whether an extraordinary distribution has been made.[70] The holding period is calculated using rules similar to those discussed above, relating to the dividend-received deduction.[71] Certain redemptions and other distributions may also be subject to the extraordinary dividend rules, even if the underlying stock is held for more than two years.[72]

Example—Mary Corporation bought 10 percent of the outstanding common stock in Don, Inc. last year, paying $100,000 for the shares. Mary Corporation estimates that the fair market value of the Don shares it owns now stands at $120,000; however, this figure cannot be proven. Don's attorneys recently won a significant court decision, and as a result the company declares a large dividend. Mary Corporation's share of the distribution amounts to $15,000. This is the first dividend Don has declared since Mary Corporation became a shareholder.

Since $15,000 is more than 10 percent of the adjusted basis of Mary Corporation's holdings, and the distribution was made within two years of Mary's becoming a shareholder, the extraordinary dividend rules apply. Mary must reduce the adjusted basis of its stock by the nontaxed portion of the dividend.[73] As a 10-percent shareholder, Mary Corporation claimed a 70-percent dividend-received deduction, amounting to $10,500 (70 percent * $15,000). This means Mary Corporation's adjusted basis in its Don shares now stands at $89,500 ($100,000 − $10,500). Had the nontaxed portion of the distribution exceeded Mary Corporation's adjusted basis in the Don, Inc. stock, the excess would have been treated as gain from the sale of the Don shares.[74]

There are exceptions to the extraordinary dividend rules of Tax Code §1059. For example, the basis reduction provisions don't apply to stock held by the shareholder-corporation for the entire period of the distributing corporation's existence, so long as certain requirements are met.[75] In addition, "qualifying dividends," which generally refer to dividends received from members of the same affiliated group, may be eligible for an exception, again provided certain requirements are satisfied.[76] Shareholder-corporations concerned about the application of the extraordinary dividend rules should look for any exceptions that may be applicable to their specific facts.

CONCLUSION

Investors who purchase stock for the dividends the corporation declares, rather than primarily to hold for appreciation in value, need to understand the rules in this chapter. Noncorporate investors should determine if the dividends they receive will be eligible for the reduced tax rates of the 2003 legislation or if ordinary income rates will apply. Corporations pay tax at regular rates on both dividends and capital gain. However, corporate investors may prefer receiving dividends in order to take advantage of the dividend-received-deduction. Corporations must be familiar with the limitations applicable to this deduction, therefore, in order to avoid unexpected tax results from an equity investment.

NOTES

[1] Corporations can claim a dividend-received-deduction. See the discussion later in this chapter.

[2] Income stock represents ownership interests in companies with histories of regular earnings and dividend payments. Typically, the share prices of these companies are relatively stable. In Pat's case, this means the stock is likely to sell for approximately the price she paid. See Downes and Goodman, *Barron's Finance and Investment Handbook* (Barron's 3d ed., 1990), at p. 19.

[3] *Id.*

[4] Taxpayers in the 10-or 15-percent brackets will pay a 5-percent tax on dividends. In 2008, qualifying dividends paid to these investors will be tax-free.

[5] Qualified foreign corporations are defined at Tax Code §1(h)(11)(C).

[6] If the mutual fund's qualifying dividend income is less than 95 percent of its gross income, only the amount of qualifying dividends the fund receives can be passed through as payouts eligible for the lower rates.

[7] In order to receive a dividend, an investor must be a shareholder as of the "record date." Once the record date is set, the stock exchange will fix the "ex-dividend" date, usually two days before the record date. An investor who buys stock on the ex-dividend date or after will not receive the next dividend payment, which instead will go to the seller. See *www.sec.gov/answers/dividen.htm*. A similar holding period requirement applies to the dividend-received-deduction. See the discussion accompanying notes 48-56.

[8] Under the 2003 legislation, dividends on stock are ineligible "to the extent that the taxpayer is under an obligation (whether pursuant to a short sale or otherwise) to make related payments with respect to positions in substantially similar or related property." Tax Code §1(h)(11)(B)(iii). This language tracks restrictions on corporations claiming a dividend-received-deduction. See the discussion accompanying notes 43-47.

[9] Extraordinary dividends are defined in Tax Code §1059(c). That section, which applies to corporate shareholders, provides that a dividend that exceeds 5 percent of the adjusted basis of preferred stock or 10 percent of the adjusted basis of other shares is extraordinary.

Aggregation rules apply, under which dividend payments may be combined in some cases. The extraordinary dividend rules applicable to corporations are discussed in the text accompanying notes 66-76 of this chapter. Note that the 2003 legislation apparently does not incorporate Tax Code §1059(a), which limits the extraordinary dividend rules applicable to corporate investors to dividends received within two years of acquisition. See Tax Code §1(h)(11)(D)(ii).

[10] Tax Code §316(a); Treasury Regulation §1.316-1(a)

[11] See Publication 564, *Mutual Fund Distributions* (2002), p. 2. Taxation of capital gains is discussed in Chapter 1.

[12] Tax Code §316(b)(1)

[13] Publication 550, *Investment Income and Expenses* (2002), p. 21

[14] Tax Code §301(c). Where a taxpayer buys stock at different times and different prices, dividend treatment is determined on a share by share basis. In other words, basis from more costly shares can't be used to try to avoid capital gain treatment on the lower basis holdings. *Johnson v. U.S.*, 435 F.2d 1257 (4th Cir. 1971).

[15] Under Tax Code §301(b), the distribution is reduced by any liability the shareholder assumes or to which the property is subject. The Treasury Regulations provide that no reduction is to be made "for the amount of any liability unless the liability is assumed" per the requirements of IRC §357(d). Treasury Regulation §1.301-1(g). Under that section, a *recourse* liability is assumed in a dividend distribution if the shareholder/dividend recipient has agreed to and is expected to satisfy the obligation. In general, a *nonrecourse* liability is treated as assumed by a shareholder/dividend recipient if the property distributed is subject to the obligation. In general, these rules apply to distributions made after January 4, 2001, but see Treasury Regulation §1.301-1(g) for exceptions.

[16] Tax Code §317(a)

[17] *T.R. Miller Mill Company v. Commissioner*, 37 BTA 43, 49 (1938) *aff'd.* 102 F.2d 599 (5th Cir. 1939)

[18] Tax Code §301(d). In some cases, the regulations provide for the basis of property received as a dividend by a *corporate* shareholder to be determined using the adjusted basis of the property in the hands of the distributing corporation. Treasury Regulation §1.301-1(h).

[19] Tax Code §316(a)

[20] Rev. Rul. 69-440, 1969-2 CB 46

[21] Rev. Rul. 64-324, 1964-2 CB 463. See Publication 550, *Investment Income and Expenses* (2002), p. 19, 22.

[22] Treasury Regulation §1.61-9(c)

[23] *Coffey v. Commissioner*, 14 T.C. 1410 (1950)

[24] Treasury Regulation §1.61-9(c). If the record date precedes the ex-dividend date, Revenue Ruling 82-11, 1982-1 CB 51, provides that the holder of the stock on the record date must report the dividend income, even if the shares are sold before the ex-dividend date.

[25] Rev. Rul. 74-562, 1974-2 CB 28

[26] Rev. Rul. 58-234, 1958-1 CB 279

[27] Publication 550, *Investment Income and Expenses* (2002), p. 52

[28] *Montgomery v. Thomas*, 146 F.2d 76 (5th Cir. 1944)

[29] *Van Brunt v. Commissioner*, 11 B.T.A. 406 (1928)

[30] Treasury Regulation §1.301-1(b)

[31] *Dynamics Corporation of America v. U.S.*, 392 F.2d 241, 247 (Ct. of Cl. 1968). In general, an accrual method taxpayer reports income when all events giving rise to a payment have occurred and the right to funds is fixed. A cash method taxpayer reports income on receipt.

[32] Treasury Regulation §1.451-2(b)

[33] *Lawrence v. Commissioner*, 143 F.2d 456 (9th Cir. 1944)

[34] Rev. Rul. 84-141, 1984-2 CB 80

[35] Rev. Rul. 56-211, 1956-1 CB 155

[36] *Cummins Diesel Sales Corporation v. U.S.*, 459 F.2d 668 (7th Cir. 1972)

[37] Tax Code §356(a). If the arrears were paid out merely incidentally to the recapitalization, the shareholder will report gain based on his share of earnings and profits, regardless of the gain or loss realized on the transaction. Treasury Reg. §1.301-1(l).

[38] Tax Code §243(a). In some cases, dividends paid by foreign corporations may be eligible for a dividend received deduction. See Code §245.

[39] Tax Code §243(d)(2); Treasury Regulation §1.243-2(b)

[40] Tax Code §243

[41] Tax Code §246. For this purpose, taxable income is determined according to the rules of Code §246. For example, the income calculation does not reflect the dividend received deduction, any deduction for net operating losses, and also deductions for capital loss carrybacks. See Code §246(b)(1).

[42] Treasury Regulation §1.246-2(b)

[43] Tax Code §246(c)(1)

[44] Treasury Regulation §1.246-5(b)(1)

[45] Treasury Regulation §1.246-5(b)(1)

[46] Treasury Regulation §1.246-5(b)(1)

[47] Treasury Regulation §1.246-5(b)(1)(ii)

[48] Corporations can only use capital losses to offset capital gains. Tax Code §1211(a).

[49] Tax Code §246(c)(1)

[50] Under Tax Code §246(c)(2), dividends paid on preferred shares held for 90 days or less during the 180-day period surrounding the ex-dividend date are not eligible for the dividend received deduction. This rule applies only if the dividends are attributable to a period or periods greater than 366 days. *Id.*

[51] Tax Code §246(c)(3)

[52] Tax Code §246(c)(4)

[53] According to the Regulations, whether an asset represents "substantially identical stock or securities" is dependent on the facts and circumstances. In general, taxpayers can rely on the wash sales rules, found in Code §1091, and the short sale rules of Code §1233. Treasury Regulation §1.246-3(c)(2).

[54] Tax Code §246(c)(4)(A). The same result applies if the taxpayer is under a contract to sell or has made but not closed a short sale of substantially identical stock or securities. *Id.*

[55] A qualified covered call option does not reduce the holding period. Code §246(c)(4).

[56] Tax Code §246(c)(4)(C). Recall the discussion in the text, previously, of the term "substantially similar or related property." Generally, this means a two-part test is satisfied: 1. the value of the stock and property primarily reflect the performance of a single firm or enterprise, the same industry or industries, or the same economic factors; and 2. changes in fair market value of the stock track, directly or indirectly, changes in the value of the prop-

erty. Treasury Regulation §1.246-5(b)(1). The risk of loss is diminished if changes in the values of the stock and positions are expected to vary inversely. Treasury Regulation §1.246-5(b)(2). For examples, see Treasury Regulation §1.246-5. Treasury Regulation §1.246-5(c)(1) contains rules regarding the application of these provisions to a portfolio of stocks.

[57] Tax Code §246A

[58] Tax Code §246A(c). The ex-dividend date is the first day of the ex dividend period, meaning the date on which the stock goes ex dividend. Securities sold ex dividend are not entitled to share in the most recently declared dividend. In other words, if the stock is purchased during the ex dividend period, the dividend payout is made to the seller, not the buyer. Usually, stock prices fall when the ex dividend period starts. Prices may rise gradually as the next dividend date approaches. See *www.investorwords.com.*

[59] Tax Code §246A(c)

[60] Tax Code §246A(d)(3). Under Code §246A(d)(3), portfolio indebtedness can include amounts received from a short sale.

[61] Rev. Rul. 88-66, 1988-2 CB 34

[62] Tax Code §246A(d)(4)

[63] Tax Code §246A(f) authorizes the issuance of regulations disallowing the interest deduction instead of reducing the dividend received deduction where the borrower on the debt is a person other than the corporation receiving the dividends.

[64] Tax Code §246A(b)

[65] Tax Code §246A(e)

[66] To avoid extraordinary status, the stock must be held for more than two years before the "dividend announcement date." Tax Code §1059(a). The dividend announcement date is the date on which the corporation declares, announces or agrees to the dividend, whichever is earliest. Code §1059(d)(5).

[67] Tax Code §1059(c)

[68] Tax Code §1059(d)(1)

[69] Tax Code §1059(c)(4). The value must be shown as of the day before the ex-dividend date.

[70] Tax Code §1059(c)(3)

[71] Tax Code §1059(d)(3)

[72] See Tax Code §1059(e) for the rules applicable in these cases. Note that dividends paid on "disqualified preferred stock" also are treated as extraordinary, regardless of the holding period. Code §1059(f).

[73] Under IRC §1059(d)(1), the basis reduction occurs at the beginning of the ex-dividend date of the distribution triggering the basis reduction.

[74] Tax Code §1059(a)

[75] Tax Code §1059(d)(6). This exception does not apply to distributions, like partial liquidations and certain redemptions, described under Code §1059(e)(1). Treasury Regulation §1.1059(e)-1(a).

[76] Tax Code §1059(e)(2). This exception does not apply to distributions, like partial liquidations and certain redemptions, described under Code §1059(e)(1). Treasury Regulation §1.1059(e)-1(a)

9 | TAXATION OF REDEMPTIONS

INTRODUCTION

When an investor sells stock that he owns in a publicly traded corporation, any gain or loss derived from the transaction is treated as a capital gain or loss. Stock is generally sold to a third-party investor, or the corporation itself may be buying back its own shares from the market. In either case, the shareholder's percentage of ownership in the corporation has diminished in proportion to the amount of stock sold.

When a shareholder sells stock owned in a closely held corporation, to a third party, capital gain treatment applies to that transaction as well. However, when the shareholder sells his stock back to the issuing corporation itself, the nature of the transaction is not as clear. A corporation may redeem its stock with cash, securities, or other property.[1] Consequently, it experiences a reduction in the amount of assets owned. The shareholder may or may not experience a change of percentage ownership resulting from the redemption. If a change in percentage ownership occurs, the transaction is treated as a capital gain. If no change in percentage ownership occurs, then the distribution is treated as a dividend.

Example 1—Florence owns 25 percent of the stock in Your Design, Inc. Her basis in the stock is $10,000. The corporation has earnings and profits of $100,000. If Your Design redeems all of her stock for $18,000, Florence has an $8000 gain. Because her ownership is terminated in the corporation as a result of the redemption, it is treated as a capital gain, the same as any other sale.

Example 2—John owns all of the stock of Fly High, Inc. with a basis of $80,000. Fly High has earnings and profits of $150,000. John redeems 25 percent of his shares for $100,000. Since this transaction results in no change of ownership (John is still the sole shareholder), but merely a reduction in corporate assets, the redemption is treated as a dividend.

This chapter discusses the various circumstances in which a stock redemption is treated as a capital gain. This is important for investors who want to maximize their after-tax return from stock holdings. If capital gain treatment applies, the amount received is offset by the shareholder's basis, and the difference is reported as capital gain income. For individuals, this income may be subject to taxation at favorable long-term rates. Corporate investors may prefer dividend treatment, because of the dividend-received deduction, as discussed in Chapter 8. In either case, the potential tax consequences arising from a redemption should be one of the considerations weighed before a stock investment is made.

REASONS FOR A STOCK REDEMPTION

A shareholder may find a stock redemption desirable for a number of reasons:

1. A shareholder may want to withdraw from a corporation and not sell his stock to an outside party. The purpose would be to give complete ownership to the remaining shareholders.
2. A shareholder may be required to sell his stock back to the corporation by the terms of a buy-sell agreement.
3. A shareholder may not wish to withdraw but to merely reduce his percentage ownership. This is common when the shareholder is thinking about retiring, beginning another business, or is in failing health and other family members own the remaining stock.
4. There may not be a market for the stock. Therefore, a shareholder's only alternative is to have the corporation redeem the stock.
5. A shareholder may deliberately wish to reduce the amount of assets owned by a corporation. Breaking apart the assets and selling them individually may bring higher prices. If he/she subsequently wishes to sell the company, a lower selling price can be asked, making the sale easier to accomplish.
6. If a shareholder dies, a corporation may have an agreement to buy back his stock to provide funds for estate, funeral, and administrative expenses.

7. Shareholder discord and hostility may prompt a shareholder to redeem some or all of his shares.

CONSTRUCTIVE OWNERSHIP OF STOCK

Determining whether a redemption qualifies for capital gain involves an understanding of who is actually the owner of the shares. The rules of constructive ownership of stock under §318 apply, which may complicate a situation. Under these rules a person is considered as owning the stock owned directly or indirectly by or for:

- Members of the family, which is defined as a spouse (other than one who is legally separated from the individual under a decree of divorce or separate maintenance), children (including legally adopted children), grandchildren, and parents.[2] The same stock that is attributed to one family member by these rules cannot be reattributed to another family member.

  Example—Matthew, his wife Beth, their son Willie, and grandson, Nicholas each own 25 percent of the stock of Big Box Corp. In calculating the family attribution rules for Nicholas, he is deemed to own 50 percent of the shares of Big Box. He is only treated as owning the actual shares owned by his father, Willie. The shares owned by his grandparents, Matthew and Beth, are not attributed to him because they are not actually owned by Willie.

- A partnership or estate. Partnership or estate holdings are considered as owned proportionately by the partners or beneficiaries.[3] An S corporation is treated in the same manner as a partnership.[4]

  Example—Serina owns 50 percent of Great Lakes, a partnership. She also owns 40 shares of the 100 shares of stock outstanding in Gymnastics, Inc., and the Great Lakes partnership owns the other 60 shares of the stock outstanding. Serina is deemed to own 70 shares of the stock in Gymnastics, Inc.

- A trust. Trust stock is considered to be owned proportionately by its beneficiaries.[5] This does not apply to tax exempt employees' trusts under §501(a).

- A corporation. When 50 percent or more of the value of the stock in the corporation is owned, directly or indirectly, by or for any person, such person is considered as owning any stock owned by the corporation in the same proportion.[6]

Example—Emily owns 60 percent and Melissa owns 40 percent of the stock of Sing Songs, Inc. Sing Songs owns 1000 shares of Great Recordings, Inc. Emily is treated as owning 600 shares of Great Recordings, and Melissa is treated as owning none of the shares due to her owning less than 50 percent of the value of the stock of Sing Songs.

In applying the 50-percent ownership test, stock constructively owned by a shareholder is added to the stock actually owned.[7]

Example—Take the same facts as above except that Emily is Melissa's mother. Emily and Melissa are treated as each owning 100 percent of the stock of Sing Songs and 1000 shares of Great Recordings, Inc.

- If any person has an option to acquire stock, that stock will be considered as being owned by that person.[8]

Stock constructively owned by a partnership, estate, trust, or corporation may not be reattributed to another partner, beneficiary, or shareholder.[9]

TAX TREATMENTS OF STOCK REDEMPTIONS

As previously stated, sales of stock to a third party result in capital gains or losses. Redemption of stock by a minority shareholder in a closely held corporation also results in capital gains because the transaction has the same result as sales to a third party. However, redemptions by shareholders owning large percentages of the stock are treated differently. If there are ample earnings and profits[10] within the corporation, and if the percentage of ownership does not change in a significant way, then the redemptions are treated as dividends to the extent of earnings and profits.

When redemptions are treated as dividends, current regulations do not provide any explicit guidance regarding the determination of the shareholders' basis of the stock redeemed. Proposed regulations under 26 CFR Part 1 state that the Code does not permit basis to offset any portion of the redemption distribution that is treated as a dividend. This is the same as in regular situations when a corporation pays a dividend and the shareholder retains his/her basis in the stock. The proposed regulations state that in cases where a distribution is treated as a dividend, the unutilized basis of the redeemed stock should not disappear and should be taken into account for federal income tax purposes at some time. Additionally, any tax benefit associated with the unutilized basis of redeemed stock should remain with the taxpayer that owns the investment. The proposed regulations are trying to prevent taxpayers from basis shifting. An example would be shifting basis among family members who each own stock in the same corporation or from a nontaxpayer shareholder to a taxpayer shareholder. These regulations would apply to partial and complete redemptions. A loss on unutilized basis would be recognized when the shareholder has sufficiently reduced his or her actual and constructive ownership interest in the redeeming corporation. The latest that the loss would be recognized is the final inclusion date, which is the last date a business action can take place. An example would be the date a corporation transfers its assets in complete liquidation.

Rules exist for determining whether a redemption is treated as a sale or exchange qualifying for capital gain treatment or as a distribution taxed as a dividend. Under §302, there are five categories that qualify for capital gain treatment:

(1) Redemptions in full termination of a shareholder's interest

(2) Substantially disproportionate redemption of stock

(3) Redemption that is not essentially equivalent to a dividend

(4) Redemption from a noncorporate shareholder in partial liquidation of the distributing corporation

(5) Redemption to pay death taxes[11]

Redemptions in Full Termination of a Shareholder's Interest

Redemptions in full termination of a shareholder's interest occur when all of the stock owned by a shareholder is redeemed. This includes all classes of stock owned by the shareholder and encompasses both voting and nonvoting stock.

Example—Yevonne owns 50 of the 100 shares outstanding of common stock of Wonderful Wedding Cakes, Inc. She also owns 50 of the 200 shares outstanding of preferred, nonvoting stock. The other shareholders are unrelated to her. She redeems all 50 shares of her common stock and all 50 shares of her preferred stock. This is a complete redemption of her interest in the corporation and qualifies for capital gain treatment.

Example—Using the same facts in the above example, Yevonne redeems 50 shares of her common stock and 20 shares of her preferred stock. This is not a complete redemption of her interest, even though the preferred stock is nonvoting. Therefore the redemption does not qualify as a full termination of a shareholder's interest.

Although a complete termination may seem straightforward, the transaction may be affected by the rules of constructive ownership discussed above. However, the family attribution rules may be waived if the following requirements are met:

- Immediately after the distribution, the shareholder has no interest in the corporation (including an interest as officer, director, or employee), other than an interest as a bondholder or other creditor;[12]
- The shareholder does not acquire any interest in the corporation (other than stock acquired by bequest or inheritance) within 10 years from the date of the distribution; and
- The shareholder must notify the IRS of any interest he or she acquires in the corporation within the 10-year period other than by bequest or inheritance and must retain appropriate records.[13] An agreement, in the form of a separate statement, must be filed with the IRS in duplicate and signed by the shareholder. It is then attached to the first tax return filed by the shareholder for the taxable year in which the distribution took place. The agreement should state that the shareholder has not acquired, other than by bequest or inheritance, any interest in the corporation since the terminating distribution. Additionally, the shareholder agrees to notify the IRS within 30 days of any such acquisition that occurs within 10 years from the date of the distribution.[14]

Example—Linus owns 50 percent of the stock in Charlie's Sporting Goods, Inc. His wife, Lucy owns the remaining shares. Even if all of Linus' stock is redeemed, the transaction will not qualify as a complete termination. This is because Linus is treated as owning all of his wife's shares. However, if Linus meets the conditions described above and files the appropriate documentation, he can waive the attribution rules. This means Linus will receive capital gain treatment when shares are redeemed, even though his wife owns all of the remaining shares of Charlie's Sporting Goods, Inc.

There is an exception to the waiver of the family attribution rules. This exception was implemented to prevent family members from transferring stock among themselves in order to qualify a transaction as a complete redemption. The exception is that the family attribution rules are not waived if:

(1) Any portion of the stock redeemed was acquired, directly or indirectly, within the 10-year period ending on the date of the redemption from a person related to the shareholder; or

(2) Any related person owns stock at the time of the redemption and that person acquired the stock, directly or indirectly, from the redeeming shareholder within 10 years of the redemption. If the stock was acquired in the same transaction as the redemption, then the transaction is acceptable.[15]

Example—Continuing with the same facts as in the above example, assume that Linus transferred Charlie's Sporting Goods, Inc. stock to his son two years before the redemption of his remaining shares. Linus no longer is able to waive the family attribution rules. He will not be treated as completely terminating his investment in Charlie's, even though he no longer owns any of the stock directly.

A person's interest as a creditor, after a complete termination of shareholder interest distribution, is valid only if the rights of that person are not greater or broader in scope that what would be necessary for the enforcement of his claim of the debt. This debt must not be proprietary or be subordinate to claims of general creditors. Additionally, payments and interest on the debt must not be based on the amount of corporate earnings.[16]

Substantially Disproportionate Redemptions

A redemption is treated as an exchange or sale qualifying for capital gain treatment if it is substantially disproportionate with respect to the shareholder. To be considered "substantially disproportionate," the following requirements must be met:

- The shareholder must own less than 50 percent of the total combined voting power of all classes of voting stock immediately after the redemption.[17]
- The ratio of voting stock owned by the shareholder immediately after the redemption is less than 80 percent of his or her ratio of ownership before the redemption;
- The ratio of common stock (voting or nonvoting) owned by the shareholder immediately after the redemption is less than 80 percent of his/her ratio of ownership before the redemption.[18] Addi-

tionally, the plan must not be made for the purpose of effecting a series of redemptions that do not, in the aggregate, meet the first three requirements.[19]

> **Example**—Lois, Clark, and Jimmy are three unrelated share-holders. Clark owns 500 shares and Lois and Jimmy each hold 200 shares of the outstanding voting common stock of Daily Planet, Inc. Clark decides to have Daily Planet redeem 300 of his shares. Prior to the redemption, Clark owned 55.56 percent (500/900) of the outstanding stock and afterwards he owns 33.33 percent (200/600) of the outstanding stock. Since Clark owns less than 50 percent of the voting stock and less than 80 percent of the percentage of voting common stock owned by him before the redemption (80 percent X 55.56 percent = 44.45 percent), the redemption qualifies as a substantially disproportionate redemption.

These requirements can be met only if voting stock is redeemed. However, if a redemption does qualify as being substantially disproportionate, the simultaneous redemption of nonvoting preferred stock is included as a sale or exchange qualifying for capital gains treatment.[20]

Additionally, the redemption of nonvoting stock actually owned by the shareholder and voting common stock constructively owned by the same shareholder is considered a redemption of both voting and nonvoting stock for purposes of these regulations.[21] If no common stock is owned, directly or indirectly, then a redemption of voting preferred stock can qualify as a substantially disproportionate redemption even though the shareholder does not experience a reduction in common stock ownership.[22]

Redemptions That Are Not Essentially Equivalent to Dividends

A redemption must result in a meaningful reduction of the shareholder's proportionate interest in the corporation in order to quality as "not essentially equivalent to dividends."[23] Factors to be considered in determining whether the distribution results in a meaningful reduction in a shareholder's proportionate interest in a corporation include:

- A shareholder's right to vote and exercise control
- A shareholder's right to participate in current earnings and accumulated surplus
- A shareholder's right to share in net assets in liquidation[24]

Tax law does not provide safe harbor rules to determine when a redemption is not essentially equivalent to a dividend. The Supreme Court's decision in *Maclin P. Davis* identified some of the criteria to be used in making this determination. The Court maintained that: (1) a business purpose is irrelevant, (2) §318 attribution rules must be used to determine dividend equivalency, and (3) a redemption of part of a sole shareholder's stock is always essentially equivalent to a dividend.

Example—Chris, his wife Polly, and their two sons Mitchell and Jessie each own 500 shares of the 2000 outstanding common shares of Habitat, Inc. Chris also owns 500 shares of the outstanding preferred stock. Chris purchased the preferred stock 20 years ago for $150,000 to inject working capital into the corporation to qualify for a 20-year loan for a corporate mortgage. Chris had an agreement with the corporation that the preferred stock would be redeemed when the mortgage was repaid. The mortgage was repaid this year and the 500 shares were redeemed. Because of the family attribution rules, Chris is deemed to own all of the stock owned by Polly, Mitchell, and Jessie both before and after the redemption. Despite the fact that there was a legitimate business purpose to the issuance and redemption of the preferred stock and not one of tax avoidance, Chris did not reduce his proportionate ownership in Habitat, and the redemption does not qualify as "being not essentially equivalent to a dividend."

Redemptions of Common Stock   Redemptions of common stock by sole shareholders do not result in any reduction of ownership and do not qualify as a reduction that is not essentially equivalent to a dividend.[25]

Redemptions of common stock by majority shareholders who continue to maintain control after the redemption generally must be recognized as dividends. However, whether majority shareholders are in control after a redemption depends on the facts and circumstances of the situation and not solely on whether the shareholder owns more than 50 percent of its stock. State law regarding control should be consulted.

Redemptions from minority shareholders are more likely to result in a redemption that is not essentially equivalent to a dividend. The reason is that the shareholder who does not control a corporation has no power to distribute any of its earnings and profits.[26]

Example—Meaningful reduction of ownership. Florence is a minority shareholder in a publicly held corporation, Winron, Inc. Winron redeems some shares owned by Florence. After the redemption, Florence owns .0001113 percent of the stock outstanding. Previously, she held

.000105735 percent of the stock outstanding. Florence holds 95 percent of her stock after the redemption. The redemption is a meaningful reduction of Florence's proportionate interest in Winron, and, therefore, it is not considered as being essentially equivalent to a dividend.

Example—No reduction in shareholder's interest.

Consider the facts above except that Winron, Inc. offers to buy 150,000 shares of its common stock from its shareholders for $25 per share. Winron has 1,000,000 shares outstanding and 5000 shareholders. About 3000 shareholders redeemed 100,000 shares of their stock in response to this offer, including Florence, who redeems 200 of the 2000 shares she owned in response to this tender offer. Prior to the offer, Florence's proportionate interest in Winron was .2 percent (2,000/1,000,000), and after the redemption it was .2 percent (1,800/900,000). Therefore, there was no meaningful reduction in Florence's interest in Winron, and the redemption is essentially equivalent to a dividend.

Redemptions of Preferred Stock If a shareholder has a controlling interest in a corporation and decides to redeem his preferred stock, he or she still has the ability to maintain the dollar amount of preferred dividends he received by influencing the corporation to declare a common stock dividend. This redemption would essentially be equivalent to a dividend. Whether a shareholder owns preferred stock with voting rights, or is convertible into common stock, or provides participation in management decisions in any way is all based on the circumstances of each individual situation.

Example—Randy owns 75 percent of the common stock of Handmade Wood Products, Inc. and 100 percent of the nonparticipating, nonvoting, nonconvertible preferred stock. Handmade Wood Products redeems 50 percent of his preferred stock. There is no meaningful change of Randy's interest in the corporation as a result of this transaction because he is still the majority shareholder and can influence corporate decisions. Therefore this redemption is essentially equivalent to a dividend.

The redemption by a corporation of any of its nonvoting, nonconvertible, nonparticipating preferred stock that is not "section 306 stock"[27] and that is owned by an individual who doesn't own any of the corporation's common stock qualifies as "not essentially equivalent to a dividend" under Section 302(b)(1) of the Code.[28]

Example—Gary owns all of the preferred nonvoting, nonconvertible, nonparticipating stock of Thruway Electricians, Inc. He owns none of the common stock of the corporation. Thruway redeems 10 percent of his preferred stock. Since the rights represented by the redeemed shares were yielded to the common shareholders of the corporation and could not be recovered through the taxpayer's continued stock ownership, the redemption does qualify as "not essentially equivalent to a dividend."[29]

Redemptions from Noncorporate Shareholders in Partial Liquidation of a Corporation

A redemption will qualify for capital gain treatment as a sale or exchange if it is a redemption of stock held by a shareholder who is not a corporation and in partial liquidation of the distributing corporation.[30] This category of redemptions applies only to individuals, partnerships, estates, and trusts. Qualification for this category of redemption is determined at the corporate level, and the redemption is pursuant to a plan that occurs within the taxable year in which the plan is adopted or within the succeeding taxable year.[31] A redemption can qualify as a partial liquidation whether or not it is pro rata with respect to all of the shareholders.[32]

Example—Alex, Nicholas, Christina, and Kate each own 500 of the 2000 outstanding shares of common stock of Uniforms, Inc. Uniforms, Inc. had two divisions—one that sells uniforms to health-care professionals and the other to restaurant employees. The board of directors of Uniforms, Inc. drew a plan to liquidate their restaurant uniform division. They sold that division to a third-party purchaser for cash during the same taxable year as when the plan was adopted. The distribution of the proceeds of the sale will qualify for sale or exchange treatment subject to capital gains. It does not matter if Uniforms, Inc. redeems half of the stock held by each shareholder or all of the stock held by two shareholders.

A formal plan should be adopted so that there is no confusion about the intention to partially liquidate. This plan should be recorded in the corporate minutes by the board of directors and indicate the details of the redemption. IRS Form 966 must be filed by the corporation within 30 days of the adoption of the plan containing the following information:

- Name and address of the corporation
- Place and date of incorporation
- Date of the adoption of the resolution or plan and dates of any amendments or supplements to the plan
- The internal revenue district in which the last income tax return of the corporation was filed and the taxable year it covered[33]

Requirements of a Partial Liquidation   The number of shares of stock considered redeemed in a partial liquidation, regardless of the number of shares actually surrendered, is computed based on the fair market value of the stock of the distributing corporation before and after the distribution.[34] If the stock is from a closely held corporation, it is necessary to value the stock by valuing the underlying assets and by computing the number of shares considered redeemed.[35] Factors to consider in the valuation of the stock of a closely held corporation include:

(a) The nature of the business and the history of the enterprise from its inception

(b) The economic outlook in general and the condition and outlook of the specific industry in particular

(c) The book value of the stock and the financial condition of the business

(d) The earning capacity of the company

(e) The dividend-paying capacity

(f) Whether the enterprise has goodwill or other intangible value

(g) Sales of the stock and the size of the block of stock to be valued

(h) The market price of stock of corporations in the same or a similar line of business having their stocks actively traded in a free and open market, either on an exchange or over-the-counter[36]

An independent, competent, certified business valuator should perform the valuation.

Example—Partial liquidation of a publicly traded corporation. Flossie owned 100 shares of Dental Equipment, Inc., all of which were represented by a single stock certificate. Her adjusted basis for each share of stock was $40. Flossie received $5000 as a partial liquidating distribution but does not actually give up any Dental Equipment stock. Therefore, the number of shares Flossie is treated as surrendering is dependent on the fair market value of the Dental Equipment holdings. The mean between the highest and lowest quoted selling price per share of Dental's stock on the exchange just prior to the time that the stock was traded ex distribution was $100. A public announcement of the distribution in partial liquidation had been made by Dental Equipment, Inc. prior to the date the distribution was first made available to the shareholders.

The amount of stock deemed to be surrendered by Flossie is determined by the relationship between the per-share amount distributed to her

($5000/$100 = 50) and the per-share fair market value of the stock immediately before the distribution ($100). Flossie is deemed to have surrendered one-half of her 100 shares (50) of Dental Equipment, Inc. in exchange for the $5000 distribution. Under §1001, she recognized a gain of $3000 ($5000 distribution less her basis of $2000 for the 50 shares deemed surrendered ($40 adjusted basis per share X 50 shares)).[37]

Example—Partial liquidation of a closely held corporation. Assume the same facts as in the previous example except that Dental Equipment, Inc. is held by only 10 shareholders. Immediately before Dental Equipment, Inc. transferred funds to be distributed to each shareholder, each share of its outstanding stock had a value of $95, which was determined by an outside business valuator. Flossie is deemed to have surrendered 52.63 shares of Dental Equipment, Inc. in exchange for the $5000 distribution. ($5000/$95 = 52.63 shares) Under §1001 of the Code, the taxpayer recognized a gain of $2894.80 ($5000 − $2,105.20 ($40 basis per share X 52.63 shares)).[38]

Actual surrender of stock certificates is not necessary when there is a pro rata distribution by a corporation of the net proceeds of the sale of all assets of one of its two divisions resulting in contraction of the business.[39]

§302 Safe Harbor

A safe harbor refers to a provision of the tax law under which taxpayers can be reasonably confident of receiving specific favorable tax treatment, provided they satisfy what are typically fairly mechanical tests. One such safe harbor rule offers partial liquidation treatment under §302(e)(2) for a redemption if the following standards are met:

1) The redemption is attributable to the distributing corporation's ceasing to conduct a qualified trade or business or the redemption consists of the assets of that business, and
2) Immediately after the redemption, the redeeming corporation is actively engaged in the conduct of a qualified trade or business.

The term "qualified trade or business" means, in this context, any trade or business that was:

(A) Actively conducted throughout the five-year period ending on the date of the redemption, and
(B) Not acquired by the corporation within the five-year period ending with the redemption.[40]

Example—Couch Potato Chips, Inc. has three divisions: potato chips, premade sour cream dips, and cheese sticks. Each of these divisions has been in business for more than 10 years. Couch purchased the premade sour cream dips division three years ago, and the cheese sticks division six years ago. A redemption from the cheese sticks division may be distributed to the shareholders as a partial liquidation, but a transaction involving the premade sour cream dip operation would not. This is because Couch Potato Chips acquired the sour cream division within the past five years.

Contraction of the Corporate Business

A partial liquidation of a corporation occurs when there is a genuine contraction of the corporate business. One example of a contraction is the distribution of unused insurance proceeds recovered as a result of a fire that destroyed part of the business, causing a cessation of a part of its activities.[41]

A contraction of the corporate business does not have to be the elimination of a business, division, or subsidiary. A reduction of activities in a single business will qualify as long as the result is a significant reduction of the corporation's employees, services, income, or assets (other than the cash distributed).[42]

Example—Very Timely Videos, Inc. offered a comprehensive line of foreign and domestic videos produced over the last 10 years. Three video stores moved into the area, causing severe competition. In response, the shareholders of Very Timely Videos, Inc. eliminated five employees, reduced its floor space, changed the merchandise it carried to eliminate several producers of foreign films, and disposed of a number of its computers, counters, inventory, desks, and chairs. Under a plan that the shareholders adopted, the corporation would focus on discount videos. There was no strategy for growth. It subsequently paid cash to its shareholders, pro rata, in redemption of part of its outstanding common stock. This redemption qualifies as a genuine contraction of a business.

Working Capital of a Terminated Business Activity   A redemption qualifies as a partial liquidation if the redemption does not exceed the net proceeds from the sale of the business assets plus the portion of working capital reasonably attributable to the terminated business activities. Additionally, the working capital must no longer be required in the operation of the continuing business activities.[43] In determining the amount of working capital reasonably attributable to the operation of the business activity terminated, all pertinent factors will be considered. However, the amount of working capital used in the business activity just prior to its termination will be the primary consideration.[44] A substantial increase in the amount of assets, such as cash, inventories, accounts receivable, etc., may indicate a scheme to secure partial liquidation treatment of a distribution. The IRS may argue that the partial liquidation is really a dividend.

Subsidiaries   Special rules apply to partial liquidations involving termination of a subsidiary. IRC §346(a) of the Code provides, in part, that a distribution will be treated as a partial liquidation of a corporation if it is in redemption of part of the stock pursuant to a plan that is carried out within the subsequent taxable year.[45] The business activities of a subsidiary are not generally considered to be business activities of its parent corporation. Under normal circumstances, the mere fact that one corporation owns all the stock of another corporation is not sufficient to attribute the business of the subsidiary to the parent corporation.[46]

However, Reg. §1.346-1(a)(2) makes a clarification that the distribution must result from a genuine contraction of the business. A genuine contraction of the business occurs when a corporation liquidates the assets of a subsidiary and then distributes the proceeds of the liquidation to its shareholders. The distribution is considered to be in complete liquidation of the subsidiary only if:

(1) The parent corporation receiving the proceeds of the sale must have been the owner of the stock from the date of the adoption of the plan of liquidation through receipt of the proceeds;

(2) The distribution by the subsidiary to the parent corporation is in complete cancellation or redemption of all of its stock, and the transfer of all the property occurs within the taxable year;

(3) The distribution may be one of a series of distributions by the subsidiary in complete redemption of all of its stock in accordance with a plan under which the transfer of all the property is to be totally completed within 3 years.[47]

Redemptions to Pay Death Taxes

IRC §303 provides that, in certain cases, a distribution in redemption of stock that must be included in the value of the gross estate of a decedent shall be treated as a distribution in full payment in exchange for the redeemed stock.[48] The amount distributed that can qualify as a redemption to pay death taxes is limited to the sum of:

(1) Estate, inheritance, legacy, and succession taxes (including any interest collected) imposed because of the decedent's death, and

(2) The amount of funeral and administration expenses allowable as deductions to the estate.[49]

In order to qualify as a redemption to pay death taxes, the distribution must be an amount in excess of (1) 35 percent of the value of the gross estate of the decedent, or (2) 50 percent of the taxable estate.[50] The 35-percent value of the gross estate means 35 percent of the excess of the value of the gross estate over the amounts allowable for deductions for funeral and administration expenses.[51] To fulfill the 35-percent or 50-percent requirements, stock of two or more corporations shall be treated as the stock of a single corporation if more than 75 percent of the value of the outstanding stock of each corporation is included in determining the value of the decedent's gross estate.[52] Additionally, the stock must constitute 20 percent or more of the outstanding stock of each corporation.[53]

Example—The gross estate of a decedent has a value of $1,500,000 and a taxable estate of $1,200,000. The total of death taxes and funeral and administrative expenses is $300,000. The gross estate includes the following two stocks valued as follows:

Green Acre	Common Stock	$500,000	50% of outstanding stock
Black Acre	Common Stock	$200,000	20% of outstanding stock

The stock of both corporations is treated as the stock of a single corporation because they have a value in excess of $525,000 ($1,500,000 X 35 percent or 50 percent X $1,200,000). The distribution by both of the above corporations of amounts not exceeding, in the aggregate, $300,000, in redemption of the common stock of the corporation will be treated as a payment in exchange for the redeemed stock.

The time limit to qualify as a redemption to pay taxes is that a distribution must be made after the death of the decedent and:

(A) Before 90 days after the expiration of the statute of limitations for assessment of the federal estate tax.[54] This period is three years and nine months.

(B) If a petition of redetermination of a deficiency in estate tax has been filed with the Tax Court, at any time before the expiration of 60 days after the decision of the Tax Court becomes final, or

(C) By the last installment of estate tax due if an election has been made to extend the time for payment of estate taxes attributable to a closely held corporation.

The 2001 Tax Relief Act repealed the estate tax and the generation-skipping tax. This Act is subject to a phase-in period lasting through 2009 and includes rate reductions and increased exemption amounts.[55] Assuming this repeal takes effect, redemptions under §303 will be limited to funeral and administrative expenses, plus any state estate or inheritance taxes that apply.

Reporting Requirements for the Shareholder Redeeming Stock

There is little guidance as to the exact information required, but a shareholder must report the facts and circumstances regarding a distribution received in redemption of stock. A separate statement should be attached to the tax return for the taxable year when the distribution occurred. The statement should list the details of the distribution, whether the distribution should be treated as a sale or exchange or as a regular corporate distribution (dividend), whether it is a complete or partial liquidation, the date and description of any property received, and how the fair market value of the property was determined.[56]

Individual Shareholders   Individuals report distributions treated as regular corporate distributions as dividends on the front page of Form 1040. Additionally, if the total amount of interest and dividends is greater than $ 1,500, Schedule B, Part II indicating the name of each distributing corporation and the amount must be listed. Nontaxable distributions should also be listed there. Capital gain distributions are listed on Schedule D. If the taxpayer does not need Schedule D to report any other capital gains or losses, then the capital gain distribution should only be reported on Page 1 of Form 1040, and CGD (capital gain distribution) should be written to the left of the amount. If the redemption of stock is a sale or exchange, depending on the holding period, it is reported on Part I of the Form 1040, Schedule D, if it is short-term (less than 1 year) or Part II if it is long-term (one year or more).

Corporate Shareholders Corporations report dividends on the first page of Form 1120 and on Form 1120, Schedule C. As an incentive to invest, corporations are allowed a dividend-received deduction, which is also calculated on Schedule C. The dividend-received deduction, discussed in Chapter 8, allows corporate shareholders to deduct from 70 percent to 100 percent of certain dividends paid to them, provided various conditions are met. If a redemption is treated as a sale or exchange, the redemption is reported in either Part I or Part II of the Form 1120, Schedule D, depending on the holding period in the stock redeemed.

EFFECTS ON THE CORPORATION REDEEMING THE STOCK

A corporation generally does not recognize a gain or loss with respect to a partial redemption of its own stock for cash.[57] If a corporation distributes property (other than an obligation of the corporation) in redemption of its stock, and the fair market value of the property exceeds its adjusted basis, then gain shall be recognized as though it was sold to an outside party at its fair market value.[58]

Example—Stovroff-Taylor, Inc. redeems 500 shares of its stock from its shareholder in exchange for property that has a fair market value of $600,000. The property was acquired two years ago for $350,000. Stovroff-Taylor must recognize a long-term gain of $250,000.

If the property distributed is subject to a liability or if the shareholder assumes a liability of the liquidating corporation in connection with the distribution, then the fair market value shall be treated as not less than the amount of the liability.[59]

Example—Assume the same facts as above except that Stovroff-Taylor is subject to a liability of $675,000 on the property. Stovroff-Taylor must recognize a long-term gain of $325,000 as a result of the redemption.

A corporation may not recognize a loss in cases where property has depreciated in value.[60]

Effect on Earnings and Profits

There are two types of adjustments that must be made to the corporation's earnings and profits after a redemption of stock.

The first adjustment deals with distributions of appreciated property for redemptions of stock. Earnings and profits are increased by the amount by which the fair market value of the property exceeds the adjusted basis of the redeeming corporation.[61]

The next adjustment applies to all redemptions treated as a dividend distribution. Earnings and profits are decreased by: (a) the amount of cash distributed, (b) the adjusted basis of the property (other than appreciated property),[62] and (c) the fair market value of appreciated property distributed.[63]

Example 1—Popsicles Galore, Inc. redeems 100 shares of its stock from Joannie in exchange for property with a fair market value of $500 and an adjusted basis in the hands of Popsicles of $400. Popsicles also redeems 100 shares of its stock from Jacque for property with a fair market value of $500 and an adjusted basis of $550. The earnings and profits of Popsicles are increased $100 ($500 − $400 fair market value less basis resulting in a gain) and decreased by $1050 (fair market value of $500 of property distributed to Joannie + $550 of adjusted basis of property distributed to Jacque). The net adjustment is a decrease of $950 to earnings and profits.

In cases where the corporation distributes its own debt obligations in redemption of its stock, earnings and profits are decreased by the principal amount of the obligation.[64] However, when the obligations have original issue discount, the decrease is the aggregate issue price of the obligation.[65]

Example 2—Popsicles Galore, Inc. redeems 100 shares of stock from Rebecca in exchange for a note of the corporation having a principal amount of $500 and fair market value of $500. Earnings and profits and reduced by $500.

If any property distributed in redemption of stock is subject to a liability, or if a shareholder assumed a liability of the corporation in connection with the distribution, then earnings and profits will be increased by the amount of the liability assumed.

Example 3—Popsicles Galore, Inc. redeems 100 shares of stock from Colette in exchange for property with a fair market value of $500, an adjusted basis in the hands of Popsicles of $400 and subject to a liability of $50. The earnings and profits of Galore are increased by $100 (difference between the fair market value and the adjusted basis) and decreased by $450 (fair market value less the liability), resulting in a net decrease of $350.

If a redemption is treated as a sale or exchange, the decrease in earnings and profits cannot exceed the redeemed stock's share of the earnings and profits.[66] Earnings and profits are decreased pro rata to the amount of the corporation's outstanding stock that is redeemed and cannot be decreased by more that the amount distributed.

Example 4—Referring to Example 1, Popsicles Galore, Inc. redeems 100 of the 200 shares of its only outstanding stock. Popsicles has $1000 of earnings and profits, and the fair market value of its assets is $2000. Popsicles redeems all of Jacque's stock for $1000 in cash, which will terminate Her interest in Popsicles. The earnings and profits are decreased by only $500 as a result of this pro rata redemption.

Reporting Requirements of the Corporation Redeeming the Stock

A corporation must file Form 966 with the IRS 30 days after an adoption of any plan for dissolution or liquidation. A certified copy of the plan plus any amendments must be attached to Form 966.[67] Additionally, Form 1099-DIV must be provided to each shareholder to which distributions were made. Form 1096 must summarize all Forms 1099-DIV and be sent to the IRS by February 28th (or March 31st if filed electronically) of the year following the calendar year in which the distributions were made.

CONCLUSION

In summary, tax planning is crucial when a redemption of stock in a closely held company is being contemplated. For individuals, the savings in taxes might be substantial when the transaction is treated as a sale or exchange qualifying for capital gain rates versus dividends. However, as the discussion of the dividend-received deduction found in Chapter 8 suggests, corporate shareholders may prefer dividend treatment. Shareholders contemplating redemptions need to understand the tax rules that will apply, in order to be able to predict the after-tax consequences of the proposed transaction.

NOTES

[1] §317 This does not include stock in the corporation making the distribution.

[2] §318(a)(1)

[3] §318(a)(2)(A) Likewise the reverse is true. §318(a)(3)(A) states that stock owned, directly or indirectly by or for a partner or a beneficiary of an estate shall be considered as owned by the partnership or estate. In this case, all of the stock owned by a partner is considered as being owned by the partnership regardless of the amount of the interest in the partnership that the partner owns.

[4] §318(a)(5)(E)

[5] §318(a)(2)(B) This also includes grantor trusts whereby the grantor is considered the owner. Likewise under §318(a)(3)(B) stock owned directly or indirectly by or for a beneficiary of a trust shall be considered as owned by the trust, unless such beneficiary's interest in the trust is a remote contingent interest. A contingent interest will be considered remote if, under the maximum exercise of discretion by the trustee in favor of the beneficiary, the value of the interest, computed actuarially, is 5 percent or less of the value of the trust property.

[6] §318(a)(2)(C) Likewise, under §318(a)(3)(C) a corporation is considered as owning the stock owned, directly or indirectly, by a person who owns 50 percent or more of the value of the stock in a corporation.

[7] Reg.§1.318-1(a)(3)

[8] §318(a)(4)

[9] 318(a)(4)(C)

[10] Earnings and profits are not specifically defined in the codes and regulations. However, the term refers to the economic income of a corporation and how it relates to the ability to pay dividends. Normally, distributions are considered to come from earnings and profits. If the corporation has no earnings and profits, then distributions are considered as being a return of capital. If a shareholder's capital has been totally returned, then the distribution is considered a capital gain.

[11] §303(a) (1) and (2)

[12] According to the regulations, a person will be considered a creditor if his rights are not greater or broader than necessary to enforce his claim. The claim cannot be proprietary or subordinate to the claims of general creditors. If the amount of payments due under the obligation is dependent on corporate earnings, the person is not a creditor. See Treasury Regulation §1.302-4(d).

[13] §302(c)(2)

[14] Reg. §1.302-4(a) Additionally, if the shareholder fails to file the agreement, the IRS will grant a reasonable extension of time for filing the agreement if there was a reasonable cause for not filing the agreement.

[15] §302(c)(B) The objective is to eliminate the avoidance of tax motive.

[16] Reg. §1.302-4(d) If any of these variables are present, the person may not be considered a creditor, and the debt could be classified as a shareholder interest.

[17] §302(b)(2)(B) This is the primary limiting factor and the remaining requirements then follow.

[18] 302(b)(2)(C)

[19] §303(B)(2)(D)

[20] Reg.§1.302-3 The preferred stock cannot be tainted stock. Tainted stock is §306 stock that is subject to ordinary income. The circumstances under which stock is tainted fall within four categories, each with their own set of rules. These categories are: (1) stock received as a nontaxable stock dividend, (2) stock received in a corporate reorganization or corporate division, (3) stock having a transferred or substituted adjusted basis, and (4) stock acquired in certain transfers to controlled corporations. Stock distributed by a corporation having no earnings and profits is not tainted stock.

[21] Rev. Rul 77-237, 1977-2 C.B. 88

[22] Rev. Rul 81-41, 1981-1 C.B. 121 This ruling specifically addresses the requirement

that the shareholder's percentage of common stock ownership after a redemption must be less than 80 percent of the percentage owned immediately before the redemption. The Senate Finance Committee Report accompanying the enactment of Section 302 states: ". . . the Code only applies to a redemption of voting stock or to a redemption of both voting stock and other stock, but does not apply to the redemption solely of nonvoting stock. Therefore, both the legislative history and the regulations accompanying Section 302(b)(2) indicate that the provision should apply to the redemption of voting preferred stock."

[23] Rev. Rul 78-401, 1978-2 C.B.127

[24] Id.

[25] Rev.Rul. 78-422, 1978-2 C.B. 129

[26] Rev. Rull. 76-364, 1976-2 C.B. 91

[27] §306 stock is defined as stock, other than common stock, which was distributed as a nontaxable dividend, received in a corporate reorganization or separation, or acquired in an exchange if the receipt of money would have been treated as a dividend. It is applies to all stock having a substituted or transferred basis of §306 stock.

[28] Rev. Rul. 77-426, 1977-2 C.B.87

[29] Id, this Revenue Ruling examines the facts and circumstances of U.S. v Maclin P. Davis, 25 AFTR 2d 70-827, 70-1 USTC ¶9289 (USSC, 1970)

[30] §302(b)(4)

[31] §302(e)(1)

[32] §302(e)(4)

[33] Reg. §1.6043-1 Failure to file Form 966 does not prevent a qualifying redemption from receiving partial liquidation treatment. However, a corporation may be subject to penalties for willful failure to supply required information under §7203.

[34] Rev. Rul 77-245, 1977-1 C. B. 105, This ruling also refers to Rev. Rul. 59-240 for guidance in determining value for publicly traded stock and Rev. Rul. 56-513. Rev. Rul. 56-513 and 59-240 clarified for closely held corporations.

[35] Id.

[36] Rev. Rul. 59-60, 1959-1 C. B. 237. This revenue ruling is the cornerstone of all valuations particularly estates, gifts, valuations relative to divorce cases, and sales.

[37] Adapted from an example provided in Rev. Rul 77-245, 1977-1 C.B. 105

[38] Adapted from an example provided in Rev. Rul 77-245, 1977-1 C.B. 105

[39] Rev. Rul. 81-3, 1981-1 C.B. 125

[40] §302(e)(3)

[41] Reg. §1.346-1(a)(2)(iii). Additionally, the distribution of funds attributable to a reserve for an expansion program which has been abandoned does not qualify as a partial liquidation within the meaning of §346(a).

[42] Rev. Rul. 78-55, 1978-1 C.B. 88

[43] Rev. Rul. 60-232, 1960-2 C.B. 115

[44] Id.

[45] Rev. Rul. 75-223, 1975-1 C.B. 109

[46] Rev. Rul. 75-223, 1975-1 C.B. 109

[47] §332(b) There is no gain or loss recognized by a parent corporation receiving property in complete liquidation of its subsidiary.

[48] Reg. §1.303-1 reiterates §303. The 2001 tax legislation (the Economic Growth and Tax Relief Reconciliation Act of 2001) repeals the estate tax as of January 1, 2010. How-

ever, absent Congressional action, the repeal will become ineffective on January 1, 2011, meaning the estate tax laws that existed prior to the 2001 tax legislation will be reinstated.

[49] §303(a)

[50] Reg. §1.303-2(a)

[51] §303(b)(2)(A)

[52] Reg. 1.303-2 For purposes of the 75-percent requirement, stock which, at the decedent's death, represents the surviving spouse's interest in community property shall be considered as having been included in determining the value of the decedent's gross estate.

[53] §303(b)(2)(B) This stock can include the surviving spouse's interest and the surviving spouse as community property or as joint tenants, tenants by the entirety, or tenants in common.

[54] §303(b)(1)(A)

[55] There is strong belief within the accounting community that this repeal will be modified or reversed prior to 2010.

[56] Reg. §1.302-2(b) The Reg. Merely indicates that all the facts and circumstances should be reported. Therefore, one is to infer that all of the details that the IRS needs to make a determination whether or not the transaction was appropriately treated should be included.

[57] §311(a)

[58] §311(b)

[59] §336(b) This section is referenced by §311(b)(2)

[60] §311(a)

[61] §312(b)

[62] §312(a)

[63] §312(b)

[64] §312(a)(2)

[65] Id.

[66] §312(n)(7)

[67] §6043(a)(1)

10 DISTRIBUTIONS OF STOCK AND STOCK RIGHTS

INTRODUCTION

A stock dividend occurs when a distributing corporation makes a distribution of its own stock. Alternatively, a corporation might make a distribution of rights, enabling recipients to acquire stock in the future under specified terms. If the distribution is made using stock of a different corporation, or securities of the distributing corporation, it represents property and is taxed under the rules discussed in Chapter 8 of this book.

In general, a distribution of stock or stock rights in the distributing corporation is tax-free, although there are exceptions to this rule. When preferred or sometimes certain other stock is distributed, the shareholder also pays no tax. However, a later sale of these kinds of shares received tax-free may generate dividend income, even if the stock is a capital asset in the shareholder's hands. This means that the sale proceeds will be taxed at dividend tax rates. Also, a shareholder will not be able to offset income from the sale of the preferred or other stock with capital loss arising from other transactions.[1]

GENERAL RULES FOR DISTRIBUTIONS OF STOCK AND STOCK RIGHTS

Under IRC §305, a dividend paid using stock or stock rights in the distributing corporation generally is tax-free.

Example—David owns 100 shares of Lockport Company common stock, representing ownership of 100 percent of the corporation. He receives a stock dividend of 50 additional common shares, which he intends to give to his wife, Kathy. David is not taxed on the Lockport dividend.[2] Because he owned 100 percent of the company both before and after the distribution, receipt of the 50 shares does not represent income to David.[3] If his adjusted basis in the original 100 shares was $100 per share, his overall basis in the stock continues to be $10,000. However, David's basis per share changes. Since the new shares are identical to David's existing holdings, his basis in each share of stock now becomes $67 ($10,000 ÷ 150 = $67).[4] David's holding period in the new shares he receives dates back to the date he acquired the original stock.[5]

If David had received a distribution of preferred stock instead of common shares, the dividend would still be tax-free in most cases. (Under §306, discussed later in this chapter, a subsequent disposition of the preferred shares might generate dividend income.) The basis allocation now would be calculated using the fair market values of the common and preferred shares.[6] For example, assume that the fair market value of David's common stock is $15,000 and the value of the preferred shares is $5000. David's new basis in his original common stockholdings will be $7500. This is calculated by multiplying David's adjusted basis by a fraction consisting of the value of the common shares divided by the total value of the common and preferred holdings {$10,000 × $15,000/($15,000 + $5000)}. This means the adjusted basis of David's preferred shares is $2500 {$10,000 × $5000/($15,000 + $5000)}.

The results for David also would apply if he had received stock rights instead of a distribution of the actual shares. This is because §305 defines the term "stock" to include stock rights. Where rights are received, however, the rules regarding calculation of basis are somewhat different. A 15-percent test is applied, under which a stockholder must allocate basis to the rights received in a tax-free distribution if the value of the rights is 15 percent or more than the value of the underlying stock.[7]

Example—Sue owns 150 shares of common stock in Alabama Corporation. The fair market value of her shares is $15,000, and Sue's adjusted basis in the holdings is $10,000. Sue receives a distribution of 75 stock rights. The rights enable Sue to buy Alabama common stock at a specified rate and have a fair market value of $2000.[8] Under the general rule of §305, Sue is not required to recognize income upon receipt of the rights. Since the value of the rights is less than 15 percent of the value of the underlying stock (15 percent × $15,000 = $2250), Sue also is not required to reallocate any of her basis in her Alabama holdings to the rights received, although she can elect to do so.[9] However, if the value of the rights were

$2500, Sue would be required to make an allocation. Her basis in the rights would be $1429 ($10,000 $\times$ $2500/$17,500). Sue's basis in her original Alabama shares would drop to $8571 ($10,000 $\times$ $15,000/$17,500).

If a shareholder is required or decides to allocate basis to rights received in a nontaxable distribution, the amount allocated would reduce any gain recognized if the shareholder later sells the rights without exercising them. Likewise, the allocation would increase the basis of any shares acquired by using the rights. However, if the rights expire without being exercised, the shareholder cannot claim a loss.[10] Instead the basis is reassigned back to the underlying shares on which the rights distribution was made.

Example—Tom receives a distribution of 10 rights to buy stock in Harrison Company. The rights have a total value of $800. Since the value of Tom's underlying Harrison stock is $4000, he must make an allocation of his $3600 adjusted basis in his Harrison shares. Therefore Tom allocates basis of $600 to the rights ($3600 $\times$ $800/$4800). Tom sells four of the rights for $250. Because his basis in the four rights is $240 {($600/10) $\times$ 4}, he recognizes a gain of $10 on the sale. Of the remaining six rights, Tom exercises three. His basis in the new Harrison stock he receives is the price he paid for the additional shares plus $180, which is the basis of the rights Tom surrendered in order to receive the new stock.[11] Because of a change in market conditions, Tom lets the three remaining rights expire without being exercised. Tom cannot claim a loss. Instead, the $180 basis of the expired rights is added back to the basis of Tom's original Harrison shares. This means Tom's basis in his initial Harrison holdings is now $3180. This is the $3600 original basis, less the $600 allocated to the rights when they were distributed, plus the $180 allocated to the rights that now have expired.

TAXABLE DISTRIBUTIONS OF STOCK OR STOCK RIGHTS

There are exceptions under §305 of the Tax Code, under which distributions of stock or stock rights will generate taxable income. In most cases, these rules apply to both actual and "deemed" distributions.[12] A deemed distribution is a transaction like a change in conversion ratio, a change in redemption price, a recapitalization, or similar dealing with the potential to increase the proportionate interests of some shareholders in the earnings and profits or assets of the corporation. These transactions are treated as a distribution for stockholders whose proportionate interests are increased.[13]

For example, assume a corporation increases the conversion ratio under which its Class B shares can be exchanged for its Class A holdings. The corporation also pays a taxable cash dividend on the Class A shares. Even though the B investors did not receive any actual distribution, their proportionate interests in the company have increased. This is because they will receive a greater number of A shares if they surrender their B holdings. The increase is treated as a "deemed" distribution on which the B investors will receive dividend treatment.[14]

Distributions Payable in Stock or Property

The first exception to the rule providing for tax-free stock and rights distributions applies where any of the shareholders can elect to receive the distribution in either property or stock. In that case, the dividend is taxable to all the shareholders, even if made entirely in stock or stock rights.[15] If the election can only be made as to some of the shares, only part of the distribution will be taxable.[16] Investors who participate in a dividend reinvestment plan, allowing them to acquire stock instead of receiving cash dividends, have a taxable distribution equal to the fair market value of the stock received.[17] Note that the deemed distribution rules do not apply to this exception. In other words, in order for a shareholder to be required to recognize income because the stock dividend included an option to receive property, an actual distribution must be made.[18]

Example—Rich is one of 20 shareholders, each of whom owns 5 percent of the common stock in Technidish Corporation. Technidish declares a dividend, which its shareholders can elect to receive in common shares or securities (debt) of the corporation. None of the stockholders chooses to receive the dividend in securities. Nonetheless, Rich will be taxed on the fair market value of the stock shares he receives, apparently at a 15 percent rate. Under §305(b), a taxable distribution of stock or rights is to be treated as a distribution of property under Code §301. The 2003 tax legislation specifically amended §301 to include a reference to the new reduced tax rates applicable to dividends received by individuals. Consequently, it appears Rich's dividend will be taxed at the 15-percent rate, assuming it otherwise qualifies under the new rules.[19]

Disproportionate Distributions

Disproportionate distributions of stock or rights also will generate taxable income. A distribution or series of distributions will be disproportionate if the effect will be that some shareholders receive property while others see an increase in their proportionate interests in the assets or earnings and profits of the corporation. Note that both of these elements must be present in order for the distribution to be taxable. In other words, an increase in the proportionate interests of some shareholders that is not accompanied by a property distribution to others will not trigger income recognition under Tax Code §305.[20]

Example—Bill owns all of the Class A common stock in DeSales, Inc. Bonnie owns all of the outstanding Class B common shares. Each share of the A and B stock participates equally in the corporation's earnings and profits and is entitled to an equal share of corporate assets. DeSales declares a stock dividend on the Class A stock but pays a cash dividend on the B shares. Even though Bill receives only Class A common shares, the distribution to him is taxable. This is because Bill's interest in the earnings and profits and assets of DeSales increases as a result of the distribution.[21] Since the dividend is taxable, Bill's adjusted basis in the new shares is equal to fair market value.[22] His holding period in the new stock starts with the distribution and does not date back to the acquisition of the original shares.[23]

Assume instead that Bonnie's class B shares were nonconvertible and limited and preferred as to dividends. In that event, a stock dividend on Bill's common shareholdings would not be treated as taxable even if the corporation simultaneously declared a cash dividend on Bonnie's shares. This is because Bill already was entitled to the residual equity in the corporation. In other words, the stock dividend distributed to Bill did not increase his proportionate interest in the DeSales earnings or assets.[24]

Dividend treatment under the disproportionate rules can arise in unexpected situations. For example, one or a series of distributions can trigger application of this rule. This means unrelated distributions could cause stock dividends to become taxable.[25] According to the regulations, a corporation that pays cash dividends on one class of common stock and quarterly stock dividends on another class of common is making taxable stock distributions. These rules put a premium on dividend planning.[26] Likewise, paying interest on a convertible debenture can be treated as a property distribution. As a result, a corporation making an otherwise tax-free distribution of stock would be viewed as distributing taxable shares under the disproportionate rules. This is because under the regulations, securities convertible into stock are treated as outstanding shares. Therefore the corporation is making a property distribution on some shares (the interest payments), while also declaring stock dividends.[27]

A deemed stock distribution can trigger taxable income under the disproportionate distribution rules of the Tax Code. For example, assume a corporation adopts a plan under which it will periodically redeem some of its outstanding shares in transactions that will not qualify for sale treatment.[28] Since the redemptions will be taxed as dividends, they will be treated as property distributions made by the corporation to the redeeming shareholders, while at the same time the proportionate interests of the remaining stockholders increase. This means the remaining shareholders will be treated as receiving a deemed stock dividend that will be subject to tax under the disproportionate distribution rules. The regulations indicate that this treatment will not apply to redemptions made pursuant to established business practices, such as buying stock from small stockholders for later sale to employees.[29]

Where the deemed rules do apply, however, shareholders receiving these "phantom" distributions have taxable income without having collected any corresponding proceeds from the corporation with which to pay the resulting tax. Other kinds of transactions, including changing stock conversion ratios or recapitalizing shares, can have a similar result, meaning shareholders who hold proportionate interests in the corporation that are increased as a result of the transaction may be treated as receiving taxable distributions.[30] In other words, corporations need to consider the impact of these transactions on all shareholders, not just those actually participating in whatever is being planned. Often transactions like redemptions and recapitalizations involve considerable negotiation among the parties in order to structure the transaction; the tax consequences for everyone should be a part of the discussion.

Distributions of Common and Preferred Stock

An actual or deemed distribution of common and preferred stock can trigger taxable income, even though the dividend consists solely of stock in the distributing corporation. Under the Tax Code, a distribution or series of distributions that will result in some common shareholders receiving common stock and some common shareholders receiving preferred shares is subject to tax.[31] Essentially, the preferred stock is viewed as analogous to property, so that the distribution has a disproportionate effect, similar to the discussion above.

Example—Christine holds all of the Class A common stock in Garden Corporation, while Andersen owns all of the Class B common shares. Garden declares a stock dividend under which Christine will receive additional common stock while the distribution to Andersen will consist of Class C preferred shares. The receipt of the preferred shares by Andersen will be viewed as a distribution of property, taxable under Code §301. This means Andersen will recognize dividend income equal to the fair market value of the preferred shares received, assuming Garden has sufficient earnings and profits. Although Christine received only common stock in the distribution made to her, she also will be taxed on the fair market value of the dividend, presumably at the reduced dividend rates of the 2003 legislation.[32]

A preferred stock recapitalization, often used to shift control of a family-owned corporation to the younger generation, can result in some shareholders receiving preferred stock while common shares are issued to others.[33] Further, under the deemed distribution rules, a recapitalization can generate taxable dividend treatment. However, the regulations provide that the distribution of stock in a recapitalization undertaken to shift control of the distributing corporation will be tax-free. This is because the recapitalization is a single and isolated transaction.[34]

Distributions of Convertible Preferred Stock

The Tax Code also provides that distributions of convertible preferred stock are subject to taxation.[35] This exception to the rule providing for tax-free dividend distributions overlaps with the exception discussed above. Where a dividend dispensing preferred shares to some stockholders and common stock to others is subject to taxation, a corporation could easily evade the rule by using solely convertible preferred shares to make the distribution. If the option to convert the preferred shares must be exercised fairly soon after the stock is issued, the dividend is essentially equivalent to a distribution in which some shareholders receive preferred stock and others (those electing to convert) receive common.

Under the Tax Code, a distribution of convertible preferred shares is taxable if it will have a disproportionate effect. The regulations provide that a dividend of preferred stock convertible into common shares is likely to generate disproportionate results if two conditions are met. First, the conversion opportunity must expire "within a relatively short period of time" after the distribution. Second, considering factors like the dividend rate, redemption provisions, marketability of the convertible shares, and the conversion price, it is expected that some shareholders will choose to convert the stock and others will not.[36]

Example—Hugh is one of 100 shareholders who own common stock in Eggert Company. Eggert declares a dividend, payable in preferred shares that are convertible into common. The shares are convertible for a period of 20 years and pay dividends that are consistent with market conditions. Because there is no basis for predicting how many of the shares will be converted, the stock received by Hugh will be tax-free.[37] This means Hugh will allocate some of the basis of his original stockholdings to the new convertible preferred shares, based on the relative fair market values. In addition, Hugh's holding period for the new stock will date back to the day on which he acquired the original shares. If Hugh elects to convert his preferred holdings, his basis in the new stock will be equal to his basis in the converted shares, plus any additional consideration that Hugh was required to pay in order to make the conversion.

Distributions on Preferred Stock

In general, a stock distribution of any kind that is made on preferred shares is taxable.[38] For purposes of this rule, stock that participates in corporate growth to any significant degree is not "preferred." According to the regulations, preferred stock is stock that has certain limited rights and privileges, usually with respect to dividends and liquidation payments. Regardless of what legal rights may technically exist, if there is little or no chance that the shares will participate in current or expected earnings and upon the liquidation of the corporation, the shares are preferred. This means distributions of stock dividends made by the corporation on the shares will be taxable to the shareholders.

Example—Lucy holds preferred stock in Roseco. Under the Roseco organizational documents, the preferred stock is to enjoy certain specified preferences with respect to both dividends and liquidation distributions. However, in both cases, once payments made to the holders of common stock exceed certain defined targets, the preferred shareholders are entitled to share in any additional payments made. Roseco distributes a stock dividend to Lucy and the other preferred shareholders. At the time of the distribution, neither the corporation's past nor projected earnings have triggered or are likely to trigger the rights of the preferred stockholders to additional dividend payments. Further, the value of Roseco's assets makes it unlikely that holders of Roseco preferred stock will receive anything beyond the preference to which they are otherwise entitled if the corporation liquidates. Based on these facts, Lucy probably will not be able to avoid characterization as a holder of preferred stock. Despite whatever rights Lucy might have on paper, she will be unable to argue that her shares actually participate with the common shareholders in earnings and liquidation. This means stock dividends made to Lucy will be taxable.[39]

Deemed distributions on preferred shares also will create tax liability for the preferred shareholders. However, if an increase in the conversion ratio of convertible preferred stock is made solely to take into account a stock dividend or stock split on the underlying issue into which the preferred shares can be converted, no taxable income will arise.[40] A deemed distribution on preferred shares may involve a redemption premium. This means the preferred stock can be redeemed at an amount higher than the price for which it was issued. In general, principles similar to those involved with original issue discount bonds (discussed in Chapter 13) are used to determine whether the premium will trigger the deemed distribution rules and, if so, how the premium will be recognized.[41]

Example—Dan buys preferred stock in Grover, Inc. The stock pays regular dividends, and Dan buys his shares for $44,600. Dan can redeem his stock in five years, at a price of $45,000. Using the de minimis rules for original issue discount, Dan's stock is not treated as having a redemption premium.[42] This is because the excess Dan will receive when the shares are redeemed, beyond the price he paid for them, is only $400. This amount is less than $562.50 (¼ of 1 percent of the redemption price of $45,000 times 5, the number of complete years from the date of issue to the date the stock can be redeemed). Because Dan qualifies for the de minimis exception, he can ignore the $400 premium until his shares are redeemed. Had Dan paid only $44,000 for the shares, the redemption premium would have exceeded the de minimis amount, and Dan would have been required to report the premium over the five years he holds the stock, on an economic accrual basis. In other words, Dan would be treated as receiving deemed distributions on his preferred shares during his five-year holding period, using calculations similar to the constant interest rate method found in the original issue discount rules of Tax Code §1272.[43]

The regulations provide that these rules can apply even if the preferred shares can be acquired by someone other than the issuer. For example, Dan would still be required to recognize the premium on the preferred shares he bought for $44,000 where he could sell the stock in five years to a corporation in the same affiliated group as the issuing corporation. (This assumes the arrangement was devised to avoid tax under the §305 rules.)[44] Where the issuer has the right to redeem the shares, a deemed distribution of the premium occurs if, based on all the facts and circumstances, redemption is "more likely than not" to occur. This rule won't apply, however, if the premium is really a penalty for premature redemptions.[45]

Deemed distributions also can occur in the context of other transactions involving preferred stock. For example, a recapitalization, where preferred shareholders surrender their old stock, with dividends in arrears, and receive new shares with a value (or liquidation preference, if greater) higher than the issue price of the old shares can trigger the deemed distribution rules.[46] In this case the distribution would be equal to the lesser of the dividend arrearage or the spread between the value and the issue price of the preferred shares.[47] This means a reorganization likely expected to be tax-free now would be taxable, at least for the preferred stockholders receiving the deemed distribution. Since the distribution would create tax liability without an actual, corresponding cash payment by the corporation that could be used to settle the tax, corporations and investors should be alert to situations that have the potential to invoke these rules.

IRC SECTION 306 STOCK

The general rule of Tax Code §306 permits stock distributions to be received tax-free unless an exception applies. This creates an opportunity for some shareholders to try to avoid dividend treatment on funds indirectly received from a corporation.

Example—Margaret owns 100 percent of the common stock in Smyth Company. Margaret receives a tax-free distribution of nonvoting preferred stock. The stock has a value of $10,000 and is not convertible. Margaret sells her preferred shares to Josephat, an unrelated party who does not otherwise own an interest in Smyth. Because the stock is a capital asset in Margaret's hands, she recognizes capital gain on the sale. At some later date, Josephat's shares are redeemed by Smyth, at a modest premium. Since Josephat's only interest in Smyth is the preferred shares that have been redeemed, he is treated as completely terminating his interest in the corporation, and the redemption qualifies as a sale. (See the discussion of corporate redemptions in Chapter 9). This means Josephat also receives capital gain treatment. The effect of the transaction, absent special rules, is that Margaret is able to indirectly extract earnings from her corporation as capital gain despite the fact that she owned 100 percent of the voting stock throughout. Although under the 2003 tax legislation capital gain and dividend tax rates for individuals are equivalent, Margaret's plan would allow her to use capital losses that she could not otherwise offset against her dividend income.

What Is Section 306 Stock?

Tax Code §306 operates to taint certain stock received in a tax-free distribution. The effect of the taint is to generate dividend treatment for the shareholder when the stock is later disposed of in a taxable transaction. This means the dividend treatment Margaret would have received had she just redeemed some of her nonvoting preferred shares, instead of selling them to Josephat, is not avoided. Instead of generating capital gain, a later disposition of Margaret's tainted shares produces dividend results. In other words, despite Margaret's efforts, she probably will be required to recognize dividend income when she sells her preferred stock to Josephat. As a result, the consequences of the transaction will be similar to what the tax treatment would have been had Margaret simply received a cash dividend distribution from Smyth.

The dividend income taint described above only applies to what is called "§306 stock." This is stock, other than common stock issued as a dividend on common shares, that was received in a distribution wholly or partly tax-free under the §305 rules discussed above.[48] A tax-free distribution of rights can trigger the §306 rules because the word "stock" is defined to include stock rights.[49] Stock that has a basis determined by reference to §306 holdings falls within the §306 rules. This means, for example, that new shares received in a tax-free exchange for §306 stock also will be tainted.[50] Where §306 shares are transferred by gift, the donee receives the taint from the donor.[51] However, someone who buys stock that is treated as §306 shares in the seller's hands does not receive tainted holdings. This is because the buyer takes a cost basis in the shares purchased from the seller.

Example—Richard holds common stock in Black Rock, Inc. He receives a tax-free distribution of preferred shares. These shares are considered §306 stock, meaning a sale or redemption is likely to generate dividend income for Richard. In an effort to purge the taint, Richard contributes the §306 shares to a newly organized corporation, Blue Rock, and takes back all of the Blue Rock common shares. This transaction is tax-free under §351 of the Code, and Richard takes a substituted basis in his Blue Rock shares. In other words, the basis of Richard's Blue Rock holdings is determined by reference to the basis he had in the Black Rock stock. As a result, Richard's Blue Rock shareholdings inherit the taint of the Black Rock shares he formerly held. When Richard sells his Blue Rock shares to a third-party buyer, he is likely to recognize dividend income, even if the shares are a capital asset in his hands. However, the Blue Rock holdings will not be §306 stock in the hands of the person who bought the shares from Richard.[52]

Preferred stock received wholly or partially tax-free in a reorganization, where the effect of the receipt was substantially the same as a stock dividend, also is included in the definition of §306 stock.[53] A transaction has substantially the same effect as a stock dividend where the proportionate interest of each shareholder in the corporation's equity remains the same.[54]

Example—Rose holds all of the common stock in Gypsum Company. Gypsum engages in a recapitalization, and as a result Rose surrenders her existing common shares. In exchange, Rose receives new common stock and also preferred shares. Since Rose's proportionate interest in Gypsum is unchanged by the recapitalization, her preferred shares will be treated as §306 stock.[55]

A tax-free stock dividend will not be characterized as §306 stock if the distributing corporation had no earnings and profits at the time of the distribution.[56] This is because the §306 stock is not being used as a device to extract profit from the corporation without paying tax at dividend rates. As discussed in Chapter 8, a taxable distribution will generate dividend income for the shareholders only if the corporation making the distribution has earnings and profits at the time. In other words, had the distributing corporation paid out cash to the shareholders, instead of the preferred shares it did use, they would not have had been subjected to dividend treatment. Since cash could have been received without reporting dividend income, the stock distributed instead will not generate dividend treatment when later sold. However, this rule applies only if no part of a cash distribution would have been treated as a dividend. If a corporation declaring a stock dividend has even minimal earnings and profits, the entire distribution is tainted. Obviously this means that a corporation attempting to avoid the distribution of §306 stock on the basis of no earnings and profits needs to make careful calculations.

Dispositions of §306 Stock

The Tax Code provides that a redemption of §306 stock by the distributing corporation is treated as a dividend distribution. This means the redeeming stockholder will report dividend income to the extent of the corporation's earnings and profits in the year of redemption. Any amount received in excess of the dividend income portion is handled as a tax-free return of capital. Thereafter, the shareholder reports capital gain for the remainder of the distribution, assuming the stock was a capital asset.[57]

Example—Diane owns preferred stock in Lamb Company, which she received as a tax-free dividend distribution several years earlier. In the current year, Diane elects to redeem her Lamb preferred shares. Diane receives $25,000 as a result of the redemption distribution. Her adjusted basis in the Lamb preferred stock was $11,000. Lamb's earnings and profits in the year the stock was paid out were minimal. Based on its E & P balance in the current year, however, Diane will have to report $8000 of dividend, presumably taxed under the reduced 2003 rates. The next $11,000 of the redemption distribution is treated as a tax-free return of capital to Diane. This leaves $6000 that has yet to be handled {$25,000 − ($8000 + $11,000)}. This amount is reported by Diane as capital gain if the Lamb stock is a capital asset in Diane's hands.

If Diane were a corporation, the reduced 2003 rates would not apply to the dividend portion of the distribution. However, she could claim a dividend-received deduction in connection with the redemption transaction. (The dividend-received deduction is discussed in Chapter 8.) If instead Diane is an individual but she had only received $5000 when she redeemed her preferred shares, she would still have to report the entire amount paid to her as dividend because of Lamb's earnings and profits in the year of redemption. Her $11,000 of unused basis could not be claimed as a loss. Instead, it would be reallocated to any remaining Lamb stock Diane owns.[58]

Rather than redeem her Lamb shares, Diane may elect to sell or exchange them. A taxable disposition of §306 stock in a transaction other than a redemption can also generate dividend income consequences.[59] In a nonredemption distribution, however, the amount of dividend income is measured by reference to the distributing corporation's earnings and profits in the year of distribution, and not the year the shareholder sells or exchanges the preferred shares.[60] This means that in order to determine the amount of the sale proceeds that will be taxed under the dividend income rules, a stockholder selling §306 shares must know the fair market value of the stock at the time it was distributed.[61]

Example—John holds §306 stock that was issued to him in a prior year in a tax-free transaction. This year John receives an offer to sell his shares, which have an adjusted basis of $6500, for $9000. In the year John received the stock, his ratable share of earnings and profits in the corporation making the distribution was $4000. At the time of the dividend, the fair market value of the preferred shares John received was $4200. Therefore John must report dividend income of $4000, the lesser of John's share of E & P or the value of the §306 stock when it was distributed. The $5000 of sale proceeds remaining is a tax-free return of capital, leaving John with $1500 of unrecovered basis. John will add the $1500 to the basis of his remaining stock in the distributing corporation.[62] Had John sold his shares for $12,000, he would have reported $4000 of dividend income and $6500 as recovery of capital. This would have left $1500 {$12,000 − ($4000 + $6500)} for John to report as capital gain, assuming the stock was a capital asset for John.[63]

Dispositions Not Triggering Ordinary Income

Some transactions involving §306 stock will not generate ordinary income. For example, if a shareholder sells her entire interest in the corporation, including the §306 shares, in a taxable transaction, the proceeds will not be tainted. The buyer cannot be a person whose stock would be attributed to the seller under the attribution rules. (The attribution provisions, found at §318 of the Tax Code, treat stock that is held by certain persons, like family members of the taxpayer, as actually owned by the taxpayer. These rules are discussed in Chapter 9.) This means, for example, that the purchaser of the stock cannot be a member of the buyer's family.[64]

Example—Sandy holds §306 preferred shares and also common stock in Botanical Corporation. She sells all of her shares to Walter. Since Sandy has disposed of her entire interest to a buyer not within the attribution rules of IRC §318, the income Sandy reports on the sale transaction is eligible for capital gain treatment and can be offset by capital losses Sandy may have. However, if Sandy and Walter are married, the exception to §306 treatment no longer applies, since Walter's holdings would be treated as owned by Sandy under the §318 attribution rules. This means Sandy would report dividend income on the sale of her preferred stock, up to her share of Botanical's earnings and profits in the year the stock was distributed or the fair market value of the shares at the time of the dividend, whichever is lesser.

The attribution rules also complicate the question of whether the stockholder actually sold his entire interest in the corporation.

Example—Regina sells all her shares in Heise Corporation to Henry. Henry is unrelated to Regina, under §318, and the stock she sells to him includes both common shares and §306 stock received several years ago in a tax-free distribution. The remaining stock in Heise, representing a 50-percent ownership interest, is held by Regina's husband, Ken. Regina is likely to recognize dividend income in connection with the sale of her §306 stock to Henry. This is because under the attribution rules, Regina is treated as owning Ken's stock. This means the sale to Henry did not terminate Regina's interest in Heise, and she cannot rely on the exception to §306 treatment for shareholders who sell their entire interest.

If an investor redeems all of his shares, the proceeds also are not tainted, assuming the redemption would qualify as a complete termination of the shareholder's interest or as a partial liquidation. Where a redemption otherwise terminates a stockholder's investment, it is possible to waive the family attribution rules discussed above if certain conditions are met.[65] This means that if Regina redeemed her shares rather than selling them and met all the requirements to waive attribution, she would not be treated as owning Ken's stock. As a result, Regina would report capital gain on the redemption, even for the §306 shares.

A disposition arising because of a complete liquidation of the corporation escapes the §306 taint.[66] Dispositions not involving gain recognition also do not generate ordinary income or dividend treatment under the §306 stock rules. However, these kinds of transactions, like gifting §306 preferred shares, involve a continuation of basis. This means that the taint of §306 is not eliminated but continues until a later disposition.[67]

Example—Rich holds §306 stock that he received in a tax-free distribution from National Corporation. Rich gives these shares to his niece, Darlene. Because a gift typically does not generate recognition of income, Rich is not required to report gain because of this transaction. However, Darlene takes Rich's basis in the National shares she now owns. This means that Darlene "inherits" the taint from Rich and may have dividend income if she disposes of the shares in a taxable transaction.

The Tax Code also exempts from §306 treatment transactions that are not principally designed to avoid income tax.[68] For this exception to apply, both the initial distribution of the §306 shares and the later redemption or disposition must meet the tax avoidance test. However, only the later disposition or redemption of the §306 shares must be for nontax avoidance reasons if the transaction also involves a prior or simultaneous sale, etc., of the underlying holdings on which the §306 stock was distributed.[69] In either case the test is subjective, and the IRS is unwilling to issue guidance on whether specific transactions qualify.[70] This makes reliance on a nontax avoidance purpose difficult or at the very least somewhat risky, as illustrated by the court case on which the following example is based.

Example—Fireovid received both common and preferred shares at the time of incorporation. Later, the capital structure of the corporation was changed to accommodate two new investors. Because control of the corporation was to be divided equally among the three participants, Fireovid and the new stockholders received equal amounts of common stock. However Fireovid also received additional preferred shares, reflecting his larger capital contribution. These additional shares fell within the scope of §306. Later, one of the new investors demanded increased control, so Fireovid and the other new investor sold some of their common shares. At a later date, the corporation redeemed 451 of the 600 shares of preferred stock Fireovid held.

Fireovid argued that §306 should not apply to the redemption proceeds, on the grounds that the preferred stock was issued for business reasons. This argument was unsuccessful. This is because instead of issuing the preferred stock to him when the two new stockholders made their investments, the corporation could have paid a cash dividend to Fireovid. He then could have transferred the dividend back to the corporation, in the form of a loan. Since the dividend would have forced Fireovid to recognize dividend income, the court apparently concluded that tax avoidance was the motivation for issuing a preferred stock dividend to him instead.[71]

The *Fireovid* case illustrates the difficulty that can be encountered in trying to avoid §306 treatment, even where transactions are prompted by legitimate business reasons. In general, taxpayers concerned about dividend consequences on a sale or redemption of stock received as a tax-free dividend need to move with caution. The effects of IRC §306 mean that even if investors manage to avoid taxation when stock dividends are received, unexpected tax results may occur on a later disposition, depending on the circumstances involved.

CONCLUSION

Many taxpayers are generally familiar with the rules regarding taxation of stock dividends and expect that shares distributed by a corporation in which they hold an equity investment will be received tax-free. However, there are exceptions to the general rule, some of which will trigger taxation when the dividend is paid out. The dividend provisions also can impact an investor later, as where §306 stock is sold after a tax-free distribution, but dividend income must be reported. Taxpayers who rely only on general knowledge of the tax law in this area do so at their own risk and may be disappointed by the tax treatment of what they had thought was a tax-free stock distribution.

NOTES

[1] Noncorporate taxpayers can use up to $3000 of capital losses to offset ordinary income each year. The limitation drops to $1500 for taxpayers who are married but file separate returns. Code §1211.

[2] Tax Code §305(a)

[3] *Eisner v. Macomber*, 252 U.S. 189 (1920)

[4] Tax Code §307(a)

[5] Tax Code §1223(5)

[6] Treasury Regulation §1.307-1

[7] Tax Code §307(b)

[8] The rights are to be valued as of the date of distribution. Treasury Regulation §1.307-2. A shareholder who receives a rights distribution often will receive a statement from the distributing corporation, explaining the tax consequences of the distribution.

[9] An election is made by attaching a statement to the tax return for the year in which the rights were received. Once made, the election cannot be revoked. A taxpayer cannot make an election for only some of the rights received in a specific distribution on stock that is all in the same class. Treasury Regulation §1.307-2.

[10] Treasury Regulation §1.307-1(a). Under this regulation, allocations are to be made to rights only if the rights are sold or exercised.

[11] Tom's holding period for the shares he acquired by exercising the rights starts with the date of exercise, even though the underlying rights were received tax-free. Tax Code §1223(6).

[12] Treasury Regulation §1.305-7(a)

[13] Treasury Regulation §1.305-7(a)

[14] Treasury Regulation §1.305-3(e), Example 6. Under the regulations, a change in the conversion ratio or price of convertible preferred stock or debt will not trigger the deemed distribution rules, under certain circumstances. Treasury Regulation §1.305-7(b). A recapitalization will generate a deemed distribution if it is part of a plan to periodically increase

a shareholder's proportionate interest. Likewise, a recapitalization in which a stockholder's proportionate interest is increased by exchanging preferred shares with dividend arrearages for other stock will trigger the deemed distribution rules. Treasury Regulation §1.305-7(c)

[15] Tax Code §305(b)(1); Treasury Regulation §1.305-2(a)

[16] Treasury Reg. §1.305-2(b), ex. 1

[17] Rev. Rul. 76-53, 1976-1 C.B. 87

[18] Treasury Regulation §1.305-7(a)(2)

[19] See the discussion of the 2003 reduced dividend tax rates in Chapter 8. These rates do not apply to corporations that own stock.

[20] Tax Code §305(b)(2)

[21] Treasury Regulation §1.305-3(e), Ex. 1

[22] Treasury Regulation §1.301-1(h)(1) provides for a fair market value basis for non-corporate shareholders; a similar rule for stockholders that are corporations can be found at Treasury Regulation §1.301-1(h)(2)(i).

[23] Under Tax Code §1223, the holding period of stock received in a distribution dates back to the holding period of the underlying shares only if the basis of the distributed stock is determined under Tax Code §307. Code §307 only applies to tax-free distributions.

[24] Treasury Regulation §1.305-3(e), Ex. 2

[25] The regulations do not require the stock and property distributions to be related in order to trigger income recognition under this rule. Treasury Regulation §1.305-3(b)(2).

[26] Treasury Regulation §1.305-3(b). The regulations provide that if more than 36 months pass between receipt of the property and the stock, the distributions will not be combined to support characterization of the stock dividend as disproportionate. However, if the distributions are pursuant to a plan, the 36-month rule does not apply.

[27] Treasury Regulation §1.305-3(b)

[28] Taxation of redemptions is discussed in Chapter 9. If a redemption does not qualify for sale treatment under Tax Code §302, it is treated as a dividend pursuant to Tax Code §301.

[29] Treasury Regulation §1.305-3(e). Isolated redemptions that are not part of a periodic plan will not trigger deemed stock distributions under Tax Code §305(c). *Id.*

[30] Under Treasury Regulation §1.305-7(a), the transaction will be treated as a taxable dividend distribution where the shareholder's proportionate interest in the corporation increases and the transaction has the effect of a disproportionate distribution, a distribution of common and preferred stock, etc. See Treasury Regulation §1.305-7(a). This can apply also to changes in share redemption prices or other transactions having similar effects. *Id.*

[31] Tax Code §305(b)(3). Under Treasury Regulation §1.305-4(a), distributions made within 36 months of each other can be combined, resulting in taxable income where some common shareholders receive common stock and others preferred. A longer period may apply if a plan exists.

[32] Treasury Regulation §1.305-4(b), Ex. 1

[33] Typically, older shareholders surrender common stock in exchange for preferred, while younger family members receive common.

[34] Treasury Regulation §1.305-3(e), ex. 12. A preferred stock recapitalization may result in characterization of the preferred stock received by the older shareholders as §306 stock. (This can occur where the older shareholders do not give up all their common shares.)

As discussed later in this chapter, this means a later sale or redemption may generate dividend income. Tax Code §306

[35] Tax Code §305(b)(5). A deemed distribution can also trigger dividend taxation under this provision. Treasury Regulation §1.305-7(a)

[36] Treasury Regulation §1.305-6(a)

[37] Treasury Regulation §1.305-6(b), ex. 1

[38] Tax Code §305(b)(4)

[39] Treasury Regulation §1.305-5(d), Example 9

[40] Tax Code §305(b)(4). In Revenue Ruling 83-42, the same adjustment was accomplished by making an actual distribution of common shares to the holders of the convertible preferred. The distribution was taxed, since the form of the transaction involved a distribution made with respect to preferred stock. Rev. Rul. 83-42, 1983-1 C.B. 76

[41] IRS Publication 550, *Investment Income and Expenses* (2002), at p. 20

[42] The original issue discount rules are discussed in Chapter 13. In general, these rules require taxpayers who hold bonds issued at a discount to recognize interest income equal to the amount of discount that accrues during the taxable year. However, where a discount is small, it is treated as "de minimis," and these rules don't apply. Instead, the discount is recognized when the bond is sold or matures. See the discussion of the de minimis rules, in Chapter 13.

[43] *Id.*

[44] Treasury Regulation §1.305-5(b)(1)

[45] Treasury Regulation §1.305-5(b)

[46] Treasury Regulation §1.305-7(c)(1)

[47] Treasury Regulation §1.305-7(c)(2). If the liquidation preference exceeds the value of the stock, the deemed distribution is the lesser of the dividend arrearage or the difference between the liquidation preference and the issue price of the surrendered preferred shares. *Id.*

[48] Tax Code §306(c)(1)(A). Neither §306 of the Tax Code nor the associated regulations define what is meant by "common stock." Revenue rulings issued under other parts of §306 indicate that factors such as whether the stock is redeemable by the corporation and whether it represents an unrestricted interest in the corporation's equity growth are important considerations in deciding if the shares are common. Rev. Rul. 79-163, 1979-1 C.B. 131. In Revenue Ruling 57-132, "common stock" that had no voting rights and was redeemable at the corporation's option was treated as preferred shares tainted by Tax Code §306. Rev. Rul. 57-132, 1957-1 C.B. 115. However, in Revenue Ruling 76-386, voting shares on which the corporation held a right of first refusal were held to be common stock and therefore outside the scope of Tax Code §306. Rev. Rul. 76-386, 1976-2 C.B. 95. Common stock convertible into preferred shares is not treated as common. Tax Code §306(e)(2)

[49] Tax Code §306(d)(1). Under Tax Code §306(d)(2), stock acquired through the exercise of such rights can also be tainted.

[50] Tax Code §306(c)(1)(C). For special rules regarding convertible shares, see Tax Code §306(e)(1).

[51] Under Tax Code §1015, a donee's basis for determining gain is the donor's adjusted basis. Different rules apply if gifted property is sold at a loss.

[52] Under Tax Code §306(c)(1)(C), the Black Rock shares held by Blue Rock would also be tainted. This means Blue Rock would report ordinary income or dividend treatment upon

a later sale or redemption of the Black Rock preferred shares Richard contributed. Treasury Regulation §1.306-3(e). See Tax Code §304, discussed in Chapter 11, for rules applicable if Richard's stock is redeemed by Black Rock. See also Proposed Rules, *Redemptions Taxable as Dividends,* 67 FR 64331, October 18, 2002, for proposed new provisions governing Tax Code §304 transactions.

[53] Tax Code §306(c)(1)(B)

[54] Rev. Rul. 76-386, 1976-2 C.B. 95. See also Treasury Regulation §1.306-3(d) (receipt of stock has the effect of a stock dividend if a cash distribution paid out instead of the shares would have generated dividend treatment).

[55] Where §306 stock is received in a corporate reorganization under Tax Code §368, its basis and holding period are determined by the reorganization rules. The adjusted basis of the taxable property received is equal to its fair market value. The adjusted basis of stock received in a reorganization is the basis of the property surrendered, increased by gain recognized and decreased by loss recognized and by the fair market value of boot received. Tax Code §358.The holding period for the stock includes the holding period of the property surrendered in the exchange. Tax Code §1223(1).

[56] Tax Code §306(c)(2)

[57] Tax Code §306(a)(2)

[58] See Treasury Regulation §1.302-2(c) (requiring an adjustment to the basis of the remaining shares where a stock redemption is treated as a dividend). The IRS is considering changing this rule by treating the unused basis as a loss, to be recognized according to specific timing rules. See Proposed Rules, *Redemptions Taxable as Dividends,* 67 FR 64331, October 18, 2002.

[59] Tax Code §306(a)(1) provides for ordinary income treatment. However, the 2003 tax legislation amended this section by adding language specifically qualifying the income under the reduced dividend tax rate rules, assuming all other requirements are met. Tax Code §306(a)(1)(D)

[60] Tax Code §306(a)(1). Where stock acquired through stock rights that fell within the scope of §306 is sold, the dividend is measured by the earnings and profits at the time the rights were distributed. Treasury Regulation §1.306-3(b).

[61] If the terms and conditions of the stock have changed substantially since the distribution, the fair market value is whichever is greate—the value at the time the shares were distributed or the value at the time the changes occurred. A similar rule applies for determining the stock's ratable share of the corporation's earnings and profits. Tax Code §306(g)

[62] Treasury Regulation §1.306-1(b)(2), Example 2. The IRS is considering changing this rule. See Proposed Rules, *Redemptions Taxable as Dividends,* 67 FR 64331, October 18, 2002

[63] Treasury Regulation §1.306-1(b)(2), Example 1.Where §306 stock is sold rather than redeemed, the Tax Code provides for ordinary income treatment. Tax Code §306(a)(1)(A). On first glance, this appears to be a distinction without a difference. The 2003 legislation expressly authorizes §306 "ordinary income" to be treated as a dividend under the new reduced rate rules, meaning most individual shareholders will report these amounts at a 15-percent rate. However, the language is important for two reasons. First, a corporate shareholder that sells §306 stock does not receive a dividend and therefore presumably cannot qualify for the dividend-received-deduction. Second, unlike a redemption of §306 shares, a sale of this stock apparently does not produce a reduction in the earnings and prof-

its of the distributing corporation to reflect the amount of the stock distribution or the later sale. This means the shareholder must report dividend income without reducing the potential for dividend treatment in the future. These consequences may mean a redemption of §306 stock is preferable to a nonredemption disposition, assuming the corporation is in a position that permits it to reacquire some of its shares. Under the 2003 law, the IRS is authorized to extend dividend treatment in nonredemption dispositions of 306 shares to other provisions beyond the reduced dividend tax rate rules. Tax Code §306(a)(1)(D). Investors should watch for any guidance that may be issued on these questions.

[64] Tax Code §306(b)(1)

[65] Tax Code §306(b)(1). (The taxation of stock redemptions, including complete terminations and partial liquidations, is discussed in Chapter 9.) A waiver of family attribution rules apparently is not possible for nonredemption dispositions under Tax Code §306.

[66] Tax Code §306(b)(2)

[67] Tax Code §306(b)(3). This provision also applies to stock received in a tax-free reorganization. However, where the reorganization also involves gain recognition, because property other than stock (referred to as "boot") is received, ordinary income/dividend treatment will apply. Treasury Regulation §1.306-3(d)

[68] Tax Code §306(b)(4). The language of the statute speaks of transactions "not in pursuance of a plan having as one of its principal purposes the avoidance of Federal income tax."

[69] Pursuant to Tax Code §306(b)(1), a transaction involving a complete termination of the shareholder's interest also avoids ordinary income or dividend treatment under §306. However, if stock is owned by a family member, for example, a shareholder who sells his stock might be unable to qualify for complete termination treatment because of the attribution rules of Tax Code §318. Likewise, a shareholder may hold more than the §306 stock and the underlying stock on which the §306 shares were distributed. This could occur where a corporation has several classes of stock outstanding.

[70] See, for example, Rev. Proc. 2003-3, 2003-1 I.R.B. 113, §4.01(24)(Jan. 6, 2003).

[71] *Fireovid v. U.S.*, 462 F.2d 1281(3d Cir. 1972). The regulations suggest the nontax avoidance exception for certain dispositions of §306 stock may apply "to the case of dividends and isolated dispositions of §306 stock by minority shareholders." Treasury Regulation §1.306-2(b)(3)

11

REDEMPTION RULES FOR RELATED CORPORATIONS

INTRODUCTION

Capital gain recognition applies when a shareholder sells stock that he or she owns in one corporation to another corporation. However, when the shareholder has a controlling interest in both corporations, the situation becomes more complicated. There is a concern that a shareholder may be attempting to pluck earnings and profits from one of the corporations at capital gains rates. Therefore, §304 was enacted, requiring that a sale of stock from one controlled corporation to another controlled corporation be treated as redemption of stock. If the redemption meets all of the requirements, it is treated as a sale. Otherwise, if sufficient earnings and profits exist, it is treated as a dividend.

IRC §304 applies to sales of stock involving brother-sister corporations and parent-subsidiary groups. This chapter defines these corporations and discusses the application of §304 rules. Investors holding stock in publicly traded corporations aren't likely to encounter a §304 problem because they can sell their shares on the market to an unrelated buyer. However, shareholders in a closely held corporation need to recognize the impact of these rules on their holdings if capital gain treatment is desired.

BROTHER-SISTER AND PARENT-SUBSIDIARY CORPORATIONS

Brother-sister controlled groups exist when two or more corporations are owned by five or fewer persons who are individuals, estates, or trusts, and these persons have:

(A) At least 50 percent of the total combined voting power of all classes of stock entitled to vote or at least 50 percent of the total value of shares of all classes of stock of each corporation, and

(B) More than 50 percent of the total combined voting power of all classes of stock entitled to vote or more than 50 percent of the total value of shares of all classes of stock of each corporation, taking into account the stock ownership of each person only to the extent that such stock ownership is identical with respect to each corporation.[1]

Parent-subsidiary controlled groups exist when one or more chains of corporations are connected through stock ownership with a common parent corporation, and:

(A) One or more of the other corporations owns stock that possesses more than 50 percent of the total combined voting power of all classes of stock entitled to vote or more than 50 percent of the total value of shares of all classes of stock of each of the corporations, except the common parent corporation, and

(B) The common parent corporation owns more than 50 percent of the total combined voting power of all classes of stock entitled to vote or more than 50 percent of the total value of shares of all classes of stock of at least one of the other corporations, excluding in the calculation stock owned directly by the other corporations.[2]

DETERMINING CONTROL

The first step in determining whether the related corporation stock sale rules apply is to ensure that the control requirements are met. Control is defined, for brother-sister corporations and for parent-subsidiary groups, as having ownership of stock possessing at least 50 percent of the total combined voting power of all classes of stock entitled to vote, or at least 50 percent of the total value of shares of all classes of stock.[3]

Example—Dolittle Corporation has 1000 shares of voting common stock with a fair market value of $150 per share and 50 shares of nonvoting preferred stock with a fair market value of $300 per share. A shareholder would be in control of Dolittle if he or she owned 500 shares of the common stock (50 percent ownership of the voting power). Additionally, a shareholder would be in control if he or she owned all of the preferred stock (fair market value $15,000) and 450 shares of the common stock (fair market value $67,500).

Constructive Stock Ownership Rules and Determining Control

The constructive ownership rules of §318, as discussed in Chapter 9, apply for purposes of determining control with some modifications. The corporation to shareholder attribution rule is modified from 50-percent to 5-percent ownership. This means that a person owning 5 percent or more in value of the stock in a corporation is deemed to own a proportionate amount of stock owned directly or indirectly by the corporation.[4] The shareholder to corporation rules discussed in §318(a)(3)(C) are modified in two ways:

(1) 5 percent is also substituted for 50 percent ownership,[5] and

(2) If a shareholder owns between 5 percent and 50 percent in value of a corporation, then the corporation is deemed to own only a proportionate amount of the stock of any other corporation that is owned by the shareholder.[6]

Consequently if 50 percent or more of the value of the stock is held by a shareholder, then the corporation is treated as owning all of the stock owned, directly or indirectly, by the shareholder. If between 5 percent and 50 percent of the value of the stock is owned by a shareholder, the corporation is treated as owning a proportionate amount of the stock owned directly or indirectly by the shareholder. If less than 5 percent of the value of the stock of a corporation is owned by a shareholder, the corporation is treated as owning none of the stock owned directly or indirectly by the shareholder.[7]

Example—First Rate Corporation has 1000 shares of common stock outstanding, 60 percent of which is owned by Adam, 37 percent by Eve, and 3 percent by Luigi, who are unrelated shareholders. First Rate owns 90 percent of the stock of Second Rate Corporation. Besides owning First Rate Corporation, Adam, Eve, and Luigi also own shares in the following corporations, respectively:

Adam is the sole shareholder of Good Sailing, Inc.
Eve is the sole shareholder of Better Sailing, Inc.
Luigi is the sole shareholder of Best Sailing, Inc.

In determining control, the following applies:

- First Rate Corporation is treated as owning 100 percent of the shares of Good Sailing, Inc., 37 percent of the stock of Better Sailing, Inc. and none of the stock of Best Sailing, Inc.
- Adam is treated as owning 54 percent of the stock of Second Rate Corporation (90 percent × 60 percent), Eve is treated as owning 33.3 percent (90 percent × 37 percent) of the stock of Second Rate Corporation, and Luigi is treated as owning none of the stock of Second Rate.

If a person is in control of a corporation that in turn owns at least 50 percent of the total combined voting power of all stock of another corporation or the total value of all its shares, then the person shall be treated as in control of the other corporation.[8]

Example—Joanne owns 50 percent of the stock of New Age IT Discovery, Inc. New Age owns 50 percent of the stock of Nice Calculators, Inc. Joanne is deemed to be in control of Nice Calculators, Inc. even though she is considered as owning 25 percent of the stock of Nice Calculators (50 percent × 50 percent) under the corporation to shareholder attribution rules.

BROTHER-SISTER CORPORATION STOCK SALES

If a corporation acquires stock of another corporation, in return for property, from one or more persons in control of both corporations, then the property will be treated as being received in redemption of stock of the acquiring corporation.[9] Stock redemptions between a brother-sister corporation are treated as a sale or exchange or as a regular corporate distribution, but the qualifying criteria is applied with respect to the shares of the corporation that issued the stock that is sold.[10]

Example—Joanne is in control of New Age IT Discovery, Inc. and Nice Calculators, Inc. She sells 500 shares of IT stock to Nice Calculators for $100,000. The $100,000 is considered a redemption of the stock Nice Calculators. For purposes of determining whether this transaction is treated as a sale or exchange or as a corporate distribution, the rules of redemption are applied to the stock of New Age IT Discovery, Inc. (The redemption rules are discussed in Chapter 9.)

In any case in which two or more persons, in the aggregate, control two corporations, §304(a)(1) will apply to sales by those shareholders of stock in either corporation to the other corporation. However, the sales by each of the shareholders must be related to each other whether or not they were made simultaneously.[11]

Example—Chester owns 42 percent of the outstanding stock of Plasma Corporation, and Colette, an unrelated shareholder owns 10 percent of the outstanding stock. Chester and Colette also own 25 percent and 15 percent, respectively, of the outstanding stock in Teflon Corporation. Chester sells 150 shares of his Plasma stock to Teflon. Seven months later, Colette sells 95 shares of her Plasma stock to Teflon Corporation. If these two sales are related to each other, then the brother-sister stock sale rules will apply. If the sales are not related, then the brother-sister stock sale rules do not apply since neither shareholder is in control of either corporation.

Constructive Ownership Rules

In determining whether a redemption from a brother-sister corporation stock sale is a sale or exchange or a dividend, the constructive ownership rules are further modified from those used to determine control. The 50-percent limitation is eliminated, resulting in all shareholders being treated as owning a proportionate amount of stock owned by the corporation[12] Conversely, the corporation is treated as owning all of the stock that is owned by any of its shareholders.

Example—Chester owns 30 percent of the outstanding stock of Plasma Corporation. Chester also owns 40 percent, each, of Teflon Corporation and Polymer Corporation and Plasma owns 25 percent, each, of Teflon Corporation and Polymer Corporation. Chester is treated as owning 47.5 percent of the stock of Teflon Corporation and Polymer Corporation (40 percent actually and 30 percent $\times$ 25 percent constructively). Plasma is treated as owning 65 percent of the stock of Teflon Corporation and 65 percent of Polymer Corporation (25 percent actually and 40 percent constructively). Therefore, Chester and Plasma Corporation are in control of both Teflon Corporation and Polymer Corporation in applying the brother-sister stock sale rules.

Basis of Stock in a Sale or Exchange

If a brother-sister stock sale is classified as a sale or exchange, the property received by the selling shareholder is treated as being received in exchange for the stock of the acquiring corporation.[13] The basis of each share of the shareholder's stock in the acquiring corporation will be the same as the basis of each share before the entire transaction.[14] The holding period of the stock that is considered to have been redeemed is the same as the holding period of the stock actually surrendered.[15] The basis and holding period of the stock to the acquiring corporation is considered the same as the basis and holding period of the stock of the issuing corporation that is sold.[16]

Example—First Rate Corporation and Second Rate Corporation each have outstanding 100 shares of common stock. Adam owns one-half the stock of First Rate, and he and Eve each own one-half the stock of Second Rate. Adam and Eve are unrelated. Adam sells 30 shares of the stock of First Rate to Second Rate for $35,000 with a basis to him of $10,000. After the sale, Adam is considered as owning 35 shares of First Rate Corporation (20 shares are owned directly by him and 50 percent of 30 shares owned by Second Rate Corporation are attributed to him). He owned 50 percent of the stock of First Rate before the sale, and after the sale he only owns directly and constructively 35 percent of the stock. The redemption is substantially disproportionate under the rules discussed in Chapter 9, and, therefore, he realizes a capital gain of $25,000. The basis to Adam for the stock of Second Rate Corporation is not changed as a result of the entire transaction. The basis to Second Rate for the stock of First Rate Corporation is $35,000, Adam's basis plus the gain recognized by him.[17]

Basis of Stock Treated as a Dividend

When a brother-sister stock sale is considered as a corporate distribution (dividend), the selling shareholder and the acquiring corporation are treated as though they entered a §351 transfer. Under this rule, no gain or loss is recognized if property is transferred to a corporation by one or more persons solely in exchange for stock of the corporation and the person(s) is in control of the corporation. The selling shareholder's basis in the stock contributed is considered transferred to the acquiring corporation. The acquiring corporation then redeems its stock to the selling shareholder, and the adjusted basis in the stock is added to the adjusted basis of the acquiring corporation's stock owned by the selling shareholder.[18] If the amount distributed exceeds the earnings and profits of both the issuing and acquiring corporations, then the excess amount is treated as a return of capital and reduces the shareholder's adjusted basis in the stock of the acquiring corporation.[19]

Example—Pat owns 500 shares of Soccer, Ltd. and 500 shares of Golf,

Ltd. and is in control of both corporations. Her adjusted basis in Soccer is $100,000 and $120,000 in Golf. Each corporation has earnings and profits of $50,000. Pat sells 200 shares of Soccer, Ltd. to Golf, Ltd. for $110,000. If the redemption is treated as a regular corporate distribution (dividend), then Pat is treated as receiving a dividend of $100,000 ($50,000 earnings and profits from each Soccer, Ltd. and Golf, Ltd.). Her basis in Golf is reduced by $10,000.

PARENT-SUBSIDIARY STOCK SALES

A parent-subsidiary relationship exists if one corporation owns at least 50 percent of the voting power or 50 percent of the total value of all the stock in the subsidiary. If a shareholder sells stock he or she owns in a parent corporation to a subsidiary corporation, the transaction is treated as a distribution in redemption of part or all of the shareholder's stock in the parent corporation.[20] The redemption is treated as a sale or exchange qualifying for capital gains treatment or as a regular corporate distribution treated as a dividend. The sale of the parent's stock to the subsidiary is considered to be a redemption of the parent's stock.[21]

Example—Nursing Consultants, Inc. has 100 shares of common stock outstanding as follows: 75 shares owned by Liz, 20 shares by her daughter, Sarah, and 5 shares by her daughter, Laura. Nursing Consultants owns the stock of Doctor Consultants, Inc. Liz sells her 75 shares of Nursing Consultants, Inc. to Doctor Consultants, Inc. This is a redemption of Nursing Consultants' stock, even though Doctor Consultants, Inc. distributes the cash to Liz. A complete termination of Liz's interest in Nursing Consultants, Inc. occurs and the amount received from the sale will be treated as payment in exchange of the stock.[22]

Redemption treated as a Regular Corporate Distribution (Dividend)   If a parent-subsidiary stock sale does not qualify as a sale or exchange, then the redemption is treated as a regular corporate distribution or dividend to the extent of earnings and profits and is taxed as ordinary income.[23] The property received by the selling shareholder in exchange for his/her redemption of stock of the parent is considered as being distributed by the subsidiary to the parent, to the extent of the subsidiary's earnings and profits and then by the parent to the selling shareholder to the extent of the parent's earnings and profits.[24] Therefore, the distribution is a dividend to the extent of the combined earnings and profits of both the parent and the subsidiary.

Example—Liz owns 60 of the 100 outstanding shares of Nursing Consultants, Inc. Nursing Consultants is in control of Doctor Consultants, Inc. Nursing Consultants has earnings and profits of $20,000, and Doctor Consultants has earnings and profits of $25,000. Liz transfers 20 of the shares of Nursing Consultants to Doctor Consultants for $50,000. The $50,000 is considered as being paid from Doctor Consultants to Nursing Consultants to the extent of $25,000, thereby increasing the earnings and profits of Nursing Consultants. Subsequently, Nursing Consultants is then deemed as distributing the $45,000 to Liz as a dividend. The remaining $5000 is considered a return of capital and reduces Liz's basis in her remaining stock. If there is no basis left, then the remaining $5000 would be a capital gain.

Application of the Constructive Ownership Rules to Parent-Subsidiary Stock Sales

The constructive ownership rules that apply to the parent-subsidiary stock sales are the same as those discussed earlier that are applicable to brother-sister corporation stock sales. All of the shareholders of a corporation are treated as owning a proportionate amount of stock owned by the corporation. However, a corporation is treated as owning all of the stock owned by any of the shareholders.

Basis of Stock in a Sale or Exchange

When a parent-subsidiary stock sale qualifies as a sale or exchange, the selling shareholder's adjusted basis in the stock is subtracted from the amount of the distribution to determine the amount of gain realized. There is no adjustment made to the basis of the remaining stock.

Example—Gary owns 75 shares in Electrician Supplies Corp. His basis in the stock is $100 per share. Electrician Supplies Corp. is in control of Wiring, Inc. Gary transfers 25 shares of Electrician Supplies stock to Wiring, Inc. for $125 per share. Gary recognizes a gain of $25 per share for a total of $625. His basis in the remaining 50 shares that he owns in Electrician Supplies Corp. remains $100 per share.

Basis of Stock in a Regular Corporate Distribution (Dividend)

When a parent-subsidiary stock sale does not qualify as a sale or exchange, and is, therefore, treated as a regular distribution or dividend, the selling shareholder's basis for his or her remaining stock in the parent corporation will be increased by the amount of the basis of the stock of the parent corporation sold to the subsidiary.[25]

Example—Gary owns 75 shares of Electrician Supplies Corp. Electrician Supplies is in control of Wiring, Inc. Gary has an adjusted basis in Electrician Supplies Corp. of $1000 per share. Electrician Supplies and Wiring, Inc. have earnings and profits of $25,000 and $50,000 respectively. Gary sells 25 shares of Electrician Supplies to Wiring, Inc. for $75,000, which is treated as a dividend. After the sale, Gary has an adjusted basis of $1500 per share. ($75,000 total basis/50 shares that Gary continues to own.)

CONCLUSION

Redemptions qualifying for sale and exchange treatment discussed in Chapter 9 are further complicated by related corporation stock sale rules. Due to the effects of §306 tainted stock discussed in Chapter 10, tax-free stock dividends often result in unfavorable tax consequences upon disposition of the stock. Shareholders who commonly control either brother-sister corporations or parent-subsidiary corporations should be aware of the various regulations that exist for related corporations.

In view of the maze of dividend and stock regulations, an investor might be inclined to pursue the bond markets. Chapter 12 discusses investments in debt instruments.

NOTES

[1] §1563(a)(2) and §265(f)(1) which changes the 80-percent ownership requirement to 50 percent.

[2] §1563(a)(1) and §265(f)(1)

[3] §304(c)(1)

[4] §304(c)(3)(B)(I) is a modification of §318(a)(2)(C)

[5] §304(c)(3)(B)(ii)(I)

[6] §304(c)(3)(B)(II)(II)

[7] Id.

[8] §304(c)(1)

[9] Reg. §1.304-2(a). The stock received by the acquiring corporation shall be treated as a contribution to the capital of that corporation.

[10] §304(b)(1) delineates the rules for determinations of which stock, the issuing corporation or the purchasing corporation, must be evaluated against the rules of §302(b).

[11] Reg. §1.304-2 The determination of whether the sales are related to each other is dependent on the facts and circumstances surrounding the sales. The fact that the sales may occur during a period of one or more years shall be disregarded, provided the other facts and circumstances indicate related transactions.

[12] §304(b)(1)

[13] Reg. 1.304-2

[14] Id.

[15] Id.

[16] Id.

[17] The example was based on Example (3) of Reg. §1.304-2

[18] §304(a)(B)

[19] §351(c)(2)

[20] §304(a)

[21] Reg. 1.304-3 The determination whether the amount received shall be treated as being received in payment in exchange for the stock shall be made by applying §303 or §302(b) with reference to the stock of the parent corporation.

[22] Adapted from example in Reg. 1.304-3. The rules of §302(c)(2) apply whereby a liquidating shareholder may not obtain an interest in the corporation, other than by bequest or inheritance, for 10 years.

[23] §316(a)

[24] §304(b)(2)

[25] Reg. 1.304-3(a)

PART THREE

Investments in Debt Instruments

12 INVESTING IN DEBT OR EQUITY

INTRODUCTION

At its most basic level, making money through investments often involves a choice between stock and debt. For example, let's say that Ed has $20,000 that he wants to invest. He is considering purchasing Tire Company bonds, which pay interest at 6.2 percent, compounded annually. The bonds are secured by collateral owned by Tire Company, and Ed views them as a relatively low-risk investment. If Ed buys $20,000 worth of bonds, he will earn $1240 of interest annually. Assuming Ed's marginal tax rate is 30 percent, his after-tax earnings will amount to $868 per year ($1240 * .3 = $372). For a three-year investment period, Ed's total gain would amount to $2604.

Alternatively, Ed is considering buying Tire Company common stock. Historically the company has paid dividends of roughly 7.5 percent on its common shares. In the past two years, however, Tire's dividends on its outstanding common stock have averaged 3 percent. For Ed this would amount to $510 after-tax, assuming a 15 percent dividend tax rate. Published reports indicate Tire is devoting substantial sums of money to development of a new, more fuel efficient tire, which it hopes to introduce within three years. Ed anticipates that if Tire is successful, his stock will increase in value by 45 percent. This means his $20,000 investment could be sold for a $9000 capital gain. At a 15-percent tax rate, Ed would pay $1350 of taxes, leaving a profit of $7650 plus after-tax dividend payments of $510 for each of the three years Ed owns the stock before selling. If Ed invests in the Tire bonds instead, he would have after-tax income of $868 annually. Assuming the bonds are paying interest at roughly market rates, Ed would report minimal gain or loss if he sells them at the end of three years. If Tire's development efforts are unsuccessful, Ed anticipates his common stock would drop in value by at least 10 percent.

NONTAX CONSIDERATIONS

In deciding whether the Tire Company debt or equity represents the better investment, Ed should weigh not only the tax consequences of his decision but also the nontax considerations. For example, debt traditionally has been viewed as less risky than equity because a corporation that is liquidating generally must pay its creditors before any moneys can be distributed to the shareholders. In Ed's case, the risk of holding debt was reduced even further because Tire Company's obligation was backed by collateral that could be used to retire the bonds if the company's cash flow does not support repayment. Debt may provide a more reliable stream of income for Ed because interest payments typically are not dependent on the existence of profits.

Ed and the other common stockholders would own a residual interest in Tire. This means they are entitled to whatever is left after the corporation's legal obligations are satisfied. A shareholder's return is dependent on the success of the corporation's business. As a stockholder, Ed would be paid dividends, while the Tire Company bonds would throw off interest. (The tax consequences of dividends are discussed in Chapter 8.) Ed also would enjoy voting rights in connection with his equity investment. If Tire liquidates, it would make arrangements to satisfy its outstanding debt and then distribute anything that remains to Ed and the other common shareholders.[1] Viewing the liquidating distribution as a percentage of Ed's original stock investment, the payment may be more or less than what the Tire Company creditors receive.

If Tire has preferred stock outstanding, those shares likely would occupy a hybrid position, somewhere between the company's debt and equity. Usually, preferred stock has a preference as to both dividends and liquidating distributions, meaning holders of these shares receive payment before amounts are disbursed to common stockholders. However, preferred stock is often limited in its participation. In other words, ceilings may exist on the amount preferred stockholders receive through either dividends or liquidating distributions.

TAX CONSEQUENCES OF INTEREST

Interest paid on debt[2] is ordinary income for all taxpayers, meaning it is not eligible for taxation at favorable capital gain or qualified dividend rates. Interest has been defined by the courts as the cost of using money.[3] An interest rate may be fixed or variable. If a bond pays less interest than market rates would dictate, it will be sold for a discount. In other words, a bond with a $10,000 face value that pays 4.5 percent interest, when market rates for comparable obligations are 5.75 percent, will sell for less than $10,000. Depending on the size of the discount, the holder of the bond may have to report income under the original issue discount or market discount rules. (These rules are discussed in Chapter 13.) Interest payments should be distinguished from other payments an investor may receive. For example, "interest" being paid to an investor who also provides services may actually represent compensation for the services being performed.[4] Where the IRS challenges the characterization of payments as interest, the federal courts will examine the facts surrounding the payment in order to determine why it was made.[5]

Bonds often are sold between interest payment dates. In that case, the amount received by the seller represents not only payment for the bond itself but also compensation for the interest accrued as of the sale date. The regulations require that the portion of the amount realized that is attributable to the accrued interest must be reported as interest income. This means the seller may wind up recognizing both ordinary income and capital gain on the sale of a bond.

Example—Linda sells Alleghany, Inc. bonds to Jennifer. The bonds were issued to Linda three years ago, for their face value of $12,000. The instruments pay 5 percent interest on June 30th and December 31st of each year. As of the sale date, accrued interest amounts to $300. Linda sells the bonds for $12,500. She reports $300 of interest income and $200 of capital gain, assuming the bonds are a capital asset in Linda's hands. If Linda sells the bonds for $12,200 instead, she apparently is required under the regulations to report $300 of ordinary income, attributable to the interest, and $100 of capital loss [$12,200 amount received − $300 (interest income) = $11,900 amount realized on the sale].[6] When Jennifer receives the first interest payment of $600 on the Alleghany bonds, she will report only $300 of ordinary income. This is the total amount of the interest payment less the interest Linda already reported.[7]

If the Alleghany bonds Linda sells are in default at the time of Jennifer's purchase, the price Jennifer pays probably covers both the bond itself and the accrued but unpaid interest. Under the regulations, Jennifer will not be taxed if the outstanding interest is received later. Instead, the interest payments are treated as a return of Jennifer's capital, and they reduce her basis in the Alleghany bonds. However, interest arising after Jennifer's purchase is taxable.[8]

If bonds carry an interest rate that is higher than the market, they will sell at a premium. In other words, a bond with a $10,000 face value that pays interest at an annual rate of 8.25 percent will sell for more than $10,000 if market interest rates are only 7.5 percent. Under the Tax Code, an investor who pays a premium for a bond, debenture, or other evidence of debt[9] may elect to amortize it currently.[10] A premium exists where the investor's basis in the bond exceeds the total of all moneys to be received after its acquisition, other than payments of qualified stated interest.[11] The constant yield method is used for the amortization calculation. If an investor elects this option, his or her basis in the bond is reduced each year by the amount of the premium that is being amortized.

Example—Ken buys a taxable bond when it is issued on January 1, 2002, for $51,175.[12] When the instrument matures on December 31, 2006, the bond will pay $50,000. Therefore Ken has paid a premium of $1175.[13] The bond pays qualified stated annual interest each year of 6 percent per year. The yield on the bond is 5.45 percent.[14] Assuming an annual accrual period, Ken can elect to amortize the premium he has paid on the bond according the calculations in Table 12-1.

What this chart means is that if Ken sells his bond at the end of 2002, for $51,000, he will report a gain of $36. This is because Ken's basis in the bond is $50,964, after taking into account the amortization calculation. In 2002 Ken will be paid stated interest of $3000, but he will offset this amount by $211, reflecting the amount of the premium attributable to year 2002.[15]

The election to amortize premium is made by showing the amortization on the tax return for the first year in which an investor makes the election. A statement also should be attached showing that the investor is exercising the option to amortize under §171 of the Tax Code. The election is binding, meaning it can be revoked only with IRS approval, and will apply to all taxable bonds the investor holds during or after the year of election.[16] If the election is made, the investor shows an offset for bond premium on the Form 1040, Schedule B, where interest income is reported. (See Chapter 13.) If the amortization of the premium exceeds the bond's

TABLE 12-1

Date	Beginning Balance	Actual Interest (5.45%)	Stated Interest (6%)	Difference	Ending Balance
1/1/02					$51,175
12/31/02	$51,175	$2,789	$3,000	$211	50,964
12/31/03	50,964	2,777	3,000	222	50,742
12/31/04	50,742	2,765	3,000	235	50,507
12/31/05	50,507	2,753	3,000	247	50,260
12/31/06	50,260	2,739	3,000	261	50,000

stated interest, the investor may be able to claim a miscellaneous itemized deduction for the difference, depending on the total interest reported and the total premium amortized in prior years.[17]

If Ken elects not to amortize the $1175 premium he paid on the bond, he will report the full amount of stated interest as income each year. When the bond matures, Ken will have a capital loss because he will receive $50,000 in settlement of an investment for which he paid $51,175. In most cases it is advantageous to amortize because this permits reduction of interest taxed at ordinary income rates while minimizing capital losses.[18] Also, amortization permits Ken to deduct the premium sooner than if he waits to claim a loss when the bond is sold or matures.

DISPOSITION OR RETIREMENT OF STOCKS AND BONDS

Unless a nonrecognition rule applies, a stockholder who sells or exchanges her shares will report taxable gain or loss equal to the difference between the amount realized and the stock's adjusted basis. A redemption of shares that qualifies under the rules discussed in Chapter 9 also will receive sale or exchange treatment. Assuming the stock is a capital asset in the shareholder's hands, this means she will report capital gain or loss. However, if a redemption is treated as a dividend, then ordinary income or dividend treatment will apply, depending on whether the 2003 dividend rules are applicable, up to the stockholder's share of the corporation's earnings and profits. The 2003 rules for reporting dividend income are discussed in Chapter 8.

A sale or exchange of a bond generally is also expected to be taxable.[19] This means that like a stock sale, the investor must recognize gain or loss equal to the difference between the amount realized and his or her adjusted basis in the bond.[20] If the debt is a capital asset in the investor's hands, the resulting gain or loss will be capital in nature. However, accrued market discount[21] will trigger recognition of ordinary income. Declaration of a dividend on stock at the time of a sale or exchange will also generate ordinary income or dividend recognition for either the buyer or seller, depending on the circumstances. (These rules are discussed in Chapter 8.)

When a bond is sold or exchanged, the resulting gain may be taxed as ordinary income to the extent of unaccrued original issue discount. This rule applies where at the time the bond was issued originally there was an intention to call the instrument before maturity.[22] This intention can be found in either oral or written understandings between the issuer and the original holder of the debt.[23]

Example—Judith holds a bond issued by Realco, Inc. She purchased the instrument at the time it was issued, for $9673. Documents drafted at the time included an understanding that the bond would be called prior to its stated maturity. The bond has a face value of $10,000 and pays stated interest of 6.2 percent. The market rate is 7 percent. Using the original issue discount rules, Table 12-2 shows the tax results of Judith's investment for the first two years.

Assume Judith sells the Realco bond in December of 2004 for $9850. The total original issue discount on the instrument was $327 ($10,000 − $9,673). Of this amount, Judith reported $118 of discount as ordinary income during 2002 and 2003. This means that Judith's total gain of $59 ($9,850 − $9,791) will be treated as ordinary income even if the bond is a capital asset for Judith. However, these rules do not apply to tax-exempt obligations[24] or to debt instruments that are publicly offered.[25] In other words, had the Realco bond Judith bought been sold publicly, her gain of $59 would have been eligible for capital gain treatment.

Similar rules apply under the Tax Code to gain arising from the sale or exchange of short-term obligations. A short-term obligation is an instrument with a fixed maturity date of one year or less from the date of issue.[26] These rules, which are discussed in further detail in Chapter 15 of this book, ensure that taxpayers do not turn what is really interest income on short-term bonds into short-term capital gain by selling the instruments before they mature. Although short-term capital gain is not eligible for favorable capital gain treatment, it can offset capital losses that a taxpayer might not otherwise be able to use currently.

TABLE 12-2

Date	Beginning Balance	Actual Interest (7%)	Stated Interest (6.2%)	Difference	Ending Balance
1/1/02					$9,673
12/31/02	$9,673	$677	$620	$57	9,730
12/31/03	9,730	681	620	61	9,791

The retirement of a bond is considered an exchange, under Tax Code §1271.[27] The term "retirement" includes cancellation of the debt prior to maturity.[28] This means amounts received when a bond is retired or cancelled are eligible for capital gain treatment if the debt instrument is a capital asset in the holder's hands. Where bonds are disposed of at a loss, other than by sale or exchange, the law is less clear.

Three sections of the Tax Code may be applicable.

1. §1271—Retirement of a Bond

If the bond is considered to be "retired," the §1271 rules apply, meaning an exchange has occurred.[29] The investor claims a long- or short-term capital loss, depending on the holding period of the debt instrument.

2. §165—Worthless Securities

Losses falling under these rules will be characterized as arising from a sale or exchange of a capital asset occurring on the last day of the tax year. A "security," for purposes of §165, is defined as corporate stock and also includes "a bond, debenture, note, or certificate, or other evidence of indebtedness, issued by a corporation or by a government or political subdivision thereof, with interest coupons or in registered form."[30] The bad debt rules of §166, discussed below, do not apply where debt instruments falling within this definition of a security become worthless.[31]

3. §166—Bad Debts

The rules for deduction of bad debts under §166 depend on whether the instrument represents a business or nonbusiness obligation. For corporations, all obligations are considered to be business related. This means a corporation can take a deduction for wholly or partially worthless debts, equivalent to the adjusted basis of the obligation in the corporation's hands.[32] The deduction reduces the corporation's ordinary income.

The rules regarding business bad debts are the same for investors who are not corporations. However, individuals and other noncorporate investors can deduct nonbusiness bad debts only when the obligation is completely worthless; there is no deduction for a partially worthless loan. In addition, a nonbusiness bad debt is deducted only as a short-term capital loss, regardless of the investor's holding period for the debt instrument.[33] An obligation arising for investment reasons is considered nonbusiness. This means, for example, that a shareholder who loans money to a financially distressed corporation, hoping the infusion of cash will save the company and protect his original stock investment, holds a nonbusiness bad debt if the loan is not repaid.

The difference between these code sections has to do with the character of the loss. It appears § 1271 applies where a payment has been received in final settlement of the debt, meaning an exchange has occurred.[34] If that distinction is correct, that would mean an investor who receives nothing in connection with a debt instrument will claim either a bad debt or a loss because of a worthless security, depending on whether the instrument is a registered bond, bears interest coupons, or otherwise meets the definition of security described above, under § 165. These possible results are summarized in Table 12-3 as follows:

TABLE 12-3

Code Section	Tax Result
§ 1271 Retirement	Long- or short-term capital loss, depending on the investor's holding period
§ 166 Business bad debt	Deduct against ordinary income where debt is wholly or partially worthless.
§ 166 Nonbusiness bad debt	Deduct only when wholly worthless, as a short-term capital loss
§ 165 Worthless security	Capital loss arising on the last day of the tax year the security became worthless

Most corporate investors probably would prefer bad debt treatment. This is because all of a corporation's bad debts are considered business related and therefore will generate ordinary income deductions. Corporations can only deduct capital loss against capital gain; there is no offset against ordinary income comparable to the $3000 rule that applies to individuals.[35] Also, a corporation unable to use its capital losses currently can carry them back three years and forward five; if the losses are not used during that period they expire.[36] By comparison, ordinary losses can become part of a corporation's net operating loss. These can be carried back two years or carried forward 20.[37]

For individuals and other noncorporate investors, the most favorable treatment also is as a bad debt, assuming the obligation can be characterized as business-related. If the obligation is considered a business bad debt, an investor can claim a deduction against ordinary income, even for a partially worthless obligation. Further, even the nonbusiness bad debt rules generate a short-term capital loss. Since short-term capital gain is taxed at higher rates than long-term, most taxpayers prefer to treat capital losses as short-term, rather than long.

Example—Phil is an investor in Phoenix Inc., a corporation in serious financial difficulty. Phil holds Phoenix bonds for which he paid $10,000. If Phil receives $500 in settlement of the Phoenix obligations, he will claim a capital loss equal to $9500, assuming §1271 applies. If Phil bought the Phoenix bonds two years ago, the loss will be long term. Assuming Phil has $9500 or more of capital gain, his loss will have a value to him of $1900 ($9,500 * 20 percent), if net capital gain is taxed at a 20 percent rate.

Phil can claim an ordinary loss of $10,000, under §166, if his Phoenix obligations represent a business bad debt. (This assumes Phil receives no amount in settlement of the bonds.) If Phil is in a 30-percent tax bracket, the loss has a value to him of $3000. This means Phil saves $600 by not receiving the $500 payment. ($3000, value of ordinary loss, − {$500 payment plus $1900 savings from long-term capital loss}).[38] Even if the Phoenix bonds represent an investment, Phil's short-term capital loss under the bad debt rules will offset short-term capital gain, which is taxed at ordinary income rates.

If the worthless securities rules of §165 apply instead, the loss will be treated as arising on the last day of the tax year. This may mean the investor has a long-term rather than short-term loss.

Example—Kathleen, a calendar-year taxpayer, holds bonds issued by Occuther, Inc. The bonds fit within the definition of security found in IRC §165(g)(2). Kathleen purchased the instruments on July 1, 2002. In February of 2003, newspapers report that Occuther is responsible for enormous amounts of debt that have not been shown on the company's balance sheet. Additional problems come to light and by May the company has defaulted on its bonds. If on June 15, 2003 Kathleen accepts a final payment in settlement of the Occuther debt she holds, she will be treated as having made an exchange for the bonds, assuming §1271 applies. Kathleen will report a short-term capital loss, if the bonds are capital assets, equal to the difference between her basis and the amount of the settlement that she received. However, if the worthless securities rules apply instead, Kathleen's loss will be treated as arising on December 31st of 2003. This means any loss Kathleen reports in connection with the bonds will be long term.

Apart from issues arising because of losses on debt, tax consequences also arise where bond terms are significantly modified, because of market conditions or the issuer's financial circumstances, for example. These transactions may be treated as exchanges. In other words, a debt restructuring or modification can produce taxable gain or loss for the bondholder, depending on how the terms of the instrument as altered compare to the debt's original provisions. An exchange can even occur where the changes are effected without an actual surrender of the original bonds and issuance of new ones. This can happen where a creditor agrees to a waiver of one of the terms of an existing debt instrument.[39] A debt exchange generally does not arise where the terms of the instrument originally provided for changes to be made, although there are exceptions to this rule.[40] For example, a change in the obligor on the instrument is considered to be a modification, even if the original instrument provided for this possibility.[41]

Under the Treasury Regulations, exchanges occur where "significant modifications" have taken place.[42] A modification is defined as any alteration of a legal right or duty of the issuer or holder of a bond or other debt instrument.[43] The regulations contain specific rules that are used to determine whether certain kinds of modifications are significant. For example, under the rule applicable to changes made to the timing of payments, an alteration is significant if it results in a "material deferral" of the payments that were to be made under the original terms of the instrument.[44] Other specific rules apply to changes in yield, changes in the nature of the instrument, changes involving the financial and accounting covenants, and changes involving the obligor or the security on the instrument.[45]

Where no specific rule exists, the regulations contain a general test to be applied to determine if a modification is significant. This test focuses on whether the change altered the legal rights or duties to a degree that is economically significant, considering all the facts and circumstances.[46] All changes not subject to a specific rule are taken into account collectively in deciding whether or not a significant modification has occurred under the general rule.

Example—Joanne holds a 20-year debt instrument, issued at par by Book Treasures, Inc. The obligation provides for payment of $100,000 at maturity, with annual interest payments of 10 percent. At the beginning of the 11th year, Joanne and Book Treasures agree to defer all remaining interest payments until the instrument matures, with compounding. The yield on the obligation continues to be 10 percent.

Under the regulations, the change in Joanne's Book Treasures instrument is a significant modification.[47] This means that Joanne will be required to report gain or loss in connection with the transaction, equal to the difference between the value of the holding as modified and her basis in the original instrument. Although loss recognition may not be problematic for Joanne from a tax perspective, reporting gain could have unexpected tax consequences, particularly since Joanne did not receive any cash proceeds in connection with the Book Treasures transaction, and the interest payments on the bond now are deferred. In other words, investors who hold bonds or other debt instruments need to consult the exchange rules of §1001 and the accompanying regulations before agreeing to modifications in the obligations.

SPECIFIC PROVISIONS APPLICABLE TO STOCK

In choosing between debt and equity, an investor also should consider certain specific tax rules that are applicable to stock. These rules include §1244, which allows an investor to claim an ordinary loss in connection with small business stock, and §1202, which provides a 50-percent exclusion when qualified small business stock held for more than five years is sold. Tax Code §1045 permits investors to rollover gain arising from the sale of certain stock where other qualified replacement shares are purchased within 60 days. Depending on the circumstances, these provisions could make an investment in equity more attractive than holding debt, because of the potentially substantial tax advantages they represent. However, in all cases the provisions are limited to stock in only certain qualifying small corporations. This means these opportunities probably are unavailable to shares issued by large, publicly traded companies. Also, only certain shareholders can qualify.

Tax Code §1244

If stock represents a capital asset for an investor, then the gain arising from its sale is eligible for favorable capital gain taxation. However, any loss generated by the disposition of the stock is treated as capital loss, which can be deducted only to the extent of capital gain, plus, for individuals, $3000.[48] IRC §1244 alters this statutory scheme by allowing losses from the sale of §1244 stock to be treated as ordinary, up to certain limits.

Example—Lorraine owns stock in Bassett Company that she purchased three years ago. The stock has an adjusted basis of $125,000. Lorraine is an investor, and her shares are capital assets. This means if Lorraine sells the stock for $185,000, she will report $60,000 of capital gain. Assuming a 20-percent long-term capital gain tax rate, Lorraine will pay $12,000 of tax because of the Bassett stock sale, leaving her with after-tax proceeds of $173,000. Assuming Lorraine is otherwise in a 35-percent tax bracket, if the gain were not eligible for long-term capital treatment she would pay $21,000 in tax. This would leave only $164,000 of after-tax proceeds.

Assume instead that the Bassett investment loses money and Lorraine decides to sell her shares for $80,000. If the $45,000 loss is capital, Lorraine can use it only to offset capital gain, plus $3000 of ordinary income. Assuming Lorraine has $45,000 of long-term capital gain resulting from other transactions, the Bassett loss has a tax value to her of $9000 ($45,000 * 20 percent), again at a 20 percent capital gain rate. By comparison, if Lorraine could claim the $45,000 loss as ordinary, it would create tax savings for her of $15,750 ($45,000 * 35 percent assumed marginal tax rate).[49]

Shareholders that are corporations are not entitled to ordinary loss treatment under §1244. Stock owned by partnerships can qualify, but only for partners who are individuals and who owned partnership interests at the time the stock was acquired and at the time the partnership sustained the loss.[50] S corporations are not treated as partnerships for purposes of these rules, meaning an S corporation shareholder will not be able to claim ordinary loss in connection with the sale by the corporation of stock that otherwise would qualify under §1244.[51]

In order to claim ordinary loss treatment, the stock must have been issued originally to the shareholder. An investor who acquires stock by gift, by purchase from another shareholder, or as a result of inheritance cannot take advantage of these rules. Similarly, stock purchased by an investment firm and later resold to individual investors would not qualify.[52] The amount of ordinary loss that can be claimed in any tax year under §1244 is limited to $50,000 unless a joint return is filed, in which case the ceiling is $100,000.[53] Losses incurred beyond these limits are capital. The $100,000 and $50,000 amounts apply on a per-taxpayer basis. In other words, an investor who in one year sells §1244 stock held in several corporations can deduct only a total of $50,000 or $100,000 of ordinary loss, depending on which limit applies. Where losses are expected to be more than the limit, an investor should consider selling the shares over more than one tax year.

Ordinary loss treatment can only be claimed for stock that qualifies under the §1244 rules. This means three requirements must be met.

1. At the time the shares were issued, the corporation must have qualified as a "small business corporation." A domestic corporation is a small business corporation if the total amount of money and other property received for stock, as capital contributions, and as paid-in surplus is $1,000,000 or less.[54] If at the time the shares were issued the corporation met this requirement, the stock does not become ineligible later simply because the company subsequently exceeds the $1,000,000 ceiling. Instead, shares issued after the limit is passed fall outside §1244, meaning the corporation will have both §1244 and non-§1244 stock outstanding. For purposes of determining the amount of property received by a corporation, an asset's adjusted basis is used, rather than its fair market value. This amount is further reduced by any liability to which the property is subject or which the corporation assumes in connection with the asset's receipt.[55]

2. Shares qualifying under §1244 must have been issued for money or property. The term "property" does not include stock or securities[56] or services. The Tax Code specifically provides that increases in stock basis due to capital contributions or for other reasons are not eligible for §1244 treatment.[57] In other words, an existing shareholder who plans on investing more money or property should receive separate stock certificates evidencing additional shares issued, in order to qualify the new investment under the §1244 rules.

3. The last test to be met under §1244 is a gross receipts test. During the five most recent tax years ending before the loss arose, the corporation must have derived more than 50 percent of its total gross receipts from sources other than royalties, rents, interest, etc.[58] The term "gross receipts" means the total amount accrued or received

(depending on whether the corporation uses the accrual or cash method of accounting) and includes amounts received from investments and from the sale of any kind of property. Receipts are not reduced by returns, allowances, costs, or other deductions.[59] Amounts received in wholly nontaxable exchanges are not counted, but receipts from the sale of stock or securities are included, to the extent of gains.[60] The gross receipts test does not apply if the corporation reports losses during the applicable testing period.[61]

An investor who wants to preserve the possibility of an ordinary loss in connection with his or her stockholdings should keep adequate records documenting that the stock qualifies under the §1244 rules. This should include, for example, receipts showing the stock was originally issued to the investor and also that the shares were received for cash or property. It is also helpful if the corporation maintains records documenting to whom the shares were issued, the date of issuance, the amount and type of consideration received for the stock, etc.[62] This may be a caution that many investors would prefer to ignore. After all, few people invest in a corporation with the expectation of losing money. Nonetheless, assembling the appropriate records at the time the stock is issued can help ensure that an investor can make the best possible tax advantage from a loss, however unexpected.

Tax Code § 1202

Under the 2003 rules, most individuals who sell a capital asset held more than one year expect a 15-percent tax rate to apply.[63] Tax Code §1202, however, allows an investor to exclude 50 percent of the gain from the sale of qualifying small business stock. (If the corporation is a "qualified business entity" and other requirements are met, an exclusion of 60 percent applies.[64]) The remaining gain is taxed at a top rate of 28-percent, assuming the shares are a capital asset.[65]

Example—John buys stock that qualifies under the §1202 rules. His adjusted basis in the shares is $900,000, and he has held the stock for seven years. John sells his investment for $8,900,000, realizing a gain of $8,000,000. Under the §1202 rules, John can exclude 50 percent of his gain, meaning he will be taxed on $4,000,000. John will pay tax of $1,120,000 ($4,000,000 * 28 percent), leaving $7,780,000 of proceeds after tax ($8,900,000 − $1,120,000).[66] If the sale proceeds instead were handled under the 2003 capital gain rules, John would pay a tax of $1,200,000

(15 percent * $8,000,000). This would leave $7,700,000 after-tax. John saves $80,000 because of §1202. (If John's capital gain rate were 20%, his savings would be $480,000.)

In order to qualify for the 50-percent exclusion, John must hold his stock for more than five years.[67] An investor who transfers property for §1202 shares is treated as acquiring the stock on the date of the exchange. However, in certain cases a stockholder may be able to claim a holding period longer than the period of time the stock was actually in his possession. This applies, for example, where qualifying stock was acquired as a gift or inheritance or when the stock was received by converting other shares in the same corporation that also qualified under the §1202 requirements.[68]

The total amount of gain that can be excluded under §1202 in any one tax year is subject to a limitation. The limit is whichever is greater: $10,000,000, reduced by gain taken into account under §1202 in prior years as to stock of the same issuer, or 10 times the adjusted basis of the qualifying stock issued by the corporation and disposed of during the tax year.[69] In John's case this limit would be $10,000,000 because that number is greater than 10 times his adjusted basis (10* $900,000 = $9,000,000). Had John sold some of his shares in an earlier year in a sale that qualified for the exclusion, the $10,000,000 figure would have been reduced by the eligible gain taken into account in the earlier year.

Example—Continuing with the facts above, assume instead that John sold $1,000,000 worth of stock last year and the remainder in the current year. Further assume that his basis in the shares sold last year was $101,124, meaning his total gain on that sale was $898,876. Assuming no change in the value of John's holdings, his gain in the current year is $7,101,124 ($7,900,000 − $798,876). The exclusion limit that applies to John this year is the greater of $7,988,760 (10* John's adjusted basis of $798,876) or $9,101,124. This latter figure is calculated by reducing the $10,000,000 limit that otherwise would apply by the total amount of gain John realized in connection with the sale last year of stock in the same corporation.

The limit applies to the total amount of gain that can be excluded. In other words, if John's limit is $10,000,000, the most he can exclude is $5,000,000. For purposes of calculating the total gain eligible for exclusion, the basis of stock received in exchange for property cannot be less than the property's fair market value.[70]

Example—Rob forms Heat Co. by contributing property with an adjusted basis of $1,000,000 and a fair market value of $1,500,000. The transaction qualifies under Tax Code §351, meaning Rob recognizes no gain on the transfer. Under Code §358, Rob's adjusted basis in his Heat Co. shares is $1,000,000, the basis of the property contributed. However, for purposes of the 50-percent exclusion, Rob's basis in the shares is $1,500,000, the fair market value of the property at the time of contribution. This rule ensures that the gain inherent in the asset at the time Rob transferred it falls outside §1202.

If after five years Rob sells his shares for $2,600,000, his total gain will be $1,600,000 ($2.6 million amount realized − $1 million adjusted basis). However, only $1.1 million of the gain ($2.6 million − $1.5 million adjusted basis under §1202) will be eligible for the 50-percent exclusion. This means at most Rob will be able to exclude $550,000 (50 percent of $1.1 million), leaving Rob with a total of $1,050,000 to report ($1.6 million − $550,000 exclusion). Of this amount, $550,000 will be taxed at a 28-percent rate, generating a liability of $154,000. The remaining $500,000 will be taxed under the regular capital gain rules.[71] Rob will owe a total of $254,000 in tax because of the sale ($154,000 + {20 percent * $500,000}), assuming capital gains are taxed at 20 percent. If Rob had sold the stock after only four years, §1202 would not apply. Rob would owe tax of $320,000, assuming no change in the stock values between the fourth and fifth years ($1.6 million gain * .2 = $320,000 tax). This means Rob saves $66,000 by using the 50-percent exclusion.

The rule limiting the basis of qualifying shares to the fair market value of contributed property also applies to later contributions made after the shares were originally issued to the stockholder. However, the basis limitation is calculated without considering the effect of the later property transfer.[72]

Example—Jerry holds stock qualifying under §1202 in Baker, Inc. Jerry's adjusted basis in his shares is $900,000, and he is the sole stockholder of the company. One year after organizing Baker, Jerry makes an additional capital contribution, by transferring property with an adjusted basis and value of $140,000. Jerry's total basis for purposes of §1202 is $1,040,000 ($900,000 + $140,000 attributable to the later property contribution). Under §1202(b), the limit on the amount of gain Jerry can exclude is the greater of $10,000,000 (assuming no prior sales of stock in Baker) or $9,000,000. This latter number is 10 times Jerry's adjusted basis, not including the later capital contribution. If Jerry had transferred all the property when the stock was issued originally, his limit would be $10,400,000.

Of the amount of income excluded under §1202, 42 percent is treated as a preference under the alternative minimum tax rules.[73] (If the holding period of the stock begins after 2000, the preference is 28 percent. See the discussion of the alternative minimum tax in Chapter 5.) In Rob's case, for example, this means he will have a preference equal to $231,000 (42 percent * $550,000), assuming he acquired the stock before 2001. Investors need to consider the potential impact of this preference when weighing a possible investment in §1202 stock.

Although C corporations cannot use §1202, qualifying shares held by pass-through entities, like partnerships and S corporations, are eligible for the exclusion at the partner or shareholder level. In order for this to occur, however, the partner or shareholder must have owned the interest in the pass-through entity at the time the qualifying stock was acquired and at all times thereafter until the entity disposed of the qualifying shares.[74] Investors who hold interests in mutual funds also qualify for pass-through treatment of the exclusion under these rules.

In order to take advantage of §1202, an investor must hold "qualified small business stock."[75] This term is defined differently than a "small business corporation," which is the language used in §1244, discussed above. The requirements under IRC §1202 are as follows:

1. The stock must have been issued by a domestic C corporation after August 10, 1993. (This is the date §1202 was enacted.) A C corporation is taxed under the regular rules applicable to corporations.

2. The stock was originally issued to the investor for money, property, or services. However, shares issued in exchange for other stock or in exchange for underwriting services will not qualify.[76] Investors who hold §1202 stock by gift or inheritance are nonetheless treated as satisfying the original issuance requirement. Likewise, a partner who receives §1202 shares from a partnership will satisfy the rules, provided the partner held his partnership interest at the time the stock was acquired and at all times thereafter until the distribution.[77]

3. The corporation is a "qualified small business." This means the total gross assets of the corporation at all times on or after August 10, 1993 and before the shares were issued amounted to no more than $50 million. In addition, immediately after issuance of the shares, the gross assets, now including the consideration received in exchange for the stock, do not exceed the $50 million figure. Gross assets are defined to include cash plus the aggregate adjusted bases of other property held by the corporation.[78] Aggregation rules ap-

ply, under which corporations that are members of the same parent-subsidiary controlled group are combined in applying the $50 million test.[79] This prevents taxpayers from avoiding the asset limitation by dividing up operations into several smaller companies.

4. The corporation must meet the "active business" requirement for substantially all of the investor's holding period.[80] Under this requirement, a corporation must use at least 80 percent of its assets in the active conduct of one or more qualified trades or businesses. The 80-percent test is applied by value. A qualified trade or business does not include operations involving the performance of services in fields like health or law. Also excluded are banking and similar financial services, farming operations, restaurants and hotels, and also certain businesses for which percentage depletion is allowable. A parent corporation is treated as owning a ratable share of a subsidiary's assets and conducting a ratable share of the subsidiary's activities.[81] Certain corporations cannot satisfy the active business requirement, including DISCS and mutual funds.[82]

The $50-million-dollar ceiling on gross assets means many investors in large corporations will be unable to take advantage of the §1202 exclusion. For those taxpayers who do qualify, however, the benefits of §1202 can be substantial.[83] Investors who hold potentially eligible stock should try to ensure that it qualifies. For example, an investor considering selling stock that has appreciated in value after owning the shares for four years might want to consider keeping the stock an additional year to satisfy the five-year holding period requirement. The cost of complying with §1202, as where a taxpayer does hold shares beyond the date on which she otherwise would sell, should be compared with the potential benefits in deciding whether to pursue the exclusion.

Tax Code §1045

Tax Code §1045 is a rollover provision. This section permits an investor who sells qualified small business stock to defer the recognition of gain, provided replacement qualified small business shares are purchased within the 60-day period beginning with the sale.

Example—Pat holds qualified small business stock in Pendleton Co. Her adjusted basis in the shares she owns is $800,000 and the stock has a fair market value of $1,500,000. Pat decides to sell her Pendleton shares. Even though she will realize a gain of $700,000 on the transaction, Pat will not have to report any income, so long as she reinvests the proceeds in qualified small business shares within 60 days of selling the Pendleton stock. If Pat buys qualifying replacement shares in Lock Company for $1,600,000 one month after the Pendleton sale, she will not recognize any gain. Pat's basis in her new Lock shares will be $900,000. This is the price she paid for the new stock less the deferred gain ($1,600,000 − $700,000).[84]

In order for Pat to take advantage of the deferral provisions of §1045, certain requirements must be met. These are as follows:

1. The investor cannot be a corporation.[85]
2. The stock being sold must have been held more than six months as of the date of sale.[86] The holding period rules that were discussed above, under §1202, apply. This means, for example, that an investor picks up the holding period of the prior owner of qualifying shares where the stock was received by gift or inheritance. Similarly, an investor holding qualifying stock received through a partnership distribution includes the partnership's holding period, under the provisions described previously.
3. The investor elects to use §1045 before the due date, with extensions, of the tax return for the year the qualifying stock was sold. The election is made on the Schedule D. The entire amount of gain is shown on the form. On the line immediately below where the gain is reported, the deferred gain is entered as a loss, with the label "Section 1045 rollover."[87] An investor can elect rollover treatment for only some of the qualifying sales that occur in the same tax year. However, once made, the election cannot be revoked without IRS consent.

Many of the rules discussed under §1202 also apply to rollovers pursuant to Code §1045. For example, pass-through treatment of the rollover is available for noncorporate partners or S corporation shareholders in connection with the sale of qualifying shares owned by an eligible pass-through entity, provided certain conditions are met.[88] Where an investor acquires stock in exchange for property, the basis of the shares for §1045 purposes cannot be less than the property's fair market value at the time of the exchange. In order to use IRC §1045, the shares must represent "qualified small business stock." This means the requirements discussed above, including the active business rules, the original issuance provision, the gross asset test, etc., all apply.[89]

Assuming that all the prerequisites to rollover treatment are satisfied, the election to defer recognition of gain in connection with the sale of qualifying stock usually makes sense. This is because time value of money principles always favor delaying payment of income tax. However, in some cases an investor may want to recognize the gain currently. This might be the case if the investor anticipates that she will be in a higher tax bracket when the replacement shares are sold or if capital losses are available that could be used to offset gain arising from the sale.

CONCLUSION

A taxpayer looking to invest money is initially confronted with the very basic decision of whether to hold equity or debt. In many cases debt may represent a more secure investment. However, the tax law does contain various benefits, like the 50-percent exclusion of §1202, that are available only for equity holdings. This means a taxpayer, evaluating whether a potential return on a particular stock justifies what otherwise might be an increased risk associated with the shares, needs to consider whether any special tax rules apply and also whether he or she would qualify. This is because the tax consequences will affect his or her after-tax return.

NOTES

[1] If the corporation is insolvent or in bankruptcy, it is unlikely that either the creditors or the stockholders will receive back the full value of their investment.

[2] For tax purposes, the distinction between debt and equity is not always clear, particularly where an instrument has features that resemble both. In 1969 Congress enacted Tax Code §385, directing the IRS to issue regulations providing guidance in this area. Among the factors to be considered were the debt/equity ratio of the corporation, whether the instrument was convertible, the existence of subordination features, any relationship between stock ownership and debt holdings, and also the terms of any debt, including interest rates, etc. The IRS issued regulations that were later withdrawn; currently no regulations exist under this Code section.

[3] *Deputy v. DuPont*, 308 U.S. 488, 498 (1940)

[4] Characterizing compensation for services as interest income would inflate a taxpayer's investment income, thereby permitting a greater deduction of investment expenses. (See Chapter 4 for a discussion of the limitations on deduction of investment expenses.) Also, this might reduce any Social Security or self-employment taxes owed.

⁵ See, for example, *Fort Howard Corp. v. Comm'r.*, 103 T.C. 345 (1994), finding that payments made in connection with a leveraged buyout were compensation for services and not interest.

⁶ Treasury Regulation §1.61-7(d). Under the original issue discount rules, ordinary income on the sale of certain debt instruments is limited to the amount of gain recognized. See, for example, Tax Code §1271(a)(3) (short-term government obligations) and Tax Code §1271(a)(4) (short-term nongovernment obligations). If these rules were to apply to Linda, she would report $200 of interest income and no loss. However, since the Alleghany bonds had a fixed maturity date of more than one year from the date of issue, they are not short-term. Tax Code §1271(a)(4). Although a similar limit applies to the amount of ordinary income recognized on the sale of a market discount bond, Tax Code §1276(a)(1), Linda's bonds fall outside the market discount rules. See Tax Code §1278(a)(1).

⁷ If Alleghany sends Jennifer a Form 1099-INT showing the full $600 of interest income, Jennifer should report that amount on her Form 1040, Schedule B. The $300 of accrued interest is subtracted from Jennifer's interest income subtotal, so that the net result is the $300 of income Jennifer actually received. IRS Publication 550, *Investment Income and Expenses* (2002), at p. 18.

⁸ Treasury Regulation §1.61-7(c). If Jennifer is an accrual method taxpayer, generally she will report the interest income when it becomes due, when it is received, or when it has been earned, whichever occurs first. Rev. Rul. 77-135, 1977-1 C.B. 133. If Jennifer uses the cash method of accounting, she will report the income when it is actually or constructively received, under the cash method. IRS Publication 550, *Investment Income and Expenses* (2002), at p. 16.

⁹ Tax Code §171(d). Excluded from the definition are instruments that represent stock in trade for the taxpayer, that would properly be considered inventory or that are held primarily for sale to customers in the ordinary course of the taxpayer's trade or business. *Id.*

¹⁰ There is no option for the holders of tax-exempt bonds; the Tax Code requires amortization. Tax Code §171(c). Under Treasury Regulation §1.171-2, the allocable premium on a tax-exempt bond offsets the stated interest. Any excess premium is a nondeductible loss. An investor's basis in a tax-exempt bond is reduced by the premium amortized. Treasury Regulation §1.171-2(c), Example 4.

¹¹ IRS Publication 550, *Investment Income and Expenses* (2002), at p. 31. "Qualified stated interest" generally refers to interest unconditionally payable in either cash or property, at least annually, at a single fixed rate. Treasury Regulation §1.171-1(a), incorporating Treasury Regulation §1.1273-1(c).

¹² The issuer of Ken's bond will offset its interest deduction by the amount of premium allocable to the period when the interest obligation arose. If the allocable premium exceeds the interest attributable to the period, the issuer will report ordinary income, subject to certain limits. The issuer also uses the constant yield method to amortize the premium. Treasury Regulation §1.163-13

¹³ Special rules apply for calculating the premium when a bond is callable. Tax Code §171(b). If a bond is convertible, the premium does not include any amounts attributable to the value of the conversion feature. *Id.* Where a bond is received in exchange for property and the basis of the bond is determined by reference to the basis of the property, the basis of the bond is limited to its fair market value after the exchange. Tax Code §171(b)(4). Also see §171 for rules applicable to bonds exchanged in reorganizations.

[14] The yield is the discount rate that when used in calculating the present value of payments to be made under a bond gives a result equal to the investor's basis. This information should be available from an investor's broker or tax advisor. IRS Publication 550, *Investment Income and Expenses* (2002), at p. 32

[15] If Ken holds tax-exempt bonds, he would reduce his basis in the bond by the amount of the amortization calculation. *Id.* at 31. If Ken is a dealer in taxable bonds or otherwise holds them for sale to customers in the ordinary course of his trade or business, he also is not permitted to deduct the amortizable bond premium. *Id.*

[16] Where an investor makes an election in a year after the year of acquisition, the premium for the year(s) the election was not in effect cannot be amortized retroactively. For example, assume the total premium on a bond is $1,000, $300 of which is attributable to the years prior to the year of election. The investor will be able to amortize only $700. The $300 of unamortized premium will remain part of the bond's basis and will after the calculation of gain or loss at disposition. Treasury Regulation §1.171-4

[17] IRS Publication 550, *Investment Income and Expenses* (2002), at p. 32. Amounts that can't be deducted because of this limitation are carried forward. *Id.*

[18] For individuals like Ken, capital losses can only be used to offset capital gains and up to $3000 of ordinary income. Tax Code §1211. (Note that if Ken is married but files a separate return, he can only offset $1500 of ordinary income with capital loss.) Since capital gain often is eligible for taxation at lower rates, a taxpayer generally wants deductions that reduce ordinary income, rather than capital gain. If Ken were a corporation, the capital loss could only be used to offset capital gain. *Id.* However, Ken's capital gain would not be taxed at preferential rates.

[19] Certain exchanges involving bonds may be tax-free under the reorganization rules. This would include transactions qualifying as recapitalizations under Tax Code §368(a)(1)(E).

[20] Where an exchange of debt-for-debt occurs, the amount realized generally is equal to the issue price of the new securities. Treasury Regulation §1.1001-1(g)

[21] The market discount rules are discussed in Chapter 13. Also taxed as ordinary income is accrued but unpaid interest. See the discussion accompanying note 6.

[22] Tax Code §1271(a)(2)

[23] Treasury Regulation §1.1271-1(a)(1) refers to a "written or oral agreement or understanding not provided for in the debt instrument . . ." If the debt is part of an issue, the understanding must be between the issuer and "the original holders of a substantial amount of the debt instruments in the issue." *Id.*

[24] Tax Code §1271(a)(2)(B)

[25] Treasury Regulation §1.1271-1(a)(2). A public offering is defined in Treasury Regulation §1.1275-1(h). Other exceptions include debt purchased at a premium and also certain debt instruments sold through private placement memoranda. See Tax Code §1271 and the accompanying regulations for a more complete discussion of the exceptions to this rule.

[26] Tax Code §1271(a)(3) (government obligations) and §1271(a)(4) (nongovernment obligations)

[27] Tax Code §1271(a). It is also possible to have a partial retirement in connection with a prepayment. See Treasury Regulation §1.1275-2(f), discussing "pro rata prepayments."

[28] *McLain v. Comm'r.*, 311 U.S. 527 (1941)

[29] Tax Code §1271(a). This section applies to the retirement of any "debt instrument." A

"debt instrument" is defined under the regulations as "any . . . contractual arrangement that constitutes indebtedness under general principles of Federal income tax law." Treasury Regulation §1.1275-1(d)

[30] Tax Code §165(g)

[31] Tax Code §166(e)

[32] Tax Code §166(a)

[33] Tax Code §166(d). Under the rules applicable to capital gains and losses, short-term losses are first used to offset short-term gains, which are otherwise taxed at regular income tax rates. Long-term losses, by comparison, first offset long-term capital gain. For individuals, long-term capital gain may be eligible for taxation at favorable rates. This means an investor with both long- and short-term capital gain would prefer losses arising from the retirement of a bond to be treated as short-term.

[34] See *McClain v. Commissioner*, 311 U.S. 527 (1941).

[35] Tax Code §1211(a)

[36] Tax Code §1212

[37] Tax Code §172(b). For tax years ending in 2001 and 2002, NOLs can be carried back five years.

[38] If Phil refuses the $500 settlement, he probably will be treated as nonetheless receiving it, if he is a cash method taxpayer. This is because of the doctrine of constructive receipt. An accrual method investor must recognize income when all events have occurred that fix the right to receive the income and the amount can be determined with reasonable accuracy. Treasury Regulation §1.451-1(a)

[39] Rev. Rul. 87-19, 1987-1 C.B. 249

[40] Treasury Regulation §1.1001-3(c)(1)

[41] Treasury Regulation §1.1001-3(c)(2)

[42] Treasury Regulation §1.1001-3(b)

[43] Treasury Regulation §1.1001-3(c)(1). See Treasury Regulation §1.1001-3(c)(2)(iii) for rules applicable where a change occurs because of the exercise by the issuer or holder of an option to modify terms of the instrument.

[44] Treasury Regulation §1.1001-3(e)(3)

[45] Treasury Regulation §1.1001-3(e). Under the regulations, a significant modification may occur where the cumulative effect of two or more changes would be significant. See Treasury Regulation §1.1001-3(f)(3). However, changes to several terms of an instrument that do not separately trigger a significant modification under one of the specific rules are not combined. Treasury Regulation §1.1001-3(f)(4)

[46] Treasury Regulation §1.1001-3(e)(1)

[47] Treasury Regulation §1.1001-3(g), Ex. 4

[48] Tax Code §1211. For persons who are married but file separately, the $3,000 limit is reduced to $1,500.

[49] This example assumes there are no other restrictions limiting Lorraine's use of the deduction.

[50] Treasury Regulation §1.1244(a)-1(b)(2). The ordinary loss deduction is limited to the lesser of the individual's share of partnership losses at the time the stock was issued or the share at the time the loss was sustained. *Id.* In other words, an individual who was a 20-percent partner at the time the partnership acquired the stock but whose interest later increased to 30 percent would only be able to claim 20 percent of the partnership's §1244 loss as or-

dinary. For both individuals and partnerships, the stock must have been held continuously since issuance. *Id.*

[51] *Rath v. Commr.*, 101 T.C. 196 (1993)

[52] Treasury Regulation §1.1244(a)-1. This rule also means partners who receive distributions of stock otherwise qualifying under §1244 cannot claim ordinary loss upon a later sale. In other words, the partnership should sell the shares and distribute the proceeds, rather than making a distribution of the actual stock.

[53] Tax Code §1244(b)

[54] Foreign corporations do not qualify under §1244. Tax Code §1244(c). Amounts received for the stock in question are included in applying the $1 million limitation. Tax Code §1244(c)(3)(A)

[55] Tax Code §1244(c)(3). If at the time of contribution the adjusted basis of property exceeds its fair market value, and the basis of the stock in the investor's hands is determined by reference to the basis of the property, the basis for purposes of §1244 is reduced by the difference. Tax Code §1244(d)(1). For example, assume an investor contributes property with a value of $100 but a basis of $120 in a tax-free transaction falling under Code §351. The investor's basis in the stock is $120, Tax Code §358, but his basis for purposes of Code §1244 is $100.

[56] Tax Code §1244(c)(1)(B). Under the regulations, stock received tax-free under Tax Code §305 as a stock dividend on §1244 shares also qualifies under the §1244 rules. In addition, stock received tax-free in a recapitalization (Tax Code §368(a)(1)(E)) or a Type F reorganization (Tax Code §368(a)(1)(F)) in exchange for §1244 shares also qualifies. Treasury Regulation §1.1244(d)-3

[57] Tax Code §1244(d)(1)

[58] Tax Code §1244(c)(1)(C). If the corporation has been in existence for less than five years, the test is applied using the number of years the corporation has existed. If the loss arises during the corporation's first year, the period before the loss is used. Tax Code §1244(c)(2). What constitutes "rent," "royalties," "dividends," "interest," etc., is defined in Treasury Regulation §1.1244(c)-1.

[59] Treasury Regulation §1.1244(c)-1

[60] Treasury Regulation §1.1244(c)-1(e). If a stock or security is sold at a loss, the gross receipt is treated as zero. The loss cannot be used to offset gain from other stock or security sales. *Id.*

[61] Tax Code §1244(c)(2)(C). Dividends-received and net operating loss deductions are not included in determining whether a corporation's deductions exceed its gross income. *Id.* Under the regulations, a corporation not required to meet the gross receipts test because of losses must show that it is "largely an operating company." Treasury Regulation §1.1244(c)-1(e)(2)

[62] Treasury Regulation §1.1244(e)-1

[63] Tax Code §1(h)

[64] Tax Code §1202(a)(2). This provision will sunset as of December 31, 2014. *Id.*

[65] Tax Code §1(h)(5). Restrictions apply under Tax Code §1202 where investors hold qualifying stock and an offsetting short position at the same time. In general, these rules deny the exclusion unless certain conditions are met.

[66] If John's marginal tax rate were less than 28 percent, the lower rate would apply.

[67] Tax Code §1202(b)(2)

[68] Tax Code §1202(f) (stock acquired by conversion of other qualifying shares in the

same corporation); Tax Code §1202(h) (stock acquired by gift or inheritance). An investor who receives qualifying shares through distribution by a partnership assumes the partnership's holding period, provided the investor was a partner at the time the qualifying stock was acquired by the partnership and at all times thereafter until the distribution. Tax Code §1202(h)(2)(C)

[69] Tax Code §1202(b)(1). For married persons who file separate returns, the $10,000,000 figure is replaced by $5,000,000. Tax Code §1202(b)(3)

[70] Tax Code §1202(i). "Property" does not include money or stock. *Id.*

[71] Under Tax Code §1(h)(5), "§1202 gain" is taxed at a 28-percent rate. Section 1202 gain is defined as the gain that would be excluded, except for the 50-percent limitation, less the gain actually excluded under Code §1202. Tax Code §1(h)(8). For Rob, the gain that would have been excluded is $1.1 million ($2.6 million − $1.5 million, adjusted basis for §1202) and the actual exclusion is $550,000.

[72] Tax Code §1202(b)(1)

[73] Tax Code §57(a)(7)

[74] Under Tax Code §1202(g), the shares must meet the qualified small business requirements, treating the partnership as though it were an individual, and the 5-year holding period rule must be satisfied. Tax Code §1202(g). Where an investor's interest in a pass-through entity increases, as where an S corporation shareholder buys additional stock, see Tax Code §1202(g)(3). Under that provision, the exclusion is limited to the investor's original ownership interest in the pass-through entity at the time the entity acquired the qualifying shares.

[75] Tax Code §1202(a)

[76] Tax Code §1202(c)(1). Certain redemptions surrounding the issuance of new stock may trigger disqualification under the §1202 rules. This would occur, for example, where the issuer buys back stock from either the investor or taxpayers related to the investor within the four-year period surrounding the date on which the new shares were issued. "Significant" redemptions also disqualify newly issued shares. See generally Tax Code §1202(c)(3) and Treasury Regulation §1.1202-2. A taxpayer who exchanges qualified small business stock in a reorganization (Tax Code §368) or as part of an incorporation transaction may be able to treat the shares received as qualified. See the rules at Tax Code §1202(h)(4).

[77] Tax Code §1202(h). See the discussion at note 74 where an investor's interest in a pass-through entity changes.

[78] When property is contributed to a corporation on a tax-free basis under Tax Code §351, the corporation generally assumes the shareholder's basis in the asset rather than a fair market value figure. However, for purposes of §1202, the basis of contributed property is its fair market value right after the contribution. Tax Code §1202(d).

[79] Tax Code §1202(d)(3)

[80] Tax Code §1202(c)(2)

[81] Tax Code §1202(e)(5). A 50-percent ownership standard applies in determining if a parent-subsidiary relationship exists. *Id.*

[82] Tax Code §1202(e)(4). If more than 10 percent of the total value of a corporation's assets consists of real property not used in the active conduct of a qualified trade or business, the corporation will fail the active business test. Tax Code §1202(e)(7)

[83] Gain from the sale of §1202 stock is reported on Form 1040, Schedule D, in part II, relating to long-term capital gains and losses. IRS Publication 550, *Investment Income and*

Expenses (2002), at p. 60. A qualified small business also must agree to certain reporting requirements. Tax Code §1202(d)(1)(C)

⁸⁴ Tax Code §1045(b)(3). No deferral is available if the gain from the sale of qualified small business stock would be treated as ordinary income. Tax Code §1045(a). Under the rollover rules, gain is recognized only to the extent the amount realized on the sale exceeds the cost of the replacement stock. Tax Code §1045(a). In other words, in order for Pat to avoid recognizing gain because of the sale of her Pendleton shares, she must reinvest at least $1.5 million, the amount she received for the Pendleton holdings.

⁸⁵ Tax Code §1045(a)

⁸⁶ Tax Code §1045(a)

⁸⁷ Rev. Proc.98-48, 1998-2 C.B. 367, §3.01

⁸⁸ Rev. Proc. 98-48, 1998-2 C.B. 367, §2.03. The pass-through entity may make the election if it buys qualifying replacement shares within the 60-day time period. An individual who holds an interest in a pass-through entity while it owned qualifying shares and who buys qualified small business stock within 60 days of the entity's disposition can elect rollover treatment as to his portion of the pass-through gain. *Id.*

⁸⁹ According to the IRS, the replacement shares must meet the active business requirement for at least six months after the purchase. IRS Publication 550, *Investment Income and Expenses* (2002), at p. 60.

13 ORIGINAL ISSUE DISCOUNT AND MARKET DISCOUNT BONDS

INTRODUCTION

The payment of interest is compensation for the use of money. When a person borrows money, there is usually evidence of this transaction through use of a bond, debenture, note, or certificate. Prior to 1982, there were no consistent tax regulations that gave guidance to the timing and calculation of interest. Corporations would issue bonds to investors at a price below the amount payable at maturity. The discount was understood to be the charge for the amount loaned. Cash basis taxpayers, who generally invested in these bonds, could defer recognition of interest income until maturity, when bond proceeds were received. If the issuing corporation used the accrual method of accounting, however, it took deductions for the interest expense as the interest accrued over the life of the bond, rather than at the end, when the obligation matured. (An accrual method taxpayer in general deducts expenses when they become fixed and determinable, even though payment has not yet been made.)[1] This meant that a mismatch occurred, with the issuing corporation claiming deductions before the bondholders recognized the corresponding income.

Through the Tax Equity and Fiscal Responsibility Act in 1982 and the Tax Relief Act of 1984, Congress took steps to ensure that the income and expense incurred by the issuer and investor would be matched within the same tax period. The rules relating to imputed interest and the time value of money will be discussed in this chapter.

IDENTIFICATION OF INTEREST

In lending transactions, it is expected that interest will be charged for the use of money loaned. However, interest may be charged in many different ways. For example, a lender agrees to make a loan of $3000 for two years at interest of 7 percent. Alternatives include:

1. A two-year note calling for an interest rate of 7 percent, compounded semiannually
2. A note with a principal amount of $3000 that indicates stated interest at 7 percent payable at maturity
3. Lender gives the borrower $2565 in exchange for a note with a principal amount of $3000 and no stated interest due at maturity

The economic reality is the same for each alternative. In the third example, the difference between the amount received and amount due at maturity is the discount, which is equivalent to interest. This is generally referred to as original issue discount (OID). Interest is calculated either under the qualified stated interest provisions or under rules similar to the OID rules.

Qualified Stated Interest

Qualified stated interest (QSI) is interest that is unconditionally payable in cash or in property (other than debt instruments of the issuer) and is payable at least annually at a single fixed rate.[2] Qualified stated interest accrues ratably over the accrual period (or periods) to which it is attributable, and accrues at the stated rate for the period(s).[3] The amount of QSI usually varies over the term of the loan since it is based on the outstanding principal. As payments reduce the principal balance, the corresponding interest due on the principal also decreases.

Example—A bond is issued on January 1, 2000 for $100,000. It matures five years later on December 31, 2004. Principal payments are due at the end of the third though the fifth years of $33,333 and interest is payable annually at a rate of 7 percent. Exhibit 13-1 shows the payments due under this obligation.

All of the interest constitutes qualified stated interest because it is at a stated rate of interest, due in cash, and payable annually. It does not matter that the amounts of interest paid change each period. Additionally, as long as interest is unconditionally payable when due, at a single rate of interest, and paid along with principal, it is qualified stated interest.

Example—Assume the same facts as in the previous example except that payments of $24,200 are due each year. All of the payments shown as

EXHIBIT 13-1

Year	Balance of Principal at beginning of Year	Interest Due	Principal Due	Total Payment
2000	100,000	7,000		7,000
2001	100,000	7,000		7,000
2002	100,000	7,000	33,333	40,333
2003	66,667	4,667	33,333	38,000
2004	33,334	2,333	33,334	35,667

interest due are deducted by the issuer and taxable to the bondholder. Payments of both interest and principal are shown in Exhibit 13-2.

Interest is unconditionally payable only if reasonable legal remedies exist to compel timely payment. Alternatively, the debt instrument may otherwise provide terms and conditions that make the likelihood of late payment (other than that made within a reasonable grace period) or nonpayment a remote contingency.[4] The lending transaction must reflect an arm's-length transaction between the borrower and lender. Additionally, the possibility of nonpayment due to default, insolvency, or similar circumstances is ignored in considering whether interest is unconditionally payable.[5]

If the debt instruments state that the payment of interest will be made at irregular intervals, then the rate used to determine the payment must be calculated to account for these unequal intervals. This is necessary to satisfy the single fixed rate test.

Example—Assume a debt instrument for $100,000, at an interest rate of 8 percent with a term of three years. It provides for quarterly payments

EXHIBIT 13-2

Year	Balance of Principal at beginning of Year	Interest Due	Applied To Principal	Total Payment
2000	100,000	7,000	17,200	24,200
2001	80,000	5,600	18,600	24,200
2002	60,000	4,200	20,000	24,200
2003	40,000	2,800	21,400	24,200
2004	20,000	1,400	22,800	24,200
		$ 21,000	$ 100,000	$ 121,000

of interest during the first two years, and a payment at the end of the third year. The quarterly interest payments of $1943 are equivalent to 7.77 percent compounded quarterly, which equates to a single fixed rate of 8 percent, compounded annually. Therefore, all of the interest is qualified stated interest.

If a debt instrument provides for equal payment intervals, except that the first or final payment period differs in length from the other payment intervals, then the irregular intervals will be considered to be made at a fixed rate. However, the value of the rate on which the payment is based must be adjusted in some reasonable manner to take into account the length of the interval.[6]

If a debt instrument allows an alternative payment schedule upon the occurrence of one or more contingencies, then the determination of whether the interest is qualified stated interest is made by analyzing the original and each alternative payment schedule as if it were the debt instrument's sole payment schedule.[7] Under this analysis, the debt instrument provides for qualified stated interest to the extent of the lowest fixed rate at which qualified stated interest would be payable under any payment schedule

Example—On January 1, 2000 Therese issues a 10-year note to Beth for $100,000 that provides for a $100,000 principal payment at maturity and annual interest payments of $10,000. Additionally, Therese has the option, exercisable on January 1, 2003, to lower the annual interest payments to $8000. The note also gives Beth the unconditional right to place a put option on the debt instrument back to Therese, exercisable on January 1, 2003, in return for $100,000. If the payment schedule was determined by assuming that the issuer's option will be exercised and the put option will not be exercised, and this was the sole schedule, then only $8000 of each annual interest payment would be qualified stated interest. Under any other payment schedule, the debt instrument would provide for annual qualified stated interest payments of $10,000. Accordingly, only $8000 of each annual interest payment is qualified stated interest, and the excess is included in the note's stated redemption price at maturity.[8]

Stepped interest rates occur when a debt instrument contains interest that is payable at different fixed rates over the life of the debt. It may start at one rate during the first year and then increase by a percentage point each subsequent year up to a maximum rate. Qualified stated interest is the lowest constant rate throughout the entire term of the debt that is unconditionally payable. The excess stated interest is included in the debt instrument's stated redemption price at maturity.

EXHIBIT 13-3

Year	Principal Outstanding	Stated Interest Payable	Qualified Stated Interest	Nonqualified Stated Interest
2000	100,000	4,000	4,000	-
2001	100,000	5,000	4,000	1,000
2002	100,000	5,000	4,000	1,000
2003	100,000	6,000	4,000	2,000
2004	100,000	6,000	4,000	2,000
				$ 6,000

Example—Therese issues a $100,000 note to Beth payable in five years with the full principal due on maturity and interest payments of $4000 the first year, $5000 annually for the next two years, and $6000 annually for the last two years. Exhibit 13-3 is a schedule of interest payments.

The stated redemption price at maturity includes $6000 of the non-qualified stated interest.

A bond might provide for no interest payments for the first year, and thereafter semiannual payments of 5 percent, for example. This kind of obligation is referred to as an interest holiday debt instrument and is treated similarly to stepped interest rate obligations. Interest holiday debt instruments are written to include no interest payments for a period of time referred to as the holiday period. After this period, interest is payable at market or slightly higher than market rates. None of the interest paid is considered qualified stated interest because the lowest rate paid over the life of the debt is zero percent. Therefore all interest and principal payments are included in the stated redemption price at maturity.[9]

ORIGINAL ISSUE DISCOUNT

Original issue discount is the excess (if any) of the stated redemption price at maturity over the issue price.[10] The purpose of the original issue discount rules is to have tax accounting for interest closely aligned with generally accepted accounting principles as commonly used. Obligors of a debt obligation should not be allowed to deduct interest as an expense before it has been economically earned. Likewise, holders of debt instruments should be required to include in gross income interest that is economically earned and accrues, at least, on an annual basis.

Stated Redemption Price at Maturity

The term "stated redemption price at maturity" means amounts due at maturity, including interest and other amounts payable, other than qualified stated interest.[11] Therefore, all the payments required by the instrument over the full term of the debt, except for qualified stated interest, is included in the stated redemption price at maturity.

Exceptions to the Original Issue Discount Rules

IRC §1272 states that the holder of any debt instrument must include in gross income an amount equal to the sum of the daily portions of the original issue discount for each day during the taxable year on which the holder held the instrument.[12] Exceptions to the original issue discount rules include:

- Tax-exempt obligations
- U. S. Savings Bonds
- Short-term obligations having a fixed maturity date not more than one year from the date of issue (These are discussed in Chapter 15.)
- Obligations issued by natural persons (meaning not trusts or corporations, for example) before March 2, 1984, and
- Loans between natural persons not made in the course of a trade or business of the lender that do not exceed $10,000[13]

These exceptions do not apply if the principal purpose of the loan is tax avoidance.[14] A husband and wife are treated as one person for purposes of these rules. If they lived apart at all times during the taxable year in which the loan is made, they are treated as two individuals.[15]

There is a De Minimis Rule, which states that original issue discount that is less than ¼ of 1 percent of the stated redemption price at maturity multiplied by the number of complete years to maturity shall be treated as zero, and all of the interest is treated as qualified stated interest to both holder and issuer.[16]

Example—Serina buys a bond issued by Gymnastics Equipment

Corp. She pays $99,000 for the instrument, which is a five-year obligation. The bond pays annual interest of 5 percent each year and will return $100,000 at maturity. Even though the Gymnastics bond has a discount of $1000, Serina will not have to report any income under the OID rules. This is because the $1000 discount is less than ¼ of 1 percent X $100,000 X 5 years ($1250).

Issue Price

In order to determine the amount of OID within a debt instrument, it is first necessary to determine its issue price. There is a hierarchy of rules to apply in the determination of the issue price of debt. Debt instruments are separated into three general categories:

1. Debt instruments issued for money
2. Publicly traded debt instruments issued for property
3. Debt instruments issued for publicly traded property[17]

Debt Instruments Issued for Money　　If a substantial amount of the debt instruments in an initial public offering is issued for money, then the issue price is the first price at which a substantial amount of the debt instruments is sold.[18] Debt instruments in an issue may be sold to different buyers at different times and at prices greater or less than the amount paid by the holder. This price differential between the issue price of the substantial public offering and subsequent sales of the debt instruments creates a premium or discount on subsequent sales.

　　Example—John purchased publicly traded bonds for an issue price of $100,000 at a qualified stated rate of 8 percent payable semiannually, maturing in five years. One year later he sold these bonds through his broker for $105,000. The difference of $5000 is a premium John received, which is taxed as a long-term capital gain.

　　If an issue consists simply of a single debt instrument that is issued for money, the issue price of the debt is the amount paid for the instrument.[19]

　　Two or more debt instruments are part of the same issue if the debt instruments:

(a) Have the same credit terms;
(b) Are issued pursuant to a common plan beginning with the date on which a single transaction or a series of related transactions occur;

(c) Are issued within a period of 13 days beginning with the date on which the first debt instrument was issued (other than to a bond house, broker, or similar person or organization acting in the capacity of an underwriter, placement agent, or wholesaler); and

(d) Are issued on or after March 13, 2001.[20]

The term "money" refers to the functional currency of the issuer.[21] If the issuer is from the United States, then money is the U.S. dollar.

The issue date is the first settlement date on which a substantial amount of the debt instruments in the issue is sold for money.[22]

Publicly Traded Debt Instruments Issued for Property That is Not Publicly Traded   If a substantial amount of a debt instrument is issued for property, then the issue price of each debt instrument is the fair market value of the debt instrument determined on the issue (first) date.[23] Additionally, the debt instrument must be traded on an established market.

A debt instrument or property is traded on an established market if, at any time during the 60-day period ending 30 days after the issue date, the instrument fits into one of the following four categories:

1. Exchange-listed property that is listed on (a) a national securities exchange registered under Section 6 of the Securities Exchange Act of 1934; (b) an interdealer quotation system sponsored by a national securities association registered under Section 15A of the Securities Exchange Act of 1924; and (c) The International Stock Exchange of the United Kingdom and the Republic of Ireland, Limited; the Frankfurt Stock Exchange; the Tokyo Stock Exchange; or any other foreign exchange or board of trade that is designated by the Commissioner in the Internal Revenue Bulletin.[24]

2. Market-traded property that is traded either on a board of trade designated as a contract market by the Commodities Futures Trading Commission or on an interbank market;[25]

3. Property appearing on a quotation medium if it appears on a system of general circulation (including a computer listing disseminated to subscribing brokers, dealers, or traders) that provides a reasonable basis to determine fair market value by disseminating either recent price quotations (including rates, yields, or other pricing information) of one or more identified brokers, dealers, or traders or actual prices of recent sales transactions.[26]

4. Readily quotable debt instruments where price quotations are readily available from dealers, brokers, or traders.[27] The regulations do not specify what is considered a readily quotable debt instrument. However, they do delineate four guidelines covering what is not considered as readily quotable. These include:

   (i)   The issuer or guarantor of the debt has no other outstanding debt that is traded on an established market;[28]

   (ii) The original stated principal amount of the issue that includes the debt instrument does not exceed $25 million;[29]

   (iii) The conditions and covenants relating to the issuer's performance with respect to the debt instrument are materially less restrictive than those in all of the issuer's other traded debt;[30] or

   (iv) The maturity date of the debt instrument is more than three years after the latest maturity date of the issuer's other traded debt.[31]

Debt Instruments That Are Not Publicly Traded Issued for Publicly Traded Property If a substantial amount of debt instruments is issued for property that is traded on an established market, the issue price of each debt instrument in the issue is the fair market value of the property, determined as of the issue date.[32] Property includes a debt instrument, stock, security, contract, commodity, or nonfunctional currency.[33] The issue date is the first date on which a substantial amount of the debt instrument is issued for traded property.[34]

Other Debt Instruments If an issue of debt instruments does not fit within any of the three rules discussed above, then the issue price of each debt instrument is determined as if the debt instrument were a separate issue. Each individual instrument would be analyzed under the above rules. If these rules are not applicable, then the debt instrument would be subject to the rules under §1274.[35] If this section is not applicable, then the rules of §1273(b)(4) would apply to equate the issue price with the stated redemption price at maturity.[36]

MECHANICS OF OID CALCULATIONS

OID occurs when the stated redemption price of a debt instrument exceeds its issue price. This happens when (a) a debt instrument is issued for payments of qualified stated interest and the stated principal amount due at maturity is issued at a discount, (b) a debt instrument has a zero coupon calling for a single payment to be made at maturity that includes both principal and interest, and (c) a debt instrument calls for payments of interest other than qualified stated interest prior to maturity.

The holder of any debt instrument having OID must include in income an amount equal to the sum of the daily portions of OID that have accrued for each day during the taxable year on which the holder had the debt instrument.[37] It doesn't matter which regular method of accounting the holder uses.[38] The basis of a debt instrument in the hands of the holder is increased by the amount of OID included in the holder's gross income and decreased by the amount of any payment from the issuer to the holder under the debt instrument other than a payment of qualified stated interest.[39] These increases and decreases to basis are used in the computation of gain or loss upon disposition of the debt instrument. Generally, the issuer is permitted to deduct OID as it is amortized with the amount being the same as that which is includable in the holder's income.[40]

The Constant Yield Method

With certain exceptions, the amount of OID includable in the income of the holder of a debt instrument for any taxable year is determined using the constant yield method.[41] The steps involved in the constant yield method include:

(1) Determine the debt instrument's yield to maturity;
(2) Determine the accrual periods;
(3) Determine the OID allocable to each accrual period;
(4) Determine the daily portions of OID.[42]

Yield to Maturity of a Debt Instrument The yield to maturity of a debt instrument is the discount rate that, when used in computing the present value of all principal and interest payments to be made under the debt instrument, produces an amount equal to the issue price of the debt instrument.[43] The yield must be constant over the term of the debt instrument and, when expressed as a percentage, must be calculated at least to two decimal places.[44] The present value of any amount may be calculated using the formula:

$$PV = \text{Amount payable in the future} \times (1 + r)^{-n}$$

in which:

> r = annual percentage rate, expressed in decimal form, divided by the number of compounding periods in a year; and
> n = the number of compounding periods in the period from the date as of which the present value is sought to the date the amount payable in the future is due.

Example—Your Design, Inc. issues five-year bonds for $100,000 compounded quarterly at a rate of 8 percent. The present value of the bond is calculated as follows:

$$PV = \$100{,}000 \times (1 + .02)^{-20}$$
$$PV = \$67{,}297.13^{45}$$
r = .02 which is 8%/4 (the number of compounding periods in a year)
n = −20 which is the total number of compounding periods over
the term of the debt instrument (5 years X 4 periods per year)

Accrual Periods   An accrual period is an interval of time over which the accrual of OID is measured. Accrual periods may vary in length over the term of the debt instrument, provided that each accrual period is no longer than one year. Additionally, each scheduled payment of principal or interest must occur either on the first or final day of an accrual period.[46] In general, the computation of OID is simplest if accrual periods correspond to the intervals between payment dates provided by the terms of the debt instrument.[47] In computing the length of accrual periods, any reasonable counting convention may be used, such as, 30 days per month/360 days per year.[48]

OID Allocable to Each Accrual Period   The OID allocable to an accrual period is calculated by multiplying the adjusted issue price (AIP) of the debt instrument at the beginning of the accrual period by the yield (Y), and subtracting any qualified stated interest (QSI) that may be allocable to the accrual period.[49] In performing this calculation, the yield must be stated appropriately taking into account the length of the particular accrual period.[50]

The calculation may be stated as follows:

$$OID = (AIP \times Y) - QSI$$

The adjusted issue price (AIP) is the issue price at the beginning of the first accrual period.[51] Thereafter the AIP is the issue price increased by the amount of OID includable in gross income and decreased by the amount of any payment previously made on the debt instrument other than for qualified stated interest (QSI).[52]

Example—On July 1, 2000, Yevonne purchases at original issue, for $675,564.17, a debt instrument that matures on July 1, 2005, and provides for a single payment of $1,000,000 at maturity. The yield of the debt instrument is 8 percent, compounded semiannually. Accrual periods may be of any length, provided that each accrual period is no longer than one year and each scheduled payment of principal or interest occurs either on the first or final day of an accrual period. The yield to maturity to be used in computing OID accruals in any accrual period, however, must reflect the length of the accrual period chosen. A yield based on compounding "b" times per year is equivalent to a yield based on compounding "c" times per as indicated by the following formula:

$$r = c \, ((1 + i/b) - 1)^{53}$$

where:

i = the yield based on compounding b times per year expressed as a decimal

r = the equivalent yield based on compounding c times per year expressed as a decimal

b = the number of compounding periods in a year on which i is based

c = number of compounding periods in a year on which r is based

Assume that Yevonne decides to compute OID on the debt instrument using semiannual accrual periods. The OID allocable to the first semiannual accrual period is $27,022.56 ($675,564.17 X 8 percent/2). There is no QSI and the daily portion of OID for the first semiannual accrual period is $150.13 ($27,022.56/180).[54] Exhibit 13-4 illustrates the calculation of OID for each year.

In determining the OID allocable to an accrual period, if an interval between payments of QSI contains more than one accrual period, then the amount of qualified stated interest payable at the end of the interval is allocated on a pro rata basis to each accrual period in the interval. Also, the adjusted issue price at the beginning of each period in the interval must be increased by the amount of any QSI that has accrued prior to the first day of the accrual period but is not payable until the end of the interval.[55]

Example—On July 1, 2000, Colette purchases at original issue, for $90,000, Child Care Corporation's debt instrument that matures on Sep-

EXHIBIT 13-4

Accrual Period	Adjusted Issue Price (AIP)	AIP x Yield (8%/2)	Qualified Stated Interest	OID
2001	675,564	27,023	-	27,023
2001	702,587	28,103	-	28,103
2002	730,690	29,228	-	29,228
2002	759,918	30,397	-	30,397
2003	790,314	31,613	-	31,613
2003	821,927	32,877	-	32,877
2004	854,804	34,192	-	34,192
2004	888,996	35,560	-	35,560
2005	924,556	36,982	-	36,982
2005	961,538	38,462	-	38,462

2005	961,538	
OID	38,462	
Maturity	$ 1,000,000	

tember 1, 2010, and has a stated principal amount of $100,000 payable on that date. The debt instrument provides for semiannual payments of interest of $3000 payable on September 1 and March 1 of each year, beginning March 1, 2001. The yield is 7.44 percent compounded semiannually. The OID allocable to the first seminannual accrual period equals $90,000 X 7.44 percent/2 (accrual periods per year) minus $3000 (qualified stated interest) = $348.[56] A table to accrue OID can be set up as shown in Exhibit 13-5.

The OID allocable to the final accrual period is the difference between the amount payable at maturity (not including QSI) and the AIP at the beginning of the final accrual period.[57]

If there is an initial shorter period, and all other accrual periods are of equal length, the amount of OID allocable to the initial period may be computed using any reasonable method.

Example—On May 1, 2000, Beth purchases at original issue for $80,000, Pet R Us Corporation's debt instrument maturing on July 1, 2004. The debt instrument provides for a single payment at maturity of $250,000. Beth computes OID using six-month accrual periods ending on January 1 and July 1 of each year and an initial short two-month accrual period from May 1, 2000 through June 30, 2000. The yield on this instrument is 11.53

Exhibit 13-5

Accrual Period	Adjusted Issue Price (AIP)	AIP x Yield (7.44%/2)	Qualified Stated Interest	OID
2001	90,000	3,348	3,000	348
2001	90,348	3,361	3,000	361
2002	90,709	3,374	3,000	374
2002	91,083	3,388	3,000	388
2003	91,472	3,403	3,000	403
2003	91,874	3,418	3,000	418
2004	92,292	3,433	3,000	433
2004	92,725	3,449	3,000	449
2005	93,175	3,466	3,000	466
2005	93,641	3,483	3,000	483
2006	94,124	3,501	3,000	501
2006	94,626	3,520	3,000	520
2007	95,146	3,539	3,000	539
2007	95,685	3,559	3,000	559
2008	96,245	3,580	3,000	580
2008	96,825	3,602	3,000	602
2009	97,427	3,624	3,000	624
2009	98,051	3,648	3,000	648
2010	98,699	3,672	3,000	672
2010	99,370	3,697	3,000	630

2010	99,370
OID	630
Maturity	$ 100,000

percent, compounded semiannually. Beth may use any reasonable method to compute OID for the initial short period. One such method is to calculate the amount of OID based on the following formula:

$$\text{OID short} = \text{IP} \times (i/k) \times f[58]$$

Where:

OID short = the amount of OID allocable to the initial short accrual period

IP = the issue price of the debt instrument

i = the yield to maturity expressed as a decimal

k = the number of accrual periods in a year

f = a fraction whose numerator is the number of days in the initial short accrual period, and whose denominator in the number of days in a full accrual period.

Under this method, the amount of OID for the initial short accrual period is $ 1,559 ($80,000 X (11.53 percent/2) X (61/180)).

Another reasonable method is to calculate the amount of OID for the initial short accrual period using the yield based on bimonthly compounding. Under this method, the amount of OID for the initial short period is $1,508.38 ($80,000 X (11.31 percent/6)).[59]

Daily Portions of OID   Daily portions of OID are determined by allocating to each day in an accrual period the ratable portion of the OID calculated for that period.[60] The holder of the debt instrument includes in income the daily portions of OID for each day the debt instrument is held during the taxable year.[61]

Demand Obligations   Demand obligations are loans that include principal payments with a fixed amount and interest at a fixed rate compounded or paid at intervals of no more than one year.[62] However, they are uncertain as to time. The lender may demand full payment at any time according to the terms of the agreement. The yield of a demand obligation is equal to the stated rate of interest if the issue price of the instrument is equal to the stated principal amount and interest is paid or compounded at a fixed rate over the entire term of the obligation.[63]

Example—Pat lends Tim $100,000. Tim must repay the loan within 90 days after Pat's demand for repayment, which can occur any time after the first 18 months of the loan. The total amount of the principal demanded by Pat, along with interest at an annual rate of 7 percent compounded annually on the outstanding principal balance, would be due. Since none of the interest is QSI, all of the interest accrues as OID.

DEBT INSTRUMENTS PURCHASED AT A PREMIUM

A purchaser is often willing to pay a premium for a debt instrument that pays stated interest at a rate that is higher than the current market rates for an equivalent debt instrument. It doesn't matter whether the debt is purchased when it was originally issued or subsequently. A debt instrument is purchased at a premium if its adjusted basis, immediately after its purchase by the holder, exceeds the sum of all amounts payable on the instrument after the purchase date, not including payments of qualified stated interest.[64] The amount of premium that a purchaser would be willing to pay is measured by the sum of the present values of the interest payments on the current debt instrument that exceed the payments that would be due at the current market rates of interest, discounted to the date of purchase.

Example—A debt instrument of $10,000 payable at maturity in three years provides for annual interest payments of $1000. The market rate for a similar debt instrument is 8 percent. A stream of three annual payments of $200 ($1000 − $800) discounted at a rate of 8 percent compounded annually is $515.40, the premium a purchaser would be willing to pay.

Treasury Regulation §1.171-2 states that a holder amortizes a bond premium by offsetting the qualified stated interest allocable to an accrual period with the bond premium allocable to that same period. This offset occurs when the holder takes the qualified stated interest into account under the holder's regular method of accounting. A bond premium allocable to an accrual period is determined using the constant interest rate method.[65] The steps involved in this method are: (1) determine the holder's yield; (2) determine the accrual periods; and (3) determine the bond premium allocable to the accrual period.[66]

Example—Calli purchases on January 1, 2000, a taxable bond for $110,000 maturing on January 1, 2007, with a stated principal amount of $100,000, payable at maturity. It provides for unconditional payments of interest of $10,000 payable on January 1 of each year. Calli uses the cash receipts and disbursements method of accounting, and decides to use annual accrual periods ending January 1 of each year. The amortization of the bond premium would be as shown in Exhibit 13-6.

The bond premium allocable to the accrual period ending on January 1, 2001, is the excess of the qualified stated interest ($10,000) over the product of the adjusted acquisition price at the beginning of the period ($110,000) and Calli's yield (8.07 percent, compounded annually). Therefore, the bond premium for the period ending January 1, 2001 is $1,123 ($10,000 − $8877).[67]

Calli receives an interest payment of $10,000 on January 1, 2001. However, she will only report income of $8877, which is the QSI ($10,000) offset by the bond premium for the period ($1123). The basis of the bond is reduced by the premium. This same procedure is followed each year using

EXHIBIT 13-6

Accrual Period	Adjusted Acquisition Price (AAP)	AAP x Yield (AAP x 8.07%)	QSI	Premium
2001	110,000	8,877	10,000	1,123
2002	108,877	8,786	10,000	1,214
2003	107,663	8,688	10,000	1,312
2004	106,352	8,583	10,000	1,417
2005	104,934	8,468	10,000	1,532
2006	103,403	8,345	10,000	1,655
2007	101,747	8,211	10,000	1,747

2007	101,747
Premium	(1,747)
Maturity	$ 100,000

the bond premium allocable to that year. This would be reported on Schedule B of Calli's Form 1040 of her tax return. The total interest of $10,000 would be reported. All interest income listed on Line 1 should then be subtotaled. Then enter the amount $1123 of bond premium, as a subtraction from the subtotal, and identify this amount as "ABP Adjustment." Exhibit 13-7 is an example of her Schedule B of Form 1040 of her tax return.

DEBT INSTRUMENTS PURCHASED AT A DISCOUNT

Market discount means the excess of the stated redemption price of the bond at maturity over the basis of the bond immediately after its acquisition.[68] The debt instrument is acquired after its original issue at a discount. This debt instrument may or may not have OID. Market discount rules do not apply to (a) short-term obligations; (b) United States savings bonds; and (c) installment obligations.[69]

The taxpayer may elect one of several methods to accrue market discount on bonds. The first method is to accrue it ratably on a daily basis and the second is the constant interest rate basis.[70] An election made to accrue bond discount using the constant interest rate basis is irrevocable.

Exhibit 13-7

Schedules A&B (Form 1040) 2002   OMB No. 1545-0074   Page **2**

Name(s) shown on Form 1040. Do not enter name and social security number if shown on other side.

Calli Doe

Your social security number

999-33-5555

Schedule B-Interest and Ordinary Dividends

Attachment Sequence No. **08**

		Amount
Part I Interest (See page B-1 and the instructions for Form 1040, line 8a.)	**1** List name of payer. If any interest is from a seller-financed mortgage and the buyer used the property as a personal residence, see page B-1 and list this interest first. Also, show that buyer's social security number and address ▶	
	Bond Interest	10,000
	Bank Interest	2,000
	Bank B Interest	1,000
	Bank C Interest	3,000
	** Subtotal **	16,000
	ABP Adjustment	-1,123

Note. If you received a Form 1099-INT, Form 1099-OID, or substitute statement from a brokerage firm, list the firm's name as the payer and enter the total interest shown on that form.

2	Add the amounts on line 1	**2**	14,877
3	Excludable interest on series EE and I U.S. savings bonds issued after 1989 from Form 8815, line 14. You **must** attach Form 8815	**3**	
4	Subtract line 3 from line 2. Enter the result here and on Form 1040, line 8a ▶	**4**	14,877

Note. If line 4 is over $1,500, you must complete Part III.

		Amount
Part II Ordinary Dividends (See page B-1 and the instructions for Form 1040, line 9.)	**5** List name of payer. Include only ordinary dividends. If you received any capital gain distributions, see the instructions for Form 1040, line 13 ▶	

Note. If you received a Form 1099-DIV or substitute statement from a brokerage firm, list the firm's name as the payer and enter the ordinary dividends shown on that form.

6	Add the amounts on line 5. Enter the total here and on Form 1040, line 9 ▶	**6**	

Note. If line 6 is over $1,500, you must complete Part III.

		Yes	No
Part III Foreign Accounts and Trusts (See page B-2.)	You must complete this part if you **(a)** had over $1,500 of taxable interest or ordinary dividends; OR **(b)** had a foreign account; or **(c)** received a distribution from, or were a grantor of, or a transferor to, a foreign trust.		
	7a At any time during 2002, did you have an interest in or a signature or other authority over a financial account in a foreign country, such as a bank account, securities account, or other financial account? See page B-2 for exceptions and filing requirements for Form TD F 90-22.1		X
	b If "Yes," enter the name of the foreign country ▶		
	8 During 2002, did you receive a distribution from, or were you the grantor of, or transferor to, a foreign trust? If "Yes," you may have to file Form 3520. See page B-2		X

For Paperwork Reduction Act Notice, see Form 1040 instructions.

Schedule B (Form 1040) 2002

DAA

Example—Daily Basis. A debt instrument with a stated principal amount of $10,000 payable at maturity is issued on January 1, 2000. It matures on January 1, 2010 and bears a 7-percent coupon payable semiannually beginning with July 1, 2000. Its issue price is $10,000. The debt instrument is purchased on April 5 for $7980. The market discount of $2020 accrues at a rate of .5682 per day ($2020/3555 days to maturity).

Example—Constant Interest Rate Basis. A debt instrument is issued for $92,760 on January 1, 2000 with a stated principal amount of $100,000 payable at maturity on January 1, 2010 and bearing an 8-percent coupon payable semiannually. Its yield is 9 percent compounded semiannually. On January 1, 2002, when the adjusted issue price is $93,460, Joanne purchases the debt instrument for $90,845, providing for a payment at maturity of $100,000. Its yield is 9.75 percent compounded semiannually. Market discount would be accrued as shown in Exhibit 13-8.

Other approaches in using the constant interest rate method are to treat the debt instrument as a zero coupon and calculate OID for each accrual period. Then accrue the market discount, or calculate the ratio that OID for

---

EXHIBIT 13-8

Accrual Period	Beginning Adjusted Issue Price (AIP)	9.75 Yield	Issue Price on Date of Purchase	9% Yield OID	Market Discount
7/1/2002	90,845	429	93,460	206	223
1/1/2003	91,274	450	93,666	215	235
7/1/2003	91,723	472	93,881	225	247
1/1/2004	92,195	494	94,105	235	260
7/1/2004	92,689	519	94,340	245	273
1/1/2005	93,208	544	94,585	256	288
7/1/2005	93,752	570	94,842	268	303
1/1/2006	94,322	598	95,110	280	318
7/1/2006	94,920	627	95,389	293	335
1/1/2007	95,548	658	95,682	306	352
7/1/2007	96,206	690	95,988	319	371
1/1/2008	96,896	724	96,307	334	390
7/1/2008	97,619	759	96,641	349	410
1/1/2009	98,378	796	96,990	365	431
7/1/2009	99,174	835	97,354	381	454
1/1/2010	100,009	875	97,735	398	477

each accrual period has to total OID and apply this to total market discount to calculate the market discount accrual.

Accrued market discount is not included in income of the holder until the instrument is disposed of. Any gain derived on the disposition of any market discount bond shall be treated as ordinary income to the extent it does not exceed the accrued market discount on the bond.[71]

ELECTION TO TREAT ALL INTEREST ON A DEBT INSTRUMENT AS OID

The holder of a debt instrument may elect to include in gross income all interest that accrues on the instrument by using the constant yield method.[72] For purposes of this election, interest includes stated interest, acquisition discount, OID, de minimis OID, market discount, de minimis market discount,[73] and unstated interest, as adjusted by any amortizable bond premium or acquisition premium.[74]

A debt instrument subject to this election is treated as if (1) the instrument is issued for the holder's adjusted basis immediately after its acquisition by the holder; (2) the instrument is issued on the holder's acquisition date; and (3) none of the interest payments provided for in the instrument are qualified stated interest payments.[75]

The primary advantage in making this election is the ease of computation. All of the interest is treated as one unit and is calculated with the constant interest method. The disadvantage is that income is recognized on market discount prior to disposition of the instrument.

The election must be made for the taxable year in which the holder acquires the debt instrument. A statement is attached to the income tax return of the holder indicating that a §1272-3 election is made and identifying the debt instruments subject to the election.[76] A holder may make the election for a class or group of debt instruments by attaching a statement describing the type or types of debt instruments being designated for the election.[77]

DEFERRAL OF INTEREST DEDUCTIONS

Net direct interest expense on debt taken to purchase market discount bonds is deductible only to the extent that it exceeds the portion of the market discount allocable to the days that the taxpayer held the bond during the taxable year.[78] Net direct interest expense is the excess of:

1. The amount of interest paid or accrued during the taxable year on indebtedness used to purchase the debt instrument, over
2. The aggregate amount of interest (including OID) includable in gross income for the taxable year with respect to the debt instrument.[79]

A taxpayer may make an election to treat any accumulated disallowed interest expense as paid in the current taxable year up to net interest income.[80]

CONCLUSION

Original Issue Discount is present in many debt instruments. The holder must include OID in income for each day that the debt instrument was held, regardless of whether he/she is an accrual or cash-basis taxpayer. The issuer will usually issue Form 1099 OID indicating the amount of accrued OID for the taxable year. Understanding the OID rules behind these transactions enables the taxpayer to plan for the tax liabilities associated with them.

NOTES

[1] In order to claim a deduction, economic performance also must occur. For example, if a taxpayer is obligated to pay for the use of property, economic performance occurs when the property is used. Tax Code §461(h)

[2] Reg. 1.1273-1 This also applies to property that will be constructively received under §451.

[3] Reg. 1.466-2(b)

[4] Reg. §1.1273-1(c)(ii)

[5] Id.

[6] Reg. §1.1273-1(c)(B)

[7] Reg. §1.1273-1(c)(2)

[8] This example was adapted from Reg. §1.1273-1(f) Example 4

[9] Reg. 1.1273-1(d)(4)(B)

[10] §1273(a)(1)

[11] §1273(a)(2)

[12] §1272(a)(1) This applies to all debt instruments issued after July 1, 1982.

[13] §1272(a)(2)

[14] §1272(a)(2)(ii)

[15] §1272(a)(2)(iii)

[16] §1273(a)(3)

[17] §1273

[18] Reg. §1.1273-2(a)(1)

[19] Reg. §1.1273-2(a)(1)

[20] Reg. §1.1275-1(f)(1)

[21] Reg. §1.1273-2(a)(1) In some cases money includes nonfunctional currency as described in §1.988-2(b)(2).

[22] Reg. §1.1273-2 The Reg. indicates that the issue date is actually the first settlement date or losing date. However, losing date is not described. The issue is the first date on which a substantial amount of the debt instruments is sold.

[23] Reg. §1.1273-2(b)

[24] Reg. §1.1273(f)

[25] Reg. §1.1273(f)(3)

[26] Reg. §1.1273(f)(4) A quotation medium does not include a director or listing of brokers, dealers, or traders for specific securities, such as yellow sheets, that provides neither price quotations nor actual prices of recent sales transactions.

[27] Reg. §1.1273(f)(5)(i)

[28] Reg. §1.1273(f)(5)(ii)(A)

[29] Reg. §1.1273(f)(5)(ii)(B)

[30] Reg. §1.1273(f)(5)(ii)(C)

[31] Reg. §1.1273(f)(5)(ii)(D)

[32] Reg. §1.1273(c)(1)

[33] *Id.* There are circumstances when nonfunctional currency is treated as money rather than as property. See §1.988-2(b)(2).

[34] *Id.*

[35] This section deals with the determination of the issue price in the case of certain debt instruments issued for property.

[36] Reg. §1.1273-2(d)

[37] §1272(a)(1)

[38] Reg. §1.1272-1(a)(1)

[39] Reg. §1.1272-1(g)

[40] Reg. §1.163-7(a)

[41] Reg. §1.1272-1(b)(1)

[42] *Id.*

[43] Reg. §1.1272-1(b)(1)(i)

[44] *Id.*

[45] A business calculator, computer, or the present value tables in any finance book may be used for these calculations. The results may be slightly different due to rounding.

[46] Reg. §1.1272-1(b)(1)(ii)

[47] *Id.*

[48] *Id.*

[49] Reg. §1.1272-1(b)(1)(iii)

[50] *Id.*

[51] Reg. §1.1275-1(b)(1)

[52] *Id.*

[53] Reg. 1.272-1 Example 1

[54] Facts are from Example 1 in Reg. §1.1271-1(j)

[55] Reg. §1.1272-1(b)(4)(i)
[56] Facts are from Example 2 in Reg. §1.1271-1(j)
[57] Reg. §1.1272-1(b)(4)(ii)
[58] Reg. §1.1272-1 Example 3
[59] Facts are from Example 3 in Reg. §1.1271-1(j)
[60] Reg. §1.1272-1 (b)(1)(iv)
[61] *Id.*
[62] Reg. 1.1272-2(d)
[63] *Id.*
[64] Reg. §1.1272-2(b)(2)
[65] Reg. §1.171-2(3)
[66] *Id.*
[67] The facts of this example were taken from Example 1 in Reg.§1.171-2(c). However, the amount of premium calculated in the example is $1,118.17. This is due to the yield being carried out to a greater amount of decimal places. The final year's premium is calculated to be the remainder of the portion that is not amortized.
[68] §1278(a)(2)
[69] §1278(a)(B)
[70] §1276(b)
[71] §1276(a)
[72] Reg. §1.1272-3
[73] De minimis market discount is similar to de minimis OID. Under §1278(a)(2)(C), if the market discount is less than ¼ of 1 percent of the payments remaining due on the market discount bond (other than qualified stated interest), multiplied by the number of complete years to maturity, measured from the date the instrument is acquired, market discount is treated as zero.
[74] *Id.*
[75] Reg. §1.1272-3(c)
[76] Reg. §1.1272-3(d)
[77] *Id.*
[78] §1277(a)
[79] §1277(c)
[80] §1277(b)(A)

14

VARIABLE RATE DEBT INSTRUMENTS

INTRODUCTION

The original issue discount rules, discussed in Chapter 13, describe how an investor who purchases a bond at a discount recognizes income as the bond matures. Normally, a taxpayer who uses the cash method of accounting expects to be taxed on income when it is received.[1] However, the OID rules force even cash-method investors to recognize income on bonds issued at a discount as the income accrues, rather than at the end, when the instrument is liquidated.

Example—Beau spends $95,105 for a Texas Company bond that has a face value of $100,000. The bond pays interest at a rate of 6 percent, compounded annually, and matures in five years. The market rate for comparable obligations is 7.2 percent. Since the amount of original issue discount is more than $1250,[2] Beau must report income beyond the interest payments he receives, as shown in Table 14-1.

Based on this chart, Beau will have a total income in 2002 from the bond of $6848. The $4895 discount he received at purchase ($100,000—$95,105) is amortized over the life of the instrument, based on the constant interest rate method, rather than being recognized at the end, when the instrument matures. Both the amount of the discount and the amortization calculation are affected by the stated interest rate the bond pays. In other words, Beau would be willing to spend more for the bond if it carried a higher rate of interest.[3]

Rather than purchase a bond bearing a constant rate of interest, Beau instead might invest in an obligation that pays at a floating rate. For example, the bond's interest could be tied to the average yield of T-notes with a specified maturity, plus a certain number of basis points. Alterna-

TABLE 14-1

Date	Beginning Balance	Actual Interest (7.2%)	Stated Interest (6.2%)	Difference	Ending Balance
1/1/02					$95,105
12/31/02	$95,105	$6,848	$6,000	$848	95,953
12/31/03	95,953	6,909	6,000	909	96,862
12/31/04	96,862	6,974	6,000	974	97,836
12/31/05	97,836	7,044	6,000	1,044	98,880
12/31/06	98,880	7,119	6,000	1,119	100,000

tively, an instrument could provide for annual interest equal to the one-year London Interbank Offered Rate (LIBOR) at the end of each year the bond is outstanding. The existence of bonds paying variable rates of interest means special rules are needed to calculate the amount of original issue discount, if any, and the schedule under which the discount will be amortized. These rules are found in the Treasury Regulations issued under Tax Code §1275.[4] In general, the rules work by converting the variable interest into an equivalent fixed rate. Appropriate adjustments are made in later periods if the interest actually paid or accrued differs from the fixed equivalent.

REQUIREMENTS FOR VARIABLE RATE DEBT INSTRUMENTS

The first step in understanding the variable rate debt instrument regulations is to recognize when they apply. Several requirements must be met under these rules.[5]

1. Principal Payments—The first test limits the spread between the noncontingent (fixed) principal payments and the issue price.[6] Under this provision, the issue price of the instrument cannot exceed the total noncontingent principal payments by more than a specified amount. That amount is whichever is lesser of the following two calculations:
   A. 15 percent of the total noncontingent principal payments OR
   B. .015 times the product of the total noncontingent principal payments and the number of complete years to maturity from the issue date.[7]

Example—Russell buys a five-year bond issued by Flagstaff, Inc. that pays a variable rate of interest. The issue price of the obligation is $10,600 and at maturity the instrument will pay $10,000 plus an additional amount tied to a contingency. Russell's Flagstaff obligation falls under the variable rate debt instrument rules. The $600 gap between the instrument's issue price and the total noncontingent principal payments is less than $750. The $750 figure is the lesser of 15 percent of the noncontingent principal payments (15 percent * $10,000 = $1500) or .015 times the product of the noncontingent principal payments and the number of complete years to maturity from issue (.015* $10,000 * 5).

2. Stated Interest—In order to qualify as a variable rate debt instrument, an obligation can only provide for certain types of stated interest. Additionally, the interest must be paid or compounded at least annually.[8] The regulations approve four potential interest rate structures:
   a. One or more qualified floating rates
   b. A single fixed rate and one or more qualified floating rates
   c. A single objective rate or
   d. A single fixed rate and a single objective rate that is a qualified inverse floating rate[9]

A debt instrument that pays interest at a fixed rate for an initial period of one year or less and thereafter at either a qualified floating rate or an objective rate will be treated as paying interest at a single qualified floating or objective rate. For this rule to apply, however, the value of the floating or objective rate on the issue date must be intended to approximate the fixed rate used initially. An interest rate structure meeting a 25-basis-point test is presumed to satisfy the requirements.[10]

Example—Mary buys a bond issued by Southwest Company for $5000. In the first year the bond will pay 4-percent interest. Thereafter, the obligation bears interest under an arrangement that represents a qualified floating rate. As of the issue date, the value of the floating rate is 4.15 percent. Mary's Southwest bond will be treated as paying interest at a single qualified floating rate. This is because on the date of issue, the value of the variable rate (4.15 percent) does not differ from the value of the fixed rate (4 percent) by more than .25 percent.

Qualified Floating Rates

A qualified floating rate means changes in the value of the rate can reasonably be expected to measure changes in the cost of newly borrowed moneys in the same currency.[11] The rate can track current variations in the borrowing costs of the specific issuer of the instrument or changes for issuers generally. Examples of qualified floating rates include a rate equal to the one-year LIBOR at the end of each year the debt instrument is outstanding, and interest at a rate of a specified number of basis points plus the current value, at year-end, of the average yield on one-year Treasury securities.[12] Interest tied to the value of a commodity index or to a percentage of the value of the Standard & Poor's 500 Index does not qualify, as these indices are not expected to track changes in the cost of newly borrowed funds.[13]

Interest tied to a multiple of a qualified rate also is acceptable, provided it falls within certain parameters. Specifically, the regulations approve the use of multiples between .65 and 1.35. That means, for example, that a bond paying annual interest equal to twice the current value, at year-end, of the average yield of one-year Treasury securities would not be treated as having a qualified floating rate.[14] However, if the same bond provided for interest at 1.25 times the one-year Treasury rate, it would meet the requirements.

Debt instruments paying qualifying floating rates of interest may include a cap, which is a limit on the maximum stated interest rate the issuer is required to pay. A floor, by comparison, sets a lower limit and can be used to ensure at least a specified minimum return for investors holding the obligations. When a governor is included in the terms of a debt instrument, the amount by which a stated interest rate can rise or fall is restricted. Use of any of these devices, in general, means that the debt instrument does not bear a qualified floating rate of interest. However, the regulations contain exceptions that permit the use of these tools in some cases. For example, a cap, floor, or governor that is fixed for the life of the debt instrument is acceptable. Also, a cap not reasonably expected as of the issue date to cause the yield of the instrument to be significantly less than without the cap qualifies. Similar exceptions exist for floors and governors.[15] The regulations give no details about how these rules are implemented, other than to say that the reasonable expectations as to the effect of a cap, floor, or governor are determined as of the issue date.

Objective Rates

An objective rate of interest is a rate, other than a qualified floating rate, that is determined using a single fixed formula and that is based on objective financial or economic information.[16] Examples of structures that qualify as objective rates include interest equal to the percentage increase, if any, in the value in the prior year of an index based on the prices of several actively traded commodities. Interest payments of 2 percent plus the annual percent change in the Consumer Price Index also would be treated as an objective rate.[17] Rates tied to the issuer's profits do not qualify because the interest payments are dependent on information unique to the issuer.[18] Although interest equal to 2.5 times the value of one-year LIBOR, as of the payment date, is not a qualified floating rate because the multiple is too high,[19] this arrangement would represent an objective rate.[20]

The regulations prohibit arrangements involving significant front- or back-loading of interest from qualifying as objective rates. Specifically, if it is reasonably expected that the average value of the rate during first half of the debt instrument's term will be significantly more or significantly less than the value during the last half, the obligation does not bear interest at an objective rate.[21] For tax-exempt instruments, a variable rate meets the definition of an objective rate if it is a qualified inflation rate. This means the rate measures current changes in inflation based on a general inflation index. Tax-exempt obligations that pay variable interest at a qualified inverse floating rate also are treated as bearing an objective rate of interest.[22]

Qualified Inverse Floating Rates

Qualified inverse floating rates are relevant not only for tax-exempt instruments but also for obligations that use these arrangements in combination with a single fixed rate. An objective rate is a qualified inverse floating rate if it is equal to a fixed rate reduced by a qualified floating rate. Additionally, the variations in the rate must reasonably be expected to inversely reflect current changes in the qualified floating rate.[23] According to the regulations, a debt instrument paying annual interest at year-end equal to 12 percent less the value of one-year LIBOR as of the payment date is a qualified inverse floating rate where the value of one-year LIBOR as of issue is 6 percent. This is because the rate can be expected to inversely reflect current changes in one-year LIBOR. However, if the value of LIBOR were 11 percent as of issue, the rate would not meet the requirements because it is not likely to inversely reflect contemporaneous changes in one-year LIBOR.[24]

3. Other Requirements—In addition to rules regarding stated interest and principal payments, a variable rate debt instrument must meet a current value test. This means the instrument must provide that a qualified floating rate or objective rate in effect during the obligation's term must be set at a current value of that rate. A current value is a value from any date no earlier than three months before the first day the value is in effect and no later than one year following that first day.[25] Under this test, for example, a debt instrument that provided for payment of interest equivalent to the applicable federal rate from a date six months before the start of the accrual period when the rate is in effect would not qualify as a variable rate debt instrument. In general, the regulations also prohibit contingent principal payments, meaning the variable rate rules do not apply where uncertainties exist as to both the payment of interest and principal.[26]

REPORTING INTEREST AND ORIGINAL ISSUE DISCOUNT FOR VARIABLE RATE DEBT INSTRUMENTS

Calculation of interest and original issue discount for variable rate debt instruments depends upon the type of obligation involved.

Annual Payments of Interest at a Single Variable Rate

The first set of rules applies to variable instruments that call for stated interest at a single qualified floating rate or at an objective rate, unconditionally payable or constructively received at least annually.[27] Under these rules, all stated interest is treated as qualified stated interest. The amount of qualified stated interest and original issue discount accruing during a period is calculated by assuming that interest is payable at a fixed rate. In the case of a qualified floating or a qualified inverse floating rate, the rules assume a fixed rate equal to the value of the floating rate as of the issue date. If the variable rate instrument calls for an objective rate of interest, the rules use a fixed rate that reflects the yield reasonably expected for the obligation. The qualified stated interest allocable to a period is increased or de-

TABLE 14-2

Date	Value	Actual Interest	Stated Interest	Difference	Value
12/31/01					$96,691
12/31/02	$96,691	$5,608	$4,000	$1,608	98,299
12/31/03	98,299	5,701	4,000	1,701	100,000

creased, as necessary, to reflect interest actually paid during the accrual period.[28]

Example—On December 31, 2001, Judy buys a bond issued by Runner Company for $96,691. The instrument matures on December 31, 2003, at which time Judy will receive $100,000. Interest on the bond is to be paid annually, at a rate equal to the one-year LIBOR on the payment date. On the date of issue, one-year LIBOR is 4 percent, compounded annually. The rates as of December 31, 2002 and December 31, 2003 are 4 percent and 6.5 percent, respectively.

Judy is treated as purchasing a bond paying 4 percent interest, based on the value of the LIBOR as of the issue date. The yield on the bond is 5.8 percent, and the original issue discount amounts to $3309. Per Table 14-2, Judy will report a total of $5608 of income as of December 31, 2002.

On December 31, 2003, Judy will have $1701 of original issue discount. Her qualified stated interest is $6500 (6.5 percent, value of annual LIBOR, * $100,000). The additional $2500 of income Judy receives because of the LIBOR increase is treated as additional qualified stated interest.[29]

Other Variable Instruments (Except Those Providing a Fixed Rate)

Debt instruments not subject to the rules described above and that do not provide for a fixed rate of interest[30] are subject to a second set of rules. Obligations falling within this category would include instruments with multiple qualifying floating rates or investments with a single variable rate, the interest on which is not received actually or constructively at least annually. A four-step process applies to determine interest and original issue discount accruals.

Step 1. To begin, a fixed-rate substitute is determined for each variable rate provided by the instrument. For qualified floating rates, the substitute is the value of each rate as of the issue date.[31] A similar rule applies to qualified inverse floating rates. For objective rates, like interest tied to increases or decreases in a commodity index, a fixed rate reflecting the yield reasonably expected on the instrument is used.[32]

Step 2. The next step is to construct equivalent fixed-rate debt. This will have the same terms as the variable instrument, except the fixed rates, determined as above, are substituted for the actual interest obligation.[33]

Step 3. The amount of qualified stated interest and original issue discount are calculated next, based on the equivalent fixed-rate debt instrument. These amounts are treated as though the investor held the equivalent fixed obligation.[34]

Step 4. The last step of the process is to make adjustments for the actual variable interest rates carried by the instrument. This means qualified stated interest or original issue discount is increased if interest actually paid or accrued during the period is more than what was assumed for the fixed-rate equivalent. Similarly, qualified stated interest or OID is decreased where the actual interest is less than the assumed amounts. The adjustment is made to qualified stated interest where such interest is provided for in the equivalent fixed obligation and the increase or decrease is reflected in the amount actually paid. In all other cases, the adjustment is made to the original issue discount accruing during the period.[35]

Example—Tom buys a bond issued by NuMed, Inc. Tom will receive $100,000 when the instrument matures in two years. The bond provides for interest at different qualifying floating rates for each year the obligation is outstanding. As of the issue date, the value of these rates, compounded annually, is 4 percent for the first year and 5.5 percent for the second. Tom pays $100,000 for the instrument, which is expected to yield a return of 4.732 percent, again reflecting annual compounding.

Working through the steps described above, Tom is treated as having purchased a bond paying interest of 4 percent for the first year and 5.5 percent in the second. These numbers reflect the values of the qualifying floating rates as of the date of issue. Tom's discount on the bond is $1500. This amount is amortized as shown in Table 14-3.

Tom's bond has original issue discount even though the issue price and the amount payable at maturity are both $100,000, because of the increase in interest payments that Tom receives in the second year.[36] Assuming Tom actually is paid $4000 of interest in Year 1, he must report income of $4732, equal to his interest and the OID he is required to amortize.

If instead the actual payments of interest Tom receives from NuMed

TABLE 14-3

Date	Value	Actual Interest	Qualified Stated Interest	Difference	Value
Beginning					$100,000
12/31/Year 1	$100,000	$4,732	$4,000	$732	$100,732
12/31/Year 2	$100,732	$4,766.64	$4,000	$766.64	$101,498.64

differ from the 4 percent and 5.5 percent estimates used when the bond was issued, Tom must adjust the qualified stated interest he otherwise would report. For example, assume Tom's interest income actually amounts to $3800 in Year 1 and $5600 in Year 2. Tom would reduce the $4000 of qualified stated interest he expected to recognize in Year 1 by $200 and increase the $4000 for Year 2 by $100. If Tom's debt instrument did not provide for qualified stated interest, the adjustment would be made to original issue discount he otherwise would report.[37]

Variable Instruments with a Single Fixed Rate

A variable rate debt instrument can be structured to provide for a single fixed rate of interest in combination with either a qualified floating rate(s) or a qualified inverse floating rate. For example, a five-year bond might pay interest equal to 6 percent, compounded annually, for the first three years and for the last two years annual interest equal to one-year LIBOR as of the payment date. Where this type of structure is used, the regulations treat the instrument as if it provided for either a qualified floating or inverse floating rate, depending on the kind of variable rate the obligation bears.[38] In other words, the fixed rate is replaced with a qualified floating or inverse floating rate equivalent, and then the analysis proceeds as described above.[39]

Example—Mary buys a three-year bond issued by Orange Corp. for $100,000. The bond will pay Mary $100,000 when it matures. It provides for interest at a fixed rate of 7 percent for the first two years and at a qualified floating rate of one-year LIBOR plus 100 basis points in the final year. At issue, assume that Mary's bond has a value approximately the same as an otherwise identical debt instrument calling for interest equal to one-year LIBOR as of the payment date for the first two years. The value of LIBOR at the time is 6 percent.

TABLE 14-4

Date	Value	Actual Interest	Qualified Stated Interest	Difference	Value
Beginning					$100,000
Year 1	$100,000	$6,313	$6,000	$313	100,313
Year 2	100,313	6,333	6,000	333	100,646
Year 3	100,646	6,354	6,000	354	101,000

Mary's bond is treated as though it required interest equal to the value of one-year LIBOR for Years 1 and 2. The equivalent fixed-rate debt instrument has interest payments of $6000 for the first two years and $7000 in the last year. The issue price and stated principal are both $100,000. The qualified stated interest amounts to $6000. The yield on the bond is 6.313 percent, and the instrument has original issue discount of $1000.

Table 14-4 summarizes the tax consequences of Mary's bond.

As was the case for Tom, Mary has original issue discount because of the structure of the interest payments on Orange Corp. bonds. In Year 1, she will recognize qualified stated interest equal to $7000 ($6000 assumed paid by equivalent fixed-rate bond plus additional $1000 also received) and original issue discount of $313. In Year 2, Mary's income from the Orange bond will total $7333 ($6000 plus $1000 plus $333). If in the final year LIBOR has a value of 6 percent, Mary will report $6354 of income. Mary will recognize no gain when she surrenders the bond at maturity ($100,000 principal − $100,000 basis = 0 gain.)[40]

INVESTMENT CAUTIONS

Variable rate debt instruments may lead to unexpected tax consequences. For example, in Mary's case, assuming the actual interest payments are exactly what were expected at the outset, operation of the original issue discount rules requires her to recognize an additional $313 of interest in Year 1. This is the result even though the equivalent fixed-rate instrument would not pay the additional $1000 of interest income until Year 3. If Mary already is familiar with the OID rules, their application in the context of a variable rate debt instrument should not be surprising. However, if Mary is unaware of the original issue discount provisions, she is likely to be disappointed by the tax consequences of her investment. The OID rules are discussed in detail in Chapter 13 of this book; that material should be consulted in combination with the analysis of the current chapter for a more complete understanding of these provisions.

NOTES

[1] Most taxpayers use either the cash or accrual methods of accounting. Under the cash method, income is recognized when actually or constructively received. By comparison, an accrual method taxpayer recognizes income when it is earned and does not wait for receipt of the actual payment.

[2] If the discount on a debt instrument is less than ¼ of 1 percent of the stated redemption price at maturity multiplied by the number of complete years to maturity, the OID rules do not apply. Tax Code §1273(a)(3)

[3] For example, if the stated interest on the Texas Company bond were 6.5 percent, Beau would have paid $97,144 for the instrument, again assuming a market rate for comparable obligations of 7.2 percent. His total year 2002 income from the bond would have amounted to $6994, of which $494 would have been amortization of Beau's discount.

[4] The material contained in this chapter is based on the final version of the variable rate debt instrument regulations, as amended by T.D. 8674. In general, these regulations are effective August 13, 1996, although some provisions applied as of June 14, 1996. See T.D. 8674, 1996-2 C.B. 84.

[5] If a debt instrument provides for changeable rates of interest but does not meet the variable rate requirements, it is handled under the rules provided for contingent payment debt obligations. Treasury Regulation §1.1275-5(a). Likewise, an obligation that otherwise would qualify as a variable rate debt instrument but which is subject to Tax Code §1274 (issued for nonpublicly traded property) is subject to the contingent payment rules. Treasury Regulation §1.1275-5(a)(6).This rule does not apply to tax-exempt obligations. *Id.* The contingent debt instrument regulations are found at Treasury Regulation §1.1275-4. Under these rules, contingent debt instruments issued for money or publicly traded property are reported using the "noncontingent bond method." In general, this involves taking interest on the instrument into account whether or not the amount of the payment is fixed or determinable in the tax year. A projected payment schedule is used to determine the amount of interest to be taken into account. Where the actual amount of the contingent payment differs from what was projected, adjustments are made. Treasury Regulation §1.1275-4(b)(2). The regulations also contain rules that apply to contingent payment debt instruments issued in exchange for nonpublicly traded property. Treasury Regulation §1.1275-4(c)

[6] Revisions to the variable rate debt instrument rules made by T.D. 8674, 1996-2 C.B. 84, added a prohibition against "any principal payments that are contingent" (except as allowed under the test described in the text of this chapter). Treasury Regulation §1.1275-5(a)(5). "Contingent" is defined by reference to Treasury Regulation §1.1275-4(a), which applies to contingent payment debt instruments. Under that regulation, a payment is not contingent because of the possibility of impairment due to insolvency, default, or similar circumstances. Treasury Regulation §1.1275-4(a)(3). Likewise, "remote or incidental" possibilities do not render a payment contingent. Treasury Regulation §1.1275-4(a)(5)

[7] Treasury Regulation §1.1275-5(a)(2). If the instrument is an installment obligation, the weighted average maturity is used instead of the number of complete years to maturity from the issue date. *Id.*

[8] Treasury Regulation §1.1275-5(a)(3)

[9] *Id.*

[10] Treasury Regulation §1.1275-5(a)(3)(ii)

[11] Treasury Regulation §1.1275-5(b). Where an instrument provides for two or more qualified floating rates that are reasonably expected to have the same value over the obligation's term, the rates together are treated as a single qualified floating rate. See Treasury Regulation §1.1275-5(b)(1) for rules.

[12] Treasury Regulation §1.1275-5(d). In both cases, the regulations note that the proposed rate can reasonably be expected to measure contemporaneous changes in the cost of newly borrowed moneys. *Id.*

[13] Treasury Regulation §1.1275-5(d). Likewise, a bond bearing an interest rate based on the issuer's profits does not qualify. *Id.*

[14] Treasury Regulation §1.1275-5(b)(2). Debt instruments bearing interest equal to a qualified floating rate times a multiple between .65 and 1.35, plus or minus a fixed rate, also would qualify. *Id.*

[15] Treasury Regulation §1.1275-5(b)(3). Floors or similar arrangements "not reasonably expected as of the issue date to cause the yield on the debt instrument to be significantly more than the expected yield determined without the floor" can be used. *Id.* Additionally the regulations approve governors "not reasonably expected as of the issue date to cause the yield on the debt instrument to be significantly more or significantly less than the expected yield determined without the governor". *Id.*

[16] Treasury Regulation §1.1275-5(c)(1)

[17] Treasury Regulation §1.1275-5(d), Example 10, refers to the Consumer Price Index, U.S. City Average, All Items, for all Urban Consumers, seasonally unadjusted. Under the example, the rate cannot go below 0.

[18] Treasury Regulation §1.1275-5(c)(1) also applies to information within the control of the issuer. Additionally, the restriction encompasses information in the control of or unique to a party related to the issuer, under the related party rules of Tax Code §§267(b) and 707(b)(1). *Id.*

[19] See the discussion accompanying note 14.

[20] Treasury Regulation §1.1275-5(d). Objective rates also include rates based on one or more qualified floating rates, Treasury Regulation §1.1275-5(c)(1), and rates tied to the cost of borrowed moneys in a foreign currency. Treasury Regulation §1.1275-5(d), Example 8.

[21] Treasury Regulation §1.1275-5(c)(4). The regulations do not define the term "significantly." Under the regulations, an interest rate tied to a fixed percentage of the S & P 500 Index would not qualify as an objective rate. See Treasury Regulation §1.1275-5(d), Example 5.

[22] Treasury Regulation §1.1275-5(c)(5)

[23] Treasury Regulation §1.1275-5(c)(3). Restrictions described in Treasury Regulation §1.1275-5(b)(3), relating to caps, floors, and governors, are disregarded for purposes of this analysis. *Id.*

[24] Treasury Regulation §1.1275-5(d), Example 9

[25] Treasury Regulation §1.1275-5(a)(4)

[26] Treasury Regulation §1.1275-5(a)(5). Under Treasury Regulation §1.1275-5(a)(2), the issue price of an instrument cannot exceed the total noncontingent principal payments by more than the lesser of 15 percent of principal or .015 times the product of the principal and the number of complete years to maturity. See the discussion in the text accompanying note 6.

[27] Treasury Regulation §1.1275-5(e)(2). The interest must be unconditionally payable in cash or property other than debt instruments of the issuer or received constructively at least annually.

[28] Treasury Regulation §1.1275-5(e)(2). Although a qualified inverse floating rate may qualify as an objective rate, Treasury Regulation §1.1275-5(c)(3), inverse rates are treated like qualified floating rates for this rule. Both take a fixed rate equal to the rate as of the issue date.

[29] Treasury Regulation §1.1275-5(e)(3)(v), Example 3

[30] Per Treasury Regulation §1.1275-5(a)(3)(ii) if the instrument calls for a fixed initial rate of one year or less followed by a qualified floating rate or an objective rate, the fixed and subsequent floating or objective rate may be treated as one single qualified floating or objective rate. See the discussion accompanying note 10.

[31] Where an instrument provides for multiple qualified floating rates with different periods between the dates on which interest is adjusted, the fixed rate substitutes must be based on periods of equal length. Per the example in the regulations, where an instrument initially provides for interest based on the value of the 30-day commercial paper rate on each payment date, followed by interest tied to the value of the quarterly LIBOR on each date of payment, the fixed rates should reflect either 90-day commercial paper rates and quarterly LIBOR or 30-day commercial paper and monthly LIBOR. Treasury Regulation §1.1275-5(e)(3)(i)

[32] Treasury Regulation §1.1275-5(e)(3)(i). As discussed in the text, the term "objective rate" includes qualified inverse floating rates. However, for purposes of developing a fixed rate substitute, qualifying inverse floating rates are treated differently than other kinds of objective rates. *Id.*

[33] Treasury Regulation §1.1275-5(e)(3)(ii)

[34] Treasury Regulation §1.1275-5(e)(3)(iii)

[35] Treasury Regulation §1.1275-5(e)(3)(iv)

[36] Treasury Regulation §1.1273-1. See Chapter 13 of this book for a discussion of the de minimis rules for original issue discount.

[37] Treasury Regulation §1.1275-5(e)(3)

[38] Under Treasury Regulation §1.1275-5(a)(3)(ii), a debt instrument providing for a fixed rate of interest for a limited initial period, followed by a qualified floating rate or an objective rate is treated as a single qualified floating rate or objective rate, provided certain conditions are met. See the discussion accompanying note 10.

[39] Per the regulations, the qualified floating rate or qualified inverse floating rate replacing the fixed rate must be such that the fair market value of the variable instrument as of the issue date would be approximately the same as the value of an otherwise identical instrument that provides for a qualified floating or inverse floating rate rather than the fixed rate. Treasury Regulation §1.1275-5(e)(4)(i)

[40] Treasury Regulation §1.1275-5(e)(4). The regulations contain special rules that apply to bonds with reset obligations. In other words, a debt instrument may provide that interest

is to be reset by means of an auction, for example, at a specified future date or upon the occurrence of some event. For variable rate debt instruments with this kind of an interest structure, any original issue discount is accrued as though each reset period were a separate obligation. In other words, the instrument is treated as maturing on the day immediately preceding the reset for an amount equal to the reset value and then being reissued thereafter. See Treasury Regulation §1.1275-5(f).

15

SHORT-TERM OBLIGATIONS

INTRODUCTION

Under the OID provisions (discussed in Chapter 13), investors who buy bonds issued at a discount must recognize income by accruing that discount using the effective interest method. In other words, instead of waiting until the bond matures to recognize the income the discount represents, the income is reported and taxed over the bond's life. These rules do not apply to short-term obligations, defined as debt instruments with a fixed maturity date of one year or less from the date of issue.[1] Without special rules, however, the exclusion of short-term obligations from the OID provisions would represent very favorable tax treatment for investors. For example, discount income on a short-term instrument would not be recognized until the bond was retired. In some cases, a taxpayer might be able to report that discount as short-term capital gain, rather than ordinary income. Further, depending on the application of the investment interest rules,[2] an investor might buy short-term instruments with borrowed funds. This would give her a current deduction for the interest paid on the loan while not recognizing the discount the investment generates until later.

Example—Ralph, a cash method taxpayer,[3] buys bonds with a face amount of $100,000 from Burro Company. The obligations will mature 300 days from the date of issue. Ralph makes the purchase on October 31, 2002, paying $95,000. With daily compounding, the yield on the bonds is 6.24 percent. Unless special rules apply, Ralph will not recognize any income until the Burro instruments mature in 2003. Assuming sufficient investment income from other sources, if Ralph financed the acquisition through a loan, he also will take a deduction in 2002 for his current interest expense. This means Ralph has managed to both defer income recognition and take a current deduction in connection with his Burro investment. Moreover, when the bonds are retired Ralph will be treated as having made an exchange.[4] This means the resulting income will be reported as short-term capital gain, again unless special rules apply. Although short-term capital gain is taxed at the same rates as ordinary income, it can be used to offset short-term capital loss that Ralph otherwise might not be able to deduct currently.

To prevent these results, Congress has adopted various rules regarding short-term debt instruments. For example, Tax Code §1271 operates to characterize some or all of the gain arising from the sale or exchange of short-term obligations as ordinary income, even though the instruments might represent capital assets in the investor's hands. By comparison, Tax Code §1281 requires an investor to report income currently in connection with the discount at which a short-term obligation was acquired. Restrictions on interest deductions for loans associated with certain short-term debt investments are found at Tax Code §1282. The effect of all of these rules is to limit the tax advantages associated with short-term obligations. However, planning opportunities still exist for some cash method investors.[5]

GOVERNMENT AND NONGOVERNMENT OBLIGATIONS

In the case of both Code §1271 and §1281, the rules differ for short-term government versus nongovernment obligations. A short-term government obligation is defined as any obligation of the federal government, any of its possessions, a state, a political subdivision of a state, or the District of Columbia with a fixed maturity date of one year or less from the date of issue. This definition would include Treasury bills, for example. However, tax-exempt bonds, like those issued by states, are not treated as government obligations.[6] A six-month certificate of deposit or a corporate bond that matures within one year of issue are examples of short-term nongovernment obligations.[7]

TAX CODE §1281

To understand Tax Code §1281, two issues must be considered: First, when does the section apply and second, where applicable, how does it work?

When Does Tax Code §1281 Apply?

Application of Tax Code §1281 depends on who the taxpayer is and also on the type of debt instrument involved. All short-term obligations held by investors who use the accrual method of accounting fall within the §1281 rules, as do the short-term instruments owned by banks and mutual funds.[8] Also included are short-term obligations held primarily for sale to customers in the ordinary course of business or that are identified by the investor as being part of a hedging transaction.[9] Income from a short-term obligation that is a stripped bond or stripped coupon held by the person who stripped the bond or coupon also must be reported using the Code §1281 rules.[10]

Special rules apply for pass-through entities, like partnerships and S corporations. If, for at least 90 days during the tax year, 20 percent or more, by value, of the interests in the entity are held by investors that are subject to Tax Code §1281, then the §1281 rules apply to the pass-through entity as well. In other words, if an accrual method taxpayer owns 25 percent of the stock in an S corporation for at least 90 days in the tax year, the corporation's short-term obligations are subject to §1281, even if none of the other shareholders is an investor included in the rules described above. This provision applies as of the first taxable year in which the 20-percent test was met and continues until the first tax year after the year in which the test is failed and the IRS consents to the termination. Even where the 20-percent test is not met, a pass-through entity that was formed to avoid the Code §1281 rules will be subject to them.[11]

Operation of Tax Code §1281

An investor who holds a short-term obligation subject to §1281 must include in current-year income a portion of the discount attributable to the instrument. This is done by determining the total amount of the discount and then calculating the appropriate share. Where a government instrument is involved, the investor reports the sum of the daily portions of the "acquisition discount" for each day of the tax year on which the obligation was held.[12] Acquisition discount is the excess of the stated redemption price at maturity over the taxpayer's basis[13] The daily portion is determined using a ratable method by dividing the discount by the number of days after the day the investor acquired the obligation, up to and including the date of maturity.[14]

Example—Hank Corporation, an accrual method taxpayer, buys short-term government obligations that will mature in 275 days. The purchase is made on September 1, of Year 1. The stated redemption price at maturity of the instruments is $1,000,000 and Hank paid $960,000 for the investment. The yield to maturity is 5.42 percent. The acquisition discount is $40,000 ($1 million less Hank's basis of $960,000), and the daily portion is $145 ($40,000 / 275 days). If Hank is on a calendar year-end, it will report $17,600 of income on its Year One tax return ($145 * 121 days), even though none of this is received until Year Two, when the obligation matures.

Under the example above, Hank is treated as receiving an equal amount of the $40,000 discount on the government obligations for each day on which the instruments are held. Instead of this ratable method, an investor can elect to accrue the discount using a constant interest rate method.[15] This election is irrevocable, but only applies to the specific instruments the investor chooses.[16] In other words, it is possible to make this election for some but not all the short-term obligations that a taxpayer holds.

Example—Continuing with the facts above, Hank Corporation elects to report the $40,000 using the constant interest rate method instead of accruing this amount ratably. The corporation's yield to maturity is determined using Hank's cost in acquiring the obligations and daily compounding is assumed. This means Hank Corporation will report $17,399 attributable to the discount in Year One ($977,399 accrued value of the bond, as of December 31, Year One, less $960,000). By using the constant interest rate method, Hank Corporation reports $201 less income during the first year. In general, discount accrues more slowly by making the constant interest rate election.

For short-term nongovernment obligations, the calculations required by Code §1281 are based on original issue discount.[17] Both OID and acquisition discount are similar, in that they start with the instrument's stated redemption price at maturity. However, for short-term obligations, OID measures the difference between that amount and the instrument's issue price or adjusted issue price, depending on whether the obligation was acquired after original issue. By comparison, acquisition discount captures the difference between the stated redemption price at maturity and the investor's basis. For publicly offered debt instruments not issued for property, the issue price is the initial offering price to the public at which a substantial amount of the debt instruments are sold.[18] The adjusted issue price of an obligation is the sum of the issue price plus all prior adjustments under the OID rules.[19]

Investors can elect to accrue acquisition discount instead of OID for nongovernment short-term obligations. This election is helpful where an instrument is purchased after its issue, for more than the obligation's adjusted issue price as of the acquisition. However, the election applies to all short-term obligations acquired on or after the first day of the tax year for which the election is effective and to all later years. Revocation is only with IRS permission.[20]

Example—Pyrak Corporation holds a nongovernment obligation subject to Tax Code §1281. The bond was issued on May 31, 2002, and will mature in one year. The adjusted issue price of the obligation at the time of Pyrak's acquisition is $94,500. The stated redemption price at maturity is $100,000. Pyrak bought the bond on September 30, 2002, from its original holder for $96,500.

If the §1281 calculations use OID numbers, Pyrak will accrue income based on discount of $5500 ($100,000, stated redemption price at maturity, less adjusted issue price of $94,500). However, if the acquisition discount is used instead, the accrual will be based on the $3500 difference between the stated redemption price at maturity and Pyrak's basis. Assuming Pyrak is on a calendar year-end, the company will accrue discount as of December 31, 2002, of $2082 if the OID numbers are used and daily portions are calculated on a ratable basis ($5500/243 = $22.63 per day * 92 days bond held by Pyrak in 2002 = $2082). Pyrak's adjusted basis in the bond at maturity will be $102,000 ($96,500 purchase price plus $5500 accrued discount.)[21] As a result, when the bond matures, Pyrak will recognize a capital loss of $2000 ($100,000, amount received, less $102,000, adjusted basis).[22]

If instead Pyrak elects to use the acquisition discount figures, the company's income in 2002 from the short-term obligation will amount to $1325, again assuming the ratable accrual method. This number is smaller than the $2082 included in income at year-end under the OID numbers because the original holder sold the instrument to Pyrak for more than its adjusted issue price. Between 2002 and 2003, Pyrak will accrue a total discount of $3500, meaning its basis in the bond at maturity will be $100,000 ($96,500 + $3500). The corporation will recognize no gain or loss from the redemption itself.

In the Pyrak example, the election to use the acquisition discount numbers was helpful because it meant the corporation recognized less income in 2002. The OID figures would have resulted in more accrual in the first year but a short-term capital loss in the second. For most investors, this result is less favorable, both because of the time value of money and because of the restrictions on the use of capital losses. However, if instead Pyrak bought the nongovernment obligation for less than its adjusted issue price, the election to use the acquisition discount calculation would have resulted in greater income recognition in the first year.

Example—Again assume the facts above, except that Pyrak buys the short-term instrument for $92,000. If the corporation has elected to use acquisition discount, it now is required to accrue $3029 in 2002 ($8000 acquisition discount/243 total days held by Pyrak = $32.92 accrual per day * 92 days held in 2002). This is $947 more than the $2082 reported using the OID numbers. This is because the $92,000 figure represents a discount when compared to the instrument's adjusted issue price at the time of Pyrak's acquisition. Had the OID numbers been used instead of the acquisition calculation, Pyrak would have accrued a total of $5500 in discount, as noted above. The corporation's basis in the bond would stand at $97,500 when the instrument matures. This means Pyrak would recognize capital gain of $2500 when the short-term obligation is redeemed, assuming the instrument represents a capital asset in the corporation's hands.

Where Pyrak buys the bond for $92,000, the election to use acquisition discount is unfavorable and should not be made. Unfortunately, Pyrak may not have a choice if it elected this treatment earlier, in connection with another short-term obligation. This is because these elections can be revoked only with IRS consent. For that reason, an investor must be cautious in making this decision.

TAX CODE §1271 RULES FOR SHORT-TERM OBLIGATIONS

Unlike Tax Code §1281, which requires current recognition of accrued discount while an investor holds an obligation subject to its provisions, Code §1271 operates to characterize gain arising from the sale or exchange of a short-term obligation as ordinary income. These rules apply only to short-term obligations that are not subject to the rules found at Tax Code §1281.[23] The amount of gain from the sale of a taxable government short-term instrument that is treated as ordinary is based on acquisition discount. As with Code §1281, this is defined as the excess of the stated redemption price at maturity over the investor's basis. The rule applies only to the investor's ratable share. This is calculated by multiplying the discount by a fraction. The numerator of the fraction is the number of days the investor held the obligation, and the denominator is the number of days from when the investor acquired the instrument up until maturity.[24] Gain from the sale of nongovernment short-term instruments is reported using original issue discount principles, again like Code §1281. The ratable share for a nongovernment obligation is based on the number of days the investor held the instrument, divided by the total number of days from original issue until maturity.[25] For both government and nongovernment short-term obligations, an investor can elect to accrue the discount using a constant interest rate method.[26]

Example—Karl, a cash method taxpayer, holds government bonds that he purchased for $96,000. The bonds were issued on September 1, 2002, and Karl acquired them at that time. The instruments are scheduled to mature in one year and are not subject to the provisions of Code §1281. Karl will not report any income in connection with the bonds when his 2002 tax year ends, on December 31st. When the bonds are retired, Karl will recognize ordinary income of $4000, equal to his acquisition discount ($100,000 stated redemption price at maturity, less $96,000, Karl's adjusted basis). If Karl instead sells the bonds on April 1, 2003 for $98,500, he will report a total gain of $2500 on the sale. Of this amount, $2323 will be treated as ordinary income, assuming Karl uses a ratable share calculation (212/365 * 4000). If Karl elects a constant interest rate method, he will report ordinary income of $2303 in connection with the sale ($98,303, accrued value as of April 1, less $96,000, adjusted basis).

If Karl had sold the bonds on April 1 for $95,000, he would report a short-term capital loss of $1000 on the disposition, assuming the bonds are capital assets in Karl's hands. This is because Code §1271 only operates to require recognition of ordinary income to the extent of the gain realized on the sale. Where a short-term obligation is sold at a loss, no ordinary income arises.

If Karl held nongovernment bonds, he would measure his income by using original issue discount, the difference between the stated redemption price at maturity and the obligation's issue price. Unlike Code §1281, there apparently is no option to use acquisition discount instead of OID for nongovernment obligations.

Example—Bob buys a nongovernment bond that will mature on June 30, 2003. The bond was issued on September 1, 2002; Bob purchased the instrument on January 31, 2003. This means the original holder owned the bond for 152 days before the sale to Bob. The bond will pay $10,000 at maturity, and its issue price was $9100. Bob bought the obligation for $9400. The adjusted issue price at the time of Bob's acquisition is $9553. This is the sum of the issue price of $9100 plus $453 of original issue discount.

The $453 was reported as ordinary income by the original holder of the bond at the time of the sale to Bob (Using a ratable calculation − $900/302 = $2.98 discount per day * 152 days = $453). When the bond matures, Bob will report gain of $600. This is the difference between the amount received ($10,000) and his adjusted basis ($9400). Of this amount, $447 will be ordinary income to Bob.

TAX CODE §1282 INTEREST DEDUCTION RESTRICTIONS

Tax Code §1282 limits the deduction an investor can claim for "net direct interest expense" related to a short-term obligation. "Net direct interest expense" is defined as interest paid or accrued on a loan incurred or continued to buy or carry a short-term obligation.[27] The deduction is limited to the amount by which the expense exceeds the daily portions of the original issue discount or acquisition discount plus any other interest that accrues on the instrument during the year but that is not included in income because of the taxpayer's method of accounting.[28] In other words, this section disallows an interest deduction to the extent an investor is accruing but not reporting interest income. In the year the investor disposes of the obligation, interest disallowed earlier becomes deductible.[29]

Where a short-term instrument is subject to Code §1281, an investor is required to accrue income currently and therefore reports discount even in a year where there is no disposition of the instrument. (As discussed above, the amount reported is equal to the daily portions of the acquisition or original issue discount, depending on whether a governmental or nongovernmental obligation is involved.) Consequently, the law specifically exempts §1281 short-term obligations from the deduction limits of Code §1282.[30] An investor can elect to have the §1281 rules apply to instruments that would not normally be subject to those provisions, in order to avoid the interest deduction limits. However, this election applies to all short-term obligations acquired by the investor in the year of election and for all years thereafter until revocation. The election can be revoked only with IRS consent.[31]

Example—On June 30, 2002, Louise bought a short-term obligation that is not subject to the accrual requirements of Tax Code §1281. The instrument will mature in 300 days. Louise paid $94,500 for this investment and financed part of the purchase price using a loan. Interest on the loan in the current year amounts to $800. Since the short-term obligation falls outside the scope of Code §1281, Louise is not required to accrue any of the

$5500 discount in the current year. However, she can elect to do so, in order to deduct the $800 of interest she paid on the loan used to finance part of her investment. In Louise's case, this election would require her to report $3336 of accrued discount, using a constant interest rate method.

For Louise, a decision to have the investment treated as a Code §1281 short-term obligation would be unfavorable. Barring unusual circumstances, it can generally be expected that this election should not be made. This is because the election is helpful only where the interest deductions on the loan used to acquire or carry the instrument exceed the income on the obligation, as represented by the accrued discount, plus the accrued interest. Moreover, like the election discussed earlier to accrue acquisition discount instead of OID on a nongovernment obligation under the Code §1281 rules, an election here will apply to all short-term obligations held by the investor thereafter. This plus the limits on election revocation both point to the need for careful analysis before choosing this option.

PLANNING OPPORTUNITIES

As a rule, investors can expect larger returns when they are willing to commit funds for longer periods of time. However, for a variety of reasons an investment of one year or less may be advantageous because of liquidity needs, for example, or based on what a taxpayer believes future investments will yield. Short-term obligations represent a viable investment vehicle where a longer horizon is either unattractive or unworkable. Moreover, for ordinary investors who are on the cash method of accounting, short-term instruments offer some degree of tax deferral, even with all of the restrictions found in Tax Code §1281 and §1271.

Example—Charles buys short-term instruments issued by Abel Corporation, using funds he received from the sale of another investment. The instruments were issued to Charles on September 30, 2002 and will mature in one year. Charles is a cash method taxpayer, and he is not holding the obligations primarily for sale to customers in the ordinary course of his trade or business. Further, the instruments do not represent stripped bonds or coupons and are not part of a hedging transaction. This means the Abel bonds that Charles holds are not subject to the income recognition rules of Code §1281.

Charles bought the Abel instruments for $950,000. They will pay $1,000,000 at maturity. Using a ratable calculation, $137 of this discount accrues each day Charles holds the obligations ($50,000/365 = $137). If he is on a calendar year-end, this means the value of Charles's investment has grown by $12,600 by December 31, 2002 ($137 * 92 days). However, none of this income is reported until the bonds are redeemed in 2003. If Charles is in a 35-percent tax bracket, he will delay paying $4411 in tax ($12,600 * 35 percent) for a full year.

Had Charles purchased the Abel bonds with borrowed moneys, his interest deductions would be limited, under Tax Code §1282. Further, if Charles used the accrual method of accounting, or otherwise was subject to Code §1281, he would be required to report income as the discount accrues. Even in the example as given, where Charles enjoys some degree of tax deferral, he still will have to report ordinary income in connection with the discount on the Abel investment when the obligations are redeemed, where he might otherwise have expected all short-term capital gain. All of this means that if Charles is not familiar with the tax rules applicable to short-term obligations, he is likely to be disappointed with the after-tax results of his investment.

NOTES

[1] Tax Code §1272(a)(2)

[2] The investment interest rules, in general, limit the deduction of interest paid or accrued on loans allocable to property held for investment to net investment income. See Chapter 4 for a discussion of these rules.

[3] Most taxpayers use either the cash or accrual methods of accounting. Under the cash method, income is recognized when actually or constructively received. By comparison, an accrual method taxpayer recognizes income when it is earned, and does not wait until the later receipt.

[4] Tax Code §1271(a)(1)

[5] See the discussion at the conclusion of this chapter.

[6] Tax Code §1271(a)(3); Tax Code §1283(a)(1)(B)

[7] For purposes of the Code §1281 rules, a short-term obligation is defined as "any bond, debenture, note, certificate, or other evidence of indebtedness which has a fixed maturity date not more than one year from the date of issue." Tax Code §1283(a)(1)

[8] Tax Code §1281(b). Short-term obligations held by a common trust fund also are subject to the Code §1281 rules. Tax Code §1281(b)(1)(D)

[9] Tax Code §1281(b)(1)(E) refers to short-term obligations identified by the taxpayer under §1256(e)(2) as part of a hedging transaction.

[10] This rule also applies where the instrument is held by a person whose basis is determined by reference to the basis in the hands of the taxpayer who stripped the bond or coupon. Tax Code §1281(b)(1)(F). For example, if an investor strips a bond and then gives the resulting obligation to his son, the son would be subject to the §1281 rules, assuming he takes his father's adjusted basis in the bond.

[11] Tax Code §1281(b)(2). The Tax Code permits an investor to elect §1281 treatment for the short-term obligations he or she holds. Where this election is made, it applies to all obligations acquired on or after the first day of the tax year the election takes effect and continues to later years, unless revoked with IRS permission. The election would mean that Code §1282, which limits the deduction for interest expense arising on loans incurred or continued to purchase or carry a short-term obligation, would not apply. This is because Tax Code §1282 contains an exception for bonds subject to Code §1281. The deduction limits found at §1282 are discussed later in this chapter. See the material in the text accompanying notes 27–31.

[12] Tax Code §1281(a). Under Tax Code §1281(a)(2), an investor must take any interest payable on the obligation into account as it accrues, regardless of when it is received.

[13] Tax Code §1283(a)(2). See Tax Code §1273 for the definition of stated redemption price at maturity.

[14] Tax Code §1283(b)(1)

[15] Tax Code §1283(b)(2)

[16] Tax Code §1283(b)(2)

[17] Tax Code §1283(c)

[18] Tax Code §1273(b). For short-term obligations, the stated redemption price at maturity includes all payments to be made when the instrument matures, including what would otherwise be considered qualified stated interest. Treasury Regulation §1.1273-1(c)(5)

[19] Tax Code §1272(a)(4)

[20] Tax Code §1283(c)(2)

[21] Tax Code §1283(d)(1)

[22] If an investor acquires a bond for a premium, he or she can elect to amortize the premium amount under Code §171. (These rules are discussed in Chapter 12.) To date, no regulations have been issued under the Code provisions dealing with short-term obligations (Code §§1281–1283) and consequently it is unclear whether an investor who pays a premium for a short-term instrument can offset the daily portions of original issue discount by amortizing the premium amount.

[23] Tax Code §1283(d)(3)

[24] Tax Code §1271(a)(3)(D)

[25] Tax Code §1271(a)(4)(C)

[26] Tax Code §1271(a)(3)(E) (government obligations); Tax Code §1271(a)(4)(D) (nongovernment obligations)

[27] Tax Code §1277(c)

[28] Tax Code §1282(a)

[29] Tax Code §1282(c) refers to the rules found at Tax Code §1277(b). Under that provision, disallowed interest expense is treated as paid or accrued by the taxpayer in the year an obligation is disposed of. Tax Code §1277(b)(2). Special rules apply where the instrument is disposed of in a nonrecognition transaction. *Id.*

[30] Tax Code §1282(b)(1)

[31] Tax Code §1282(b)(2)

16 STRIPPED BONDS AND STRIPPED COUPONS

INTRODUCTION

When a bond is issued with interest coupons, it really can be viewed as a collection of separate debt instruments. Each coupon represents the right to receive an obligation equal to the amount of the interest payment due on the date specified. In addition, the bond itself entitles the holder to payment of the bond principal, also called the corpus, when the obligation matures. Taxpayers sometimes detach the coupons from the bonds in order to sell part of the obligation. Where, for example, an investor sells the underlying instrument but retains the interest coupons, the bond is said to have been "stripped."

Taxpayers found that transactions involving stripping bonds and coupons could be used to manipulate taxable income and loss. As a result, Congress adopted Code §1286, which governs stripped obligations. The §1286 rules are designed to prevent abuses where a taxpayer strips an instrument.

Example—Jean buys a bond issued by Hefei Corporation, at par. The bond will mature in five years, at which time Jean will receive a principal payment of $100,000. The coupon rate on the instrument is 8 percent, compounded semiannually. Immediately after the acquisition, Jean strips the coupons and sells the underlying bond for $67,556 [$100,000/(1.04)^{10}]. If no basis allocation is required, she will report a loss of $32,444 on the transaction ($67,556 amount realized less $100,000 purchase price). Again assuming no special rules apply, Jean will recognize no income in connection with the coupons she stripped from the Hefei instrument until payment is made or the coupons are sold. On the other hand, if Jean has net operating losses about to expire, she will sell the coupons and retain the bond. If none of the bond's purchase price is allocated to the basis of the coupons,[1] the proceeds she receives on their sale will be taxable in full.

In response to transactions like Jean's, Tax Code §1286 generally adopts three requirements. First, an investor who sells a stripped bond or stripped coupon must report any accrued but unrecognized interest income and market discount that may exist at the time of the stripping transaction. (A corresponding basis adjustment is made to take into account this income recognition.) Second, before disposition, a bondholder who sells a stripped bond or coupon must allocate his or her basis in the entire obligation, using fair market values, between the items retained and the items sold. Finally, both the seller and buyer of a stripped bond or stripped coupon are subject to the original issue discount rules. This is done by treating the stripped pieces of the instrument as separate obligations issued on the date the stripping transaction occurred. The original issue discount rules, discussed in Chapter 13 of this book, require current recognition of income when an investor holds obligations that were issued at a discount.

BOND STRIPPING IN GENERAL

Under §1286, a stripped bond is defined as a bond issued with interest coupons where a separation in ownership has occurred between the underlying instrument and any coupon not yet payable.[2] A coupon includes any right to receive interest on a bond, whether or not an actual coupon evidences the right.[3] These definitions mean a bond can be stripped by selling the right to receive one or more interest payments on the obligation or, alternatively, the right to the principal payable when the instrument matures. However, the sale of a proportionate share in both the interest and the underlying bond, as where an investor transfers half of all her rights to another, is not considered a strip. This is because the investor did not dispose of the right to receive a portion of the interest separately from the right to be paid the same proportion of principal or, conversely, the right to receive principal separately from the rights to the interest income.

Zero coupon instruments that investors obtain through the STRIPS program are considered to be stripped obligations. The term "STRIPS" refers to the Treasury Department's "Separate Trading of Registered Interest and Principal of Securities" program. This allows investors to buy separate interests in either principal or income arising under Treasury bonds and Treasury notes with original maturity dates of at least 10 years.[4]

Stripped bonds and coupons can be used for a variety of reasons. By buying a stripped obligation at a specific discount rate, an investor can lock in a particular return on his or her money. This may not be possible if instead interest is paid currently, which is then reinvested at prevailing market rates.

Example—Page has approximately $55,000 that she wants to invest for a period of six years. She would like to receive a return on her money of 10 percent, compounded semiannually. Page therefore purchases from Marc a stripped bond that will mature in six years. The obligation was originally issued to Marc, with coupons attached, by the Anhui Corporation. Marc had held the investment for four years as of the date of sale to Page. She buys the stripped bond, which has a face value of $100,000, for $55,684 $[100,000/(1.05)^{12}]$. Assuming Anhui Corporation honors its obligation, Page will receive the desired 10-percent return on her money, compounded semiannually, even if market interest rates fall to 8 percent.

If instead Page had put her funds in preferred stock that paid 5-percent dividends every six months, she would be able to reinvest the after-tax proceeds only at a rate of return (8-percent assumed market rate, compounded semiannually) less than the 10 percent she had targeted. However, if rates rise, holding the stripped Anhui obligation means Page will be unable to take advantage of the higher returns unless she liquidates her Anhui holding and reinvests the proceeds at market rates. Even then, the price at which Page sells the bond will reflect a greater discount because of the increased return offered by the prevailing markets.

Assume, for instance, that Page sells the stripped bond after one year, when interest rates are 12 percent, compounded semiannually. A buyer would be willing to pay only $55,839 for the Anhui obligation $[100,000/(1.06)^{10}]$. By comparison, had market rates stayed at 10 percent, Page could've sold the instrument at the end of one year for $61,391 $[100,000/(1.05)^{10}]$.

Stripped bonds and stripped coupons can have other uses also. For example, a stripped bond can fund an expense an investor anticipates will arise in the future.

Example—Hannah and her family live in Boomtown, where housing values are high. Her employer transfers her to a job site in Middletown for an assignment expected to last five years. Hannah sells her Boomtown residence and is able to exclude the gain under Tax Code §121. (IRC §121 allows a taxpayer to exclude up to $500,000 of gain on the sale of a home, assuming a joint return is filed and certain requirements are met.) She purchases a comparable home in Middletown for $60,000 less. Hannah uses the excess proceeds to buy a stripped bond issued by Guangzhou Corporation. The Guangzhou bond will mature in five years, at which time Hannah will receive $100,000. She plans to put these funds toward the purchase of a new home when she is transferred back to Boomtown at the end of her assignment.

TAX CONSEQUENCES OF STRIPPING TAXABLE BONDS

There is no tax impact for the issuer of a coupon-bearing bond that is later stripped by an investor. For sellers and buyers of stripped obligations, IRC §1286 imposes several requirements.

Recognition of Accrued Interest and Discount by the Seller

Under the Tax Code, a person who strips one or more coupons from a bond and then sells either the bond or a coupon must recognize income. The amount of income reported is equal to the interest accrued but not recognized while the seller held the obligation and also any accrued market discount, determined as of the time of the disposition, which has not yet been recognized.[5] (Market discount is discussed in Chapter 13.)

Example—On January 1, Year 1, Catherine buys from Cece a Beijing Company bond, for which she pays $92,420. The bond will mature in five years, at which time Catherine will receive principal of $100,000. The price paid for the bond reflects a market rate of interest of 10 percent compounded annually; the coupons pay 8 percent annually. At the end of Year 1, Catherine reports total income of $8000, consisting of the coupon interest. She has accrued discount of $1242, assuming market discount is calculated on a constant interest rate method.

Halfway through Year 2, Catherine strips the coupon that matures at the end of the fourth year and sells it. Because of the strip, Catherine is required to recognize the entire market discount that has accrued up to the point of the transaction. This amounts to $683 from Year 2 [$1366, total discount for Year 2, * .5], plus the $1242 of discount that accrued in Year 1. In addition, Catherine must report $4000, half of the amount of the coupon interest she will be paid in Year 2.[6]

As discussed in Chapter 13, in general the market discount rules operate to recharacterize income arising where a bond is purchased in the market at a discount and later sold for a gain. In the case of a stripping trans-action, however, the §1286 rules, in combination with the market discount provisions, require recognition of income.[7] In other words, Catherine will report a total of $1925 of accrued discount in Year 2, even if she ultimately recognizes a loss because of the stripping transaction. If no strip had oc-curred, the market discount rules would affect Catherine only when she later makes certain transfers of the instrument or when it's redeemed. Even then, the provisions would have no impact if the investment represented a loss.

Under §1286, the bases of an investor's stripped bond and coupons are increased by the amount of interest and discount recognized immediately before the sale. This total must be allocated by the seller, using fair market values, among the items disposed of and the items retained.[8]

Example—Continuing with the facts above, assume Catherine sold the $8000 coupon payable at the end of Year 4 for $6172. Based on market interest rates at the time of this sale, further assume the fair market values of the Beijing bond and the remaining coupons as of the Year 2 stripping transaction are as follows:

Bond: $69,496	Coupon payable 12/31/Year 2	$7,603
	Coupon payable 12/31/Year 3	$6,850
	Coupon payable 12/31/Year 4	$6,172
	Coupon payable 12/31/Year 5	$5,560

Because of the income Catherine is required to report, her new basis in all her Beijing holdings is now $98,345 ($92,420 + $4000 + $1242 + $683). Catherine must allocate this figure, among the bond and coupons, using fair market values.[9] This means the basis of the coupon Catherine sold is $6344 [$98,345 * ($6,172/$95,681)].[10] As a result, Catherine rec-ognizes a loss of $172 on the sale of the Year 4 coupon.[11] In December, when the $8000 Year 2 coupon is paid, Catherine will report $4000 of in-come, the remaining interest for Year 2 that has accrued since midyear.

Original Issue Discount Rules

The original issue discount rules apply to both the seller and buyer in a bond stripping transaction. Under Tax Code §1286, the purchaser of a stripped bond is treated as holding an instrument issued on the date of purchase and having original issue discount equal to the excess of the stated redemption price at maturity over the bond's ratable share of the price the buyer paid for all interests received.[12] A similar rule applies to stripped coupons, except that the OID is measured by reference to the amount payable on the coupon's due date, rather than the stated redemption price.[13] If a buyer acquires multiple interests, as where an investor purchases a stripped bond and one of its coupons, the ratable share of the purchase price is based on fair market values of the interests acquired as of the date of purchase.

An investor who strips a bond and sells either the underlying obligation or one or more of the stripped coupons is treated as having purchased all of the retained interests. This purchase occurs on the day of the disposition, for an amount equal to the basis allocated to each item, after adjustment for any accrued interest or discount the seller is required to report.[14] As was the case for buyers of stripped instruments, the OID is measured by the stated redemption price at maturity, in the case of a bond, or by the amount payable at the due date, where coupons are retained.[15]

Example—Ceily buys a bond originally issued by Shanghai Corp. The instrument will mature in five years from the date Ceily acquired the obligation from its original holder. The bond bears 8-percent semiannual coupons, payable on June 30th and December 31st of each year. The face value of the obligation is $100,000; the market interest rate for similar instruments at the time of Ceily's purchase is 9.5 percent, compounded semiannually. Ceily pays $94,138 for the bond and coupons.

At the end of September in Year 4, Ceily strips the remaining coupons from the bond and sells the underlying instrument to Christine. Prior to the stripping transaction, Ceily had recognized $28,000 of interest in connection with the Shanghai coupons. Again assuming use of the constant interest rate method, she also accrued $3811 in market discount, as shown in Table 16-1.

Ceily is required to report $2000 of interest accrued as of the date of the stripping transaction and disposition, assuming the strip occurred midway between the June 30th and December 31st coupon due dates. Also, she must include in income $326.50, or half of the discount of $653 that accrues from June 30th to December 31st, in the year the strip occurred. This is in addition to the $3811 of market discount that arose from the date Ceily purchased the Shanghai investment to June 30, Year 4, which she must report too.

The income Ceily is required to recognize puts her adjusted basis in her total Shanghai investment, immediately before the bond disposition, at $100,275.50. This figure must be allocated between the bond and coupons

TABLE 16-1

Date	Beginning Balance	Actual Interest (9.5%, semi.)	Stated Interest (8% semi)	Difference	Ending Balance
1/1/Year 1					$94,138
6/30/Yr 1	$94,138	$4,472	$4,000	$472	94,610
12/31/Yr 1	94,610	4,494	4,000	494	95,104
6/30/Yr 2	95,104	4,517	4,000	517	95,621
12/31/Yr 2	95,621	4,542	4,000	542	96,163
6/30/Yr 3	96,163	4,568	4,000	568	96,731
12/31/Yr 3	96,731	4,595	4,000	595	97,326
6/30/Yr 4	97,326	4,623	4,000	623	97,949

based on their relative fair market values. At the market interest rates prevailing as of the stripping transaction, assume those values are as follows:

Bond	$88,021
Coupon due 12/31/Yr 4	3,900
Coupon due 6/30/Yr 5	3,706
Coupon due 12/31/Yr 5	3,521

Using these numbers to allocate Ceily's total basis, her adjusted basis in the underlying Shanghai bond prior to its disposition becomes $89,022 [(88,021/99,148)*100,275.50]. Her bases in the three remaining Shanghai coupons are $3944, for the coupon maturing on December 31, Year 4; $3748, for the June 30, Year 5 coupon, and $3561, for the final interest coupon. If Ceily sold the Shanghai bond for its assumed fair market value of $88,021, she will report a loss of $1001 on the sale ($88,021 − $89,022).

Both Ceily and Christine will have to accrue original issue discount, since the de minimis exception is not applicable in either case.[16] To calculate her yield to maturity, Christine will use the following formula, which is found in IRS Publication 1212, on original issue discount instruments:

$$n * [(srp/ap)^{(1/\{(r/s) + m\})} - 1] \text{ where}$$

n is the number of accrual periods in 1 year;
srp stands for the stated redemption price at maturity;
ap represents the acquisition price;
r is the number of days from Christine's purchase to the end of the short accrual period;

s stands for the total number of days in the accrual period containing the stripping transaction and disposition; and
m is the number of full accrual periods from the date of Christine's purchase to maturity.[17]

Christine's yield to maturity is 10.47 percent $(2 * [(100,000/88,021)^{(1/\{(92/184)+2\})}} - 1])$. For the short period beginning at purchase and ending on December 31, Year 4, she will accrue a total of $2275.10 of discount. This is calculated using the following formula, again taken from IRS Publication 1212:

$$[ap * \{1 + (ytm/n)\}^{(r/s)} - ap]/r \text{ where}$$

ap is the acquisition price;
ytm stands for the yield to maturity, calculated above;
n is the number of accrual periods in 1 year;
r represents the number of days from purchase to the end of the short accrual period; and
s is the number of days in the accrual period containing the strip and disposition.[18]

In Christine's case, a discount of $24.73 arises on each day of the short accrual period, using the formula above. Since there are a total of 92 days in this short period, she multiplies her daily figure by 92 to calculate the total discount ($2275.10) she must report.

To determine the discount accruing during full periods, the following formula is used:

$$[ap * (ytm/n)]/p.$$

The characters in this equation have the same meanings as outlined above.[19] The term "p," not previously seen, stands for the number of days in the accrual period. In Christine's case, this formula means she will accrue $26.12 per day, or a total of $4,728.16 of discount, during the period running from December 31, Year 4 to June 30, Year 5 $[\{90,296.10 * (.104725566/2)\}/181]$. Note that the acquisition price is adjusted to reflect original issue discount accrued in prior periods ($88,021 + $2,275.10). For the period ending with the bond's maturity, on December 31, Year 5, Christine will recognize a discount of $27.04 per day $[\{95,024.26*(.104725566/2)\}/184]$. Because there are a total of 184 days in this period, Christine will report $4975.73 of OID. This amount, when added to her adjusted issue price as of June 30, Year 5, brings her total adjusted issue price in the bond to $100,000, the instrument's face value ($95,024.26 + $4975.73).

Ceily also will report original issue discount on the coupons stripped from the Shanghai bond. The first coupon matures on December 31, Year 4, at which time she will recognize a discount of $56. This is the difference between the $4000 Ceily will receive when the coupon matures and her adjusted basis in the item, after taking into account the accrued interest and discount she recognized at the time of the strip and disposition ($3944). For the second coupon, maturing on June 30, Year 5, Ceily uses the formula $n * [(srp/ap)^{(1/\{(r/s)+m\})} - 1]$—to calculate her yield to maturity. (This formula is used because the first accrual period is a short period, running from the date of the strip to December 31, Year 4.) This produces a result of 0.088672114 ($2 * [(4{,}000/3{,}748)^{(1/\{(92/184)+1\})} - 1]$). Inserting this number into the OID calculation for the first short period, $[\{3{,}748 * (1 + (0.088672114/2))^{(92/184)} - 3{,}748\}/92]$ means Ceily will accrue $.89 of discount per day, or $82.18 for the period ending December 31, Year 4. As of June 30, Year 5, when the coupon matures, she will recognize additional income of $169.82 $[\{3{,}830 * (0.088672114/2)\}/181]$. Consequently, her total adjusted issue price when the coupon is redeemed will amount to $4000 ($3830 + $169.82).

The last coupon Ceily holds matures on December 31, Year 5. Her yield to maturity on this obligation is 0.095198636 $\{2 * [(4{,}000/3{,}561)^{(1/\{(92/184)+2\})} - 1]\}$. Ceily will accrue discount of $83.77 as of December 31, Year 4 $[\{3{,}561 * (1 + (0.095198636/2))^{(92/184)} - 3{,}561\}/92]$. Her discount for the period ending June 30, Year 5, will amount to $173.49 $[\{3{,}644.77 * (0.095198636/2)\}/181]$ and $181.75 $[\{3{,}818.26 * (0.095198636/2)\}/184]$ will accrue at the end of the final period. Again, Ceily's adjusted issue price in the last coupon, as of maturity, will amount to $4000.

STRIPPING TAX-EXEMPT BONDS

At first glance, the rules for bond stripping seem inapplicable to tax-exempt bonds, since the return on these obligations is expected to be tax-free. However, holders of tax-exempt instruments do recognize income or loss if the bonds are sold. This means, for example, that investors in tax-free municipal bonds will need to accrue market discount for the periods while the instrument is held, in order to calculate the amount of ordinary income recognized on any later sale. Unlike a taxable instrument, the seller of a stripped tax-exempt bond or coupon does not recognize the interest that has accrued as of the time of the stripping transaction.[20] However, accrued but previously unreported market discount must be included in income. The seller's adjusted basis in the obligation is increased by both the reported market discount and the tax-free accrued interest.[21]

Example—Edward sells a five-year tax-exempt bond issued by Burkhardt City to Matilda, for $96,366. The bond, which has a face value of $100,000, bears interest coupons that pay $4000 on April 1 and October 1 of each year. Market interest is 9 percent. The bond was issued originally to Edward on April 1, Year 1, and sold by him to Matilda six months later, after the first coupon is paid. Midway between April 1 and October 1 of Year 4, Matilda strips the instrument and sells the coupon due on April 1, Year 6, to Mathias. Prior to the strip, Matilda accrued market discount using a constant interest rate calculation, as shown in Table 16-2.

Matilda is not required to include in income the $2000 of interest that has accrued in connection with the coupon payable on October 1 in the year of sale. However, she must report the market discount that has arisen as of the sale date. Had Matilda held the entire instrument until October 1, Year 4, the accrued market discount on the Burkhardt obligation for the April to October period would have amounted to $419. Therefore she reports $209.50, or half of this amount, in addition to the $1840 of market discount that has arisen between October 1, Year 1 and April 30, Year 4. Her basis in her Burkhardt investment now stands at $100,415.50. This amount will be allocated according to fair market values to determine Matilda's gain or loss on the sale to Mathias of the coupon due April 1, Year 6. Matilda will be treated as having purchased the Burkhardt bond and the coupons she did not sell for an amount equal to her bases in these items as of the date of the

TABLE 16-2

Date	Beginning Balance	Actual Interest (9%, semi.)	Stated Interest (8% semi)	Difference	Ending Balance
10/1/Yr 1					$96,366
4/1/Yr 2	$96,366	$4,336	$4,000	$336	96,702
10/1/Yr 2	96,702	4,352	4,000	352	97,054
4/1/Yr 3	97,054	4,367	4,000	367	97,421
10/1/Yr 3	97,421	4,384	4,000	384	97,805
4/1/Yr 4	97,805	4,401	4,000	401	98,206

sale transaction. As was the case for the April 1, Year 6 coupon Matilda sold, her bases in the retained items will reflect the discount and interest accrued because of the strip.

Under Code §1286, an investor who purchases a stripped tax-exempt obligation can only exclude the same portion of original issue discount as would have been treated as tax-free had the stripping not occurred. In other words, discount that arises not because of the original structure of the bond transaction but instead due to market conditions at the time of the later stripping is not tax-exempt. The tax-free portion of the original issue discount is determined by reducing the stated redemption price at maturity, for a bond, or, for coupons, the amount payable when the instrument is due, by the issue price. The issue price for this purpose is the figure that would generate a yield to maturity, as of the date the investor purchased the stripped obligation, equal to the lower of the following:

1. The coupon rate of interest on the bond from which the coupons were separated; or
2. The yield to maturity based on the price the investor paid for the obligation.[22]

Example—Dorothy purchased a tax-free bond issued by Eighten City, at par. Dorothy strips the bond and sells the four remaining coupons to Warren, at a time when the market rate of interest for comparable obligations is 7 percent, compounded semiannually. The bond will pay principal of $100,000 in two years, when it matures. The coupon rate of interest is 6 percent, also compounded semiannually. The strip occurred on a coupon payment date, so there was no accrued but unpaid interest. Warren paid $11,020 for the four coupons he received. The total fair market value of the coupons and corpus at the time of the strip and disposition was $98,164. This means the bond instrument itself had a fair market value of $87,144 ($98,164 − $11,020).

Dorothy is treated as having purchased the bond corpus for $88,774 as of the date of the stripping transaction. This number is calculated by allocating her total basis, $100,000, according to the fair market values of the coupons and the bond itself [(87,144/98,164) * 100,000]. The yield to maturity on the Eighten bond that Dorothy retained is 6.0433 percent, compounded semiannually [$100,000 = (1+r)^4 * 88,774]. Since this is more than the coupon rate of interest, the issue price for the tax-exempt part of the bond is calculated using the coupon rate (6 percent, compounded semiannually). As a result, Dorothy is treated as having acquired the corpus that she retained in the stripping transaction for a price of $88,849 [$100,000/(1.03)^4]. This means Dorothy has $11,151 of tax-exempt original issue discount in connection with the Eighten obligation ($100,000 − $88,849). Her total original issue discount is $11,226 ($100,000 − 88,774, adjusted basis of corpus after allocation described above). Reducing the total by the tax-exempt amount gives Dorothy taxable original issue discount of $75 to report in connection with the Eighten bond ($11,226 − $11,151).

Warren also must report OID because of his investment. He paid $11,020 for the bonds, based on a current market interest rate for comparable obligations of 7 percent, compounded semiannually. Warren therefore has total original issue discount of $980 ($12,000 − $11,020). Of this amount $849 is tax-free. This figure is determined by reducing the $12,000 Warren will receive when all the coupons are paid by the issue price, calculated using the coupon rate of interest of 6 percent, again compounded semiannually. (Like Dorothy, Warren also uses the lesser of the coupon rate of interest or the yield to maturity, based on the purchase price.[23]) This number works out to be $11,151 [{3,000/1.03} + {3,000/(1.03)^2} + {3,000/(1.03)^3} + {3,000/(1.03)^4}]. Subtracting the tax-exempt OID from the total discount means Warren will report original issue discount of $131 in connection with the coupons ($980 − $849).

Dorothy sold the Eighten items to Warren for $11,020. Her adjusted basis in the coupons was $11,226 [(11,020, fair market value of the coupons,/98,164, fair market value of the entire Eighten investment before the strip) * 100,000, Dorothy's total basis in her Eighten holding]. This means Dorothy recognized a loss of $206 on the sale (11,020 − 11,226). This loss is the same number as the amount of original issue discount Dorothy and Warren will report after the strip transaction ($75 + $131, respectively).

CONCLUSION

Stripping transactions can present other tax questions, many of which are unsettled. For example, it is unclear whether a gift of a stripped bond or stripped coupon is a disposition triggering the application of the IRC §1286 provisions. The IRS has been directed to write regulations providing for rules in cases of instruments with varying rates of interest or where put or call options are involved. To date, however, no regulations have been issued. Investors considering stripping a bond or coupon or acquiring a stripped obligation need to realize that in some cases they may be trying to predict the tax consequences of transactions where little guidance exists. [24]

NOTES

[1] See, for example, *Comm'r v. PG Lake, Inc.,* 356 US 260 (1958).

[2] Code §1286(e)(2). The term "bond" is defined broadly and refers to a "bond, debenture, note, or certificate or other evidence of indebtedness." Code §1286(e)(1)

[3] Code §1286(e)(5)

[4] IRS Publication 550, *Investment Income and Expenses* (2002), at p. 14. Stripped bonds and stripped coupons also may be available through the Resolution Trust Corporation and other government sponsored enterprises. *Id.*

[5] Code §1286(b)(1)

[6] Under Tax Code §1281, the short-term obligation rules apply to stripped bonds or stripped coupons held by the person who stripped the instrument or by someone whose basis is determined by reference to someone who stripped the instrument. Tax Code §1281(b)(1)(F). Short-term obligations are discussed in Chapter 15 of this book. In Catherine's case, the coupon due at the end of Year 2 would be treated as a short-term obligation, since it will mature in not more than one year. However, assuming Catherine is on a calendar year-end, the application of the Code §1281 short-term rules will have no impact. This is because the payment date for the Year 2 coupon is on the last day of Catherine's tax year, meaning she would have recognized that income in any event.

[7] Even without market discount, the Code §1286 rules can accelerate income recognition. For example, assume a calendar year taxpayer holds a bond that pays interest on February 1 and August 1 of each year. If on December 31st the taxpayer sells the coupon payable the following February, he must report interest on the bond that has accrued through December 31st. This is true even though without the strip and sale none of the interest represented by the February coupon would have been includible in current year income.

[8] Code §1286(b)

[9] There is some support in the regulations for using an aggregate approach for allocating basis. In other words, if a stripping transaction involves a pool of debt instruments, allocation would be made by treating the retained interests as one instrument. See Treasury Regulation §1.1275-2(c).

[10] Catherine's new basis in her holdings is $98,345. To allocate the appropriate portion of this figure to the coupon payable 12/31/Year 4, she multiplies by a fraction. The numerator of the fraction is the fair market value of the Year 4 coupon ($6,172) and the denominator is the sum of the fair market values of the bond and all the coupons ($95,681).

[11] Although the issue is not addressed by Code §1286 or the regulations, it appears this loss is capital, assuming a sale of the entire investment, without a stripping transaction, would have generated capital gain or loss.

[12] Again, some support exists for taking an aggregate approach with respect to this rule. See, for example, Treasury Regulation §1.1275-2(c), discussed above.

[13] Code §1286(a)

[14] Code §1286(b). See the discussion in the text at footnote 5 and following regarding recognition of accrued discount or accrued interest because of a bond stripping transaction. The seller's holding period for the retained items is not recalculated, meaning it dates from the time of original acquisition.

[15] IRS Publication 550, *Investment Income and Expenses* (2002), at p. 14

[16] Treasury Regulation §1.1286-1(a) incorporates the de minimis rules of the OID provisions. In general, these rules treat as zero original issue discount that is less than [Q] of 1 percent of the stated redemption price at maturity times the number of years from the date of original issue to maturity.

[17] IRS Publication 1212, *List of Original Issue Discount Instruments* (2002), at p. 14. If the period from the date of purchase to the date of maturity can be evenly divided into full accrual periods with no partial period, the formula used is: $n*[(srp/ap)^{(1/m)} - 1]$.

[18] *Id.*

[19] *Id.*

[20] Code §1286(d)(1)

[21] Code §1286(d)(1)(C)

[22] Code §1286(d)(2)

[23] Tax Code §1286 allows a purchaser of a stripped bond or stripped coupon to elect to use the original yield to maturity instead of the coupon rate of interest. If this option is elected, the issue price would be the amount producing a yield to maturity as of the purchase date equal to the lower of the original yield to maturity or the yield to maturity based on the purchase price of the stripped obligation.

[24] The IRS has issued rules governing the sale of a pool of mortgages by a lender. Where the purchaser enters into a mortgage servicing agreement with the seller/lender, it is possible the transaction will be treated as a stripping arrangement. See Revenue Ruling 91-46, 1991–2 C.B. 358 for further details. Revenue Procedure 91-49 provides rules for market discount treatment in connection with certain mortgage instruments. See 1991-2 C.B. 778.

PART FOUR

Other Financial Instruments and Financial Transactions

17 | OPTIONS AND WARRANTS

INTRODUCTION

Options and warrants offer tremendous versatility in a market that has been highly volatile and unstable. Options offer protection from declines as well as increases in the market. Additionally, they may permit an investor to buy stock at a lower price, sell at a higher price, or create additional income against a position. This chapter describes the various types of options and when they are used. It further discusses the advantages and disadvantages of each type. IRC §1234 is examined, including a breakdown of the taxation rules for investors who purchase and sell options. The use of warrants is also analyzed.

WHAT IS AN OPTION?

An option is a contract whereby the grantor undertakes an obligation to buy or to sell a specific item at an agreed-upon price. The grantor receives a premium for undertaking this obligation. Several factors determine the amount of the premium, including the current price of the underlying asset, the strike price of the option, the time remaining until expiration, and volatility of the market. An option premium on stock is priced on a per-share basis, and each option corresponds to 100 shares. Therefore, if a premium of an option is priced at 3, the total premium would be 3×100 or $300.

Example—Lulu would like to buy stock in Lake Pollute, Inc., a small, privately owned corporation. She knows that there are no shares available, and hears that one shareholder would like to sell her shares. Additionally, she heard that another buyer submitted an offer to purchase shares from the shareholder. There is another corporation, River Blue Ltd. that also has a shareholder willing to sell his shares. In order to be sure that she obtains stock in one of those corporations, she negotiates an option from the shareholder at River Blue for the opportunity to buy his shares at a price of $200,000 within 45 days. The owner agrees to sell her the option for $2500. If Lulu ultimately purchases the shares of stock in Lake Pollute, she loses her $2500. If not, then she has secured for herself the right, but not the obligation, to purchase the shares of River Blue.

Common terms used synonymously are:

- Grantor, writer, or seller
- Other party to the contract, holder, optionee, or buyer
- Agreed-upon price, exercise, or strike price

The grantor or writer of an option is said to be in a "short" position, while the holder or buyer is said to be in a "long" position with respect to the option. Option buyers have the right, but not the obligation, to buy or sell the underlying stock at a specified price until the third Friday of the expiration month.[1] If the holder does not exercise this right, then the obligation will lapse. The option holder must treat any gain or loss attributable to the sale or exchange of an option as though it has the same character as the underlying property to which the option relates.[2]

Some benefits of options include:

- Options allow investors to participate in price movements of the market without committing large amounts of money to buy the stock outright.
- Options can be used to secure a price that is more favorable than the current market price.
- Options enable grantors to earn premium income.
- Options allow investors the flexibility to determine their position relative to their individual financial situation and risk tolerance.

There are two types of options: calls and puts. The market moves up, down, and sideways. Consequently, it is important to assess market movement prior to placing a trade. If the market is going up, you can buy calls, sell puts, or buy stock. Long and short options and underlying assets can be combined in a variety of ways to limit your risk while taking advantage of market movement. Expiration dates vary from one month to more than a year. Long-Term Equity Anticipation Products (LEAPS) are options that have maturities ranging from nine months to several years.[3]

CALL OPTIONS

Call options give the buyer the right to purchase, from the grantor, an underlying asset. Strike price will vary depending on the market price of the underlying instrument. Expiration dates vary from one month to over a year. An investor may decide to buy a call or to sell a call option.

Purchasing a Call Option

When you buy a call option (go long), you are purchasing the right to buy the underlying property at whatever strike price you choose up to the expiration date. Money is made on buying a call when the market price rises above the strike price. At that point, you can exercise the call and sell the underlying property at the current price. Your profit is the difference between the market price and strike price.[4] Alternatively, an investor may choose to offset the call by selling a call with the same strike price and option date. The call's premium increases in value as the market price of the property increases above the strike price. You have the option to buy the property at the lower strike price of the call.

Example—Florence acquires a call option for $3 each to purchase 100 shares of stock from Laura of Healthy Snacks, Inc. at a strike price of $25 per share. The option expires in 45 days. During this period, the market prices reaches $35 per share and Florence decides to exercise her option. She pays $2500 for the shares. Her total basis in the shares is $2800 ($2500 + $300). She then sells the shares for $3500. Florence has a short-term capital gain of $700. If the market price fell below $25 per share, Florence would not exercise her option. She would have a short-term capital loss of $300, the premium paid for the option.[5]

If the current market price is more than the strike price, the call option is said to be in the money (ITM). If the current market price is less than the strike price, the call option is out-of-the money (OTM). If the current market prices and strike prices are the same or very close, then the call option is said to be at-the-money (ATM).

The primary benefit to purchasing calls is that the investor has a lower capital commitment than having to purchase the stock outright. Additionally, calls offer the purchaser a predetermined risk where the maximum loss is the amount of premium paid for the call option. At any time before expiration of the call option, the holder can sell the call to close out his/her position.

Bull Call Spread

Another strategy is to purchase a call option and simultaneously write a call option on the same underlying stock with the same expiration month, but at a higher strike price. This is also known as a vertical spread.[6]

Example—Refer back to the previous example except that Florence wrote a call for $3.50 and a strike price of $32 per share. The holder of her call decided to exercise the option and Florence also exercised her option. The total selling price is $3550 ($3200 strike price + $350 premium received) less her basis of $2800, resulting in a short-term capital gain of $750.

An investor will use this strategy to take advantage of a small advance in the market price of the underlying stock. Additionally, this strategy provides a hedge against losing the entire premium.

Selling a Call Option

If an investor decides to sell (go short) a call option, he/she is selling to the purchaser the right to buy the underlying property at a particular strike price during a particular time. In order to make money, the current market price must stay below the strike price. If the market price rises above the strike price, the option will generally be exercised, and the writer of the option will have to buy the underlying asset at the current price and sell it at the lower strike price. The maximum loss that a writer of a call option can incur is unlimited, depending on current market price increases during the duration of the call option.

Example—Ricardo wrote (sold) a call, for a premium of $3, to sell 100 shares of BaBaLoo Drums Ltd. at $50 per share to Lucy when the current market price is $45. The option expires in 60 days. During this period, the market price never rose over $48. Therefore, the option lapsed and Ricardo had a short-term capital gain of $300, the total premium price he received. If the current market price had risen to $52, then the option would have been exercised. Ricardo would have had to purchase the underlying asset at the price of $52 and sell it to Lucy at $50. He would have had a short-term capital gain of $100 ($300 + $5,000 − $5200).

Covered Call Options Covered calls involve either: (1) purchase of an asset and then writing a call option against this asset, or (2) writing a call option against an asset currently owned by the writer. The premium received helps offset the price of the stock. Additionally, the writer of the call continues to receive dividends from the stock. In either event, the writer of the call risks losing the stock if the current market value rises above the strike price. In exchange for the premium, the writer is obligated to sell the stock.[7]

Example—Ethel purchases 100 shares of BaBaLoo Drums, Ltd. at $50 per share and writes a 60-day call for $2 to Fred at $55 per share. Three possibilities exist at expiration.

1. The call option will expire worthless. The premium and the stock position will be retained. The basis of the stock is $4800, the purchase price of $5000 less the premium received of $200. Ethel must decide if she wishes to write another call extending further in time for an additional premium. This would lower her purchase price of the stock even more.

2. The current market price rose to $60. Fred exercises his option to buy the stock at $55. Ethel's return is calculated as follows:

Sales price received from Fred	$5,500
Plus premium received	200
Less basis in stock sold[8]	(5,000)
Short-term capital gain	$700

3. The current market price is $55. In this situation, if Fred exercises his option, Ethel will be forced to sell her stock at $55 for a net gain of $700. If Fred allows his options to lapse, then Ethel could choose to write another call going further out in time. She would obtain another premium and reduce her purchase price of the stock.

The covered call write is a strategy that many investors may use in various situations, including stock owned in a Keogh plan, margin account, cash account, or IRA. It allows the writer to be paid for assuming the obligation of selling a stock at a particular price and within a specified time.

PUT OPTIONS

Put options give the buyer the right, but not the obligation, to sell an underlying asset for a strike price until the market closes on the third Friday of the expiration month. Put options, just like call options, come in various expiration dates and strike prices, depending on the current market prices of the underlying asset.

Purchasing a Put Option

If an investor buys (goes long) a put option, he/she is purchasing the right to sell the underlying asset at the desired strike price until the expiration date. A profit can be made in one of two ways if the current market price declines.

- A put is purchased without owning the underlying stock. If and when the underlying stock falls below the strike price, the investor can exercise the put and then buy the underlying stock at a lower price to cover the transaction and exit the trade.
- A put can also be offset. If the price of the underlying stock declines, the corresponding put premium increases and can be sold at a profit.[9]

Example—Tootsie developed a new beauty cream that promises to make a person look 20 years younger. A local beauty spa guarantees (put option) an order by a deposit of $1500 to buy 500 jars of the cream in 3 months for $150 each. Tootsie's total cost for each jar is $65. Tootsie now has a guaranteed profit of $42,500 ($75,000 − $32,500). Two months later, Annette developed a competing cream, which she is selling for $100 each. If Tootsie did not have the guaranteed order (put option), she would have to reduce her price to meet her competition. Assume instead that Tootsie is approached by another beauty spa to purchase her cream for $200 each. She is under no obligation to sell her cream to the first health spa, and she is free to accept the higher market price.

The benefits to purchasing a put option include a predetermined, limited financial risk and lower up-front capital requirements. Prior to expiration of the put, an option holder can sell the put to close out the position. This is done to realize a gain from the premium or to cut a loss. Most investors holding an in-the-money put will elect to sell the option in the marketplace prior to expiration. An alternative is to purchase an equivalent number of shares, exercise the long put, and then sell them to a put writer at the option's strike price.

Protective Put Options   The protective put option strategy involves purchasing a put option at the same time that an investor owns the shares of the underlying asset from a previous purchase. The investor generally has unrealized gains in those shares and would purchase a put to protect those gains.[10]

Example—John purchased 100 shares of Moonglow Corp. two years ago for $50. The current market value of Moonglow is $75 per share. Because the stock market has not been doing well over the last year, and rumors indicate that Moonglow will be laying off some of its workers, John would like to protect his gain in this stock. He, therefore, purchases a put for $3, which enables, but not obliges, him to sell his shares for $70 per share. The put expires in 45 days. During this period, the current market value of Moonglow declines to $68. John exercises his option and sells his shares for $70. His long-term capital gain is $1700 ($7000 − $5000 − $300).

The investor retains all the benefits of continuing stock ownership during the life of the contract. However, the protective put limits the downside loss in unrealized gains since the purchase of the stock. No matter how much the current market value of the underlying stock declines, the investor has protected the price, for which he can sell his stock, during the duration of the protective put option. A put owner has the ability to adopt a wait-and-see attitude, while he/she owns the put, during sharp declines in the market. If market prices for the stock rise, then the investor can allow the protective put option to lapse, and the premium paid for the option is considered a short-term capital loss.[11] The investor is free to sell his stock and/or the put option at any time that he owns them.

Married Put Strategy A married put strategy is a hedging strategy whereby an investor purchases a put and at the same time purchases an equivalent number of shares of the underlying stock. The investor enjoys full benefits of stock ownership but has protection from immediate market downturns. Regardless of the amount of decline in the current market price of the underlying asset, the investor has a guaranteed selling price, during the duration of the put option contract, of its strike price. If there is a sudden downturn, the investor has the benefit of not having to make an immediate response.[12]

Example—Prof. Smarts purchases 100 shares of Great Gadgets, Inc. for $50 per share. At the same time, he purchases a put option on these shares for $3, at a strike price of $52, to expire in 90 days. Three possibilities exist:

1. The current market price of the shares goes up. Let's say that at the expiration of the put option, the current market value is $55. Prof.

Smarts will not exercise his option since he can get a better price on the market, and he will let the put expire. He will not recognize a capital loss of $300 for the premium that he paid. Instead, the premium is added to the basis of the underlying stock to which it is identified.[13] If he sells the stock on the open market at the current market price, he will have a short-term capital gain of $200 ($5500 − $5000 − $300).[14]

2. The current market price of the shares goes down. Assume the same facts as above except that at expiration of the put option, the current market price is $48 per share. Prof. Smarts will exercise his put option and sell the stock at the strike price of $52. His has a short-term capital loss of $100 ($5200 − $5000 − $300). However, if he did not have this put option, his loss would have been $200. ($4800 − $5000).

3. The current market price of the shares remains approximately the same as the purchase price. The put option would be allowed to lapse and the loss for the premium paid of $300 would not be recognized but would be added to the basis of the underlying stock.[15]

The investor using a married put is free to sell the underlying stock or the put option at any time during its lifetime.

Selling a Put Option

When an investor chooses to sell (go short) a put option, he/she is selling the right to sell the underlying asset at a certain strike price to the option holder. By writing a put option, the investor anticipates that the option will expire on the expiration date and be worthless. The return is the premium received, which is the maximum profit that can be obtained by selling a put option. If the current market value of the underlying stock falls below the put's strike price, the option holder will probably decide to exercise the option. The writer (seller) of the put option has the obligation to purchase those shares from the option holder at the agreed upon strike price.

Example—Winona wishes to make some extra money. She sells a put option to Poncho for $10 for 100 shares of Future Techs Corp. at a strike price of $50, due to expire in 180 days. The current market price of Future Techs is $150. Winona immediately earned $1000. However, 60 days later, there was an announcement that Future Techs experienced a computer virus prior to backing up its data. It had lost its hard drive and was unable to recapture any data. The stock immediately plunged to $40. Poncho initially purchased his shares for $55 and felt that he should exercise his put option. Winona was obligated to purchase his shares for $50 each and immediately sold them for $40. Winona did not have any gain or loss.

Premium received	$1,000
Less purchase price of stock	(5,000)
Sales price of stock	4,000
Gain/(Loss)	-0-

The put seller must always be ready to have the stock "put" to him/her. The option with little time to maturity is preferred so that there is a greater probability that the option will expire worthless. A short put may be offset by purchasing a put with the same strike price and expiration date.

Bear Put Spread A bear put spread involves the purchase of a put option on an underlying asset while simultaneously writing a put option on the same underlying asset with the same expiration date, but with a lower strike price. The buy and sell sides of this spread are opening transactions and contain the same number of contracts.[16] This spread is also known as a vertical spread and can be illustrated as follows:

Purchase a put option—the right to sell at the strike price of $100

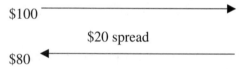

$100

$20 spread

$80

Sell a put option—the obligation to purchase the stock at the strike price of $80.

The price paid for the put with the higher strike price is somewhat offset by the premium received from writing the put with a lower strike price. The long put with the higher strike price caps the risk of the written put with the lower strike price. If the investor's written put is exercised, he/she can sell the purchased put with the higher strike price in the marketplace. The premium received will partially offset the cost of purchasing the shares from the exercise of the put option. The net cost to the investor is usually less than current market prices. The maximum profit usually occurs when the underlying asset price declines below the lower strike price, and both options expire in the money. If the underlying asset is in between the higher and lower strike prices when the puts expire, the purchased put will be in-the-money and be worth its intrinsic value (discussed later). The written put will be out-of-the-money and have no value.

Example—Lisa purchases a put from Paul for $3 for 100 shares of Kinetic Design, Inc., giving her the right to sell the stock at a strike price of $100, due to expire in 180 days. She simultaneously writes a put for $3 for 100 shares of Kinetic Design, Inc., giving her the obligation to buy the stock at a strike price of $80 from Doreen. The price paid for the put with the higher strike price is offset by the premium received from writing the put with the lower strike price. If Doreen exercises her put, Lisa must buy the stock for $80 per share. She will then be able to exercise her put from Paul and sell the stock to him for $100 per share.

Cash Secured Put (Covered Put)   A put writer is obligated to purchase a certain number of underlying shares of an asset at the put's strike price if the put option is exercised by the holder. A put writer is considered to issue a cash secured put (or covered put) if there is on deposit with his/her brokerage firm a cash amount (or other approved collateral) sufficient to cover the purchase of the shares.[17]

There are several reasons for using this strategy:

- It's an incentive to purchase the underlying shares below the current market price.
- There is a desire to retain the premium received from the sale of puts, which expire out-of-the-money.

A covered put should be written only if the investor is comfortable owning the underlying asset. The number of put contracts written should correspond to the number of shares that the investor is capable of purchasing. Otherwise, the strategy can become extremely risky.

Example—Nicholas wrote a put for $5 for 100 shares of Aqua Clean Corp. at a strike price of $100 to expire in 180 days. Nicholas had $10,000 on deposit with his broker. Ninety days later, when the current market price was $95, the option was exercised. Nicholas instructed his broker to purchase the shares at the strike price. Three scenarios could result:

1. Nicholas immediately sells the shares at no gain or loss ($9,500 − $10,000 + $500).
2. If the current market price fell below $95, then the loss would be the difference between $95 and the market price.

3. If Nicholas held on to the stock and the current market price subsequently rose to $106, the net short term capital gain would be $1100 (10,600 − $9,500).[18]

COLLAR

A collar is a strategy whereby an investor owns shares of an underlying asset and simultaneously purchases a protective put and writes a covered call on that stock. The put and the call are initially out of the money when the spread is established. The buy and sell sides of the spread are opening transactions, with the same expiration and same number of contracts. Therefore, one collar equals one long put and one written call along with owning 100 shares of the underlying asset. The primary motive is the protection of unrealized profits versus increasing returns on the upside.[19]

Example—Jackie purchased 100 shares of Cookies Galore, Inc. for $100 per share. A year later, when the fair market value was $130 per share she decided to establish a collar to protect her profit of $30 per share. She purchased a protective put for $3 per share at a strike price of $140 to expire in 90 days. She simultaneously wrote a covered call for which she received a premium of $3 per share, giving the holder of the call option the right to buy the underlying stock at $145 per share. If the stock goes down, Jackie will exercise her put option and sell her shares for $140 per share. Her long-term capital gain is $3700 ($14,000 − $300 − $10,000). Additionally, she will have a short-term capital gain of $300 for the premium received on the call that expired. If the price of the stock goes up, the purchaser of the covered call will exercise his option. Jackie then must sell her stock for $145 per share. Her long-term capital gain is $4800 ($14,500 + $300 − $10,000). She also has a short-term capital loss of $300 for the premium she paid on the protective put.

The collar offers downside put option protection at a smaller cost because the cost of the premium paid is somewhat offset by the premium received on the covered call. The unrealized profit is protected on the downside by the long put.

WARRANTS

A warrant is an option to acquire stock directly from the issuer. They are similar to call options in that they give the holder the right to acquire a specific number of shares at a predetermined price. Warrants usually have an expiration date one or several years from the date of purchase. Alternatively, they may not even have an expiration date. They are usually issued in connection with a private placement of debentures to a lender to obtain a lower interest rate.

Detachable warrants are often issued with other securities, especially debt instruments, as compensation for a reduced interest rate. Warrants can be traded in a secondary market once they are detached.

INTRINSIC AND TIME VALUE OF OPTIONS

Intrinsic value is the amount by which the strike price of an option is in-the-money.[20] It is that portion of an option's price that is not lost due to the passage of time. The intrinsic value of a put option is the amount by which the strike price of the put option exceeds the fair market value of the underlying asset. The intrinsic value of a call option is the amount by which the price of the underlying asset exceeds the strike price.

Example—An individual holding an option to acquire stock for $100 that is currently trading at $110 has an option with an intrinsic value of $10. If the value of the stock declines to $100, the option will be at-the-money. If the value of the stock declines below $100, the option will be out-of-the-money. In the last two cases, the intrinsic value of the option is zero.

Time value is the amount by which the price of an option exceeds its intrinsic value.[21] It is the portion of the premium in excess of intrinsic value. Time value of an option is predicated on how much time is left before expiration of an option. The greater the amount of time left, the greater the chance of the option being in-the-money. Time value is also a function of volatility of the underlying asset. There is a greater possibility that the option will become in-the-money some time during the life of the option contract when it is more volatile. The cost of money is another factor that affects the time value of options. Increases in interest rates tend to produce higher premiums.

EXITING AN OPTION POSITION

There are three ways to earn a profit while owning an option. The first is to exercise it, the second is to offset it with another option, and finally the third is to let it expire worthless. By exercising an option that an investor purchases, he or she is choosing to buy the underlying asset (call) or to sell (put) the underlying asset at the option's strike price. Only the purchaser of the option has the choice to exercise an option.[22]

An offsetting transaction is accomplished by writing or purchasing an option that is exactly opposite from the position held. Therefore, the writer of an option can enter into an offsetting transaction by purchasing an option on the same underlying asset with the same expiration and strike price. Conversely, the holder of an option would enter into an offsetting transaction by writing (selling) an option on the same stock with the same expiration and strike price. Offsetting transactions permit a writer and holder to terminate their positions without exercising the option or waiting for it to lapse.

If an option is not offset or exercised by the time it expires, then the option becomes worthless. If an investor wrote the option, then he/she wants it to become worthless in order to keep the premium and not be obligated to sell the underlying asset. If an investor bought the option, the premium paid is unrefundable, even though the option expired worthless.

SUMMARY OF TAX CONSEQUENCES OF BUYING AND SELLING OPTIONS

The tax rules dealing with purchasers (holders) and sellers (writers) of options are contained in §1234. Neither the purchaser nor seller recognizes any gain or loss upon the opening of a transaction. It doesn't matter whether the option is an equity or nonequity option or whether it was purchased through a dealer.

The purchaser (holder) of an option has a taxable transaction generally eligible for capital treatment (if the underlying asset is a capital asset)[23] when the option:

1. Is sold or exchanged
2. Is allowed to lapse (expire)

The exercise of a call, alone, triggers no taxable event. The premium is merely added to the purchase price and becomes part of the basis in the stock. When the purchaser of a put exercises the option, a taxable event takes place. The premium paid is subtracted by the grantor from the price of the stock in the calculation of the stock's basis. The difference between the basis and the strike price is the capital gain. (An investor would not pay a premium to incur a loss.) If an option is allowed to expire, it is treated as a taxable sale or exchange on the date of expiration.[24]

The seller (writer) of an option does not have a taxable event until the option is exercised, sold, exchanged, or expired. If the seller sells the underlying stock pursuant to exercise of a call, the premium received by the seller increases the amount realized upon the sale of the stock in determining gain or loss.[25] The gain or loss is short term or long term, depending on the holding period of the underlying stock.[26] If the option expires, the premium is short-term capital gain.[27] In the case of a put, the seller of the option would subtract the premium received from the purchase price of the stock upon exercise. The holding period begins on the date of the stock purchase, rather than on the date the put was written.[28]

Record Keeping

It is important for an investor to keep records of all transactions; especially those involved in option trading. Options may or may not be included on the 1099-B received from a broker. If they are listed, there may be no indication whether or not the option was purchased or sold or whether or not it was exercised. There is no consistency in reporting option transactions among brokerage houses. Therefore, good record keeping for tax purposes is imperative.

OPTIONS NOT SUBJECT TO §1234

IRC §1234 applies to options to buy and sell property. Property means stock and securities, commodities, and commodity futures. It does not apply to §1256 contracts that include: (a) any regulated futures contract, (b) any foreign currency contract, (c) any nonequity option, (d) any dealer equity option, and (e) any dealer securities futures contract.[29] (IRC §1256 is discussed in Chapter 18.) Additionally, §1234 does not apply to options used in hedging transactions, compensatory options, warrants, or a married put.[30]

CONCLUSION

The use of options protects investors from losses in the market as well as providing unlimited profit potential without having to own the underlying stock. Therefore, the expenditure of capital is substantially reduced while allowing participation in the market. However, risks can be substantial, especially if an investor writes a number of options without having sufficient capital to obtain the underlying stock. Caution, planning, education, and professional advice are all required for successful trading in options markets.

NOTES

[1] Optionetics, *www.optionetics.com*

[2] §1234(a)(1)

[3] Optionetics, *www.optionetics.com*

[4] The Options Industry Council, *www.optionscentral.com*

[5] Rev. Rul. 78-182, 1978-1 C.B. 265

[6] The Options Industry Council, *www.optionscentral.com*

[7] Options Learning Center presented by the Chicago Board Options Exchange, *www.cboe.com*

[8] This is for illustrative purposes. In reality, as indicated above, the premium would be subtracted from the purchase price of the stock for a basis of $4800.

[9] The Options Industry Council, *www.optionscentral.com*

[10] *Id.*

[11] §1234(b)(1)

[12] The Options Industry Council, *www.optionscentral.com*

[13] Reg. §1.1234-1(c)

[14] This is the bottom line capital gain. However, if the option lapses, then gain/loss is calculated on the option alone. Since the sale of stock did not involve the exercise of the option, the premium would not be used to determine the basis of the stock.

[15] Reg. §1.1234-1(c)

[16] The Options Industry Council, *www.optionscentral.com*

[17] *Id.*

[18] $9,500 represents the basis in the stock which is $10,000 purchase price reduced by the $500 premium.

[19] The Options Clearing Corporation, *www.optionsclearing.com*

[20] Optionetics, OptionsXPress, *http://biz.yahoo.com*

[21] *Id.*

[22] Optionetics, OptionsXPress, *http://biz.yahoo.com/opt/basics2.html*

[23] §1234(a)

[24] §1234(a)(2)

[25] Rev. Rul. 78-182, 1978-1 C.B. 265

[26] *Id.*

[27] *Id.*

[28] *Id.*

[29] §1256(b)

[30] See Reg. §1.1234-4 (hedging transactions); Reg. §1.1234-3 (compensatory options); Code §1032(a) (warrants); and Reg. §1.1234-1(c) (married puts)

18 MARK-TO-MARKET AND 60/40 RULES

INTRODUCTION

In the early 1980s, Congress enacted rules governing certain transactions that the legislators felt were manipulative practices regarding recognition of income and losses. For example, taxpayers could structure investments to create losses for the current tax year, at a cost of long-term capital gains reported later.

Example—In Year 1, Barney enters into a futures contract to buy commodity X and at the same time also enters a second futures arrangement, under which he is obligated to sell the same commodity in a different month. Barney is a calendar year taxpayer. Both of his contracts are for the same amount of X, to be sold at the same price, and each contract had the same initial cost to Barney. While he holds both positions, the price of X falls. As a result, at the end of the year Barney's contract to sell X reflects an increase in value, while his futures position requiring him to buy has generated a comparable decrease.

On December 31, Year 1, Barney closes out the depreciated futures position, and reports a loss of $2500 for tax purposes. He uses this loss to offset income from an unrelated investment. Barney continues to hold the appreciated position, under which he will sell X. At the same time as he closes out the first contract, however, Barney enters a new futures arrangement, to replace the loss position he sold. Like the liquidated investment, this agreement obligates Barney to buy X, but delivery will not occur in the same month as under the terminated position. In the following year, Barney closes out both the original (sell) and the replacement (buy) futures contracts. Because the price of the commodity has continued to fall, he reports $3300 in gain on the futures position obligating him to sell X and a loss of $800 on the replacement contract. Barney's total loss is $3300, consisting of the $2500 reported in the first year and the $800 shown on his tax return in Year 2, the year of sale.

Because Barney's income and loss are both $3300, it appears his futures investments at best represented a wash, but more likely a loss, considering transaction expenses. However, Barney actually made money, after taking into account the tax consequences of his investments, assuming that no special rule applies. He reported a short-term capital loss of $2500 in Year 1, which he used to offset a short-term capital gain. If Barney's marginal tax rate is 35 percent, this loss generated tax savings of $875 because short-term capital gain is not eligible for reduced capital gain taxation rates.[1] If Barney has no other capital gain or loss in Year 2; the $800 of short-term capital loss arising from the sale of the replacement position will offset some of the income he reports from liquidating the original appreciated contract to sell X. As a result, Barney will report $2500 of long-term capital gain from the appreciated position, assuming he held the contract for longer than one year.

If long-term capital gain is taxed at a 20-percent rate, Barney will pay $500 of tax when he closes both positions.[2] This means he has savings of $375, the difference between the value of the loss he reported in Year 1 and the additional tax he paid in Year 2. In addition, Barney managed to claim the loss in the first year of the investment, while he delayed recognition of the gain until the following year. In other words, Barney's savings are even greater than $375, taking into account the time value of money.

To combat Barney's strategy, Congress adopted two major principles. Under Code §1256, discussed in this chapter, investors holding certain kinds of contracts must report gain or loss using "mark-to-market" principles. This requires the contracts to be treated as sold on the last day of the tax year and gain or loss recognized. Assuming the contracts represent capital assets, the increase or decrease in value is reported as a mixture of short- and long-term capital gain or loss. The second principle defers recognition of certain losses. These rules are found at Tax Code §1092 and are discussed in Chapter 20.[3]

CONTRACTS SUBJECT TO SECTION 1256

The mark-to-market and 60/40 rules of IRC §1256 cover only certain kinds of investments. Specifically, the rules apply to "§1256 contracts," defined as regulated futures contracts, foreign currency contracts, nonequity options, dealer equity options, and any dealer securities futures contract.[4]

Regulated Futures Contracts

Like a forward contract, a futures contract involves an agreement for the purchase or sale of a specific amount of an asset at a specific future date, with the price set at the time the future is entered. Unlike a forward contract, futures are traded on an organized exchange, like the Chicago Board of Trade.[5] A forward contract may involve the actual delivery of the commodity or be cash-settled; the majority of futures are closed by entering into a reversing trade on a futures exchange.[6] In other words, an investor who holds a futures contract obligating him to sell a specific quantity of commodity X enters into a second futures arrangement to buy the exact same commodity, under the same terms. The original position and the offsetting position cancel each other out, and the investor therefore is under no further obligation.

Futures contracts are marked to market through the mechanism of the futures exchanges. This occurs at the end of each business day.

Example—Fritz holds a "long" position on corn. (A long position means the investor has entered into a futures contract to buy corn on some specified date.) If the price of corn increases, the value of the long position also rises. This gain is posted to Fritz's margin account. Had he held a short position, meaning a futures contract to sell, an increase in the price of corn would have reduced the value of the investment. This decrease would have generated a corresponding reduction in the margin account.[7] If the balance of the margin account falls too far, Fritz will be required to restore it. These settlements occur at the end of every trading day.[8] If, for example, on the second day of his investment the price of corn rises again, additional gain will be posted to Fritz's margin account.

The Tax Code §1256 rules apply only to "regulated futures contracts." This means the futures contract meets two requirements, both of which are consistent with the discussion above. First, the amount an investor must deposit or is permitted to withdraw from a margin account in connection with the contract is dependent on a marked-to-market system. Second, the contract must be traded on or subject to the rules of a qualified board or exchange.[9] A qualified board or exchange is a domestic board of trade designated as a contract market by the Commodity Futures Trading Commission (CFTC), plus any board or exchange approved by the Treasury. (A national securities exchange registered with the Securities and Exchange Commission also qualifies.)[10] Because futures contracts in the United States can only be traded on an exchange that the CFTC has designated as a contract market, all futures contracts traded on domestic exchanges meet this second requirement. Also, certain foreign futures exchanges have been designated by the IRS as qualified, like the Mercantile Division of the Montreal Exchange.[11]

Foreign Currency Contracts

The Code §1256 rules also apply to "foreign currency contracts." These are contracts that meet three requirements:

1. The contract must require delivery of a foreign currency that has positions traded through regulated futures contracts. Alternatively, a contract the settlement of which depends on the value of that type of foreign currency also meets this part of the definition.[12]
2. The contract must be traded on an interbank market.[13] According to the IRS, the term "interbank market" refers to an over-the-counter market that banks use to buy and sell foreign currency and financial products. This is not a formal market but instead a group of banks that hold themselves out to the public as willing to enter certain transactions.[14]
3. Additionally, the investment must be entered into at arm's length, at a price determined by reference to the price in the interbank market.[15] Referring to the legislative history, a price based on one obtained from a bank that is a substantial participant in the interbank market would meet this requirement.[16]

Example—Mike enters into a forward contract requiring him to buy Italian lire. Since Italian lire are not traded through regulated futures contracts, this investment is not subject to the §1256 rules. In other words, the mark-to-market requirements do not apply, and Mike will recognize gain or loss under the usual tax principles. However, Mike also purchases a second forward contract, obligating him to sell Canadian dollars. Because Canadian dollars are traded through regulated futures contracts, this second investment meets the first test described above. If Mike entered into the Canadian dollar agreement with a futures commission merchant who participates in the interbank market, the second test is also satisfied.[17] This means Mike will have to use the mark-to-market rules for the Canadian dollar forward contract, assuming the price for his investment was set at arm's length through the interbank market.

A taxpayer who holds a foreign currency contract with unrealized gain or loss or who disposed of such an investment during the tax year should receive a Form 1099-B, or its equivalent, from her broker, summarizing the results to be reported for tax purposes. (This form is also received by investors who hold regulated futures contracts.) A bank forward contract that has a maturity date longer than the maturities usually available for regulated futures contracts may be treated as a foreign currency contract if the three conditions described above are met.[18]

Nonequity Options

Nonequity options, also subject to the mark-to-market and 60/40 rules of Tax Code §1256, are defined as any listed option that is not an equity option.[19] This means options on debt, on commodities futures, and on currency are all nonequity.[20] A broad-based stock index option also is treated as nonequity. In other words, an option based on the Standard and Poor's 500 Index or similar group of diversified stocks or securities would be treated as a nonequity option.[21] Nonequity options include listed options on U.S. Treasury notes, on regulated futures contracts, and on commodities like grain.

For most taxpayers, the mark-to-market rules do not apply to equity options. An equity option is an option to buy or sell stock or an option that is valued directly or indirectly based on any stock or narrow-based security index.[22] This means, for example, that an option based on a composite of oil industry stocks would be treated as equity and therefore not subject to the mark-to-market and 60/40 rules. Warrants based on a stock index are treated as stock index options, where the warrants are economically and substantially identical to options based on a stock index.[23] In other words, a warrant grounded on a broad-based stock index would be treated as a nonequity option and therefore would be subject to the §1256 rules.

Example—In the current year, Jessie holds a call on A Company stock, meaning an option to buy shares in the corporation. She also owns an option on silver futures. Both contracts are held as investments. By year end, the value of the silver futures option increased by $1000, while the A Co. stock option lost $1800. Neither asset is liquidated at the end of the year. Although overall Jessie lost $800, she must report income in the current year under §1256 in connection with her silver futures investment, which is a nonequity option. However, since there is no corresponding mark-to-market rule applicable to equity options held by investors, Jessie will not be able to use the loss from the A Co. stock option to offset the gain she reports on the silver futures investment.

Dealer Equity Options

As the language suggests, the Code provision subjecting dealer equity options to the mark-to-market rules is of concern only for options dealers. An options dealer, in general, is anyone registered with an appropriate national securities exchange as a market maker or specialist in listed options.[24] A "dealer equity option" is a listed option that meets all the following requirements:

1. The option is an equity option.[25] As noted above, this would include an option to buy or sell stock, for example.
2. The option is purchased or granted by the dealer in the normal course of his or her option-dealings activities.[26] This means, for instance, that an options dealer who acquires a call on B Corp. stock for investment and not as part of his dealing operations would not be subject to the mark-to-market rules as to the B holdings.
3. The option is listed on the qualified board or exchange on which the options dealer is registered.[27]

Summarizing the discussion of nonequity and dealer equity options, the tax treatment of these investments can be described as follows:

1. Regardless of whether the taxpayer is an investor or a dealer, nonequity options are subject to the rules contained in §1256.
2. Equity options held by investors are not covered by IRC §1256. Instead, these are reported under the §1234 rules, discussed in Chapter 17.
3. Dealer equity options are subject to the provisions of §1256. However, equity options owned by the dealer as an investment are governed by the §1234 rules.

Dealer Securities Futures Contracts

The final category of §1256 contracts also affects only dealers. A dealer is required to mark-to-market any securities futures contract and also options on such contracts, provided that certain conditions are met. Specifically, the contract or option must be a part of the dealer's normal course of dealing and must be traded on a qualified board or exchange. A person is a dealer if the IRS determines that he or she performs functions with respect to securities futures contracts or options on these contracts that are comparable to the functions performed by options dealers.[28] A securities futures contract is any security future, as defined under the 1934 Securities Exchange Act.[29] In general, this term refers to a contract of sale of a single security or a narrow-based security index, to be delivered in the future.[30]

INCOME RECOGNITION UNDER THE MARK-TO-MARKET RULES

Under the mark-to-market provisions, all §1256 contracts that an investor holds at the end of the tax year are treated as though they were sold for fair market value. The resulting gain or loss must be reported for income tax purposes, even though no actual sale has taken place.[31] The legislative history behind these rules indicates that the settlement price, as determined by the appropriate exchange, generally is used as the measure of fair market value.[32] In other words, §1256 contracts are treated as though they were sold for an amount equal to the settlement price as reported by the exchange for the §1256 investment, as of the last business day of the tax year. This price does not reflect transaction costs that the investor would have incurred had an actual sale taken place.

Example—Dusty holds a regulated futures contract under which she is required to sell commodity X, meaning Dusty holds a short position. As of December 31, Year 1, the price of X has fallen, so that Dusty has $1000 of gain on her futures investment. As a result, she reports $1000 of income in the current year, despite the fact that had her short position actually been liquidated, Dusty would have included in income the $1000 reduced by the expenses of the liquidating transaction. Assume that on January 10 of Year 2 the price of X rises, so that the value of Dusty's contract drops and she closes out the investment at a loss. Dusty includes this loss in income in Year 2; the existence of the Year 2 loss has no effect on the gain she is required to report in Year 1.

The mark-to-market rules require adjustments to be made for income or loss recognized as a result of the sales deemed to occur at year-end.[33]

This adjustment prevents multiple recognition of the same gain or loss. This could occur when investments deemed to be sold at the close of the tax year are actually closed out later, in a taxable transaction.

Example—In Year 1, Ike invests in regulated futures contracts, representing a long position in corn. Ike is a calendar-year taxpayer. The contracts call for delivery of 10,000 bushels in September of Year 2 at a price of $2.25 per bushel. At year-end, the price of September corn futures has risen to $2.50 per bushel. As a result, Ike reports a gain of $2500 under the mark-to-market rules [($2.50−$2.25)*10,000]. On April 20, Year 2, when the price of September corn rises to $2.60 per bushel, Ike closes out her investment by offset. Her total gain is $3500 [($2.60−$2.25)*10,000]. However, Ike's gain for tax purposes is limited to $1000 [$2.60−$2.50)*10,000].

Had the price of September corn fallen to $2.10 per bushel on December 31, Year 1, Ike would have reported a loss in Year 1 of $1500 [($2.25−2.10)*10,000]. Again, assuming the September corn price rises to $2.60 per bushel when Ike liquidates her investment on April 20, Year 2, she now will report a gain of $5000 for tax purposes [($2.60−$2.10)*10,000]. Even though Ike paid $2.25 per bushel for the futures contract, she is treated as having acquired the September corn rights at a per-bushel cost of $2.10, the value to which her corn investment was marked down as of December 31, Year 1.

Character of Gain or Loss Recognized

There are special rules for determining the character of the gain or loss recognized under the mark-to-market system. Regardless of holding period, the Code provides that 40 percent of all gain or loss arising from §1256 contracts is short-term, with the remaining 60 percent characterized as long-term.[34] This rule only applies where §1256 contracts qualify as capital assets.[35] In other words, the 60/40 rule does not convert ordinary income or loss into capital.[36] However, the provision does cover both the deemed sales required under the mark-to-market rules and, as discussed later, any actual terminations or transfers of an investor's position.[37]

Example—Buster enters into a regulated futures contract involving a long position on silver. He also holds listed options on U.S. Treasury bonds that qualify as nonequity options under IRC §1256. At the end of the year, the value of Buster's Treasury bond options has risen by $1000, but the silver future dropped by $400. This means Buster will report $600 of long-term capital gain (60 percent * $1,000) and $240 of long-term capital loss (60 percent * $400), for a net long-term gain of $360. His net short-term gain will amount to $240 [(40 percent * $1000)−(40 percent * $400)].

In the following year, Buster liquidates his T-bond position but continues to hold the silver interest. Assume he has a gain of $800 on the termination of his listed Treasury bond options and a further gain of $500 when the silver future is marked to market at year-end. For tax purposes, Buster will report $780 of long-term capital gain [60 percent * ($800 + $500)]. His short-term gain will amount to $520 [40 percent * ($800 + $500)].

Corporate taxpayers receive only minimally preferential treatment on net capital gain.[38] As a result, characterization of 60 percent of the income arising from a Code §1256 contract as long-term capital in most cases will not represent a substantial tax saving. However, the 60/40 rule can still affect a corporation's tax liability, as in cases where the organization has long- or short-term capital losses arising from other transactions that will be used to offset the §1256 income.

Termination of Section 1256 Contracts

The termination of an IRC §1256 contract triggers application of the mark-to-market and 60/40 rules. In the example above, this means that if Buster terminated his futures investment by offset, he is treated as having sold the §1256 contract for its fair market value.[39] Presumably his basis is the initial price of the contract, adjusted to reflect the gain reported under the mark-to-market rules previously.

Similar rules apply where §1256 contracts are liquidated by other methods. For example, when an investor terminates a regulated futures contract representing a long position in wheat by taking delivery, he must take into account the fair market value of the futures investment as of the date of termination. The investor takes a basis in the wheat he acquires pursuant to the futures arrangement equal to the price paid under the futures agreement, plus or minus gain or loss recognized under §1256. Where a contract is terminated by exercise or by making delivery, again the investment is treated as though it were sold for fair market value.[40] If an investor holds a straddle that consists of two or more §1256 contracts and she takes delivery or exercises any one of them, a special rule applies. Under this rule, the remaining §1256 contract(s) are considered terminated and treated as though they were sold for fair market value. Thereafter the investor is deemed to have acquired new §1256 contract(s), with terms identical to the retained agreement(s).[41] Straddles, in general, represent offsetting positions in personal property. They are discussed in further detail later in this chapter and also in Chapter 20.

Treatment of §1256 Losses

If an individual taxpayer sells a capital asset at a loss, generally he or she is not allowed to carry the loss back to offset gain in an earlier year.[42] However, the Tax law permits a noncorporate investor with "net §1256 contracts loss" to elect to carry the losses back for three years. "Net §1256 contracts loss" is defined as the lesser of the following:

1. The taxpayer's net capital losses for the year, taking into account only §1256 contract gains or losses; or
2. The capital loss carryover for the year, determined without any carryback election under §1256.[43]

The example below, based on an illustration included in the legislative history, is useful for purposes of understanding these rules.

Example—In 2001, Sly reports the following:

- Net losses from regulated futures contracts, marked to market-($100,000)
- Short-term capital loss from non-§1256 investments-($3000);
- Long-term capital gain from non-§1256 asset—$50,000

Sly has no other capital or §1256 transactions in 2001. Under the §1256 rules, 60 percent of her futures losses are long-term and are used to offset the gain from the non-§1256 asset. Additionally, §1211[44] allows Sly to use the $3000 of short-term capital loss to offset ordinary income. This means she has $50,000 of loss not yet used, which represents her net §1256 contracts loss. Sly elects to carry this loss back to 1998. Under the Code rules, the loss carried to an earlier year cannot exceed Sly's "net §1256 contract gain" reported in that year. The definition of net §1256 contract gain is similar to the discussion above. Specifically, this gain is equal to the lesser of

1. Capital gain net income for the carryback year, calculated by taking into account only §1256 contract gains and losses; or
2. Capital gain net income for the carryback year.[45]

The loss must be carried to the earliest eligible tax year first. The 60/40 rule applies in each carryback year.[46] This means $20,000 of the $50,000 loss Sly carried back to 1998 will be short-term, while $30,000 is long-term loss. Assume that three years earlier, Sly reported §1256 gain of $50,000 and a long-term loss of $30,000 from non-§1256 sources. The $30,000 loss offset the amount of Sly's 1998 §1256 gain that is treated as long-term (60 percent * $50,000 = $30,000). This left $20,000 of short-term gain for 1998 (40 percent * $50,000), and therefore Sly can use $20,000 of carried back losses.[47] The $30,000 of unused losses will be carried back to 1999 and 2000. If she has no net §1256 contract gain in either of those years, the remaining losses are carried forward to 2002.[48]

A §1256 loss carryback cannot be used to create or increase a net operating loss in the year to which the §1256 loss is being carried. The election to carry net §1256 losses back is made by filing an amended tax return for the carryback year. Include an amended Form 6781, *Gains and Losses from Section 1256 Contracts and Straddles.*[49]

STRADDLES

Investors holding straddles need to know the tax rules that apply to these transactions. A straddle, in general, is defined as a set of offsetting positions with respect to personal property. A purchased option to buy and a purchased option to sell the same number of shares of a security, in the same period and at the same exercise price, would be considered a straddle.[50] In addition to other restrictions, investors who hold straddles may be required to defer their recognition of loss, under §1092, and also to capitalize certain interest and other costs. Straddles are discussed in further detail in Chapter 20; this chapter focuses on how the §1256 rules affect these investments.

Straddles Consisting of only §1256 Contracts

If a straddle consists solely of §1256 contracts, meaning the mark-to-market and 60/40 rules apply to each part of the transaction, the special straddle provisions of §1092 and the capitalization of interest, etc., requirements are not applicable.[51]

Example—Callie holds a straddle consisting of two §1256 contracts. In the current year, she closes out one of the positions for a loss of $4000. The remaining position, which Callie retains, shows a gain of $2200. Under the loss deferral rules of §1092, Callie normally would be able to claim only $1800 of the loss on her current-year tax return. However, since the retained position shows a gain that Callie will have to report under the mark-to-market rules, the entire $4000 loss will be recognized.

Mixed Straddles

Under IRC §1256, a straddle that consists of both non-§1256 and §1256 contracts is considered a "mixed straddle."[52] There are various tax consequences for holding mixed straddles, some of which are unfavorable.

1. If a gain exists on the §1256 contract position at year-end, this gain must be reported under the mark-to-market rules.[53] However, since these rules do not apply to the non-§1256 position, any corresponding loss on that leg of the straddle is not taken into account.

   Example—Jasmine holds a mixed straddle consisting of a §1256 contract and a non-§1256 position. At the end of the year, the §1256 contract has appreciated in value and as a result, Jasmine recognizes gain under the mark-to-market rules. However, since these rules do not apply to the non-§1256 position, none of the loss Jasmine realized on that leg of the straddle can be used to offset the gain she reports on the contract marked to market, unless she actually liquidates the non-§1256 leg in the current year.

2. Under the mark-to-market rules, a taxpayer who holds a §1256 contract that has fallen in value will recognize that loss at year-end. However, the deferral rules of IRC §1092, discussed in Chapter 20, allow this loss to be recognized only to the extent that it exceeds the unrecognized gain on the non-§1256 leg in the straddle.[54]

   Example—Continuing with the facts above, assume instead that at year-end, Jasmine's §1256 contract had dropped in value by $500 while the value of the non-§1256 leg of the straddle increased by $600. Since the mark-to-market rules do not apply to non-§1256 contracts, Jasmine is not required to include in income any of the

$600 of appreciation on the non-§1256 position. However, she also is not permitted to claim any of the $500 loss. This is because her loss does not exceed her unreported gain.

3. The "killer" rule, found in the Code §1092 regulations, converts loss from a non-§1256 contract into loss subject to the 60/40 rule, if certain conditions are met.[55]

Example—Larry owns a mixed straddle, which he acquired earlier this year. At year-end, he liquidates the investment. Larry reports a gain of $1075 on the §1256 position and a loss of $1000 on the non-§1256 leg. Since he held the straddle for less than 12 months, Larry normally would expect to report short-term capital loss on the non-§1256 position, which could be used to offset short-term capital gain that otherwise would be taxed as ordinary income. If Larry is in a 35-percent tax bracket, he would anticipate savings of $350 because of this loss. However, if $600 of Larry's loss is treated as long-term capital, he will save only $260, assuming long-term capital gain is taxed at a 20 percent rate [($400 * .35) + ($600 * .2)]. This means application of the killer rule will cost Larry $90 in tax savings. The killer rule is discussed in greater detail in Chapter 20.

Various elections can be made under the loss deferral rules of IRC §1092 to avoid some of these harsh results.[56] In addition, an investor who holds a mixed straddle can elect under §1256 to have the mark-to-market and 60/40 provisions not apply to the §1256 contract(s) in the straddle.[57] If this election is made, the investor gives up the right to report any gain from the position under the 60/40 rule. If the investor is an individual and the gain otherwise would constitute short-term capital gain, which is taxed at ordinary income rates, giving up 60/40 treatment is unfavorable.[58] However, if the §1256 position generates a short-term loss, individuals are better off avoiding application of this rule.

Example—Paula enters into a mixed straddle in March of the current year. Six months later, she reports $500 of gain on the §1256 position in the straddle, when she liquidates this part of her investment. Since Paula held the §1256 contract for less than one year, the $500 of gain is short-term, and under the normal capital gain rules would be taxed the same as ordinary income. If Paula has a 35-percent marginal tax rate, this means she must pay $175 in tax on the gain. However, if the 60/40 rule applies, 60 percent, or $300, of Paula's gain is taxed as long-term capital. Assuming a 20-percent tax rate, Paula's total tax bill on the $500 of gain will amount to $130 [($200

* .35) + ($300 * .2)]. She saves $45 because of the 60/40 rule. Paula's savings will be even greater if her long-term capital gain is taxed at 15 percent.

Assume instead, however, that Paula had liquidated both legs of the straddle, at an overall loss of $500 that was attributable to the §1256 position. If Paula's net capital gain is taxed at 20 percent, in this case, the 60/40 rule will cost her $45. This is because instead of being able to use all the loss to offset short-term capital gain taxed as ordinary income, 60 percent is treated as long-term capital loss. Therefore it will reduce income otherwise taxed at favorable long-term capital gain rates, assuming Paula has at least $300 of long-term capital gain income in the current year.

The restrictions found in Code §1092, including the loss deferral provisions and the modified short sale and wash sale rules, will apply where a taxpayer avoids the mark-to-market and 60/40 provisions by making the §1256(d) election in connection with a mixed straddle investment.[59] In order to avoid the loss deferral rules, the taxpayer also would need to identify the straddle under the §1092 provisions. This is discussed in further detail in Chapter 20.

Example—Jill invests in a mixed straddle. To avoid application of some of the provisions discussed above, she makes an election to treat the §1256 leg of her investment as a non-§1256 position. However, Jill does not identify the straddle under IRC §1092. Because of her §1256(d) election, Jill will not have to mark either position in her straddle investment to market at year-end. This means she will not have to report any gain if the position that otherwise would be treated as a §1256 contract has appreciated in value. Also, because of her election, Jill is not subject to the killer rule, which otherwise would convert non-§1256 gain or loss into items reported under the 60/40 rule. However, if in the current year Jill liquidates either straddle position at a loss, the deferral rules of §1092 will prevent her from using it currently, assuming the loss does not exceed the unrecognized gain on the retained part of the straddle investment.

The election under §1256(d) is made by checking the box labeled "Mixed Straddle Election" ("Election A") on Form 6781, *Gains and Losses from Section 1256 Contracts and Straddles*. The election can be revoked only with IRS consent.[60] In order to make the election, each position forming part of the straddle must be clearly identified as such on the day the first §1256 contract forming part of the straddle is acquired. The §1256(d) election is an alternative to the mixed-straddle elections discussed in Chapter 20.[61] In other words, the advantages and disadvantages of all the options for mixed straddles should be compared before an election is made.

EXCEPTIONS TO THE MARK-TO-MARKET AND 60/40 RULES

The §1256 provisions do not apply to certain transactions. These include the following:

1. Hedging transactions. A "hedging transaction" is defined as a transaction entered into in the normal course of a taxpayer's trade or business, primarily to manage risks relating to price changes or currency fluctuations on ordinary property the taxpayer owns or will own. It also includes transactions to manage risk of interest rate or price changes or currency fluctuations on borrowings or ordinary obligations. This means that a manufacturer that enters a short position on a commodity it produces, in order to guarantee a minimum price when the goods are sold later, is not required to mark the contract to market at year-end.[62] However, a speculator who engages in a hedging transaction to minimize the risk of the investment position she holds cannot use this exception to the §1256 rules.[63] Similarly, the exception is unavailable to "syndicates." A partnership that allocates more than 35 percent of its losses during the taxable year to limited partners would be an example of a syndicate.[64]

2. Under Tax Code §988, certain otherwise separate transactions are to be combined for tax purposes. Transactions targeted by §988 include, for example, hedging transactions that manage the risk of currency fluctuations with respect to property held by the taxpayer. The mark-to-market and 60/40 rules of §1256 do not apply to separate positions of a transaction integrated under the §988 provisions. However, the integrated transaction itself may be subject to the §1256 rules.

THE §1256 RULES

IRC §1256 was enacted by Congress as part of a package of revisions designed to prevent certain favorable treatment for investors. Taxpayers interested in acquiring §1256 assets, like regulated futures contracts or nonequity options, need to be sure their proposed investment makes economic sense, after factoring in the effect of the mark-to-market and 60/40 rules. Investors holding §1256 contracts as part of a straddle or hedging arrangement may be able to avoid the operation of these provisions in certain cases. However, qualifying for these exceptions may trigger application of other special rules, meaning caution is required.

NOTES

[1] Taxation of capital gains and losses is discussed in Chapter 1.

[2] Under the 2003 tax legislation, most individual taxpayers with long-term capital gains will be taxed at a 15-percent rate, although in some cases a 5-percent or 0-percent rate may apply. See the discussion of the 2003 tax legislation's capital gain rules in Chapter 1.

[3] Tax Code §1092 also incorporates modified wash sale and short sale rules. See Chapter 20.

[4] Tax Code §1256(b)

[5] Smithson, *Managing Financial Risk* (McGraw-Hill, 1998) at p. 89

[6] *Id.*

[7] *Id.* at p. 92–94

[8] *Id.* at 92

[9] Tax Code §1256(g)(1)

[10] Tax Code §1256(g)(7)

[11] Rev. Rul. 86-7, 1986-1 C.B. 295

[12] Tax Code §1256(g)(2)(A)

[13] *Id.*

[14] Field Service Advice Memorandum 200025020, March 17, 2000

[15] Tax Code §1256(g)(2)(A)

[16] Technical Corrections Act of 1982, (Pub. L. No. 448, 97th Cong., 2d Sess.) Conf. Rep. at 25.

[17] *Id.* The legislative history indicates that generally contracts between commercial banks and another person also are treated as traded in the interbank market. *Id.*

[18] IRS Publication 550, *Investment Income and Expenses* (2002) at p. 37. The IRS has held that a nonregulated foreign currency futures contract may qualify as a foreign currency contract. See Field Service Advice Memorandum 200025020, March 17, 2000.

[19] Tax Code §1256(g)(3). A listed option is an option traded on or subject to the rules of a qualified board or exchange. The term does not include the right to acquire shares from an issuer. Tax Code §1256(g)(5)

[20] IRS Publication 550, *Investment Income and Expenses* (2002), at p. 37

[21] *Id.* at p. 37–38. Cash-settled options based on a stock index that are traded or subject to the rules of a qualified board of exchange are nonequity if the SEC has designated the index as broad-based. *Id.* The IRS has identified other options to be treated as nonequity. See, for example, Revenue Ruling 87-67, holding that an option on the Institutional Index of the American Stock Exchange is a nonequity option. 1987-2 C.B. 212.

[22] IRS Publication 550, *Investment Income and Expenses* (2002), at p. 38

[23] Rev. Rul. 94-63, 1994-2 C.B. 188

[24] Tax Code §1256(g)(8). The IRS has authority to designate as options dealers other persons who perform functions similar to options dealers in markets the IRS has identified

as having rules adequate to carry out the purposes of §1256. Tax Code §1256(g)(8)(B), referring back to Tax Code §1256(g)(7)(C).

[25] Tax Code §1256(g)(4)(A). An equity option would include an option on a narrow-based security index. Tax Code §1256(g)(6)

[26] Tax Code §1256(g)(4)(B)

[27] Tax Code §1256(g)(4)(C)

[28] Tax Code §1256(g)(9). The 60/40 rule applies to gains or losses on dealer securities futures contracts. See the discussion later in this chapter.

[29] Tax Code §1256(g)(9), referring to Tax Code §1234B

[30] IRS Publication 550, *Investment Income and Expenses* (2002), at p. 71. Tax Code §1234B governs the tax treatment of gain or loss from the sale, exchange or termination of a securities futures contract. In general, the gain or loss is to be treated the same as gain or loss from the sale or exchange of property with the same character as the property involved in the contract. Tax Code §1234B. In other words, if the securities futures contract involves a capital asset, gain or loss on the termination of the contract will be capital. If gain or loss on a securities futures contract to sell property is treated as capital, it generally will be characterized as short-term. Tax Code §1234B(b). Gain or loss on a long securities futures contract may be long- or short-term, depending on the holding period of the contract. The term "securities futures contract" is defined by reference to the securities laws. See Tax Code §1234B(c). Exceptions may apply, as where the contract constitutes inventory. See Tax Code §1234B(a)(2).

[31] Tax Code §1256(a)(1), but see Chapter 20, discussing restrictions under Tax Code §1092 on the use of losses where an investor holds a straddle.

[32] Staff of the Joint Committee on Taxation, *General Explanation of the Economic Recovery Tax Act of 1981*, (H.R. 4242, 97th Congress, Pub. L. No. 97-34, December 29, 1981) at 296-297. (Hereinafter referred to as "1981 Bluebook".)

[33] Tax Code §1256(a)(2)

[34] Tax Code §1256(a)(3). The 60/40 rule is not applicable to gain or loss arising from dealer equity options or dealer securities futures contracts allocated to limited partners or limited entrepreneurs. Tax Code §1256(f)(4). Such gain or loss is treated as short-term. *Id.*

[35] Tax Code §1256(f)(2). Under Tax Code §1256(f)(3), gain or loss arising from trading §1256 contracts is to be treated as capital. However, this rule is not applicable where §1256 contracts are held to hedge property losses on which would be treated as ordinary. Tax Code §1256(f)(3). For purposes of determining whether any gain or loss on property would be ordinary, the fact the taxpayer is actively engaged in dealing or trading §1256 contracts on such property is not to be taken into consideration. *Id.*

[36] Under Code §1256(f)(1) property that at any time was personal property identified as part of a hedging transaction is not eligible for capital gain treatment. This means the 60/40 rule does not apply to income arising from the disposition of such property. This provision applies only to gain; no similar rule is provided for losses. The term "personal property" is defined at Tax Code §1092(d)(1) and includes personal property of a type that is actively traded. Tax Code §1092(d)(1). Identification rules apply. Tax Code §1256(e)(2). Even if the investment is not designated as part of a hedging transaction, ordinary income treatment may still apply. See Tax Code §1256(f)(2).

[37] Tax Code §1256(c)(1)

[38] Tax Code §1201 sets a maximum tax rate on net capital gain for corporations of 35 percent. See Chapter 1 for a further discussion of the capital gain rules.

[39] Tax Code §1256(c)(3). The Second Circuit has held that the mark-to-market rules apply where a taxpayer donates a Code §1256 contract to charity. See *Greene v. United States*, 79 F.3d 1348 (2d Cir. 1996).

[40] If the §1256 contract is a capital asset, the 60/40 rule will apply to the gain or loss recognized.

[41] Tax Code §1256(c)(2)

[42] An unlimited carryforward is permitted. Corporate taxpayers generally are allowed to carry losses back for three years and carryforward for five. See the rules discussed in Chapter 1.

[43] Tax Code §1212(c)

[44] Tax Code §1211(b). See the discussion in Chapter 1.

[45] Tax Code §1212(c)(5). See also IRS Publication 550, *Investment Income and Expenses* (2002), at p. 38. Under Tax Code §1212(c)(5)(B), net §1256 contract gain for tax years before the loss year is calculated without taking into account net §1256 contract loss incurred in the loss year or any year thereafter.

[46] IRS Publication 550, *Investment Income and Expenses* (2002), at p. 38

[47] The carryback rules do not apply to estates and trusts. Tax Code §1212(c)(7).

[48] Tax Code §1212(c)(6). Assume instead the investor had $50,000 of §1256 loss in 2001, plus $50,000 of long-term and $3,000 of short-term capital losses, both from non-§1256 sources. As indicated in the text, the $3,000 of short-term loss offsets ordinary income in 2001. If $20,000 of loss is used in 1998, $80,000 of loss remains. Of this amount, $12,000 is short-term (40 percent * $30,000 of unused §1256 loss) and $68,000 is long-term. This latter number is the sum of the $50,000 of long-term loss plus 60 percent of the remaining §1256 loss. 1981 Bluebook, at 307.

[49] See IRS Publication 550, *Investment Income and Expenses* (2002), at p. 38–39, regarding use of a Form 1045, *Application for Tentative Refund*, instead of filing an amended return on Form 1040X.

[50] IRS Publication 550, *Investment Income and Expenses* (2002), at p. 55. A taxpayer who buys a straddle as an investment makes money if the price of the underlying asset changes. See Smithson, *Managing Financial Risk* (McGraw-Hill 1998) at p. 296.

[51] Tax Code §1256(a)(4). This rule is not applicable if the §1256 straddle is part of a larger straddle transaction. Code §§1092 and 263(g) are discussed in Chapter 20.

[52] Tax Code §1256(d)(4). Identification requirements apply. Each position that is part of a mixed straddle must be identified before the close of the day on which the first §1256 contract constituting part of the straddle is acquired. Tax Code §1256(d)(4)(B). The definition of "mixed straddle" under Code §1092 is somewhat different. See the discussion in Chapter 20.

[53] Tax Code §1256(a)(1)

[54] Tax Code §1092(a)(1)

[55] Treasury Reg. §1.1092(b)-2T(b)(2)

[56] These elections are discussed in Chapter 20.

[57] Tax Code §1256(d)(1)

[58] As noted previously, corporate taxpayers receive only a slightly preferential tax rate on net capital gain. Tax Code §1201(a)

[59] 1981 Bluebook at p. 298

[60] See the instructions to Form 6781, *Gains and Losses from Section 1256 Contracts and Straddles*.

[61] IRS Publication 550, *Investment Income and Expenses* (2002), at p. 57–58. As discussed in Chapter 20, an investor can elect under Code §1256(d) to avoid the mark-to-market rules and also qualify the investment as an identified straddle, pursuant to IRC §1092(a)(2). This would exempt the investment from the loss deferral provisions, although the identified straddle, wash sale, and short sale rules of IRC §1092 would apply.

[62] Tax Code §1256(e). These transactions also are exempt from the deferral rules of IRC §1092 and the capitalization requirements of Code §263(g). See IRC §§1092(e) and 263(g)(3), respectively.

[63] See the further discussion of hedges in Chapter 20, at note 19.

[64] Tax Code §1256(e)(3). See also IRS Publication 550, *Investment Income and Expenses* (2002), at p. 39. Limited partners or limited entrepreneurs in a syndicate also are subject to limits on the amount of hedging loss that can be claimed. IRS Publication 550, *Investment Income and Expenses* (2002), at p. 39.

19 | WASH SALES AND SHORT SALES

INTRODUCTION

Over the years, more taxpayers have become involved in various financial transactions and investments. As the level of sophistication has increased, so has the level of tenacity for increasing profits and avoiding taxes. Investors quickly learned to offset their capital gains with capital losses to avoid taxes all together. Unfortunately, this perfectly valid tax planning technique was carried to the extreme. Investors would own blocks of stock, sell part or all of it at a loss to offset capital gains, and then immediately repurchase the shares.

As a deterrent to this practice, in 1938 Congress enacted §1091, which contains the "wash sale" rules to prevent taxpayers from claiming losses from sales of securities while the taxpayer remains in the same economic position. Additionally, §1233 was added to the arsenal of weapons to prevent abuse. The rules in this section deal with short sales where an investor borrows property and sells it to a third party. This chapter wil explore the anti-abuse rules of wash and short sales.

WASH SALES

If a taxpayer sells a stock or security at a loss and then repurchases the identical security within 30 days before, or after, the date of the sale, then no deduction is allowed for the loss.[1] This transaction is called a wash sale due to the fact that the taxpayer remains in the same economic position subsequent to the sale as before it.

Example—Sarah sells stock having a basis of $1500 on December 15,

2002 for $1000 so that she can claim a capital loss of $500 on her 2003 tax return. On January 10th, she repurchases the same stock for $980 because she feels that it is ultimately a good investment. Since she repurchased the stock within the 61-day window of 30 days before and after the sales date, she will be unable to claim any loss. Instead, her basis in the repurchased stock is $1480, her cost plus any disallowed loss ($980 + $500).

Wash sales apply not only to stock and securities, but also to contracts or options to acquire substantially identical stock or securities.[2] However, commodity futures contracts are not considered stock or securities and are, therefore, not subject to the wash sales rules.[3] These contracts are agreements regarding a specified quantity and price at which a commodity will be bought and sold at a specific date in the future.

Example—In 2003, Sharon executed transactions involving commodity futures contracts that were capital assets. These were speculative investments that involved a substantial amount of capital. During a particular month, Sharon realized a loss upon the sale of one such contract, and within a period ending 30 days after the date of the sale, she purchased another contract involving the same commodity in an equal quantity and of the same quality. Even though Sharon repurchased the identical commodity within the 61-day period surrounding the date of sale, the loss is recognized because the wash sale rules do not apply to commodity futures contracts.[4]

Determination of Basis and Holding Periods

When the wash sale rules apply, special provisions determine the basis and holding period of the replacement shares. If the price received from the old stock sale is less than the purchase price of the new stock, then the basis of the new stock is equal to the basis of the old stock plus the difference between the purchase price of the new stock and the sale price of the old stock.

Example—On June, 2002, Therese purchased 100 shares of TK Photography, Inc. for $100,000. She subsequently sold these shares for $75,000 on December 15, 2002. On January 12, 2003 she purchased 100 TK shares for $90,000. Her basis in the new shares is $115,000, which is her original purchase of $100,000 plus the difference between her selling price and repurchase price ($15,000).

If the selling price of the old stock is greater than the purchase price of the new stock, then the basis of the new stock is equal to the basis of the old stock minus the difference between the selling price of the old stock and the purchase price of the new stock.

Example—Assume the same facts as above except that Therese repurchased the shares for $70,000. The basis of the new stock is $95,000, which is the purchase price of the old shares, ($100,000) less the difference in the price received for the old shares ($75,000) over the price paid for the new shares ($70,000).

The holding period of the disposed security is carried over to the replacement security. IRC §1223 indicates that the holding period of newly acquired securities must also include the holding period of the stock from the loss sale. In the example above, Therese is treated as having acquired the replacement stock on June 1, 2002.

Varying Quantities Purchased and Sold

The regulations contain specific rules for when the amounts of stock acquired and sold during the 61-day period varies. If the amount of stock acquired within that period is equal to or greater than the amount sold, then the holding period and basis of the new shares are determined by matching them with an equal number of the loss shares. The stock that was sold will be matched with an equal number of shares of stock acquired, in an order, beginning with the earliest acquisition.[5]

Example—On September 15, 2000, Beth purchased 100 shares of stock in MSX Corporation for $5000. She sold these shares on February 1, 2003, for $4000. On each of the four days from February 15, 2003, to February 18, 2003, inclusive, she purchased 50 shares of substantially identical stock for $2000. There is an indicated loss of $1000 from the sale of the 100 shares on February 1, 2003. However, within the 61-day period, Beth purchased more than the original 100 shares of the loss stock; therefore, the loss is not deductible. The 50 shares of stock purchased on February 15th and February 16th caused the nondeductibility of the $1000 loss. The holding period for the shares purchased on February 15th and 16th begins on September 15, 2000.[6] The shares purchases of February 17th and 18th are outside of the wash sales rules. The holding period starts with Beth's acquisition date.

Alternatively, if the shares purchased within the 61-day period are less than the amount of stock or securities sold, then the stock acquired will be matched in order of their acquisition, beginning with the earliest, to the shares sold at a loss. The basis and holding period of the new shares are determined by the basis and holding period of the shares to which they are matched.[7]

Example—Yevonne purchased 100 shares of common stock of Tutti Frutti Corp. on September 21, 2003 for $5000. On December 21, 2003, she purchased 50 shares of substantially identical stock for $2750, and on December 27, 2003, she purchased 25 additional shares of such stock for $1125. On January 3, 2004, she sold for $4000 the 100 shares purchased on September 21, 2003.

There is an indicated loss of $1000 on the sale of the 100 shares. However, because Yevonne purchased 75 shares of substantially identical stock within the 61-day period, the loss on the sale of 75 of the shares ($3750 − $3000) is not deductible due to §1091. The loss on the sale of the remaining 25 shares ($1250 − $1000) is deductible, subject to §267 and §1211.[8] The basis of the 50 shares purchased December 21, 2003, is $2500 (the cost of 50 of the shares sold on January 3, 2004) + $750 (the difference between the purchase price ($2750) of the 50 shares initially acquired and the selling price ($2000) of 50 of the shares sold on January 3, 2004), or $3250. Similarly, the basis of the 25 shares purchased on December 27, 2003 is $1375 ($1250 + $125).[9]

Substantially Identical Stock or Securities

There are no guidelines to indicate what constitutes a substantially identical stock or security. All the facts and circumstances must be considered on a case-by-case basis. Generally, stocks or securities of one corporation are not considered substantially equal to the stocks or securities of another corporation. However, there may be situations where they could be considered identical. For example, in a reorganization, the stock and securities of the predecessor and successor corporations may be substantially identical.[10]

Similarly, bonds and preferred stock of a corporation are not ordinarily considered substantially identical to the common stock of the same corporation. However, where the bonds or preferred stock are convertible into common stock of the same corporation, the relative values, price changes, and other circumstances may make these bonds or preferred stock and the common stock substantially identical.[11] Preferred shares is considered "substantially" identical to the common stock if the preferred stock:

- Is convertible into common stock
- Has the same voting rights as the common stock

- Is subject to the same dividend restrictions
- Trades at prices that do not vary significantly from the conversion ratio, and
- Is unrestricted as to convertibility[12]

EXCEPTION TO THE WASH SALE RULES

The wash sale rules do not apply to the disposition of stock or securities made in connection with an individual taxpayer's trade or business. Additionally, they also do not apply to a corporation that is a dealer in stock or securities.[13] To be engaged in the business of being a trader in securities, you must meet all of the following conditions:

- You must seek to profit from daily market movements in the prices of securities and not from dividends, interest, or capital appreciation.
- Your activity must be substantial.
- You must carry on the activity with continuity and regularity.[14]

The following facts and circumstances should be considered in determining if your activity is a securities trading business.

- Typical holding periods for securities bought and sold.
- The frequency and dollar amount of your trades during the year.
- The extent to which you pursue the activity to produce income for a livelihood.
- The amount of time you devote to the activity.[15]

If your trading activities are not a business, you are considered an investor and not a trader. It does not matter whether you call yourself a trader or a "day trader."[16] If you are an investor, the wash-sales rules apply.

SHORT SALE RULES

Short sale rules were enacted to prevent the conversion of short-term gain into the more favorable long-term capital gain. Alternatively, they prevent conversion of long-term loss into short-term capital loss. Short-term loss offsets short-term gain that is taxed at ordinary rates.

A short sale is the sale of property that the seller does not possess. Property includes only stocks, securities, and commodity futures, which are capital assets in the hands of a taxpayer, but does not include any position to which §1092(b) applies.[17] A taxpayer borrows property and then sells that property to a third party. Investors who sell short believe that the price of the stock will fall. If the price does drop, the investor can buy the stock to be returned to the lender at a lower price and made a profit. If the price rises, the investor will have to buy the shares at the higher price and will incur a loss. There are no tax consequences until the taxpayer delivers identical property to the lender to close the sale.

Short Sale Transactions

Short sale transactions are generally of two different types: (1) short sale, and (2) short sale against the box.

When an investor sells short a stock, it is usually borrowed from his/her broker. The stocks come out of the broker's own inventory, from another customer of the broker, or from another brokerage company. The shares are then sold and the proceeds are credited to the investor's account. Within the time specified in the contract, the investor must buy back the same number of shares and return them to the broker. This is called covering. Sometimes the lender wants the borrowed stock back before the specified time. In this situation, the broker will have to come up with new shares to borrow or the investor will have to cover. The lender retains all of the rights associated with stock ownership. The investor must pay the lender any dividends or rights declared on the stock or securities during the term of the loan. Additionally, because the investor is borrowing the stock, the transaction is considered as buying on margin. The broker will charge interest on the loan, and the investor is subject to the rules of margin trading. These rules include:

- Establishing a minimum margin account of at least $2000.
- Borrowing cannot exceed 50 percent of the purchase price of a stock.
- Maintaining a minimum amount of equity in the margin account, ranging from 25 percent–40 percent.
- Using only marginable securities as collateral for the loan.
- Only qualifying stocks can be bought on margin.[18]

Investors enter short sales to speculate when they feel that a certain stock is overpriced. Additionally, the short sale contract may be entered to hedge other long positions with offsetting short positions. Short selling is very risky in that your losses are unlimited, but the best that an investor can gain is 100 percent of the initial investment.

Example—Rigo wishes to take advantage of an unexpected decline in the value of publicly traded Fat Burners Corp. shares. On March 1, 2003, the value of the stock is $10 per share. Rigo decides to sell Fat Burners short through his broker. The broker borrows 100 shares of Fat Burners stock for him, and Rigo proceeds to sell them on the open market. The broker holds the $1000 proceeds plus any income earned on the proceeds as collateral for Rigo's obligation to return the stock to the lender.

On June 1, 2003, the value of the stock declines to $5 per share and Rigo instructs his broker to close the short sale. The broker buys 100 shares of Fat Burners for $500 and delivers the stock to the lender. Rigo has a short-term capital gain of $500, the difference between the $1000 proceeds of the sale of the borrowed stock and the $500 purchase price of the replacement shares. If instead the value of Fat Burners shares climbed unexpectedly to $25 per share when Rigo was required to return the stock, he would have a loss of $1500. This is the difference between the $1000 Rigo earned on the short sale and the $2500 it cost him to replace the borrowed shares.

Short Sale Against the Box

A short sale against the box is where the investor owns the security but does not want to use it for delivery. So he/she borrows identical stock from the brokerage firm. This is usually done to lock in a profit while delaying the tax consequences. The sale is closed out by purchasing identical property and delivering it to the lender or, alternatively, by delivering the property already owned (held in the box) by the investor.

Interaction with Wash Sale Rules

Short sales were used by taxpayers to avoid the wash sale rules. This is because there is no taxable event until a short sale is closed. In this respect, a taxpayer could own a depreciated stock and could enter into a short sale and simultaneously buy identical stock. Without special rules, if the short sale was closed more than 30 days from that date, the wash sale rule did not apply. The replacement stock was not acquired within the 61-day-period of the initial sale. The loss incurred by closing the sale with the stock held against the box was recognized, even though the taxpayer continued to hold his position.

Regulations were enacted to stop circumvention of the wash sale rules in these circumstances. When stock held against the box is used to close a short sale, the wash sale rule is applied by treating the date the short sale was entered into as the date of sale.[19]

Example—On March 1, Dennis holds 100 shares of Arbitrators, Inc. with a basis of $1000. The price declines to $900. Dennis enters into a short sale, selling the borrowed shares at that price. On the same day, Dennis buys 100 shares of Arbitrators for $900. He waits 40 days and closes the short sale with the $1000 basis stock. His loss is $100. It would appear that the wash sale rules do not apply since the $900 basis stock was acquired more than 30 days from the date that the original 100 shares were disposed of. Under the Regulations, however, the disposition of the $1000 basis stock is deemed to have occurred on the date the short sale was entered into, and the wash sale rule applies. The $100 loss is disallowed.

Tax Consequences of Short Sales

For income tax purposes, a short sale is not considered finished until delivery of the property to close the short sale occurs.[20] Whether the recognized gain or loss from a short sale is a capital or ordinary gain or loss depends on whether the property delivered constitutes a capital asset in the hands of the taxpayer.[21] If a dealer in securities makes a short sale, ordinary gain or loss results on closing of the short sale if the stock used to close the short sale was held primarily for sale to customers in the ordinary course of his trade or business.[22] If the stock used to close the short sale was a capital asset in his hands, or if the taxpayer is not a dealer, a capital gain or loss would result.[23]

The timing of the gain or loss remains open until the borrower closes the sale. A taxpayer can use a short sale against the box as a technique to lock in a gain in one taxable year but defer the tax recognition until the subsequent year.

Example—On November 15, 2002, Olive owns 100 shares of Oil Olina Inc. that have a basis of $1000 and a fair market value of $4000. Olive wants to lock in this profit but does not want to pay the capital gains tax for the 2003 tax year. Olive enters into a short sale by having her broker sell 100 shares short. She waits until 2004 and closes the short sale by delivering to the lender the 100 shares of Oil Olina stock that she held at the time of the short sale. When the transaction is complete, Olive receives the $4000 proceeds from the sale. Olive has successfully locked in the gain of $3000 in 2003 but deferred the capital gain tax until 2004.

Anti-Abuse Rules

Taxpayers were able to use short sales as a method of converting a short-term capital gain to a long-term capital gain and converting a long-term capital loss to a short-term capital loss. However, anti-abuse rules were enacted to prevent taxpayers from using short sales for these purposes. IRC §1233 contains three special rules that affect gains and losses realized on short sales. They are known as Rule 1, Rule 2, and Rule 3.

Rule 1 indicates that, if on the date of the short sale, substantially identical property has been held by the taxpayer for less than one year, then any gain on the closing of the short sale is short-term gain.[24] This is also applicable if the taxpayer acquired substantially identical property after the short sale but before its closing.[25] The taxpayer is prevented from aging the transaction while locking in the gain at the time of the short sale.

Example—Chester buys 100 shares of Compost Galore, Inc. on January 12, 2003, at $20 per share. On June 1, 2003, he sells short 100 shares of Compost Galore at $35 per share. On January 15, 2004, Chester closes the short sale by delivering the 100 shares that he purchased on January 12, 2003, to the lender of the stock.

Chester has a realized capital gain of $1500 ($3500 − $2000). This would normally be a long-term capital gain because Chester held the property he used to close the short sale for more than one year. However, under Rule 1 of §1233, the character of the gain is short-term because on the date of the short sale, Chester owned substantially identical property for less than one year.[26]

Rule 2 indicates that the holding period of substantially identical property shall be considered as beginning on the date that the short sale is closed or, if earlier, the date of a sale, gift, or other disposition of such property.[27] This rule applies to identical property in order of its acquisition and only to the extent that the amount of such property does not exceed the amount sold short.[28]

Example—Matthew buys 100 shares of Man Power Weights, Inc. at $10 per share on February 1, 2003. He sells short 100 shares of the same stock at $16 per share on July 1, 2003. The short sale is closed on August 1, 2003, with 100 shares of Man Power stock purchased on that date at $18 per share. On February 2, 2004, he sells at $18 per share the 100 shares of Man Power purchased on February 1, 2003. The $200 ($1600 − $1800) loss sustained upon the closing of the short sale is a short-term capital loss to which Rule 2 or Rule 3 has no application. Additionally, Matthew realizes a short-term capital gain of $800 on the shares sold on February 2, 2004, which were purchased on February 1, 2003. Under Rule 2, the holding period is considered to begin on August 1, 2003, the date of closing the short sale.[29]

There is a "married put" exception to Rule 2. This exception involves property that is acquired and, on the same day, a put option is also acquired on that same property. At the same time the taxpayer identifies the property as intended to be used in exercising the option. The property's holding period is not affected by Rule 2. If the option is not exercised, the cost of the option shall be added to the basis of the property with which the option is identified.[30]

Rule 3 applies to short sales in which there are realized losses. If on the date of a short sale, substantially identical property has been held by the taxpayer for more than one year, any loss on the closing of such short sale shall be considered a loss on the sale or exchange of a capital asset held for more than one year.[31] Any capital loss is considered long term even if the taxpayer closes the short sale with property held only for the short-term period.[32] Rules 1 and 3 apply only to the extent that the amount of property used to close the short sale does not exceed the amount of substantially identical property held at the time of the short sale.[33]

Example—Liz purchases 100 shares of Nurses-R-Us, Inc. on February 1, 2002 at $10 per share. On March 1, 2003, Liz sells short 100 shares of Nurses-R-Us at $16 per share. On April 1, 2003, Liz sells the shares purchased on February 1, 2002, for $18 per share. On April 1, 2003, Liz also buys 100 shares of Nurses-R-Us for $18 per share and closes the short sale with these shares.

Liz realizes a long-term capital gain of $800 on the sale of stock purchased on February 1, 2002, and sold on April 1, 2003 ($1800 − $1000). Liz held this property for more than one year as of the date of the short sale; therefore, the gain is long term. Liz realizes a $200 long-term capital loss with respect to the short sale ($1600 − $1800). This loss is long term because, under Rule 3, on the date of the short sale, Liz held substantially identical property for more than one year. Rule 3 is applicable even though Liz closed the short sale with stock purchased on the day of the short sale.[34]

Payments Relating to Short Sales

A short seller often has to make a variety of payments associated with a short sale. The investor or short seller will have to keep the proceeds from the short sale on deposit with his/her broker. Alternatively, he/she may have to post collateral with the broker in order to free up the funds obtained from the short sale. The broker often pays interest to the seller for these deposits. These payments of interest are ordinary income to the seller and deductible by the broker.

Where stock is involved, an amount equivalent to all of the dividends distributed must be paid to the lender before the sale is closed. Where debt is involved, this amount would be equivalent to the interest earned. If the borrower is a dealer, these payments would be deductible as a business expense. If the borrower is an investor, these payments constitute an investment expense. The limits on the amount of investment interest that is deductible would apply because these payments constitute amounts paid for the use of money.[35] Interest expense is deductible only to the extent of net investment income.[36]

However, if the closing of the short sale occurs on or before the 45th day after the date of the short sale, then no deduction shall be allowed for any of these payments. The basis of the stock used to close the short sale shall be increased by the amount not allowed as a deduction.[37] In the case of an extraordinary dividend, the time period is one year instead of 45 days.[38] An extraordinary dividend is one that exceeds 10 percent of the amount realized by the seller on the sale of the borrowed common stock. The percentage is reduced to 5 percent when preferred stock is involved.[39]

The lender of the securities recognizes no gain or loss when the sale is closed. All payments received for dividends or interest are treated as ordinary income, regardless of whether or not the borrower must add these payments to basis.[40]

If the corporation, the stock of which is used in a short sale, is liquidated, then the amounts paid, which are now liquidating dividends, must be added to the basis of the stock. This is also applicable to nontaxable stock dividends.[41]

CONCLUSION

The wash sale and short sale transactions are linked by virtue of the use of substantially identical securities. For the wash sales rules to apply, substantially identical securities must be acquired within the 61-day period surrounding the date of initial sale. In case of the short sale, substantially identical property must be held at the time of the sale or acquired prior to closing the sale. Consequently, the concept of substantially identical securities has a major impact in each of these situations. Determination of what constitutes substantially identical securities is often made on a case-by-case basis. IRC §1091 and §1233 do not perfectly overlap in providing guidance. Focus seems to be placed on a taxpayer's economic rationale in acquiring specific property. Taxpayers entering into transactions that involve substituting or borrowing property must be careful of the regulations that curtail the tax effects of these transactions.

NOTES

[1] §1091(a)

[2] *Id.*

[3] Rev. Rul. 71-568, 1971-2 C.B. 312

[4] Example taken from Rev. Rul. 71-568, 1971-2 C.B.312

[5] Reg. §1.1091-1(d)

[6] Based on Example 3 in Reg. §1.1091-1

[7] Reg. 1.1091-1(c)

[8] IRC §267 deals with transactions between related persons and the disallowance of losses. IRC §1211 deals with the limit on capital losses allowable by individuals. Capital losses offset capital gains dollar for dollar. An additional $3000 is allowed against ordinary income. Any capital losses above the $3000 must be carried forward to future years to be offset by future capital gains and/or reduced by another $3000 against ordinary income.

[9] Based on Example 2 in Reg. §1.1091-1

[10] Internal Revenue Service Publication 550

[11] *Id.*

[12] *Id.*

[13] Reg. §1.1091-1(a)

[14] Internal Revenue Service Publication 550

[15] *Id.*

[16] *Id.*

[17] §1233(e)(2)(A). IRC §1092(b) deals with offsetting gains and losses from positions that are part of mixed straddles. It is discussed in Chapter 20.

[18] *www.Investopedia.com*

[19] Reg. 1.1091-1(g)

[20] Reg. §1.1233-1(a)(1)
[21] *Id.*
[22] Reg. §1.1233-1(a)(2)
[23] *Id.*
[24] §1233(b)(1)
[25] *Id.*
[26] Based on facts in Example 1 in Reg. §1.1233-1(c)(6)
[27] §1233(b)(2)
[28] *Id.*
[29] The example is based on Example (2) in Reg.§1.1233-1(c)(6)
[30] §1233(c)
[31] §1233(d)
[32] Reg. 1.1233-1(c)(4)
[33] Reg. 1.1233(c)(5)
[34] Example was based on fact pattern contained in Example 3 in Reg. 1.1233(c)(6)
[35] §163(d)
[36] *Id.*
[37] §263(h)(B)
[38] §263(h)(2)
[39] §1059(c)
[40] §1058
[41] Rev. Rul. 72-521, 1972 C.B. 178

20

STRADDLES

INTRODUCTION

According to the Tax Code, a straddle consists of offsetting positions in personal property.[1] For example, an investor who has both a long and short position in oats, with both contracts containing identical terms except for different delivery dates, is treated as holding a straddle.[2] Buying a straddle is profitable when the price of the underlying commodity either increases or decreases. This is because the price movement will cause one of the positions to become valuable. If the price changes substantially, the increase in value will be sufficient to permit the investor to make a profit, even after taking into account the costs of the straddle transaction.[3] However, barring special rules, straddles also can be used to defer recognition of income or change capital gain from short-term to long-term, making the profit eligible for taxation at the favorable long-term capital gain rates.

Example—In March, Bob buys offsetting futures contracts for corn. The contracts have identical terms, with the exception of different delivery dates. Because Bob holds offsetting positions, his investment risks are minimized. Assume that by year-end, the price of corn has risen, so that the value of Bob's long position has increased while the short position has fallen by roughly the same amount. Bob therefore sells the short position, and uses the resulting short-term capital loss to offset short-term gain from an unrelated transaction. Since short-term capital gain is taxed at ordinary income rates, Bob's tax savings because of the sale are measured by his marginal tax rate. He immediately buys a replacement short position, which calls for delivery to take place in a month different than the month that delivery was to occur under the original short contract. The replacement futures contract enables Bob to maintain his balanced position in corn. This means that he has minimized his risk by locking in his gain on the long futures investment. Assume that in the following year, the price of corn rises further, so that Bob's long position continues to increase in value while the replacement (sell) contract suffers a corresponding decrease. After waiting for a year to pass from the date of the initial investment, Bob liquidates both the original long position and the replacement short contract. The gain arising from the original investment is taxed at favorable long-term capital gain rates while the loss generated by the replacement contract offsets short-term capital gain that, as noted above, otherwise would be taxed as ordinary income.

Unless special rules apply, Bob receives very favorable tax treatment from the transactions described above. He deferred his tax obligation on the unrelated short-term capital gain he recognized in the first year of the investment. This gain was offset by the short-term loss from the original short leg of the straddle. In addition, Bob was able to use the straddle transaction to age the gain on the long position so that it would be eligible for the reduced tax rates applicable to net capital gains. He achieved this result even though he locked in his gain on this position during the first year, when he entered the replacement short arrangement.

To prevent taxpayers from achieving these results, Congress enacted various rules in the early 1980s that cover straddle transactions. One of these provisions, as discussed in Chapter 18, requires taxpayers holding certain kinds of investments to use a mark-to-market system, treating the resulting gain or loss as 60 percent long-term and 40 percent short-term.[4] In addition, Congress enacted rules deferring loss recognition, at Tax Code §1092, and requiring capitalization of certain expenses associated with straddle investments. Restrictions also were adopted that are similar to the wash sale and short sale rules described in Chapter 19. Investors need to understand all of these provisions before entering into a straddle transaction.[5]

WHAT IS A STRADDLE?

As mentioned above, the tax law defines a straddle as "offsetting positions with respect to personal property."[6] A "position" is an interest in personal property, including a futures or forward contract or an option.[7] "Personal property" is any property of a type that is actively traded.[8] This definition excludes real estate or an option to buy an identified parcel of real estate. Commodities like corn or gold (for which regulated futures contracts are traded) and also listed corporate bonds and U.S. Treasury obligations would qualify under the definition.[9] Interests in stock, like exchange-traded options, also are included. However, stock itself is treated as personal property only in limited cases. For example, stock shares represent personal property where they are part of a straddle and at least one of the offsetting positions is:

1. An option on the stock or on substantially identical stock or securities.[10]
2. A securities futures contract with respect to the stock or substantially identical stock or securities.
3. A position with respect to substantially similar or related property other than stock.[11]

Related party rules apply to prevent a taxpayer from avoiding application of the straddle rules by, for example, transferring or putting property in a spouse's name.[12] In other words, using the facts above, Bob would not escape the Code §1092 rules by holding the long position in his own name and putting the short contract under the name of his wife.

In order for a taxpayer to be treated as holding a straddle, the positions he or she owns must be offsetting. This means there is a "substantial diminution of the taxpayer's risk of loss" arising from one position because of the other position(s) held.[13] Referring back to the example appearing at the start of this chapter, Bob's long and short futures positions in corn are offsetting. This is because changes in the value of corn, the underlying commodity, will cause one of the contracts to increase in value while the other falls. According to the legislative history, diversified long positions are not treated as offsetting just because losses in one may be offset by gains in others arising from factors like changes in interest rates, for example.[14] However, little authority exists regarding how much risk reduction is "substantial."

Certain positions are rebuttably presumed to be offsetting. These include positions:

1. In the same personal property. This means an investor who owns silver and a short futures contract obligating him to sell silver holds a straddle.
2. In the same personal property although in substantially altered form. For example, a straddle includes offsetting futures positions in soybeans and soybean oil.

3. In debt instruments of similar maturities. This refers to instruments with scheduled maturities sufficiently close in time so that value changes in one will correspond substantially to changes in the value of the other.[15]

4. That are sold or marketed as offsetting, including spreads, straddles, and butterflies.

5. Where the aggregate margin requirements are less than what would be required if each position were held separately.

6. Treated as offsetting under IRS regulations.[16]

In some of the cases listed above, the transactions are presumed to be offsetting only if the value of the positions ordinarily varies inversely. This rule applies to the interests listed at #1 (in the same personal property), #2 (in the same personal property although in substantially altered form), #3 (debt instruments), and #6 (other cases described in the regulations). In other words, if a change in market conditions, for example, will affect the value of debt instruments held by an investor in the same way, the positions would not be offsetting.

LOSS DEFERRAL RULE

Code §1092 permits an investor to claim a loss in connection with a straddle only to the extent that the amount of the loss exceeds the "unrecognized gain" in offsetting positions. The term "unrecognized gain" is defined as the amount of gain that would be included in income if the position were sold on the last business day of the tax year at fair market value.[17] This gain must be reported to the IRS annually, using Form 6781, even though no tax is paid on it.[18] Losses that do not exceed unrecognized gain, meaning losses disallowed under IRC §1092, are carried over but are subject to the same limitations in subsequent tax years.

Example—Dave enters into a straddle transaction in September. On December 10th, Dave closes out one of the positions in the straddle, at a loss of $5000. As of December 31st, he has unrecognized gain in the position he retained, amounting to $5250. Because Dave's losses do not exceed his unrecognized gain, he will not be able to use any of these losses on his current year tax return. Assume that in the following year, Dave liquidates the gain position and reports income of $5300. He now is able to use the losses that arose in the prior year because he no longer has unrecognized gain. If Dave has no other investment transactions in this second year, he will use the losses to offset the income arising from disposition of the gain position, meaning he will include in income $300 in the second year because of the straddle investment.

Had Dave continued to hold the gain position throughout the second year instead of liquidating it, he would have been able to use the $5000 of loss only to the extent that it exceeded his unrecognized gain at the end of the second year. In other words, had Dave's unrecognized gain on December 31st of the second year amounted to $4000, he would have been able to claim $1000 of the loss arising from the sale of the depreciated position in the first year. He would continue to carry the remaining $4000 of unused loss to later tax years.

Exceptions to the Loss Deferral Rules

Certain investments are not subject to the loss deferral provisions of Code §1092. These include identified straddles, straddles formed solely of Code §1256 contracts, straddles consisting of qualified covered call options and the optioned stock, and hedging transactions. A transaction entered into by a taxpayer in the normal course of his or her trade or business, in order to manage the risk of a price change on ordinary property, for example, would be considered a hedge provided certain identification requirements are met.[19]

Identified Straddles   The rules for identified straddles are designed to permit investors to claim losses arising from legitimate investments made for profit. Under the Tax Code, an identified straddle is one where all of the original positions forming the investment were acquired on the same day. An identification requirement applies, under which the positions must be clearly shown in the investor's records as being part of an identified straddle transaction by the close of the day of acquisition.[20] All the positions in the straddle must be disposed of on the same day during the tax year or, alternatively, all the positions must be held as of year-end. A straddle that is part of a larger straddle transaction cannot qualify for this exception.[21]

Positions constituting an identified straddle are treated as an economic unit. In other words, positions outside the straddle are not subject to the loss deferral rules, simply because they happen to offset an investment that is part of an identified straddle.[22] Similarly, an investor who liquidates all positions of an identified straddle can claim any losses arising from the disposition, even though one of the straddle legs also offsets an outside position the investor owns in addition to the straddle. Losses from an identified straddle arise no earlier than the day on which all positions comprising the transaction are liquidated.[23]

Example—Lisa holds an identified straddle consisting of silver and a regulated futures contract representing a short position in silver. Independent of this transaction, she also owns a regulated futures contract allowing her to buy silver (a long position) as an investment. Assume that Lisa liquidates the identified straddle by disposing of both positions on the same day, recognizing loss on the short (sell) position and gain on the sale of the metal itself. She is allowed to claim the loss arising from liquidating her futures contract to sell (the short leg), even though the long futures contract represents an offsetting position. This is because the identified straddle is treated as a separate economic unit. A similar result would have applied had Lisa kept both her silver and her short futures contracts and sold the long position at a loss instead.

Straddles Consisting Solely of Code §1256 Contracts IRC §1256, discussed in Chapter 18, requires certain kinds of investments to be marked to market annually. When all of the positions in a straddle are subject to mark-to-market reporting, the investor includes both the unrecognized gain and loss in his or her annual income. This means the loss deferral rules are unnecessary because the taxpayer holding a straddle comprised of §1256 contracts is reporting the gain associated with the investment on an annual basis, in addition to losses. However, a taxpayer can choose to designate a Code §1256 straddle as an identified straddle transaction, assuming the requirements described above are met.[24] The advantage of making this designation is that loss recognized on the disposition of an outside position that offsets one of the §1256 contracts included in the straddle transaction will not be subject to the loss deferral provisions.

Example—Roger holds an identified straddle consisting of regulated futures contracts representing long and short positions in gold. Since both legs of the straddle are subject to the mark-to-market rules of Code §1256, the loss deferral provisions are not applicable. However, assume that Roger also owns gold as an investment. By designating the long and short futures gold positions as part of an identified straddle, he will be able to claim any loss that may arise when he disposes of the gold, even though the metal represents an offsetting position with respect to the short (sell) leg of the straddle. This result applies even if Roger had unrecognized gain on the sell position of the straddle at the time the gold was liquidated.

Qualified Covered Call Options   The loss deferral rules do not apply to a straddle where all of the offsetting positions consist of one or more "qualified covered call options" and the stock to be purchased from the investor under the options.[25] A qualified covered call option is an option granted by an investor to purchase stock that he or she already owns or that is acquired as part of the transaction in which the option is granted.[26] However, in order to be treated as qualified, a covered call option must meet five requirements.[27]

1. The option must be traded on an exchange regulated by the SEC.[28]
2. The option must be granted more than 30 days before expiration.[29]
3. The investor is not an options dealer who granted the option in connection with his or her options dealing activities.[30]
4. Gain or loss the investor recognizes on the option must not be ordinary.[31]
5. The option cannot be deep-in-the-money.[32]

In general, a call option that has a strike price less than the prevailing market price for the shares is considered to be "in-the-money." An option's strike price is the price at which the option can be exercised.[33] According to the tax law, a "deep-in-the-money" option has a strike price lower than the "lowest qualified benchmark." The lowest qualified benchmark generally is defined as the highest available strike price that is less than the "applicable stock price."[34] The applicable stock price is the closing price of the shares on the most recent day on which the stock was traded prior to the date the option was granted. However, if the opening price on the day the option was granted is more than 110 percent of the closing price on the previous trading day, the opening price figure is used instead.[35]

Example—Tom owns shares of stock in Bender Company. On May 15th of the current year, Tom writes a call option on his shares that will expire in July. The day before the call option was written, the closing price of Bender stock was $101 per share. The opening price on the day Tom granted the option was $105. Under these facts, the applicable stock price for Bender will be $101. This is because the opening price on the day the option was granted, $105, is less than 110 percent of the closing price on the prior day (110 percent * $101 = $111.10). Had Bender opened at a price of \$112 on the day of Tom's option transaction, the applicable stock price would have been the \$112 figure.

Assume that on May 15th, the strike prices for July call options on Bender stock are reported by the financial press to be \$90, \$95, \$100, \$105, \$110, and \$115. The lowest qualified benchmark for Bender shares is the highest available strike price that is less than \$101, the applicable stock price calculated above. This means the lowest qualified benchmark is \$100. If the strike price on the call option Tom wrote is \$95, the transaction represents a deep-in-the-money option. As a result, Tom is subject to the Code §1092 deferral rules if he liquidates either the option or the stock at a loss during the current tax year. However, if the strike price is \$105, Tom's option is not deep-in-the-money. Assuming he meets the other requirements for qualified call options, he will avoid application of the loss deferral provisions.[36]

If an investor who owns stock writes a qualified covered call option on the shares she owns with a strike price less than the applicable stock price, any loss arising from the option is treated as a long-term capital loss. This rule applies if at the time the loss was realized, gain on the sale or exchange of the stock would have qualified for long-term capital gain treatment.[37] Since long-term capital loss is used first to offset long-term capital gain, which otherwise would be eligible for taxation at favorable rates, this rule is disadvantageous to the taxpayer. In other words, an investor who closes out a qualified covered call option at a loss would prefer to characterize that loss as short-term, so that it could be used to offset short-term capital gain that would be taxed at ordinary income rates.

MODIFIED SHORT SALE RULES

Two special provisions have been adopted to prevent the use of straddles to manipulate the character or holding period of assets held by an investor.[38] One of these rules provides that losses from the disposition of a leg in the straddle are characterized as long-term if two conditions are satisfied:

1. When the taxpayer entered into the loss position, he or she held an offsetting position.
2. Gain or loss from one or more positions in the straddle would have been long-term had the position(s) been disposed of on the day the investor entered into the loss position.[39]

Example—For the past five years, Lynn has held silver as an investment. On April 1 of the current year, Lynn enters into a regulated (short) futures contract on silver that offsets her silver holdings. In July, Lynn closes out the silver future at a loss. The loss is long-term even though regulated futures contracts normally are subject to the 60/40 rule, meaning 40 percent of the loss should be treated as short-term.[40] This is because the futures contract offsets the silver, which would have generated long-term gain or loss had Lynn sold it when she acquired the futures investment. Assume Lynn's loss amounts to $1000, and her marginal tax rate is 35 percent. If long-term capital gain is taxed at a 20-percent rate, Lynn's loss will generate $200 in tax savings for her ($1000 * 20 percent). However, had Lynn been able to treat 40 percent of her loss as short-term, her total savings would have amounted to $260 [(.35 * $400) + (.2 * $600)]. This means Lynn pays an additional $60 in tax in this example because of the rule treating the $1000 as a long-term loss.

The modified short sale rules also prevent the use of straddles to age assets, in order to qualify for long-term capital gain treatment on a later disposition. Under this provision, the holding period of a position constituting part of a straddle begins on the date the straddle ends. However, this rule does not apply where the asset had already been held for over a year when the straddle was created.[41]

Example—On November 1, Year 1, Marilyn purchased silver. Two months later, on January 2 of Year 2, she entered into an offsetting short silver forward contract, which she liquidated in May. On November 10th of Year 2, Marilyn sold the silver, reporting a gain of $2000 on the transaction. The proceeds of Marilyn's silver sale are not eligible for favorable long-term capital gain treatment, even though she has owned the silver for more than 12 months as of the date of sale. Because Marilyn had not held the silver longer than one year when she created the straddle transaction, her holding period for the metal is treated as beginning in May, when the straddle was liquidated. Had she owned the silver for 13 months when she entered into the forward contract, this rule would not have applied and Marilyn would have reported long-term capital gain on the sale transaction.

COORDINATION WITH THE WASH SALE RULES

Under the wash sale provisions, a taxpayer generally is not allowed to recognize a loss from the sale or exchange of stock or securities when substantially identical instruments are acquired in a purchase or taxable transaction within 30 days before or after the sale.[42] The Treasury Regulations use similar principles for straddle transactions by adopting two rules that apply sequentially.[43] In other words, any losses that survive application of Rule 1 are then subjected to Rule 2. Rule 1 applies only where stock or securities make up one of the positions in the straddle. Rule 2 restates the basic loss deferral principles of Code §1092, in the context of the wash sale provisions.

Rule 1: The first wash sale rule bars an investor from deducting a loss on the disposition of stock or securities that constitute positions in a straddle if, within 30 days of the disposition, the investor acquires substantially identical stock or securities or enters into a contract or option to acquire such instruments. Losses disallowed because of this provision are carried over and subject to the same restrictions in later years.[44] This means an investor will be unable to take a deduction for a loss on the sale of stock or securities so long as he holds substantially identical instruments purchased within 30 days of the underlying disposition.[45]

Example—On August 1st of the current year, Lynn, an investor, bought stock in Clarke Corporation and also a put option permitting her to sell the Clarke shares. The stock and put represent offsetting positions. On October 1st, Lynn sold her Clarke stock at a loss of $1000. Ten days later, Lynn purchased new Clarke shares that were substantially identical to the stock she liquidated. By year-end, there was no unrecognized gain on either the option or the replacement Clarke shares. She continued to hold both the put and also the stock. Because Lynn bought the replacement stock within 30 days of the disposition generating the loss, she will not be allowed to claim any deduction on her current-year tax return. This is true even though there is no unrecognized gain on the put option or replacement shares at year-end, meaning the loss deferral rules of Code §1092 would not bar the deduction. If Lynn continues to hold the replacement shares throughout the following tax year, she will be unable to use the loss in that year also.[46]

Rule 2: The second rule uses wash sale principles to extend the reach of the loss deferral provisions of Code §1092. This restriction on loss use applies to the extent that certain unrecognized gain exceeds the amount of loss disallowed under Rule 1. The unrecognized gain relevant for purposes of this rule is gain on:

1. Offsetting positions to the loss position.
2. Positions that offset any successor position.
3. Successor positions.

Successor positions are positions that are or were at any time offsetting to a second position, provided certain conditions are met. Specifically, the second position must offset the loss position that was liquidated. Also, the successor must have been entered into within 30 days before or after the disposition of the loss position.[47] Losses disallowed under Rule 2 are carried over, but are subject to the Rule 1 (if applicable) and Rule 2 restrictions in the carryover year.[48]

Example—On November 20th of the current year, Suzanne purchased offsetting positions constituting a straddle. Neither position consisted of stock or securities, meaning Rule 1 is not applicable to Suzanne's investment. Ten days after her purchase, on November 30th, she closed out the sell (short) position at a loss of $400. On December 6th, Suzanne purchased a replacement short position. As of year-end, Suzanne had unrecognized gain of $10 on the replacement investment and $200 on the original long position. Suzanne's total unrecognized gain, for purposes of Rule 2, amounts to $210. This is the sum of the gain on the successor position ($10 on the replacement short contract) and the gain on the long leg of the straddle ($200), which offset the original loss position. Because of this gain, Suzanne will be able to deduct only $190 of the $400 loss against current year income under the Rule 2 provisions. If by year-end Suzanne had $10 of unrecognized loss on the replacement position and $200 of unrecognized gain on the retained long contract, she would be able to deduct only $200 of the $400 loss generated by the November 30th disposition. This is because unrecognized gains and losses are not netted to calculate the total amount of unrecognized gain at the end of the tax year.[49]

Had Suzanne's straddle consisted of stocks or securities that she had disposed of and replaced either 30 days before or after the disposition, the Rule 1 disallowance provision would have applied first. The interaction of the two rules is illustrated by the following, based on an example contained in the Code §1092 regulations.

Example—In January of the current year, Maigret purchased 200 shares of Stewart Company stock and two put options, giving him rights, in total, to sell all his 200 shares. On October 1st, when Maigret had $400 of unrealized gain on the Stewart options, he sold the underlying shares at a loss of $400. Twenty days later, Maigret purchased 100 new shares in Stewart that are substantially identical to the stock he liquidated. He also acquired a call option that offsets his existing puts but that does not give him rights to acquire property substantially identical to the shares of stock he sold. As of year-end, Maigret had $150 of unrecognized gain on his replacement Stewart stock. He also had $80 of unrecognized gain on the call position and neither gain nor loss on the put options.

In the current year, Maigret can recognize $170 of the $400 loss the sale of his original Stewart shares generated. Since he replaced half of the stock he sold within 30 days of the disposition, half the loss, or $200, is disallowed under the Rule 1 wash sale provision. Rule 2 prevents Maigret from claiming that portion of the remaining $200 loss that is equal to the excess of the total unrecognized gain on the Stewart stock and the call and put options over the loss disallowed under Rule 1.

Unrecognized gain ($150 + $80)	$230
Loss disallowed under Rule 1	$200
Difference	$ 30
Loss allowed under Rule 1	$200
Less difference calculated above	$ 30
Loss allowed after application of Rule 2	$170 [50]

The rules providing for coordination between the wash sale and straddle provisions do not apply to certain transactions, including hedges, losses on the sale of a loss position in a mixed straddle account, and losses on the sale of a position in a straddle consisting of only §1256 contracts.[51] If the sale of a loss position would have generated a capital loss, the carryover loss is capital. This is true even if the gain or loss on any successor positions would be treated as ordinary.[52]

INTEREST AND CARRYING CHARGES

Under Code §263, interest and carrying charges properly allocable to personal property forming part of a straddle are not deductible. Instead, these costs must be capitalized and added to the investor's basis in the property.[53] This rule applies not only to conventional interest expenses but also other costs associated with ownership of the property, including insurance, storage, etc. However, the amount otherwise required to be capitalized is reduced by certain income items, including interest and original issue discount reported for the year with respect to personal property included in the straddle and also dividends received on the property (reduced by the dividends-received deduction).[54] The interest capitalization rules do not apply to hedges.[55]

MIXED STRADDLES

Under the IRC § 1092 regulations, a mixed straddle is a straddle in which one but not all of the positions are § 1256 contracts. (A discussion of § 1256 contracts can be found in Chapter 18. Generally, these include investments like regulated futures contracts and nonequity options.) The positions in a mixed straddle must be held as capital assets, and the straddle cannot be part of a larger straddle arrangement.[56] The term does not include offsetting straddle positions where an election under Code § 1256(d) has been made.[57] (The Code § 1256(d) election, discussed in Chapter 18, gives a taxpayer an option to avoid using the mark-to-market and 60/40 rules for the § 1256 contracts included in a mixed straddle. However, this election does not eliminate the restrictions discussed in this chapter, including the loss deferral provisions, and the wash sale and short sale rules that govern straddles.) A taxpayer who acquires a long gold forward contract and at some later date enters into an offsetting short gold regulated futures contract holds a mixed straddle.[58]

Tax Consequences of Mixed Straddles

There are various tax results that arise from mixed straddles. To begin, as noted in Chapter 18, unless the taxpayer elects otherwise, the mark-to-market rules apply to the § 1256 positions, meaning gain existing on these contracts must be reported at year-end. This is true even though any corresponding loss on the non-§ 1256 leg is not recognized, because the mark-to-market rules won't apply to positions outside of IRC § 1256. Further, if the loss arises on the § 1256 contract, the straddle rules of IRC § 1092 will permit its recognition only to the extent that it exceeds the unrecognized gain on the non-§ 1256 position. In other words, the combined operation of the mark-to-market and straddle rules can generate very unfavorable results for taxpayers regarding the timing of gain and loss recognition.

Additional problems arise for an investor who holds a mixed straddle, as defined under the Code § 1092 regulations, because of the "killer rule." Under this provision, unless certain elections are made, 60 percent of the loss on the disposition of the non-§ 1256 position must be reported as long-term capital and 40 percent short-term. This applies if both of the conditions below are met:

1. The straddle positions that are §1256 contracts would be generate capital gain or loss upon disposition.
2. Liquidation of no other position in the straddle, apart from the §1256 contracts, would result in long-term capital gain or loss.[59]

Example—Denise holds a mixed straddle consisting of a §1256 position and a non-§1256 contract. She liquidates the non-§1256 leg of the straddle, which she had held for five months, at a loss. Even though Denise did not close out the §1256 position, the 60/40 rule will still apply, assuming the conditions above are met. This will convert loss that otherwise would be short-term capital into 60 percent long-term and 40 percent short-term. If Denise is in a 35-percent tax bracket, and her loss amounts to $2000, this rule will cost her $180, assuming a 20% long-term capital gain rate. This is because she would have saved $700 had the loss been treated as short-term and used to offset gain otherwise taxed at ordinary income rates ($2,000 * .35=$700). Under the 60/40 rule, 60 percent of the loss offsets gain eligible to be taxed under favorable long-term rates. Denise's savings under the 60/40 rule, assuming sufficient gain to use up both types of losses, would amount to $520 [($1,200 * .2) + ($800 * .35)]. Note that if Denise sells the non-§1256 position at a gain, the income will be reported as short-term capital, meaning it will be taxed at ordinary income rates.

Positions in "mixed straddle accounts" and "identified mixed straddles" are exempt from the operation of the killer rule.[60] To take advantage of these exceptions, investors need to file Form 6781 and make either "Election B," in the case of identified mixed straddles (also referred to as "straddle by straddle identification"), or "Election C," for mixed straddle accounts.[61] (Election "A," the option available under Code §1256(d), is mentioned above and discussed in greater length in Chapter 18. Mixed straddles for which Election A is chosen also avoid application of the "killer rule.") Both Elections "B" and "C" permit an investor to report the results of the §1256 leg of the mixed straddle using the 60/40 rule. This can be favorable, where a taxpayer holds the straddle for less than 12 months, for example, and otherwise would report 100 percent of the gain as short-term capital.

Straddle-by-Straddle Identification/ Identified Mixed Straddle

Under the straddle-by-straddle identification option (Election B), the investor makes a timely identification of each position that is part of a mixed straddle for which this treatment is desired.[62] The character of gain or loss arising thereafter, where all positions of the straddle are liquidated on the same day, depends on which leg in the straddle produced the net gain or loss. In other words, if the taxpayer has net gain or loss because of the §1256 contract(s), it is reported as 60 percent long-term and 40 percent short-term. However, if the net gain or loss arises from the non-§1256 positions, it is treated as short-term.[63]

Example—Anna Marie acquires a §1256 contract and an offsetting non-§1256 position.[64] The contracts are properly identified and Anna Marie chooses to report the results of the investment using the Election B alternative. Several days later, Anna Marie closes both positions on the same day, reporting a gain of $1000 on the non-§1256 position and a loss of $600 on the §1256 contract. Anna Marie nets $400; this arises from the non-§1256 position. Therefore this income is reported as short-term capital gain. Had the loss on the §1256 contract instead amounted to $1200, Anna Marie would have a net loss of $200 on the transaction. She would report this as $120 of long-term capital loss and $80 of short-term. This is because the 60/40 rule applies, since the loss is attributable to the §1256 leg of the straddle.

Although Election B permits an investor to avoid application of the killer rule, the loss deferral and other provisions of Code §1092 continue to apply. This means an investor who realizes a loss on the disposition of one leg of an identified mixed straddle may be required to defer recognition of the loss until a later year. The following example, based on the Code §1092 regulations, illustrates this point.

Example—On November 20th of the current year, Kathleen enters into a straddle consisting of a §1256 contract and an offsetting non-§1256 position. She identifies the positions on a timely basis, as required, and opts to report the transaction under Election B. On December 22nd, Kathleen enters into a second non-§1256 contract that offsets the non-§1256 position constituting part of the straddle. On December 31st, Kathleen disposes of the original non-§1256 position for a gain of $2000. She realizes a loss of $2200 on the §1256 contract when it is marked to market. Additionally, she has $200 of unrecognized gain on the non-§1256 position acquired on December 22nd. Pursuant to the identified mixed straddle rules, Kathleen must offset the $2200 loss from the §1256 position against the $2000 gain generated by the sale of the original non-§1256 position. The resulting net loss of $200 is treated as 60 percent long-term and 40 percent short-term, since it is attributable to the §1256 contract. However, this loss cannot be claimed in the current year. This is because of the $200 of unrecognized gain on the December 22nd non-§1256 contract, which qualifies as a successor position.[65]

Where all the non-§1256 contracts in an identified mixed straddle are disposed of on the same day, rules similar to those described above apply. In other words, the gains and losses arising from liquidation of the non-§1256 investments are netted. A netting process also is performed on the realized and unrealized gains and losses from the §1256 positions. The non-§1256 results then are offset against the §1256 gain or loss, to determine the overall net gain or loss from the straddle. If this gain or loss is attributable to the §1256 positions it is reported under the 60/40 rule; otherwise the investor treats the results as short-term capital gain or loss. Any gain or loss later realized on the §1256 contracts is adjusted to take into account the offset that occurred when the non-§1256 positions were liquidated.[66]

Example—In May, Marty enters into an identified mixed straddle and opts to report the transaction under Election B. On June 1st, Marty disposes of the non-§1256 position and reports a loss of $2500. He has a realized gain in the exact same amount on the §1256 leg as of the same date. Marty continues to hold the §1256 investment as of year-end, at which time his total unrealized gain amounts to $3000. As of June 1st, Marty reports no gain or loss from the identified mixed straddle investment. This is because his $2500 loss on the disposition of the non-§1256 position is offset by the unrealized gain of $2500 on the §1256 leg of the straddle. On December 31st, Marty normally would expect to report income of $3000 from his investment, under the mark-to-market rules of Code §1256. However, this figure is adjusted to reflect the gain previously used in the netting process, and as a result Marty reports income of $500. This amount will be treated under the 60/40 rule, meaning Marty will have $300 of long-term and $200 of short-term gain.[67]

If all the §1256 contracts are liquidated or deemed disposed of on the same day, the investor nets those results and also calculates the net realized and unrealized gain or loss on the non-§1256 positions. The net results from the §1256 investments are reported as short-term capital gain or loss, to the extent of the net gain or loss existing on the non-§1256 holdings. Excess §1256 gain or loss is subject to the 60/40 rule. If the netting process generates a loss, the deferral and wash sale rules of Code §1092 may defer its recognition.[68]

Example—Greg enters into an identified mixed straddle on December

1st. On December 31st, Greg disposes of the §1256 leg of the straddle at a loss of $1800; he has a comparable gain on the retained non-§1256 investment. Greg's loss is short-term, since there is $1800 of gain on the non-§1256 position. However, he is unable to claim the loss in the current year. This is because the loss deferral rules of Code §1092 allow Greg to take the deduction only to the extent the loss exceeds the unrecognized gain on the other leg of the straddle. Since Greg's unrecognized gain equals the loss arising from the disposition, no deduction is allowed in the current year.[69]

Mixed Straddle Accounts

The second option for a mixed straddle, "Election C," involves creation of one or more mixed straddle accounts. A separate account is required for each separate designated class of activities.[70] Gain or loss for each position in the account is calculated at the end of each business day,[71] and the investor nets the results from the §1256 contracts with the results of the non-§1256 positions. This leads to a figure called the "daily account net gain or loss." If this number reflects §1256 contracts, the amount is reported as 60 percent long-term and 40 percent short-term. If instead the number is attributable to the non-§1256 components of the straddle, the amount is reported as short-term gain or loss, as the case may be. Where both netting calculations produce gain, the portion of the total gain allocable to the non-§1256 contracts is treated as short-term, while the percentage attributable to the §1256 investments is reported using the 60/40 rules. A similar result applies where both netting procedures generate losses.[72] An adjustment is made to later gain or loss determined under this netting procedure, to avoid double inclusion of gain or loss already taken into account.[73]

On the last business day of the tax year, the daily account amounts are netted for each account to calculate the "annual account net gain or loss." The annual account net gain or loss for each account then is adjusted to reflect interest and other carrying charges.[74] An investor's total annual account net gain or loss is calculated by netting the annual account amounts for all the mixed straddle accounts established by the taxpayer. The net amounts retain their characterization as long-term or short-term. However, a ceiling exists under which no more than half the total annual account net gain for the year can be treated as long-term capital gain. If a taxpayer has long-term gain in excess of this ceiling, it is reported as short-term. Similarly, no more than 40 percent of the total annual account net loss can be

TABLE 20-1

Day	Net §1256 Results	Net non-§1256 Results
Dec. 27th	$100	($80)
Dec. 28th	($50)	$60
Dec. 29th	$30	($20)
Dec. 30th	($50)	$35
Dec. 31st	$50	$40

reported as short-term capital loss. Short-term loss beyond the 40-percent figure is treated as long-term.[75]

Example—In late December, Gary creates a mixed straddle account to report the results of his straddle investments. Gary's results for his investment during the current year are shown in Table 20-1.

Gary has $20 of daily account net gain from December 27th. Since this amount is attributable to the §1256 investment, it is reported as 60-percent long-term and 40-percent short-term capital gain. He also has a daily account gain on December 28th. However, because this figure reflects the non-§1256 position, it is reported as short-term. Using similar principles for the remaining days in Gary's tax year yields the results shown in Table 20-2.

Based on these figures, Gary's annual account adds up to $39 of long-term and $76 of short-term capital gain. Gary's total gain therefore is $115. No more than 50 percent of this amount can be reported as long-term. However, since $39 is less than 50 percent of $115 ($57.50), none of Gary's long-term capital gain will be recharacterized. Had the numbers been re-

TABLE 20-2

Day	Daily account net Gain or loss	Long-term gain/loss	Short-term gain/loss
Dec. 27	$20 (§1256 position)	$12	$ 8
Dec. 28	$10 (non-§1256)		$10
Dec. 29	$10 (§1256)	$6	$ 4
Dec. 30	($15)(§1256)	($9)	($6)
Dec. 31	Both legs show gain	$30	$20(§1256) $40(non-§1256)

versed, meaning Gary's totals would have amounted to $76 of long-term gain and $39 of short-term, $18.50 of his long-term gain would have been treated as short-term income.[76]

STRADDLE INVESTMENTS

Where a taxpayer anticipates market volatility, entering into a straddle transaction may represent a wise investment strategy. However, the tax rules relating to these transactions are complex. A taxpayer considering a straddle needs to understand both the basic loss deferral and interest capitalization provisions, in addition to the other rules governing these investments, like the wash sale and short sale provisions. Further, if a mixed straddle is being contemplated, the special rules and elections discussed in both this chapter and Chapter 18 should be considered. This is because an investment that generates unanticipated and unwelcome tax consequences is at a minimum less profitable than expected, but often may prove to be a money-losing strategy.

NOTES

[1] Tax Code §1092(c)(1). This definition is discussed in greater detail later in this chapter.

[2] As mentioned in Chapter 18, a futures contract obligating the holder to buy a specific commodity at a specific price is a "long" position. Conversely, a "short" position exists under a contract obligating the holder to sell the commodity.

[3] Smithson, *Managing Financial Risk* (McGraw-Hill 1998), at p. 296

[4] Tax Code §1256

[5] The loss deferral, interest capitalization, wash sale, and short sale provisions applicable to straddles are all discussed in this chapter. The mark-to-market and 60/40 rules, found in Code §1256, are described in Chapter 18.

[6] Tax Code §1092(c)(1)

[7] Tax Code §1092(d)(2). In some cases, an obligation under a debt instrument may represent a position in personal property. Proposed Regulation §1.1092(d)-1(d)

[8] Tax Code §1092(d)(1). According to the legislative history, only property or interests that can generate gain or loss on disposition are treated as personal property. That means that U.S. currency is not personal property under the straddle rules, for example. Staff of the Joint Committee on Taxation, *General Explanation of the Economic Recovery Tax Act of 1981*, (H.R. 4242, 97th Congress, Pub. L. No. 97-34, December 29, 1981) at 289. (Hereinafter referred to as "1981 Bluebook".) However, notional principal contracts may constitute an interest in personal property. See Treasury Regulation §1.1092(d)-1(c)(2).

[9] Per the legislative history, property need not be traded on an exchange or on a recog-

nized market in order to be considered actively traded. 1981 Bluebook at 289. The regulations provide that any personal property for which an established financial market exists is actively traded. Treasury Regulation §1.1092(d)-1(a). An "established financial market" includes an interbank or interdealer market, a domestic board of trade designated as a contract market by the CFTC, and a national securities exchange registered under §6 of the 1934 Securities Exchange Act. See Treasury Regulation §1.1092(d)-1(b)(1) for a complete list. (A notional principal contract is actively traded if contracts based on the same or substantially similar specified indices are purchased, etc., on an established financial market. Treasury Regulation §1.1092(d)-1(c)(1).

[10] Proposed regulations require the stock to be of a type that is "actively traded," Proposed Regulation §1.1092(d)-2(a)(1). These regulations were issued in 1995. Consequently, they do not address the 2000 amendment to the Tax Code, under which personal property also includes stock that is part of a straddle where one of the offsetting positions is a securities futures contract. See Tax Code §1092(d)(3)(B)

[11] Under IRS regulations, property is "substantially similar or related" to stock if the property and stock primarily reflect performance of a single firm, industry, or economic factor(s). In addition, changes in the stock's value must be reasonably expected to approximate, directly or inversely, changes in the fair market value of the property, a fraction of the value of the property or a multiple. See Treasury Regulation §1.1092(d)-2(a), generally, using the regulations appearing at §1.246-5. If changes in the value of the stock and the property are reasonably expected to vary inversely, the taxpayer has diminished her risk of loss. Treasury Regulation §1.246-5(b)(2). Stock in a corporation formed or used to hold positions in personal property that offset positions held by shareholders is also considered personal property. Tax Code §§1092(d)(3)

[12] Tax Code §1092(d)(4). A corporation with whom the taxpayer files a consolidated return is also related. Unless the regulations provide otherwise, if gain or loss from a position owned by a partnership, S corporation, or trust would be taken into account by the taxpayer, he or she is treated as owning the position. *Id.* The definition of related persons under the hedging rules is narrower.

[13] Tax Code §1092(c)(2). In an identified straddle, positions outside the straddle are not treated as offsetting positions within. Tax Code §1092(c)(2)(C). See the discussion later in this chapter.

[14] Diversification alone does not substantially diminish risk provided the positions are not balanced. 1981 Bluebook at p. 288. If a position offsets only a portion of another position, only part of the loss should be subject to the deferral rules. Tax Code §1092(c)(2)(B)

[15] 1981 Bluebook at p. 288. The IRS is authorized to issue regulations extending this presumption to other debt instruments. Tax Code §1092(c)(3)(A)(iii)

[16] Tax Code §1092(c)(3). Positions need not be in the same kind of personal property in order to be offsetting. Tax Code §1092(c)(2)(A)

[17] If gain has been realized on the position as of the end of the taxable year but not recognized, the unrecognized gain is equivalent to the realized gain. Tax Code §1092(a)(3)

[18] No report is necessary if a taxpayer has no losses during the tax year, Tax Code §1092(a)(3)(B)(ii). See Tax Code §1092(a)(3)(B)(ii) for a list of exceptions to the reporting requirements, including exceptions for hedges and identified straddles.

[19] The hedging exception is not useful to investors. According to the Tax Code, a hedging transaction is a transaction entered into in the normal course of a taxpayer's trade or

business. It must be used primarily to manage the risk of price changes or currency fluctuations as to ordinary property. It also includes transactions that manage risk of interest rate or price changes or currency fluctuations as to borrowings or ordinary obligations of a taxpayer. Tax Code §1221(b)(2)(A). This definition poses a number of problems for investors who hold personal property, like options or futures contracts, as investment assets. In particular, in a hedging transaction, the item hedged must constitute ordinary property, ordinary obligations, or borrowings. Property is ordinary if a sale or exchange could not generate capital gain or loss under any circumstances. Treasury Regulation §1.1221-2(c)(2). Under the tax law, however, an asset held for investment is a capital asset, meaning it will produce capital gain or loss upon disposition. Tax Code §1221. As a result, taxpayers are unable to characterize risk reduction strategies adopted in connection with investments as hedges. Further, with respect to obligations, hedges are ordinary if gain or loss arising from an obligation's performance or termination could not be capital. Treasury Regulation §1.1221-2(c)(2). A "termination" is defined by §1234A of the Tax Code. That section provides that gain or loss from the cancellation, etc., of a right or obligation concerning property that is or would be a capital asset in the taxpayer's hands is treated as capital. Likewise, gain or loss from the cancellation, etc., of a §1256 contract that is a capital asset for the taxpayer is treated as arising from the sale of a capital asset. This means an investor's obligations under a short sale of stock held as a capital asset would not be ordinary, where the short sale is the hedged item. Additionally, the hedge must involve a transaction entered into in the normal course of a taxpayer's trade or business. According to case law arising in the context of other tax issues, "taxpayers who are simply investors . . . are not considered to be engaged in a trade or business, notwithstanding the frequency, extent and regularity of their investment activity." *Asch v. Commissioner of Internal Revenue*, T.C. Memo 1986-238 (U.S. Tax Court 1986).

[20] Tax Code §1092(a)(2)(B). The regulations may provide other timing rules for identification. *Id.*

[21] IRS Publication 550, *Investment Income and Expenses* (2002), p. 56

[22] Tax Code §1092(c)(2)(C). Similarly, the interest capitalization rules of Code §263(g) are not applicable to the outside positions.

[23] Tax Code §1092(a)(2). An investor also can make an IRC §1256(d) election for an identified straddle that includes one but not all §1256 contracts. See Tax Code §1256(d), discussed in Chapter 18 (elections with respect to mixed straddles). That would mean the mark-to-market, 60/40 and loss deferral rules wouldn't apply.

[24] Tax Code §1092(d)(5). The exception for straddles consisting solely of §1256 contracts does not apply if the straddle is part of a larger straddle arrangement. Tax Code §1256(a)(4)

[25] Tax Code §1092(c)(4). This exception does not apply if the straddle is part of a larger straddle. *Id.*

[26] IRS Publication 550, *Investment Income and Expenses* (2002), p. 56. Regulations have been issued under which equity options with flexible terms, over-the-counter options, and standardized options with terms longer than one year may be eligible for qualified covered call option treatment. See Treasury Regulation §1.1092(c)

[27] A special year-end rule may apply, under which investors holding qualified covered call options might nonetheless be subjected to the loss deferral rules of Code §1092. This rule applies if three conditions are met. First the taxpayer closes a qualified covered call op-

tion or disposes of the stock at a loss during the tax year. Second, gain on the disposition of the stock or option is includible in gross income in a later tax year. Finally, the stock or options were held less than 30 days after closing the option or disposing of the stock. See Tax Code §1092(c)(4)(E).

[28] According to the statute, the option must be traded on a national securities exchange registered with the SEC or on another market that the Secretary of the Treasury determines has rules adequate for purposes of this provision. Tax Code §1092(c)(4)(B)(i)

[29] Tax Code §1092(c)(4)(B)(ii)

[30] Tax Code §1092(c)(4)(B)(iv). An options dealer is defined at Code §1256(g)(8). See the discussion in Chapter 18.

[31] Tax Code §1092(c)(4)(B)(v)

[32] Tax Code §1092(c)(4)(B)(iii)

[33] Tax Code §1092(c)(4)(F)

[34] Tax Code §1092(c)(4). If an option is granted for a period more than 90 days at a strike price that exceeds $50, the lowest qualified benchmark is the second highest available strike price that is less than the applicable stock price. If the applicable stock price is $25 or less and the lowest qualified benchmark would otherwise be less than 85 percent of the applicable stock price, then the lowest qualified benchmark is treated as 85 percent of the applicable stock price. Where the applicable stock price is $150 or less and the lowest qualified benchmark otherwise would be less than the applicable stock price reduced by $10, the lowest qualified benchmark is equal to the applicable stock price reduced by $10. Tax Code §1092(c)(4)(D).

[35] Tax Code §1092(c)(4)(G). Regulations provide that the lowest qualified benchmark for equity options with standardized terms is not affected by strike prices for equity options with flexible terms. Treasury Regulation §1.1092(c)-2(b)

[36] IRS Publication 550, *Investment Income and Expenses* (2002), p. 56

[37] IRS Publication 550, *Investment Income and Expenses* (2002), p. 56. The holding period of stock subject to a qualified covered call option granted by the taxpayer does not include any period during which the taxpayer was the grantor of the option. Tax Code §1092(f)(2)

[38] These rules do not apply to hedging transactions, straddles consisting of only §1256 contracts, and straddles included in a mixed straddle account. Temporary Regulation §1.1092(b)-2T(c)(1). See Temporary Regulation §1.1092(b)-2T(c)(2) for exceptions applicable to identified mixed straddles.

[39] Temporary Regulations §1.1092(b)-2T(b)(1). This rule also applies if the offsetting position is held indirectly, through a related person or flow through entity. *Id.*

[40] See the discussion in Chapter 18. If Lynn had held a §1256 contract for more than one year and then acquired an offsetting position, the rule requiring her to report any loss as long-term would not apply. This is because disposition of the §1256 investment would have generated 60/40 income, not long-term gain.

[41] IRS Publication 550, *Investment Income and Expenses* (2002), p. 57

[42] Tax Code §1091. The rules also apply where the taxpayer enters into a contract or option to buy substantially identical stock or securities. See the discussion of the wash sale rules in Chapter 19.

[43] Tax Code §1092(b). See Treasury Regulation §1.1092(b)-1T.

[44] IRS Publication 550, *Investment Income and Expenses* (2002), p. 56. The rule does

not apply to losses sustained by dealers in stock or securities, where the loss arose in the ordinary course of business. *Id.* Note that under the regulations, the acquisition or exchange must have involved a transaction in which all gain or loss was recognized. Temporary Regulation §1.1092(b)-T(a)(1)

[45] Temporary Regulation §1.1092(b)-1T(b)

[46] Temporary Regulation §1.1092(b)-1T(g), Ex. 20

[47] A "disposition" includes a sale, exchange, cancellation, lapse, expiration, or other termination of a right or obligation. Temporary Regulation §1.1092(b)-5T(a)

[48] IRS Publication 550, *Investment Income and Expenses* (2002), p. 57. Note that a transaction does not represent a successor position if both legs of the straddle were disposed of before the new position is entered. Temporary Regulation §1.1092(b)-1T(g), Ex. 9

[49] Temporary Regulation §1.1092(b)-1T(g), Ex. 8

[50] Temporary Regulations §1.1092(b)-1T(g) ex. 25

[51] IRS Publication 550, *Investment Income and Expenses* (2002), p. 57. Mixed straddle accounts are discussed later in this chapter. Hedges are described in note 19 of this chapter and §1256 contracts were the subject of Chapter 18.

[52] IRS Publication 550, *Investment Income and Expenses* (2002), p. 57. Otherwise, the loss is ordinary, Temporary Regulation §1.1092(b)-1T(c)(1). If the 60/40 rule would apply to the disposition of a loss position, the carried over loss is subject to the 60/40 provisions, even if gain or loss on successor positions would be 100 percent long-term or short-term capital gain or loss. Temporary Regulation §1.1092(b)-1T(c)(2)

[53] Tax Code §263(g). Proposed regulations were issued under Tax Code §263(g) in 2001. These regulations include guidance on what is "personal property" under the capitalization rules and also the type of payments that must be capitalized. In addition, the regulations discuss the operation of the capitalization rules and the cases in which an obligation under a debt instrument may constitute part of a straddle. See Proposed Regulation §1.263(g).

[54] See Tax Code §263(g)(2). Reductions also are made for amounts treated as ordinary income under Code §§1271(a)(3)(A), 1278, and 1281(a) with respect to personal property and also payments with respect to security loans includible in connection with the property. See Tax Code §263(g)(2)(B).

[55] Hedges are discussed in this chapter, at note 19.

[56] Temporary Regulation §1.1092(b)-5T(e)

[57] Temporary Regulation §1.1092(b)-5T(e)

[58] IRS Publication 550, *Investment Income and Expenses* (2002), p. 57. Note that the definition of mixed straddle under Code §1256, discussed in Chapter 18, differs somewhat from the definition provided in the Code §1092 regulations, described in this paragraph. Tax Code §1256 provides only that a mixed straddle refers to a straddle where one but not all positions are §1256 contracts, provided certain identification requirements are met. Tax Code §1256(d).

[59] Temporary Regulations §1.1092(b)-2T(b)(2)

[60] Temporary Regulation §1.1092(b)-2T(c)

[61] IRS Publication 550, *Investment Income and Expenses* (2002), p. 58

[62] IRS Publication 550, *Investment Income and Expenses* (2002), p. 58. Identification is required for each position by the earlier of the close of the day on which the straddle is established or the time the position is disposed of. *Id.* If a position is disposed of on the day the straddle is established, identification must occur by the time of disposition. *Id.* Timely

identification is presumed if an investor receives independent verification of identification. This presumption is rebuttable. Where the presumption does not apply, the burden of proof is on the taxpayer to establish timely identification. Temporary Regulation §1.1092(b)-3T(d)

[63] Temporary Regulation §1.1092(b)-3T(b)(2)

[64] If positions constituting part of an identified mixed straddle were held by the investor before the straddle was established, they are treated as though they were sold for fair market value as of the close of the last business day before the day on which the straddle was created. This means an adjustment is necessary for any later gain or loss realized with respect to the positions deemed sold. See Temporary Regulation §1.1092(b)-3T(b)(6).

[65] Temporary Regulation §1.1092(b)-3T(b)(2), Ex. 6

[66] Temporary Regulation §1.1092(b)-3T(b)(3)

[67] Temporary Regulation §1.1092(b)-3T(b)(3), Ex. 1. If Marty had reported a net loss, he would be able to claim a deduction, unless prevented by the loss deferral or wash sale rules.

[68] Temporary Regulation §1.1092(b)-3T(b)(4). Under the regulations, gain or loss on non-§1256 contracts that are part of an identified mixed straddle, held after the investor disposed all of the §1256 contracts constituting positions in the same straddle, is treated as short-term to the extent attributable to the period during which the investments were part of the straddle transaction. Temporary Regulation §1.1092(b)-3T(b)(7).

[69] Temporary Regulation §1.1092(b)-3T(b)(4), Ex. 3. The netting rules are applied at the time of disposition, meaning later changes to retained non-§1256 positions will not affect the results. Temporary Regulation §1.1092(b)-3T(b)(4), Ex. 4. See Temporary Regulation §1.1092(b)-3T(b)(5) for rules applicable where some but not all of the positions in a straddle are liquidated.

[70] Temporary Regulation §1.1092(b)-4T(b)(1). An investor can designate as a class of activities positions that a reasonable person, based on the facts and circumstances, would ordinarily expect to be offsetting. Temporary Regulation §1.1092(b)-4T(b)(2). The regulations give an example where a taxpayer engages in dealer equity options relating to XYZ stock and also in XYZ stock itself. Likewise, the taxpayer is involved in transactions in UVW stock and UVW dealer equity options. A reasonable person would not expect the XYZ investments to offset the UVW holdings. If the taxpayer wants to elect mixed straddle account treatment, two accounts will be necessary: one for the XYZ activity and one for the UVW transactions. *Id.* See Temporary Regulation §1.1092(b)-4T(b)(4) for rules applicable where impermissible designations of classes of activities are made. Other rules regarding removal or insertion of positions into mixed straddle accounts by the IRS can be found in Temporary Regulation §1.1092(b)-4T(b)(5) and (6).

Investors with a large number of straddle transactions may find Election C more convenient than the straddle-by-straddle identification method of Election B. See Temporary Regulation §1.1092(b)-4T(f) for rules regarding how to make Election C.

[71] Where a position is disposed of during the day, gain or loss is calculated using the amount received on the disposition. Positions not liquidated as of day's end are treated as though they were sold for fair market value at the close of the day. Temporary Regulation §1.1092(b)-4T(c)(1)

[72] Temporary Regulation §1.1092(b)-4T(c)(1)

[73] *Id.* Where an investor held a position prior to the creation of a mixed straddle account,

the position is treated as sold for fair market value as of the close of the last business day before the straddle account was established. This means an adjustment to later gains or losses realized with respect to these positions will be necessary. Temporary Regulation §1.1092(b)-4T(c)(5). A similar rule applies to straddle-by-straddle identifications. See note 64, above.

[74] An investor cannot deduct interest or carrying charges attributable to a mixed straddle account. Instead, these amounts are capitalized by making adjustments to the annual account net gain or loss. The charges are to be allocated on a pro rata basis between net short-term capital gain or loss and net long-term capital gain or loss. Temporary Regulation §1.1092(b)-4T(c)(3). Interest and carrying charges are reduced by interest, original issue discount, etc., includible in gross income with respect to positions in the account. *Id.*

[75] Temporary Regulation §1.1092(b)-4T(c)(4)

[76] Temporary Regulation §1.1092(b)-4T(c)(6), ex. 1. Note that this example does not include any adjustment for interest or other carrying charges.

21

NOTIONAL PRINCIPAL CONTRACTS

INTRODUCTION

Notional principal contracts (NPCs) have gained tremendous popularity because they provide participants with a number of advantages. Cash flows from each party's investment stream can be more closely matched, income from floating rates can be substituted for fixed rates on liabilities, and a party with access to low borrowing rates can sell this advantage to another party. Notional principal contracts are more flexible and provide considerable value as hedging devices that are not affected by §1256 and §1092 (where no foreign currencies are involved).

Notional principal contracts are used to reduce the cost of debt, enhance the yield on assets, and minimize the risks that are incident to fluctuating interest and foreign currency exchange rates. The two most common notional principal contracts are interest rate swaps and foreign currency swap agreements. This chapter focuses on various interest rate agreements.

NOTIONAL PRINCIPAL AGREEMENT

A notional principal contract is a financial instrument that provides for the payment of amounts by one party to another party, at designated intervals, calculated by reference to a specified index upon a notional principal amount. In exchange, the other party will pay a fixed amount at a fixed interval based on the same notional principal amount.[1] In other words, two parties are agreeing to exchange cash flows. One party usually makes payments based on a fixed rate and the other party makes payment based on a fluctuating rate of interest.

Example—On April 1, 2003, Stanley enters into a contract with Stella for a five-year period. During this time, Stanley is obligated to make a payment to Stella each April 1st, beginning April 1, 2004 in an amount equal to the London Interbank Offered Rate (LIBOR), as determined on the immediately preceding April 1, multiplied by a notional principal amount of $1,000,000. Under the contract, Stella is obligated to make a payment to Stanley each April 1, beginning April 1, 2004, of an amount equal to 4.75 percent multiplied by the same notional amount of $1,000,000. Stanley and Stella are calendar year taxpayers that use the accrual method of accounting. On April 1, 2002, LIBOR is 5 percent.

Under the terms of the swap agreement, on April 1, 2004, Stella is obligated to make a payment to Stanley of $47,500 ($1,000,000 × 4.75 percent) and Stanley is obligated to make a payment to Stella of $50,000 ($1,000,000 × 5 percent). The ratable daily portions for 2003 are the amounts of these periodic payments that are attributable to Stanley's and Stella's taxable year ending December 31, 2003. The ratable daily portion of the 4.75 percent fixed payment is $35,690 ($47,500 × 275 days/366 days). The ratable daily portion of the floating portion is $37,568 ($50,000 × 275 days/366 days). The net amount for the taxable year is the difference between the ratable daily portions of the two periodic payments or $1878 ($37,568 − $35,690). Accordingly, Stella has net income of $1878 from this swap for 2003, and Stanley has a corresponding net deduction of $1878. The $622 unrecognized balance of the $2500 net periodic payment that is made on April 1, 2004, is included in Stanley's and Stella's net income or net deduction from the contract for 2004.[2]

TYPES OF NOTIONAL PRINCIPAL CONTRACTS

Notional principal contracts are generally governed by Reg. §1.446-3 and include interest rate swaps, currency swaps, basis swaps, interest rate caps, interest rate floors, commodity swaps, equity index swaps, and similar agreements. A collar is itself not a notional principal contract, but certain caps and floors that comprise a collar may be treated as one. A contract may be a notional principal contract even though the term of the contract is subject to termination or extension.[3] Each confirmation under a master agreement to enter into an agreement is treated as a separate notional principal contract.[4]

The following is a list of definitions for the notional principal contracts listed in Reg. §1.446-3:

- Interest Rate Swap is a transaction where one party pays periodic amounts of a given currency based on a specified fixed rate. The other party pays periodic amounts of the same currency, but this payment is based on a specified floating rate that is recalculated periodically.
- Commodity Swap is a transaction in which one party pays periodic amounts of a given currency based on a fixed price. The other party pays periodic amounts of the same currency, but these payments are based on the price of a commodity, such as natural gas, gold, or a commodity futures contract.
- Equity or Equity Index Swap is a transaction in which one party pays periodic amounts of a given currency based on a fixed price or a fixed rate. The other party pays periodic amounts of the same or a different currency. However, these amounts are based on the performance of a share of an issuer, a number of shares of several issuers, or an equity index, such as the Standard and Poor's 500 index.
- Cap Transaction is a transaction whereby one party pays a single or periodic fixed amount. The other party pays periodic amounts of the same currency that are based on the excess, if any, of a specified floating rate that is reset periodically over a specified per annum rate.
- Floor Transaction is a transaction in which one party pays a single or periodic amount and the other party pays periodic amounts of the same currency. These payments are based on the excess, if any, of a specified per-annum rate or a specified price over a specified floating rate or commodity price.
- Collar Transaction is a blending of a cap and a floor where one party is the floating rate or floating commodity price payer on the cap, and the other party is the floating rate or floating commodity price payer on the floor.
- Currency Swap is a transaction in which one party pays fixed periodic amounts of one currency and the other party pays fixed periodic amounts of another currency. Payments are calculated on a notional amount. Such swaps may involve initial and/or final payments that correspond to the notional amount.[5]

An agreement between a taxpayer and a qualified business unit of the taxpayer, or among qualified business units of the same taxpayer, is not a notional principal contract because a taxpayer cannot enter into a contract with itself.[6]

SPECIFIED INDEX

A specified index is:

- A fixed rate, price, or amount.
- A fixed rate, price, or amount applicable in one or more specified periods followed by one or more different fixed rates, prices, or amounts applicable in other periods.
- An index that is based on objective financial information.
- An interest rate index that is regularly used in normal lending transactions between a party to the contract and unrelated persons.[7]

Examples of some indexes include the prime rate of a bank, the Federal Reserve Rate, LIBOR, and the rate of a Treasury Obligation such as 90-day T-Bills.

HOW ARE NOTIONAL PRINCIPAL CONTRACTS TRADED?

Notional Principal Contracts formerly were privately negotiated between the parties without the use of an exchange. The interest rates on debt instruments depended on market rates and the credit worthiness of the parties involved. In time, a network of dealers, who developed a standardized contract, was used.

The International Swaps and Derivatives Association (ISDA) is the global trade association representing leading participants in the privately negotiated derivatives industry, a business that includes interest rate, currency, commodity, credit, and equity swaps, as well as related products such as caps, collars, floors, and options. ISDA was chartered in 1985 and today numbers over 575 member institutions from 44 countries on six continents. Its most notable contributions to trading in notional principal contracts include developing the ISDA Master Agreement. This Agreement is designed to facilitate cross-product netting and allows parties to document all derivative transactions under a single master agreement. Additional contributions include producing legal opinions on the enforceability of netting, securing recognition of the risk-reducing effects of netting in determining capital requirements, promoting sound risk management practices, and advancing the understanding and treatment of derivatives and risk management from public policy and regulatory capital perspectives.

EXCLUDED CONTRACTS

There are a number of contracts that are not considered notional principal contracts. These contracts are §1256(b) contracts, which include any regulated futures, any foreign currency contract, any nonequity option, and dealer equity option and any dealer securities futures contract. Additionally, a futures contract, a forward contract, and an option are not notional principal contracts.[8] An instrument or contract that constitutes indebtedness under general principles of federal income tax law is not a notional principal contract.[9] An option or forward contract that entitles or obligates a person to enter into a notional principal contract is not one; however, payments made under such an option or forward contract may be governed by special rules of Reg. 1.446-3.

TAXATION OF NOTIONAL PRINCIPAL CONTRACTS

The net income or net deduction from a NPC for a taxable year equals the total of all of the periodic and nonperiodic payments that are recognized from that contract in that taxable year.[10] Payments made pursuant to NPCs are divided into three categories: periodic, nonperiodic, and termination payments. The regulations provide separate timing regimes for each.

Periodic Payments

Periodic payments are those made or received pursuant to a NPC that are payable at intervals of one year or less during the entire term of the contract.[11] Payments are tied to a specified index and are based on either a single notional principal amount or an amount that varies over the term of the contract in the same proportion as the NPC measures the other party's payments.[12]

All taxpayers, regardless of their method of accounting, must recognize the ratable daily portion of a periodic payment for the taxable year to which that portion relates as ordinary income.[13]

Example—On April 1, 2002, Laurie enters into a contract with Jeff, an unrelated party, under which for a period of five years, Laurie is obligated to make a fixed payment to Jeff each April 1, beginning April 1, 2003, of an amount equal to 6 percent multiplied by a notional principal amount of $1,000,000. Jeff is obligated to make semi-annual payments to Laurie each April 1 and October 1, beginning October 1, 2002, of an amount equal to one-half of the LIBOR amount as of the first day of the preceding six-month period multiplied by the notional principal amount of $1,000,000. The payments are to be calculated using a 30/360-day convention. Laurie is a calendar-year taxpayer who uses the accrual method of accounting. Jeff is a calendar-year taxpayer who uses the cash receipts and disbursements method of accounting. LIBOR is 5.5 percent on April 1, 2002 and 5.75 percent on October 1, 2002.

Under terms of the swap agreement, Jeff pays Laurie $27,500 (.5 × 5.5 percent × $1,000,000) on October 1, 2002. Additionally, Jeff is obligated to pay Laurie $28,750 (.5 × 5.75 percent × $1,000,000) on April 1, 2003. Laurie is obligated to pay Jeff $60,000 on April 1, 2003. Laurie's and Jeff's ratable daily portions for 2002 are the amounts of the periodic payments that are attributable to their taxable year ending December 31, 2002. The ratable daily portion of the 6-percent fixed amount is $45,000 (270 days/360 days × $60,000). The ratable daily portion of the floating amount is $41,875 ($27,500 + (90 days/180 days × $28,750)). Therefore, Laurie's net deduction from the contract for 2002 is $3125 ($45,000 − $41,875) and Jeff reports $3125 of net ordinary income in 2002.

The net unrecognized balance of $625 [($60,000 − ($27,500 + $28,750) − $3125] is included in Laurie's and Jeff's net income or net deduction for 2002.[14]

If the value of the specified index is not fixed until a date that occurs after the end of the taxable year, then the periodic payment is generally based on a designated index that would have been applicable as of the last day of the taxable year.[15] If a taxpayer determines that the value of the designated index as of the last day of the taxable year does not provide a reasonable estimate of the specified index, the taxpayer may use a reasonable estimate of the specified index each year.[16] However, the taxpayer and any other related person that is a party to the contract must use the same method to make the estimate consistently from year to year. This same method must also be used for financial reports to equity holders and creditors.[17] Any difference between the amount recognized and the corresponding portion of the actual payment calculated when the index becomes fixed is an adjustment to the net income or deduction for the taxable year during which the payment becomes fixed.[18]

Example—The facts are the same as in the previous example except that Jeff's obligation to make payments based upon LIBOR is determined by reference to LIBOR on the day each payment is due. LIBOR is 5.40 percent on December 31, 2002, 6.25 percent on April 1, 2003, and 6.3 percent on October 1, 2003.

On December 31, 2002, the amount that Jeff is obligated to pay Laurie is not known because it will not become fixed until April 1, 2003. The ratable daily portion of the periodic payment from Jeff to Laurie for 2002 is based on the value of LIBOR on December 31, 2002 (unless Jeff or Laurie determines that the value of LIBOR on that day does not reasonably estimate the value of the specified index). The ratable daily portion of the floating portion is $40,500 (270 days/360 days × 5.40 percent × $1,000,000). The ratable daily portion of the fixed portion remains at $45,000. The net amount for 2002 on this swap is $4500 ($45,000 − $40,500). Accordingly, Jeff has $4500 of net income from the swap in 2002, and Laurie has a net deduction of the same amount.

In 2003, Jeff makes a net payment to Laurie of $2,750 ($62,500/2 = $31,250 + $63,000/2 = $31,500 payment on floating portion − $60,000 payment on fixed portion). For purposes of determining their net income or deduction from this contract for the year ended December 31, 2003, Jeff and Laurie must adjust the net income and deduction that they recognized in 2002 by $6,563 (270 days/360 days × ($62,750 actual payment on floating amount − $54,000 assumed payment on floating amount)).[19]

Nonperiodic Payments

The regulations describe a nonperiodic payment as any payment made or received with respect to a notional principal contract that is not a periodic payment. Examples of nonperiodic payments are the premium for a cap or floor agreement (even if it is paid in installments), the payment for an off-market swap agreement, the prepayment of part or all of one portion of a swap, and the premium for an option to enter into a swap if and when the option is exercised.[20]

A method of accounting that properly recognizes a nonperiodic payment over the life of the contract is considered to clearly reflect income. Including the entire amount of such a payment in income when it is received or deferring the entire amount of the payment to the termination of the contract does not clearly reflect income and is an impermissible method of accounting.[21]

General Rule for Swaps   A nonperiodic payment that relates to a swap must be recognized over the term of the contract by allocating it in accordance with the forward rates (or, in the case of a commodity, the forward prices) of a series of cash-settled forward contracts that reflect the specified index and the notional principal amount.[22] Any reasonable method of selecting the forward rates or prices will be respected.[23]

Example—On January 1, 2001, John enters into a commodity swap agreement with unrelated counterparty Florence. Under this contract, John is obligated to make annual payments, for a term of three years, based on a fixed price of $2.35 per bushel times a notional amount of 100,000 bushels of corn. Florence is obligated to make annual payments equal to the spot price times the same notional amount. Assume that on January 1, 2001, the price of a one-year forward for corn is $2.40 per bushel, of a two-year forward $2.55 per bushel, and of a three-year forward $2.75 per bushel. To compensate for the below-market fixed price provided in the swap agreement, John pays Florence $53,530 for entering into the swap. John and Florence are calendar year taxpayers.

John must recognize the nonperiodic payment of $53,530 over the term of the agreement by allocating the payment to each forward contract in accordance with the forward price of corn. Solely for timing purposes, John treats the $53,530 payment as a loan that Florence will repay in three installments of $5000, $20,000, and $40,000, the expected payouts on the in-the-money forward contracts. Assuming annual compounding at 8 percent, the ratable daily portions are computed as shown in Table 21-1.

The ratable daily portion of the principal component is added to John's periodic payments in computing the net income or deduction from the notional principal contract for each taxable year. The time value components are needed only to compute the principal components, and are otherwise disregarded.[24]

Alternative Methods for Swaps   The determination of the timing of income and deductions of a nonperiodic payment made or received with respect to a swap may be made by use of one of the alternative methods described below. However, these methods may not be used by a dealer in notional principal contracts.

TABLE 21-1

	Expected Forward Payment	Time Value Component*	Principal Component**	Principal Balance
				53,530
2001	5,000	4,282	718	52,812
2002	20,000	4,225	15,775	37,037
2003	40,000	2,963	37,037	0

*Principal balance × 8%
**Expected forward payment − Time value component

(1) Prepaid Swaps

An up-front payment on a swap may be amortized by assuming that the nonperiodic payment represents the present value of a series of equal payments made throughout the term of the swap contract, adjusted for increases or decreases in the notional principal amount.[25] The discount rate must be the rate used by the parties to determine the amount of the nonperiodic payment. If that rate is not readily ascertainable, the discount rate used must be a rate that is reasonable under the circumstances.[26]

Under this method, an up-front payment is allocated by dividing each equal payment into its principal recovery and time value components. The principal recovery components of the equal payments are treated as periodic payments that are deemed to be made throughout the term of the swap contract.[27]

Example—On January 1, 2001, Chris enters into an interest rate swap agreement with Jim, an unrelated counterparty. For a term of five years, Chris is obligated to make annual payments at 11 percent and Jim is obligated to make annual payments at LIBOR on a notional principal amount of $1,000,000. At the time Chris and Jim enter into this swap agreement, the rate for similar on-market swaps is LIBOR at 10 percent. To compensate for this difference, on January 1, 2001, Jim pays Chris a yield adjustment fee of $37,908. Chris provides Jim with information that indicates that the amount, of the yield adjustment fee that was determined as the present value is 10 percent compounded annually, of five annual payments of $10,000 (1 percent × $1,000,000). Chris and Jim are calendar year taxpayers.

Under the alternative method, the yield adjustment fee is recognized over the life of the agreement by assuming that the $37,908 is repaid in five

TABLE 21-2

	Five Level Payments	Time Value Component*	Principal Component**	Principal Balance
				37,908
2001	10,000	3,791	6,209	31,699
2002	10,000	3,170	6,830	24,869
2003	10,000	2,487	7,513	17,356
2004	10,000	1,736	8,264	9,091
2005	10,000	909	9,091	0
	50,000	12,092	37,908	—

*Principal balance × 10%
**Level payment − time value component

level payments. Assuming a constant yield to maturity and annual compounding at 10 percent, the ratable daily portions are computed as shown in Table 21-2.

Chris also makes swap payments to Jim at 11 percent, while Jim makes swap payments to Chris based on LIBOR. The net of the ratable daily portions of the 11-percent payments by Chris, the LIBOR payments by Jim, and the principal component of the yield adjustment fee paid by Jim determines the annual net income or net deduction from the contract for both Chris and Jim. The time value components are needed only to compute the ratable daily portions of the yield adjustment fee paid by Jim, and are otherwise disregarded.[28]

(2) Other Nonperiodic Swap Payments

Nonperiodic payments on a swap other than an up-front payment may be amortized by treating the contract as though it provided for a single up-front payment (equal to the present value of the nonperiodic payments) and a loan between the parties.[29] The discount rate used in determining the deemed up-front payment and the time value component of the deemed loan is the same as the rate used in the level payment method. The single up-front payment is then amortized under the level payment method. The time value component of the loan is not treated as interest, but, together with the amortized amount of the deemed up-front payment, is recognized as a periodic payment.

Example—The facts are the same as in the previous example, but Jim agrees to pay Chris a yield adjustment fee of $61,051 on December 31,

TABLE 21-3

	Beginning Loan Amount	Time Value Component*	Present Value
2001	37,908	3,791	41,699
2002	41,699	4,170	45,869
2003	45,869	4,587	50,456
2004	50,456	5,046	55,501
2005	55,501	5,550	61,051

*Beginning loan amount × 10%

2005. Under this alternative method, Jim is treated as paying a yield adjustment fee of $37,908 (the present value of $61,051 discounted at a 10-percent rate with annual compounding) on January 1, 2001. Solely for timing purposes, Jim is treated as borrowing $37,908 from Chris. Assuming annual compounding at 10 percent, Table 21-3 shows the time value component computed.

The amortization of Jim's yield adjustment fee is equal to the amortization of a yield adjustment fee of $37,908 paid in advance, increased by the time value component of the $37,908 deemed loan from Chris to Jim. Thus, the amount of Jim's yield adjustment fee that is allocated to 2001 is $10,000 ($6,209 + $3,791 from the previous example). The time value components of the $37,908 loan are included in the periodic payments paid by Jim, but are not characterized as interest income or expense. The net of the ratable daily portions of the 11-percent swap payments by Chris, and the LIBOR payments by Jim, added to the principal components from the previous example and the time value component from this example determines the annual net income or net deduction from the contract for both Chris and Jim.[30]

General Rule for Caps and Floors A payment to purchase or sell a cap or floor must be recognized over the term of the agreement by allocating it in accordance with the prices of a series of cash-settled option contracts that reflect the specified index and the notional principal amount.[31] The option pricing used by the parties for purposes of this allocation must be reasonable. Only the portion of the purchase price that is allocable to the option contract or contracts that expire during a particular period is recognized for that period.[32] Therefore, straight-line or accelerated amortization of a cap premium is generally not permitted.[33]

Example—On January 1, 2001, when LIBOR is 8 percent, Bridget pays $600,000 to Bob, an unrelated party, for a contract that obligates Bob to make a payment to Bridget each quarter equal to one-quarter of the excess, if any, of the three-month LIBOR over 9 percent with respect to a notional principal amount of $25 million. Both Bob and Bridget are calendar-year taxpayers. Bob provides Bridget with a schedule of allocable premium amounts indicating that the cap was priced according to a reasonable variation of the Black-Scholes option pricing formula and that the total premium is allocable to the following periods:

2001	$55,000
2002	225,000
2003	<u>320,000</u>
	<u>$600,000</u>

Since the Black-Scholes model is recognized in the financial industry as a standard technique, Bob's use of this model is reasonable, and the schedule generated is consistent with the economic substance of the cap. Both Bob and Bridget may use this schedule for calculating their ratable daily portions of the cap premium. Bob recognizes the ratable daily portion of the cap premium as income, and Bridget recognizes this amount as a deduction.[34]

Alternative Methods for Caps and Floors that Hedge Debt Instruments
If a cap or floor is entered into primarily to reduce risk with respect to a specific debt instrument or group of debt instruments held or issued by the taxpayer, the taxpayer may amortize a payment to purchase or sell the cap or floor using one of the methods described below, adjusted for the increases or decreases in the notional principal amount. A dealer in notional principal contracts may not use these methods:

(1) Prepaid Caps and Floors—A premium paid up front for a cap or a floor may be amortized using the "level payment method" described above.[35]

(2) Other Caps and Floors—Nonperiodic payments on a cap or floor that are not paid up front are amortized by treating the contract as if it provided for a single up-front payment (equal to the present value of the nonperiodic payments) and a loan between the parties, as described above.[36]

(3) Special Method for Collars—A taxpayer may also treat a cap and a floor that comprise a collar as a single NPC and may amortize

the net nonperiodic payment to enter into the cap and floor over the term of the collar in accordance with other methods for caps and floors.[37]

Termination Payments

A payment made or received to finish or assign all or a part of the remaining rights and obligations of any party under a NPC is a termination payment.[38] A termination payment includes a payment made between the original parties (extinguishment), a payment made between one original party and a third party (assignment), and any gain or loss realized on the exchange of one NPC contract for another.[39]

A party to a NPC recognizes a termination payment in the year the contract is extinguished, assigned, or exchanged.[40] Additionally, any other payments that have been made or received are recognized. If the transaction involves only a proportionate share of a party's rights and obligations, then only that proportion of the unrecognized payments is recognized.[41] A termination payment made or received by an assignee is recognized as a nonperiodic payment for the NPC.[42]

Example—Termination by extinguishment. On January 1, 2001, Jeff enters into an interest rate swap agreement with Lisa, an unrelated counterparty, for a term of seven years. Under this contract, Jeff is obligated to make annual payments based on 10 percent and Lisa is obligated to make semi-annual payments based on LIBOR and a notional principal amount of $1,000,000. Jeff and Lisa are both calendar-year taxpayers. On January 1, 2003, when the fixed rate on a comparable LIBOR swap has fallen to 9.5 percent, Jeff pays Lisa $1895 to terminate the swap. The payment from Jeff to Lisa extinguishes the swap contract and is a termination payment for both parties. Accordingly, Jeff recognizes a loss of $1895 in 2003 and Lisa recognizes a gain for the same amount.[43]

Example—Termination by assignment. The facts are the same as in the above example except that on January 1, 2003, Jeff pays Kim, an unrelated party, $1895 to assume all of Jeff's rights and obligations under the swap with Lisa. In return for this payment, Kim agrees to pay 10 percent of $1,000,000 annually to Lisa and to receive LIBOR payments from Lisa for the remaining five years of the swap. The payment from Jeff to Kim terminates his interest in the swap contract with Lisa and is a termination payment. Jeff recognizes a loss of $1895 in 2003. The assignment payment that Kim receives from Jeff is a nonperiodic payment for an interest rate swap. Because this payment is not a significant nonperiodic payment, Kim amortizes the $1895 over the five-year term of the swap agreement.[44]

Anti-abuse Rule

If a taxpayer enters into a transaction for the purpose of applying the regulations to produce a material distortion of income, the Commissioner of the Internal Revenue Service may depart from these regulations. This departure may be made to the extent necessary to reflect the appropriate timing of income and deductions from the transaction.[45]

One such type of transaction is when a taxpayer enters into a notional principal contract and makes periodic payments by borrowing funds. He/she may enter into an agreement to terminate the NPC prior to the scheduled payment date of the nonperiodic payment. The taxpayer deducts the ratable daily portion of each periodic payment but does not accrue income with respect to the nonperiodic payment. Instead, he/she intends to report the income realized as capital gain upon termination of the contract. Another example is when the taxpayer uses a partnership as a party to a NPC to engage in some or all of the activities. The benefits purportedly generated by these types of transactions are not allowable for federal income tax purposes.[46]

TIMING

No guidance is provided in the regulations for when contingent nonperiodic payments made under NPCs are included on a person's tax return as income or deductions. Additionally, neither Reg. §1.446-3 nor any other section provides specific rules governing the character of the various types of payments that could be made pursuant to a NPC.[47] The following methods are considered appropriate for recognition of contingent payments: the Noncontingent Swap Method, the Full Allocation Method, the Modified Full Allocation Method, and the Mark-to-Market Method.

- The Noncontingent Swap Method provides rules for creating a payment schedule that spreads the recognition of income or deduction of this noncontingent amount over the life of the NPC on a constant yield basis.[48]
- The Full Allocation Method does not have taxpayers include or deduct any payment that is required to be made under the NPC

(periodic, nonperiodic, contingent, and noncontingent) until the taxable year in which all contingencies are resolved. When the final contingency is resolved, the parties would treat all payments as made or received in the year of the resolution of the contingency.[49]

- The Modified Full Allocation method has each party to a NPC offsetting any noncontingent payments made by that party in a taxable year against any payments received in that year with respect to the NPC. However, the party would not be able to claim a deduction if the amount received were less than the amount paid out. Any net deductions with respect to the NPC would be deferred until all contingencies are resolved.[50]

- The Mark-to-Market Method specifies that taxpayers would mark their NPCs to market and recognize gain or loss at year end, or when the contract is terminated, assigned, etc.[51]

The rules for various financial instruments are inconsistent with each other, and it is difficult to decide which rules should be applicable to new instruments. In evaluating each method, the IRS and Treasury have considered the extent to which each method reflects fundamental tax policy principles.

CONCLUSION

Notional principal contracts have been used to reduce the cost of debt, increase the yield on investments, and manage interest rate exposure. When used with other financial instruments, they alter the resulting cash flows of the asset or liability that ultimately meets the needs of the parties involved. The versatility of these instruments has also been applied in other areas such as commodity price risks. Further embellishments and applications evolve constantly.

NOTES

[1] Reg. §1.446-3(c)(i)
[2] Based on Example 1 of Reg. §1.446-3(e)(3)
[3] *Id.*
[4] *Id.*
[5] The definitions were derived from *www.isda.org*. An Introduction to the Documentation of OTC Derivatives by Allen & Overy.

[6] *Id*

[7] Reg. §1.446-3(c)(2)

[8] Reg. §1.446-3(c)(ii)

[9] *Id.*

[10] Reg. §1.446-3(d)

[11] Reg. §1.446-3(e)

[12] *Id.*

[13] Reg. §1.446-3(e)(2)

[14] This example was based on Example 2 of Reg. §1.446-3(e)(3)

[15] Reg. §1.446-3(e)(2)(ii)

[16] *Id.*

[17] *Id.*

[18] *Id.*

[19] Based on facts contained in Example 3 of Reg. §1.446-3(e)(3)

[20] Reg. §1.446-3(f)(1)

[21] Notice 89-21, 1989-1 C.B. 651 and Rev. Rul. 2002-30

[22] Reg. §1.446-3(f)(2)(ii)

[23] *Id.*

[24] Facts are taken from Example 7 in Reg. §1.446-3(f)(4)

[25] Reg. 1.446-3(f)(2)(iii)(A)

[26] *Id.*

[27] *Id.*

[28] Based on facts contained in Example 5 of Reg. §1.446-3(f)(4)

[29] Reg. §1.446-3(f)(2)(B)

[30] The example was based on facts from Example 6 in Reg.§1.446-3(f)(4)

[31] Reg. 1.446-3(f)(2)(iv)

[32] *Id.*

[33] *Id.*

[34] Example was based on the facts of Example 1 of Reg. §1.446-3(f)(4)

[35] Reg. §1.446-3((f)(2)(v)(A)

[36] Reg. §1.446-3(f)(2)(v)(B)

[37] Reg. §1.446-3(f)(2)(v)(C)

[38] Reg. §1.446-3(h)(1)

[39] *Id.*

[40] Reg. §1.446-3(h)(2)

[41] *Id.*

[42] Reg. §1.446-3(h)(3)

[43] This example is based on the facts contained in Example 1 of Reg. §1.446-3(h)(5)

[44] This example is based on the facts contained in Example 2 of Reg. §1.446-3(h)(5)

[45] Reg. §1.446-3(i)

[46] Notice 2002-35, 2002-21 I.R.B. 992 (5/28/2002)

[47] Notice 2001-44

[48] *Id.*

[49] *Id.*

[50] *Id.*

[51] *Id.*

22

FOREIGN CURRENCY DENOMINATED INSTRUMENTS

INTRODUCTION

Transactions in foreign currencies have always been very confusing. There were uncertainties regarding gains and losses arising from fluctuations in the value of currencies. Additionally, transactions were uncertain in regards to the timing, amount, and character of any recognized gain or loss.

Businesses have quickly become significantly global in scope, and today there are very few corporations of any size that do not do some foreign business. Furthermore, various foreign currency denominated instruments have been used more frequently, including foreign currency denominated debt, accounts payable and receivable, and currency contracts and swaps. Consequently, Congress found it increasingly important to resolve the many issues arising from foreign currency transactions.

The Tax Reform Act of 1986 added Subpart J, which includes §985 through §989 to the Internal Revenue Code. It was the desire of Congress to simplify the rules governing foreign currency, provide guidance for planning of legitimate transactions, and reduce opportunities for tax avoidance. This chapter will highlight the provisions of these sections of the Internal Revenue Code.

DEFINITIONS OF KEY CONCEPTS

The following discussion is a summary of key concepts that apply to foreign currency transactions.

Qualified Business Unit

A qualified business unit (QBU) is any separate and clearly identified unit of a trade or business of a taxpayer that keeps separate books and records.[1] Corporations are QBUs; partnerships, trusts, or estates are QBUs of a partner or beneficiary.[2]

Functional Currency

A taxpayer or qualified business unit must calculate income using the currency where the activities that produce income or loss are produced. There is a bias in the regulations towards using the U.S. dollar because there is an immediate recognition of taxable income or loss. Foreign functional currencies defer this recognition.

- Dollar Functional Currency—The dollar shall be the functional currency of the following taxpayers, regardless of the currency used in keeping its books and records:
  1. An individual
  2. A qualified business unit that conducts its activities primarily in dollars
  3. Territories where the dollar is the standard currency
  4. A qualified business unit that does not keep books and records in the currency of any economic environment in which a significant part of its activities is conducted
  5. A qualified business unit that produces income or loss that is (or treated as) effectively connected with the conduct of a trade or business within the US.[3]

  Additionally, any QBU that would be required to use a hyperinflationary currency[4] as its functional currency must use the dollar as its functional currency.[5] Exceptions exist for a QBU that is a branch of a foreign corporation having a nondollar functional currency that is not hyperinflationary. The QBU must adopt that functional currency.[6] Additionally, a foreign corporation or its qualified business unit branch that operates in a hyperinflationary environment is not required to use the dollar as its functional currency.[7]

- Nondollar Functional Currency—The functional currency of a QBU that is not required to use the dollar shall be the currency of the economic environment in which a significant part of the activities of the business is conducted or if the business keeps its books in that currency.[8]

The facts and circumstances considered in determining the economic environment include:

1. The currency of the country in which the QBU is a resident
2. The currencies of the unit's cash flows
3. The currencies in which the QBU generates revenues and incurs expenses
4. The currencies in which the unit borrows and lends
5. The currencies of the QBU's sales markets
6. The currencies in which pricing and other financial decisions are made
7. The duration of the unit's business operations
8. The significance and/or volume of the QBU's independent activities[9]

- Single Functional Currency for a Foreign Corporation—If a foreign corporation has two or more QBUs that do not have the same functional currency, the foreign corporation shall be treated as having a single functional currency that is different from the functional currency of one or more of its QBUs.[10] The determination of which functional currency to use shall be determined in a two-step process:

  1. Each QBU determines its functional currency under the rules outlined above.[11]
  2. The foreign corporation then determines its functional currency by applying the rules outlined above to the corporation's activities as a whole. If a QBU of a foreign corporation has the dollar as its functional currency, the QBU's activities shall be considered dollar activities of the corporation.[12]

- QBUs with Different Functional Currencies Than the Foreign Corporation As a Whole—Where the functional currency of a foreign corporation as a whole differs from the functional currency of one or more of its QBUs, each QBU shall determine the amount of its income or loss or earnings and profits (or deficit in earnings and profits) in its functional currency. That income or loss would then be translated at the appropriate exchange rate.

  Adjustments (as prescribed by the Secretary) for transfers of property, subject to changes in the exchange rates, between QBUs of a corporation having different functional currencies would be made.[13]

IRC §988 Transaction

A §988 transaction is an amount to be paid or received by a taxpayer that is denominated in a nonfunctional currency or is determined by reference to that currency.[14] The following transactions would be considered §988 transactions

- Acquisition of a debt instrument or becoming an obligor under a debt instrument[15]

  Example—On January 1, 2002, Christy Corp. borrows 500,000 British pounds (£) for a period of five years and issues a note to the lender with a face amount of £500,000. The note provides for payments of interest at an annual rate of 10 percent paid quarterly in pounds and has a stated redemption price at maturity of £500,000. This is a §988 transaction. Because Christy Corp. is an accrual basis taxpayer, the accrual of interest expense is also a §988 transaction. Finally, the acquisition of the British pounds (for purposes of establishing basis) to make payments under the note, as well as the disposition of those pounds are §988 transactions.

- Accruing, or otherwise taking into account, any item of expense or gross income or receipts that is to be paid on a subsequent date such as a payable or receivable[16]

  Example—On January 1, 2003, Darryl sells and delivers inventory to Christy Corp. for 1,000,000 Italian lira for payment on April 1, 2003. Under Darryl's method of accounting, January 1, 2003 is the accrual date. Because Darryl is an accrual basis taxpayer, the accrual of a nonfunctional currency denominated item of a receivable on January 1, 2003, for payment after the date of accrual is a §988 transaction.

- Forward contracts, futures contract, option contracts, or similar financial instruments that are tied to any currency, rather than a commodity, and are not subject to the mark-to-market rules.

  Example—On April 15, 2003, Bechtel Corp. enters into an interest swap that requires it to make payments to its counterparty based on 5 percent of a 100,000 yen principal amount in exchange for amounts based on yen LIBOR rates. This yen for yen interest rate swap is a §988 transaction.

Example—On April 15, 2003, Bechtel Corp. enters into an option contract for sale of a group of stocks traded on the Japanese Nikkei exchange. The contract is not a §988 transaction because the underlying property to which the option relates is a group of stocks and not nonfunctional currency.[17]

A taxpayer may elect to treat a §1256 contract, subject to the mark-to-market rules (see Chapter 18) as a §988 transaction. The advantage of making this election is that the taxpayer does not have to recognize unrealized gains and losses at the end of each year where 40 percent of the gains are taxed at ordinary rates. This election is made on a statement sent to the Internal Revenue Service titled "Election to Treat Regulated Futures Contracts and Non-Equity Options as Section 988 Transactions Under Section 988(c)(1)(D)(ii)" and contains the following:

(A) The taxpayer's name, address, and taxpayer identification number.

(B) The date the notice is mailed or otherwise delivered to the Internal Revenue Service Center.

(C) A statement that the taxpayer (including all members of an affiliated group or in case of an individual, all persons filing a joint return with that individual) elects to have §988(c)(1)(D)(i) and §1.988-1(a)(7)(i) not apply.

(D) The date of the beginning of the taxable year for which the election is being made.

(E) If the election is filed after the first day of the taxable year, a statement regarding whether the taxpayer has previously held a contract during the taxable year, and if so, the first date during the taxable year on which such a contract was held.

(F) The signature of the person making the election (in case of individuals filing a joint return, the signature of all persons filing such return).[18]

The time for making this election is on or before the first day of the taxable year or, if later, on or before the first day during the taxable year on which the taxpayer holds an applicable contract.

Spot Rate

A spot rate must show to the satisfaction of the District Director or the Assistant Commissioner (International) that it reflects a fair market rate of exchange, available to the public, for currency under a spot contract, in a free market, and involving representative amounts.[19] In the absence of such a demonstration, a spot rate may be determined by the District Director or the Assistant Commissioner (International), at his/her sole discretion, from a source of exchange rate information reflecting actual transactions conducted in the free market.[20] For example, a spot rate may be determined by reference to exchange rates published in the monthly issue of "International Financial Statistics" or a successor publication of the International Monetary Fund; rates published by the Board of Governors of the Federal Reserve System, newspapers, financial journals; or exchange rates quoted by electronic financial news services.

Fair Market Value

Fair Market Value is the value of an item, which must reflect an appropriate premium or discount for the time value of money.[21] For example, the fair market value of a forward contract to buy or sell nonfunctional currency shall reflect the:

(a) Present value of the difference between the units of nonfunctional currency times the market forward rate at the time of valuation, and

(b) The units of nonfunctional currency times the forward rate indicated in the contract.[22]

However, if consistent with the taxpayer's method of financial accounting, the preceding sentence shall not apply to a financial instrument that matures within one year from the date of issuance or acquisition.[23] If the use of inconsistent sources of forward or other market rate quotations results in the distortion of income, the District Director or the Assistant Commissioner (International) may determine the appropriate rate.[24]

CALCULATION OF GAIN OR LOSS

Recognition of exchange gain or loss upon the sale or other disposition of nonfunctional currency shall be governed by the recognition provisions of the Internal Revenue Code, which apply to the sale or disposition of property and are taxable events.[25] These provisions include §1001, which indicate that the computation of gain upon the disposition of property shall be the excess of the amount realized over the adjusted basis of the property. The loss shall be the excess of the adjusted basis of the amount realized. IRC §1092 delineates the rules for recognition of losses and unrecognized gain in the case of straddles (Chapter 20). For purposes of §1031, which deals with tax-free exchanges of like-kind property, an amount of one nonfunctional currency is not like-kind property with respect to an amount of a different nonfunctional currency.[26]

However, no gain or loss is recognized with respect to the following transactions:

(A) An exchange of units of nonfunctional currency for different units of the same nonfunctional currency.[27]

(B) The deposit or withdrawal of nonfunctional currency in a demand or time deposit or similar instrument (including a certificate of deposit) issued by a bank or other financial institution if such instrument is denominated in such currency.[28]

(C) The receipt of nonfunctional currency from a bank or other financial institution from which the taxpayer purchased a certificate of deposit or similar instrument denominated in such currency that matured or was terminated.[29]

(D) The transfer of nonfunctional currency from a demand or time deposit or similar instrument issued by a bank or other financial institution to another demand or time deposit or similar instrument denominated in the same nonfunctional currency issued by a bank or other financial institution.[30]

Example—Americard Systems, Inc. is a corporation on the accrual method of accounting with the U.S. dollar as its functional currency. On January 1, 2003, Americard acquires 100,000 British pounds (£) for $150,000 (£ = $1.50) On January 10, 2003, when the spot rate is £1 = $1.49, Americard deposits the £100,000 with a British financial institution in a non-interest-bearing demand account. On February 10, 2003, when the spot rate is £1 = $1.45, Americard withdraws the £100,000. On February 15, 2003, when the spot rate is £1 = $1.42, Americard purchases inventory in the amount of £100,000. No exchange loss is realized until February 15, 2003, when Americard disposes of the £100,000 for inventory.[31]

Computation of Exchange Gain or Loss

The amount realized from the disposition of nonfunctional currency should be the sum of any money received plus the fair market value of the property (other than money) received.[32] The exchange of nonfunctional currency for property (other than nonfunctional currency) shall be treated as (1) an exchange of the units of nonfunctional currency for units of functional currency at the spot rate on the date of the exchange, and (2) the purchase or sale of the property for such units of functional currency.[33]

Example—Hooks Shoes, Inc. is a U.S. Corporation with the U.S. dollar as its functional currency. On January 1, 2000, Hooks enters into a contract to purchase a shoe manufacturing machine for 10,000,000 British pounds (£) for delivery on January 1, 2003. On January 1, 2003, when Hooks exchanges £10,000,000 (which Hooks purchased for $12,000,000) for the machine, the fair market value of the machine is £17,000,000. On January 1, 2003, the spot exchange rate is £1 = $1.50. This transaction is treated as an exchange of £10,000,000 for $15,000,000 and the purchase of the machine is $15,000,000. In computing Hooks" exchange gain of $3,000,000 on the disposition of the £10,000,000, the amount realized is $15,000,000. Hooks" basis in the machine is $15,000,000. No gain is recognized on the bargain purchase of the machine.[34]

Adjusted Basis   The adjusted basis of nonfunctional currency is determined under the applicable provisions of sections 1011 through 1023 of the Internal Revenue Code.[35] Along with cost being the primary determinant of basis, these sections consider the various adjustments required in determining the basis of property of a decedent, inventory, gifts and transfers, discharge of indebtedness, and improvements made by a lessee. A taxpayer that uses a spot rate convention to determine an exchange gain or loss with respect to a receivable shall determine the basis of the nonfunctional currency received in satisfaction of such receivable in a manner consistent with that convention.[36]

The basis of nonfunctional currency withdrawn from an account with a bank or other financial institution shall be determined under any reasonable, consistently applied method. For instance, a taxpayer may use a first in first out method, a last in first out method, a pro rata method, or any reasonable method that is consistently applied.[37] However, a method that consistently results in units with the highest basis will not be accepted as reasonable.

Stock or Securities Traded on an Established Securities Market If stock or securities traded on an established securities market are sold by a cash basis taxpayer for nonfunctional currency, the amount realized with respect to the stock or securities shall be computed by translating the units of nonfunctional currency received into functional currency at the spot rate on the settlement date of the sale.[38] The basis of the stock or securities shall be determined by translating the units of nonfunctional currency paid into functional currency at the spot rate on the settlement date of the purchase.[39]

Example—On November 1, 2001, Therese, a calendar-year cash basis U.S. individual, purchases stock for £100 for settlement on November 5, 2001. On November 1, 2001, the spot value of the £100 is $140. On November 5, 2001, Therese purchases £100 for $141, which she uses to pay for the stock. Her basis in the stock is $141. On December 30, 2002, (the trade date), Therese sells the stock for £110 for settlement on January 5, 2003. On December 30, 2002, the spot value of £110 is $165. On January 5, 2003, Therese transfers the stock and receives £110 that, translated at the spot rate, equals $166. Under §453(k), the stock is considered disposed of on December 30, 2002. The amount realized is $166, the value of the £110 on January 5, 2003. Therefore, Therese's gain realized on December 30, 2002, from the disposition of the stock is $25 ($166 − $141). Therese's basis in the £110 received from the sale of the stock is $166.

An accrual taxpayer may make an election to follow the same rules as the cash-basis taxpayer. Filing a statement with the taxpayer's first return in which the election is effective shall make the election. A method so elected must be applied consistently from year to year and cannot be changed without the consent of the Commissioner.[40]

Regulations Relating to Debt Instruments

The regulations relating to debt instruments discuss interest income and expense, principal, bond premium, market discount, debt instruments, and deposits denominated in hyperinflationary currencies.

Exchange Gain or Loss on Interest and Principal Interest income received with respect to a demand account with a bank or other financial institution that is denominated in a nonfunctional currency shall be translated into functional currency at the spot rate on the date received, accrued, or pursuant to any reasonable spot rate convention consistently applied by the taxpayer.[41] Interest income or expense that is not required to be accrued by the taxpayer prior to receipt or payment shall be translated at the spot rate on the date of receipt or payment. No exchange gain or loss is realized with respect to the receipt or payment of such interest income or expense other than the exchange gain or loss realized upon disposition of the nonfunctional currency.[42] When interest income or expense is required to be accrued prior to receipt or payment, it shall be translated at the average rate for the interest accrual period or, with respect to an interest accrual period that spans two taxable years, at the average rate for the partial period within the taxable year.[43]

The holder of a debt instrument shall recognize exchange gain or loss with respect to accrued interest income on the date the interest is received or the instrument is disposed of. The amount of exchange gain or loss so realized is determined for each accrual period by (1) translating the units of nonfunctional currency interest income received with respect to such accrual period into functional currency at the spot rate on the date the interest income is received or the instrument disposed of, and (2) subtracting the amount computed by translating the units of nonfunctional currency interest income accrued at the average rate for the accrual period.[44]

The timing for recognition of accrued interest expense for the obligor is the same as indicated for the holder of the debt. The amount of exchange gain or loss realized with respect to accrued interest expense is determined for each accrual period by (1) translating the units of nonfunctional currency interest expense accrued with respect to the amount of interest paid into functional currency at the average rate for the accrual period; and (2) subtracting the amount computed by translating the units of nonfunctional currency interest paid into functional currency at the spot rate on the date payment is made or the obligation is transferred or extinguished.[45]

With respect to principal, the holder of a debt instrument shall realize exchange gain or loss on the date the principal is received or the instrument is disposed of. The principal amount of a debt instrument is the holder's purchase price in units of nonfunctional currency. However, if the holder acquired the instrument in a transaction in which exchange gain or loss was realized but not recognized by the transferor, the nonfunctional currency principal amount of the instrument with respect to the holder shall be the same as that of the transferor.[46] The amount of exchange gain or loss realized by the holder with respect to principal is determined by:

- Translating the units of nonfunctional currency principal at the spot rate on the date that payment is received or the instrument is disposed of, and

- Subtracting the amount computed by translating the units of non-functional currency principal at the spot rate on the date the holder acquired the instrument.[47]

The borrower under a debt instrument shall realize exchange gain or loss on the principal amount on the date it is paid. For purposes of computing exchange gain or loss, the principal amount of a debt instrument is the amount received by the borrower in units of nonfunctional currency.

If the obligor was in a transaction in which exchange gain or loss was realized but not recognized by the transferor, the nonfunctional currency principal amount of the instrument shall be the same as that of the transferor. The amount of exchange gain or loss realized by the obligor is determined by:

- Translating the units of nonfunctional currency principal at the spot rate on the date the taxpayer became the obligor, and
- Subtracting the amount computed by translating the units of nonfunctional currency principal at the spot rate on the date payment is made or the obligation is extinguished or transferred.[48]

Example—Serina is an individual on cash-method accounting with the dollar as her functional currency. On January 1, 2000, Serina converts $13,000 to £10,000 at the spot rate of £1 = $1.30 and loans the £10,000 to Nicholas for three years. The terms of the loan provide that Nicholas will make interest payments of £1000 on December 31, 2000, 2001, and 2002, and will repay Serina's £10,000 principal on December 31, 2002. Assume the spot rates for the pertinent dates are as follows:

Date	Spot rate (pounds to dollars)
January 1, 2000	£1 = $1.30
December 31, 2000	£1 = $1.35
December 31, 2001	£1 = $1.40
December 31, 2002	£1 = $1.45

Serina will translate the £1000 interest payments at the spot rate on the date received. Accordingly, she will have interest income of $1350 in 2000, $1400 in 2001, and $1450 in 2002. Because Serina is a cash-basis taxpayer, she does not realize exchange gain or loss on the receipt of interest income.

Serina will realize exchange gain upon repayment of the £10,000 principal amount determined by translating the £10,000 at the spot rate on the date it is received (£10,000 × $1.45 = $14,500) and subtracting from it the amount determined by translating the £10,000 at the spot rate on the date the loan was made (£10,000 × $1.30 = $13,000). Therefore, Serina will realize an exchange gain of $1500 on the repayment of the loan on December 31, 2002.

Now let us assume that Serina is on the accrual basis of accounting and that the average rates are as follows:

Accrual Period	Average Rate (pounds to dollars)
2000	£1 = $1.32
2001	£1 = $1.37
2002	£1 = $1.42

Serina will accrue the £1000 interest payments at the average rate for the accrual period. Therefore, she will have interest income of $1320 in 2000, $1370 in 2001, and $1420 in 2002. Serina determines the exchange gain or loss for each interest accrual period by translating the units of nonfunctional currency interest income received for each accrual period at the spot rate on the date received and subtracting the amounts of interest income accrued for that period. Therefore, Serina will realize $90 of exchange gain with respect to interest received under the loan, computed as follows:

Year	Spot Value Interest Received	Accrued Interest at Avg. Rate	Exchange Gain
2000	$1,350	$1,320	$30
2001	$1,400	$1,370	$30
2002	$1,450	$1,420	$30
		TOTAL	$90

Serina will realize an exchange gain of $1500 on the principal the same way as though she was a cash basis taxpayer.[49]

Payment Ordering Rules   Units of nonfunctional currency received or paid with respect to a debt instrument shall be treated first as a receipt or payment of periodic interest. Secondly, the payment is treated as a receipt or payment of original issue discount to the extent accrued, and, finally, as a receipt or payment of principal.[50] Units of nonfunctional currency treated as a receipt or payment of original issue discount are attributed to the earliest accrual period in which OID has accrued and to which prior receipts or payments have not been attributed. No portion shall be treated as prepaid interest.[51]

Treatment of Bond Premium   Bond premium shall be computed in the foreign currency in which the bond is denominated. Amortizable bond premium shall reduce interest income or expense in units of that foreign currency. Exchange gain or loss is realized with respect to bond premium by treating the portion of premium amortized with respect to any period as a return of principal.[52] With respect to a holder that does not elect to amortize bond premium under §171, the amount of bond premium will constitute a market loss when the bond matures.[53]

Market Discount Market Discount as defined in §1278(a)(2)[54] shall also be determined in the foreign currency in which the market discount bond is denominated. Accrued market discount shall be translated into functional currency at the spot rate on the date the market discount bond is disposed of. No part of such accrued market discount is treated as exchange gain or loss. Accrued market discount currently includible in income shall be translated into functional currency at the average exchange rate for the accrual period. Exchange gain or loss with respect to accrued market discount currently includible in income shall be determined in accordance with the rules relating to accrued interest income discussed above.[55]

Regulations Regarding Receivables and Payables

Except as indicated in Reg. §1.988-5, which deals with hedging transactions, exchange gain or loss with respect to receivables and payables shall be realized on the date payment is made or received. If the taxpayer's right to receive income, or obligation to pay an expense, is transferred or modified in a transaction in which gain or loss would otherwise be recognized, exchange gain or loss shall be realized and recognized only to the extent of the total gain or loss on the transaction.[56]

Determination of Exchange Gain or Loss on a Receivable Exchange gain or loss on a receivable is determined by:

(a) Multiplying the units of the foreign currency received by the spot rate on the payment date, and

(b) Subtracting from it the amount determined by multiplying the units of foreign currency received by the spot rate on the booking date.[57]

A taxpayer may also use a spot rate convention for purposes of determining the spot rate on the booking date.

Example—Happy Holiday Seasonal Sales, Inc. is a calendar-year corporation with the dollar as its functional currency. Happy Holiday is on the accrual method of accounting. On January 15, 2002, Happy Holiday sells inventory for 10,000 Canadian Dollars (C$). The spot rate on January 15, 2002, is C$1 = U.S. $.55. On February 23, 2002, when Happy Holiday receives payment of the C$10,000, the spot rate is C$1 = U.S. $.50. On February 23, 2002, Happy Holiday will realize exchange loss. The loss is computed by multiplying the C$10,000 by the spot rate on the date the C$10,000 are received (C$10,000 × .50 = U.S. $5000) and subtracting from it the amount computed by multiplying the C$10,000 by the spot rate on the booking date (C$10,000 × .55 = U.S. $5500). Happy Holiday's exchange loss on the transaction is U.S. $500 (U.S. $5000— U.S. $5500).[58]

Determination of Exchange Gain or Loss With Respect to a Payable
Exchange gain or loss realized on a payable shall be determined by multiplying the units of foreign currency paid by the spot rate on the booking date. This amount would then be subtracted from the amount determined by multiplying the units of foreign currency paid by the spot rate on the payment date. A spot rate convention may also be used to determine the spot rate on payment date.[59]

Exchange Gain or Loss on Forward Contracts, Futures Contracts, and Option Contracts

Any gain or loss is generally recognized when a contract is terminated or disposed of. If a taxpayer takes or makes delivery in connection with any §988 transaction, any gain or loss is determined as though the taxpayer sold the contract, option, or instrument on that date for its fair market value.[60] The gain or loss shall be recognized in the same manner as if the contract, option, or instrument was actually sold.

Example—On August 1, 2001, Regal Roses Corp., a calendar year corporation with the dollar as its functional currency, enters into a forward contract with Wonderful Bank to buy 100 New Zealand dollars for $80 for delivery on January 31, 2002. (This forward purchase contract is not a §1256 contract.) On November 1, 2001, the market price for the purchase of 100 New Zealand dollars for delivery on January 31, 2002, is $76. On November 1, 2001, Regal cancels its obligation under the forward purchase contract and pays Wonderful Bank $3.95 (the present value of $4 discounted at 12 percent for the period) in cancellation of the contract. Under

§1001(a), Regal realizes an exchange loss of $3.95 on November 1, 2001, because the cancellation of the forward purchase contract for cash results in the termination of Regal's contract.

Realization by Offset Generally, exchange gain or loss on a transaction shall not be realized solely because a transaction is offset by another transaction.[61] There is an exception when the taxpayer derives an economic benefit such as cash, property, or the proceeds from borrowing from any gain inherent in offsetting positions.[62] Adjustments must be made in the amount of any gain or loss subsequently realized. If a transaction is traded on an exchange, and it is the general practice of the exchange to terminate offsetting contracts, entering into an offsetting contract shall then be considered a termination of the contract.[63]

Currency Swaps and Other Notional Contracts

A currency swap contract is a contract involving different currencies between two or more parties to (1) exchange periodic interim payments on or prior to maturity of the contract, and (2) exchange the swap principal amount upon maturity of the contract.[64]

An exchange of periodic interim payments is an exchange of one or more payments in one currency for one of more payments in a different currency specified by the contract. The payments in each currency are computed by reference to an interest index applied to the swap principal amount.[65] A currency swap contract must clearly indicate the periodic interim payments, or the interest index used to compute the periodic interim payments, in each currency.[66]

The swap principal amount is an amount of two different currencies that, under the terms of the contract, is used to determine the periodic interim payments in each currency and that is exchanged upon maturity of the contract.[67]

Timing and Computation of Periodic Payments The timing and computation of periodic interim payments provided in a currency swap agreement shall be determined by treating:

* Payments made under the swap as payments made pursuant to a hypothetical borrowing that is denominated in the currency in which payments are required to be made under the swap, and

- Payments received under the swap as payments received pursuant to a hypothetical loan that is denominated in the currency in which payments are received under the swap.[68]

The hypothetical borrowing and loan is the swap principal amount. The hypothetical stated redemption price at maturity is the total of all payments provided under the hypothetical borrowing or loan other than periodic interest payments. For purposes of determining economic accrual under the currency swap, the number of hypothetical interest compounding periods are determined pursuant to a semiannual compounding convention, unless the currency swap contract indicates otherwise.[69] The principles regarding amortization of interest apply to the hypothetical interest expense and income for purposes of determining the timing and amount of the periodic interim payments. These principles do not apply to determine the time that the principal is deemed to be paid on the hypothetical loan.[70]

The amount treated as exchange gain or loss by the taxpayer with respect to the periodic interim payments for the taxable year is:

(1) The amount of hypothetical interest income and exchange gain or loss attributable to such interest income, from the hypothetical borrowing, for the year less

(2) The amount of hypothetical interest expense and exchange gain or loss attributable to the interest expense from such hypothetical borrowing for the year.[71]

Example—Lady Godzilla, Inc. is an accrual method, calendar-year corporation with the dollar as its functional currency. On January 1, 2000, Lady Godzilla enters into a currency swap with Rimaldo, Inc. with the following terms:

1. The principal amount is $150 and £100 (British pound) (the equivalent of $150 on the effective date of the contract assuming a spot rate of £1 = $1.50 on January 1, 2000).

2. Lady Godzilla will make payments equal to 10 percent of the dollar principal amount on December 31, 2000 and December 31, 2001.

3. Rimaldo will make payments equal to 12 percent of the pound principal amount on December 31, 2000, and December 31, 2001.
4. On December 31, 2001, Lady Godzilla will pay to Rimaldo the $150 principal amount and Rimaldo will pay to Lady Godzilla the £100 principal amount. Assume that the spot rate is £1 = $1.50 on January 1, 2000, 1 British pound = $1.40 on December 31, 2000, and £1 = $1.30 on December 31, 2001. Assume further that the average rate for 2000 is £1 = $1.45 and for 2001 is £1 = $1.35.

Solely for determining the realization of gain or loss, Lady Godzilla will treat the dollar payments it made as made pursuant to a dollar borrowing with an issue price of $150, a stated redemption price at maturity of $150, and a yield to maturity of 10 percent. Lady Godzilla will treat the British pound payments received as payments received pursuant to a British pound loan with an issue price of £100, a stated redemption price at maturity of £100, and a yield to 12 percent to maturity. Lady Godzilla is required to compute hypothetical accrued British pound interest income at the average rate for the accrual period and then determine the exchange gain or loss on the day payment is received with respect to the accrued amount. Accordingly, Lady Godzilla will accrue $17.40 (£12 × $1.45) in 2000 and $16.20 (£12 × $1.35) in 2001. Lady Godzilla will also compute hypothetical exchange loss of $.60 on December 31, 2000 [(£12 × $1.40) − (£12 × $1.45)] and hypothetical exchange loss of $.60 on December 31, 2001 [£12 × $1.30) − (£12 × $1.35)]. All such hypothetical interest income and exchange losses are characterized as exchange gain and loss.

Further, Lady Godzilla is treated as having paid $15 ($150 × 10 percent) of hypothetical interest on December 31, 2000, and again on December 31, 2001. Such hypothetical interest expense is characterized and sourced as exchange loss. Thus, Lady Godzilla will have a net exchange gain of $1.80 ($17.40 − $.60 − $15.00) with respect to the periodic interim payments in 2000 and a net exchange gain of $.60 ($16.20 − $.60 − $15.00) with respect to the periodic interim payments in 2001. Finally, Lady Godzilla will realize an exchange loss on December 31, 2001 with respect to the exchange of the swap principal amount. This loss is determined by subtracting the value of the units of swap principal paid ($150) from the value of the units of swap principal received (£100 × $1.30 = $130) resulting in a $20 exchange loss.[72]

Other Notional Principal Contracts fall under the same rules for determining recognition of periodic payments, nonperiodic payments, and termination payments. However, since these contracts fall under §988, income and loss under the NPC timing regulations are usually characterized as exchange gain or loss.[73]

CHARACTER OF EXCHANGE GAIN OR LOSS

Except as otherwise provided in the regulations, exchange gain or loss realized with respect to a §988 transaction shall be characterized as ordinary gain or loss.[74] A taxpayer may elect to treat any gain or loss recognized on a contract as capital gain or loss, but only if the contract:

- Is a capital asset in the hands of the taxpayer.
- Is not part of a straddle, and
- Is not a regulated futures contract or nonequity option.[75]

Requirements for Making the Election

A taxpayer elects to treat gain or loss on a transaction of §988 as a capital gain or loss by clearly identifying the transaction on its books and records on the date the transaction is entered into. No specific language or account is necessary for identifying this transaction. However, the method of identification must be consistently applied and must clearly identify the pertinent transaction as subject to §988(a)(1)(B) election. An election may be invalidated that does not comply with the preceding sentence.[76]

A taxpayer that has made this election must attach to his income tax return a statement that indicates the following:

1. A description and the date of each election made by the taxpayer during the taxable year.
2. A statement that each election made during the taxable year was made before the close of the date the transaction was entered into.
3. A description of any contract for which an election was in effect and the date such contract expired or was otherwise sold or exchanged during the taxable year.

4. A statement that the contract was never part of a straddle as defined in §1092.

5. A statement that all transactions subject to the election are included on the statement attached to the taxpayer's income tax return.[77]

HEDGING TRANSACTIONS

A §988 hedging transaction is any transaction entered into primarily to manage risk of currency fluctuations with respect to property that is held or to be held by the taxpayer. Additionally, a hedging transaction is used to manage risk of currency fluctuations with respect to borrowings made or to be made, or obligations incurred or to be incurred by the taxpayer.[78] The transaction must be identified as being a 988 hedging transaction.

A qualified hedging transaction is an integrated economic transaction consisting of a qualifying debt instrument and a hedge. If a taxpayer enters into a transaction that is a qualified hedging transaction, no exchange gain or loss is recognized by the taxpayer for the period included in the transaction.[79] The transaction shall be integrated and treated as a single transaction with respect to the taxpayer.[80]

A qualifying debt instrument means a bond, debenture, note, certificate, or other evidence of indebtedness.[81] It does not include receivables or payables.

A hedge is a spot contract, futures contract, forward contract, option contract, notional principal contract, currency swap contract, similar financial instrument, or series or combination, that, when integrated with a qualifying debt instrument, permits the calculation of a yield to maturity in the currency in which the synthetic debt instrument is denominated.[82]

The effect of integrating and treating a transaction as a single transaction is to create a synthetic debt instrument for income tax purposes, which is subject to the original issue discount provisions covered in Chapter 13.

CONCLUSION

IRC 988 and the related regulations have formed a solid foundation on which to identify and calculate exchange income and loss and the appropriate timing for this recognition. With the birth of numerous new financial instruments and the resulting effects of foreign currency transactions, familiarity with these regulations becomes increasingly more important to the investor and businessperson.

NOTES

[1] Reg. §1.989(a)-1

[2] *Id.*

[3] Reg. §1.985-1(b)(1)

[4] A hyperinflationary currency means the currency of a country in which there is cumulative inflation during the base period of at least 100 percent as determined by reference to the consumer price index of the country listed in the monthly issues of the "International Financial Statistics" or a successor publication of the International Monetary Fund. Base period means the 36 calendar months immediately preceding the first day of the current calendar year.

[5] Reg. §1.985-1(b)(2)

[6] *Id.*

[7] *Id.*

[8] Reg. §1.985-1(c)

[9] Reg. §1.985-1(c)(2)(i)

[10] Reg. §1.985-1(d)(1)

[11] *Id.*

[12] *Id.*

[13] §987

[14] Reg. §1.988-1(a)(1)

[15] Reg. §1.988-1(a)(2)(i)

[16] Reg. §1.988-1(a)(2)(ii)

[17] Based on the facts contained in Example 11, Reg.§1.988-1(a)(6)

[18] Reg. §1.988-1(a)(7)

[19] Reg. 1.988-1(d)

[20] *Id.*

[21] Reg. 1.988-1(g)

[22] *Id.*

[23] *Id.*

[24] *Id.*

[25] Reg. §1.988-2(a)(1)

[26] Reg. §1.988-2(a)(1)(ii)

[27] Reg. §1.988-2 (a)(1)(iii)

[28] *Id.*

[29] *Id.*

[30] *Id.*

[31] Facts taken from example in Reg. §1.988-2(a)(1)(iv)

[32] §1001(b) and Reg. §1.988-2(a)(2)

[33] Reg. §1.988-2(a)(ii)

[34] Example is based on facts in Reg. §1.988-2(a)(2)(C)

[35] Reg. §1.988-2(a)(2)(iii)

[36] *Id.* A taxpayer may utilize a spot rate convention determined at intervals of one quarter year or less, for purposes of computing exchange gain or loss with respect to payables and receivables, denominated in a nonfunctional currency. For example, if consistent with the taxpayer's financial accounting, a taxpayer may accrue all payables and receivables incurred during the month of January at the spot rate on December 31 or January 31 (or at an average of any spot rates occurring between these two dates) and record the payment or receipt of amounts consistent with such convention. The use of a spot rate convention cannot be changed without the consent of the Commissioner.

[37] *Id.*

[38] Reg. §1.988-2(a)(2)(iv)

[39] *Id.*

[40] Reg. §1.988-2(a)(2)(v)

[41] Reg. §1.988-2(b)(1)

[42] Reg. §1.988-2(b)(2)(B)

[43] Reg. §1.988-2(b)(2)(C)

[44] Reg. §1.988-2(b)(3)

[45] Reg. §1.988-2(b)(4)

[46] Reg. §1-988-2(b)(5)

[47] *Id.*

[48] Reg. §1.988-2(b)(6)

[49] Based on the facts of Examples 1 and 2 in Reg. §1.988-2(b)(9)

[50] Reg. 1.988-2(b)(7)

[51] *Id.*

[52] Reg. 1.988-2(b)(10)

[53] *Id.*

[54] §1278(a)(2) describes market discount as the excess (if any) of the stated redemption price of the bond at maturity, over the basis of such a bond immediately after its acquisition by the taxpayer.

[55] Reg. §1.988-2(b)(11)

[56] Reg. §1.988-2(c)(1)

[57] Reg. §1.988-2(c)(2)

[58] Based on facts contained in Example 1 of Reg. §1.988-2(c)(4)

[59] Reg. §1.988-2(c)(3)

[60] §988(c)(5)

[61] Reg. §1.988-2(d)(2)(ii)

[62] *Id.*

[63] *Id.*

[64] Reg. 1.988-2(e)(2)(ii)

[65] *Id.*

[66] *Id.*

[67] *Id.*

[68] Reg. 1.988-2(e)(iii)(A)

[69] *Id.*

[70] *Id.*

[71] *Id.*

[72] Example taken from facts in Example 1 of Reg. 1.988-2(e)(5)

[73] Reg. 1.988-2(e)(1)

[74] Reg. §1.988-3(a)

[75] Reg. §1.988-3(b)

[76] Reg. §1.988-3(b)(3)

[77] Reg. 1.988-3(b)(4)

[78] §988(d)

[79] Reg. §1.988-5(a)(1)

[80] Reg. §1.988-5(a)(9)

[81] Reg. 1.988-1(a)(2)

[82] Reg. 1.988-5(a)(4)

GLOSSARY AND CODE SECTION LISTING

The following is a brief glossary of some of the terms appearing in this volume. This section also contains a list of some of the sections of the Internal Revenue Code discussed in this book. For a more detailed listing of the contents of this text, consult the table of contents and also the index.

Accumulated Earnings Tax   This tax is imposed on corporations to ensure that companies do not maintain profits unnecessarily within the business to avoid paying tax on dividends at the shareholder level. As discussed in **Chapter 7**, the tax applies where a corporation accumulates earnings not required by the reasonable needs of the business. Under the 2003 tax legislation, the accumulated earnings tax is 15 percent times the corporation's accumulated taxable income.

Alternative Minimum Tax   The AMT is a separate tax system designed to ensure that taxpayers with economic income pay some amount of income tax. It is calculated by making a series of adjustments, additions, etc., to taxable income in order to arrive at a **tentative minimum tax**. If the tentative minimum tax exceeds the amount of income tax due under the regular system, the extra represents the alternative minimum tax the taxpayer owes. The AMT rules are discussed in **Chapter 5**.

At-Risk Rules   In general, the at-risk rules are designed to limit a taxpayer's deductions in connection with an activity to the amount he or she could lose if the activity were to fail. **Chapter 3** contains a discussion of these rules, including the taxpayers subject to the provisions, exceptions that may apply, and how losses disallowed under the at-risk limitations are treated.

Capital Gain   This is gain from the sale or exchange of a capital asset. Capital gain may be eligible for taxation at favorable rates, depending on how long the taxpayer has held the asset and certain other factors. A **capital loss** arises when a taxpayer sells a capital asset at a loss. Use of capital losses may be restricted. See **Chapter 1**.

Dividend   For tax purposes, a dividend is any distribution made by a corporation in the ordinary course of business from earnings and profits. Depending on the amount of earnings and profits at the time a corporation makes a distribution, the consequences to the shareholders might be **dividend income** , a **tax-free return of capital,** or **capital gain.** Income tax treatment of dividends is discussed in **Chapter 8**; the rules applicable to **stock dividends** are described in **Chapter 10**. Corporate shareholders who receive dividends may be eligible to claim a **dividend-received deduction,** as discussed in **Chapter 8.**

Hedge   A hedge is a transaction entered into in the normal course of a taxpayer's trade or business primarily to manage certain kinds of risk. These risks include price changes or currency fluctuations as to ordinary property and also interest rate or price changes or currency fluctuations as to borrowings or ordinary obligations. Hedges are described in **Chapter 20**. Risk reduction strategies adopted in connection with investments do not meet the tax law definition of a hedge.

Interest   Interest is the cost of using money and is reported by its recipient as ordinary income. Interest-bearing bonds may be issued at a discount or a premium, depending on how the interest the bond pays compares to market rates. (See Chapter 13 for a discussion of the original issue discount and market discount provisions.) Special rules are required where a bond is sold between interest payment dates. The consequences of holding interest-paying bonds are described in **Chapter 12**.

Investment Interest   This is interest paid or accrued on debt allocable to property held for investment. Where a taxpayer borrows money in order to acquire or hold investment assets, the deduction for interest paid on the loan is limited to net investment income. These rules are discussed in **Chapter 4**.

Mark-to-Market Rules   The mark-to-market rules, discussed in **Chapter 18**, apply to §1256 contracts. These include **regulated futures contracts, foreign currency contracts, nonequity options, dealer equity options, and dealer securities futures contracts**. Under the mark-to-market rules, a taxpayer is required to treat his or her §1256 investments as though they were sold at the end of the tax year, recognizing the resulting gain or loss. When a §1256 contract is actually sold or liquidated at some later date, an adjustment is made for the gain or loss already recognized because of the mark-to-market reporting.

Market Discount Bond   Market discount exists when the stated redemption price of a bond at maturity exceeds its basis, or tax cost, immediately after the acquisition. This means the investor acquired the debt instrument at a discount after the bond was originally issued. The market discount rules require the discount to be amortized unless an exception applies, although the discount is not included currently in the bondholder's income. Instead, gain on the disposition of these bonds is treated as ordinary income up to the amount of discount that has accrued. See the discussion in **Chapter 13**.

Option   An option is a contract under which a grantor incurs an obligation to buy or sell a specific item at an agreed-upon price. Options include **puts** and **calls**. Options are discussed in **Chapter 17**, which includes an analysis of **bull call spreads, covered call options, married puts, bear put spreads, covered puts, and collars**.

Original Issue Discount   The OID rules, described in **Chapter 13**, require investors who hold bonds issued at a discount to recognize income over the life of the investment, as the discount is amortized. A discount means the bond's stated redemption price at maturity exceeds the issue price by more than a certain amount. Some instruments are not subject to the OID provisions.

Passive Activities   The passive activity rules are designed to prevent taxpayers from using losses or credits generated by certain investments to offset income from other sources, like salary. This is done by restricting the use of **passive activity losses** and **passive activity credits**. See the discussion in **Chapter 2**.

Personal Holding Company Tax   If five or fewer individuals own more than 50 percent of a corporation's outstanding stock at any time during the last half of the tax year, the corporation may be classified as a personal holding company, assuming certain income tests are met. Personal holding companies owe a tax on undistributed personal holding company income, which must be paid in addition to the corporation's regular income tax liability. Under the 2003 legislation, the tax is imposed at a flat rate of 15 percent. See **Chapter 7** for an analysis.

Qualified Small Business Stock   A 50-percent (in some cases 60-percent) exclusion applies to gain from the sale or exchange of qualified small business stock held more than five years. Corporations must meet certain requirements in order for their shares to be treated as qualified small business stock, including a $50 million ceiling on gross assets and an active business requirement. See the discussions in **Chapter 12**. An investor who sells qualified small business stock may be able to **rollover**, or defer recognition of the gain, provided replacement qualified small business shares are purchased within certain time limits. See the discussion of IRC §1045, in **Chapter 12**.

Redemptions   A redemption occurs when a corporation acquires its own stock in exchange for money or property. As described in **Chapter 9**, if a shareholder's percentage ownership changes in a corporation as a result of a redemption, he or she may be able to treat the transaction as capital gain, depending on the circumstances. A redemption not qualifying for capital gain treatment is taxed like a dividend distribution. **Constructive ownership rules** apply in determining if a shareholder's percentage ownership has changed. Redemptions from noncorporate shareholders in **partial liquidation** of a corporation may qualify for capital gain treatment. See **Chapter 9**.

Section 1244 Stock   Loss on the sale of §1244 stock is treated as ordinary, rather than capital, meaning the limitations on the use of capital losses won't apply. Code §1244 stock must have been issued by a "small business corporation." In order to qualify as a small business corporation, a company must meet various requirements, including a $1 million ceiling on money and property received for stock, as capital contributions, and paid-in surplus, as of the time the shares were issued. Limits apply on the amount of loss eligible for §1244 treatment. See **Chapter 12**.

Short Sales   A short sale is a sale of property a taxpayer does not possess. The short sale rules of the Internal Revenue Code, discussed in **Chapter 19**, were enacted to prevent the use of these transactions to convert short-term capital gain into the more favorably taxed long-term gain or, alternatively, long-term capital loss into short-term. (The latter rule applies because individuals generally find short-term capital losses more useful for tax purposes than long-term.) Where a corporate shareholder makes a short sale of its holdings, the **dividend-received deduction** it otherwise would claim may be lost. See the discussion in **Chapter 8**.

Short-term Obligations   These are debt instruments with a fixed maturity date of one year or less from the date of issue. Short-term debt instruments are not subject to the original issue discount rules, which means taxpayers could try to use these investments to defer recognition of interest or convert the instrument's discount, otherwise reported as ordinary income, into short-term capital gain. As a result, special rules have been adopted, as described in **Chapter 15**.

60/40 Rule   The 60/40 rule applies to §1256 contracts. Under this rule, gain or loss arising from a §1256 investment that is a capital asset in the investor's hands must be recognized as 60 percent long-term and 40 percent short-term. See the discussion of this rule in **Chapters 18 and 20**.

Stock Dividend   A stock dividend is a distribution by a corporation of its own stock. (Corporations also may distribute rights, enabling recipients to acquire stock in the future under specified terms.) In general, distributions of stock or stock rights are received tax-free, although exceptions apply. See the discussion in **Chapter 10**. In some cases, later sales of stock acquired through distributions of shares or stock rights may generate **dividend income**, as noted also in **Chapter 10**.

Straddles   A straddle generally can be thought of as offsetting positions with respect to personal property. Straddles involving §1256 contracts are discussed in **Chapter 18**; **Chapter 20** is devoted to an examination of straddle investments in general. Taxpayers holding straddles may be subject to various rules, including limitations on the use of any losses the investments generate, under the **loss deferral rules** of §1092. **Short sale** and **wash sale** principles also apply to these investments. **Mixed straddles**, which consist of both §1256 and non-§1256 contracts, are discussed in both Chapters 18 and 20.

Stripped Bonds   A stripped bond is a bond issued with interest coupons attached where a separation in ownership has occurred between the underlying instrument and any coupon not yet payable. A strip can involve disposition of one or more of the interest coupons or of the right to receive the principal when the instrument matures. The tax consequences of bond stripping are examined in **Chapter 16**.

Variable Rate Debt Instruments   When the rate of interest paid by a debt instrument floats, rather than being set at a constant rate, the obligation may represent a variable rate debt instrument. Special rules are needed for these investments, in order to apply the original issue discount provisions (described in Chapter 13). See the discussion in **Chapter 14**.

Warrant   A warrant is an option to acquire stock from an issuer. Detachable warrants are often issued with other securities, including debt instruments. Detached warrants can be traded in secondary markets. See the discussion in **Chapter 17**.

Wash Sales   A wash sale occurs when a taxpayer sells stock or securities at a loss and reacquires identical instruments within 30 days before or after the sale. The use of losses arising from a wash sale is restricted, since the taxpayer essentially occupies the same economic position after the sale and purchase as before. These rules also apply to contracts or options to acquire substantially identical stock or securities. **See Chapter 19**.

CODE SECTIONS DISCUSSED

Many sections of the Internal Revenue Code are discussed in this book. However, the list below shows some of the Code provisions for which more extensive discussion is provided.

§ **55–§59** Alternative Minimum Tax. Chapter 5.

§ **163** Interest. Chapters 4, 19.

§ **165** Losses. Chapters 1, 12.

§ **166** Bad debts. Chapter 12.

§ **171** Amortizable bond premium. Chapters 12, 13.

§ **243, §§245–246A** Dividend-received deduction. Chapter 8.

§ **263** Capital expenditures. Chapters 19, 20.

§ **265** Expenses and interest relating to tax-exempt income. Chapter 4.

§ **267** Losses, expenses, and interest with respect to transactions between related taxpayers. Chapters 1, 3.

§ **279** Interest on debt incurred by corporation to acquire stock or assets of another corporation. Chapter 4.

§ **301** Distributions of property. Chapter 8.

§ **302** Distributions in redemption of stock. Chapter 9.

§ **303** Distributions in redemption of stock to pay death taxes. Chapter 9.

§ **304** Redemption through use of related corporations. Chapter 11.

§ **305** Distributions of stock and stock rights. Chapter 10.

§ **306** Dispositions of certain stock. Chapter 10.

§ **307** Basis of stock and stock rights acquired in distributions. Chapter 10.

§ **311** Taxability of corporation on distribution. Chapter 9.

§ **312** Effect on earnings and profits. Chapter 9.

§ **316** Dividend defined. Chapters 8, 11.

§ **317** Other definitions (related to dividends and distributions, etc.). Chapters 8, 9.

§ **318** Constructive ownership of stock. Chapters 9, 10, 11.

§ **332** Complete liquidations of subsidiaries. Chapter 9.

§ **465** Deductions limited to amount at risk. Chapter 3.

§ **469** Passive activity losses and credits limited. Chapter 2.

§ **532, §535** Accumulated earnings tax. Chapter 7.

§ **541–§545, §547** Personal holding company tax. Chapter 7.

§ **562–§565** Deductions for dividends paid. Chapter 7.

§ **1045** Rollover of gain from qualified small business stock to another qualified small business stock. Chapter 12.

§ **1058** Transfers of securities under certain agreements. Chapter 19.

§ **1059** Corporate shareholder's basis in stock reduced by nontaxed portion of extraordinary dividends. Chapters 8,19.

§   **1091**   Loss from wash sales of stock or securities. Chapter 19.

§   **1092**   Straddles. Chapters 18, 20.

§   **1202**   Partial exclusion for gain from certain small business stock. Chapter 12.

§   **1211**   Limitation on capital losses. Chapters 12, 19.

§   **1212**   Capital loss carrybacks and carryovers. Chapters 1, 12, 18.

§   **1221**   Capital asset defined. Chapter 1.

§   **1222**   Other terms relating to capital gains and losses. Chapter 1.

§   **1231**   Property used in the trade or business and involuntary conversions. Chapter 1.

§   **1233**   Gains and losses from short sales. Chapter 19.

§   **1234**   Options to buy or sell. Chapter 17.

§   **1244**   Losses on small business stock. Chapter12.

§   **1256**   Section 1256 contracts mark to market. Chapters 18, 20.

§   **1271**   Treatment of amounts received on retirement or sale or exchange of debt instruments. Chapters 12, 15.

§   **§1272, 1273**   Original issue discount. Chapter 13.

§   **1276–§1278**   Market discount on bonds. Chapter 13.

§   **1281–§1283** Short-term obligations. Chapter 15.

§   **1286**   Tax treatment of stripped bonds. Chapter 16.

§   **1400F**   Renewal community capital gain. Chapter 1.

§   **1563**   Definitions and special rules (relating to controlled corporations). Chapter 11.

INDEX

Note: Boldface numbers indicate tables.

ABOUT THE AUTHORS

Arlene M. Hibschweiler. JD, MBA, is a business lecturer at State University of New York at Buffalo (SUNYAB) and has taught and practiced business law for nearly twenty years. Her work has appeared in a number of professional publications, including *Journal of Accountancy, Taxation for Accountants, Personal Financial Planning,* and *The CPA Journal.*

Marion Kopin, CPA, MBA, MS Taxation, is a partner at Bechtel, Kopin & Co., where she provides tax planning and preparation advice for individuals and entities. She has more than two decades of experience and is a frequent contributor to professional publications including *Journal of Accountancy, Practical Tax Strategies,* and *Taxation for Accountants.*